EU Policies in a Global Perspective

Recent decades have seen a rise in the significance of governance layers beyond the nation-state and even Europe. Nonetheless, few efforts have been made thus far to systematically examine the EU's interaction with global policy regimes. This book maps the relative importance of EU policies in the multi-level global governance system, in comparison with national and global activities. It provides a unique comparative analysis of the EU's capacity for projecting its policies outward. Focusing on trade policy, agriculture, food safety, competition, social rights, environmental policy, transport, migration, nuclear non-proliferation or financial regulation, each chapter contributes to a better understanding of the EU's role in shaping global policies, the mechanisms it uses and the conditions leading to success or failure.

The contributors' comparative research highlights that policy export is a demanding phenomenon that faces severe limitations and frequently comes with drawbacks. Still, EU policy export played a key role in shaping the rules of the global trade regime and influenced global policy outcomes – at least to a minor extent or in technical aspects – in the majority of the covered policy areas. Overall however, this book reveals that the EU not only aims to export its policies, but interacts with its global environment in a number of distinct ways, including policy import and policy protection, to shield it from global pressures.

Concluding with a comparison of all policies on the meta-level and relevant policy recommendations, this book will be of interest to students, scholars and practitioners of European politics, European public policy, global governance and international relations.

Gerda Falkner is Head of the Institute for European Integration Research, and a professor of political science at the University of Vienna, Austria.

Patrick Müller is assistant professor at the Institute for European Integration Research (EIF) at the University of Vienna, Austria.

Routledge series on global order studies
Edited by David Armstrong
University of Exeter, UK
and
Karoline Postel-Vinay
CERI, Sciences-Po, Paris, France

This new series focuses on the major global issues that have surfaced in recent years which will pose significant and complex challenges to global governance in the next few decades. The books will explore challenges to the current global order and relate to these themes:

- The Challenge to Western Dominance
- The Challenge to International Governance
- Religion, Nationalism and Extremism
- Sustainable Growth
- Global Justice and the Poorest Countries
- The implications of the Global Economic Crisis for Future World Order

1 **Redefining Regional Power in International Relations**
   Indian and South African perspectives
   Miriam Prys

2 **Turkey between Nationalism and Globalization**
   Riva Kastoryano

3 **Contemporary Political Agency**
   Theory and practice
   Edited by Bice Maiguashca and Raffaele Marchetti

4 **1989 as a Political World Event**
   Democracy, globalisation and the international system
   Edited by Jacques Rupnik

5 **EU Policies in a Global Perspective**
   Shaping or taking international regimes?
   Edited by Gerda Falkner and Patrick Müller

EU Policies in a Global Perspective

Shaping or taking international regimes?

Edited by Gerda Falkner and Patrick Müller

LONDON AND NEW YORK

First published 2014
by Routledge

Published 2014 by Routledge
2 Park Square, Milton Park, Abingdon, Oxfordshire OX14 4RN

and by Routledge
711 Third Avenue, New York, NY 10017

Routledge is an imprint of the Taylor and Francis Group, an informa business

First issued in paperback 2015

© 2014 Gerda Falkner and Patrick Müller, selection and editorial matter; contributors their contributions.

The right of Gerda Falkner and Patrick Müller to be identified as the authors of the editorial material, and of the authors for their individual chapters, has been asserted by them in accordance with sections 77 and 78 of the Copyright, Designs and Patents Act 1988.

All rights reserved. No part of this book may be reprinted or reproduced or utilized in any form or by any electronic, mechanical, or other means, now known or hereafter invented, including photocopying and recording, or in any information storage or retrieval system, without permission in writing from the publishers.

Trademark notice: Product or corporate names may be trademarks or registered trademarks, and are used only for identification and explanation without intent to infringe.

British Library Cataloguing in Publication Data
A catalogue record for this book is available from the British Library

Library of Congress Cataloging in Publication Data
EU policies in a global perspective: shaping or taking international regimes? / edited by Gerda Falkner and Patrick Müller.
    pages cm. – (Global order studies)
    Includes bibliographical references and index.
    1. European Union countries–Foreign relations. 2. European Union countries–Politics and government. 3. Security, International–International cooperation. 4. Diplomatic negotiations in international disputes. I. Falkner, Gerda.
    JZ1570.A5E864 2013
    341.242'2–dc23
                                                                    2013019979

ISBN 978-0-415-71149-4 (hbk)
ISBN 978-1-138-95643-8 (pbk)
ISBN 978-1-315-86741-0 (ebk)

Typeset in Times New Roman
by Wearset Ltd, Boldon, Tyne and Wear

Contents

List of figures vii
List of tables viii
Notes on contributors ix
List of abbreviations xi

1 **The EU as a policy exporter? The conceptual framework** 1
  PATRICK MÜLLER AND GERDA FALKNER

2 **The EU in trade policy: from regime shaper to status quo power** 20
  DIRK DE BIÈVRE AND ARLO POLETTI

3 **The EU's Common Agricultural Policy: a case of defensive policy import** 38
  CARSTEN DAUGBJERG AND CHRISTILLA ROEDERER-RYNNING

4 **Food safety: the resilient resistance of the EU** 58
  VESSELA HRISTOVA

5 **Competition policy: the EU and global networks** 76
  MARCO BOTTA

6 **Social rights: the EU and the International Labour Organization (ILO)** 93
  GUIDO SCHWELLNUS

7 **EU environmental policy: greening the world?** 111
  KATHARINA HOLZINGER AND THOMAS SOMMERER

Contents

8 **Transport policy: EU as a taker, shaper or shaker of the global civil aviation regime?** 130
MARCIN DĄBROWSKI

9 **Migration policy: an ambiguous EU role in specifying and spreading international refugee protection norms** 149
FLORIAN TRAUNER

10 **Nuclear non-proliferation: the EU as an emerging international actor?** 167
PATRICK MÜLLER

11 **EU financial market regulation: protecting distinctive policy preferences** 186
ZDENEK KUDRNA

12 **Comparative analysis: the EU as a policy exporter?** 205
GERDA FALKNER AND PATRICK MÜLLER

Index 230

Figures

12.1 The significance of governance levels in ten policies 207
12.2 Number of policies classified highly significant at each level of governance 210

Tables

1.1	Significance of governance levels over time (Policy X)	6
1.2	Mechanisms of EU policy export	8
1.3	Vertical EU export – mechanisms and conditions	11
1.4	Horizontal EU export – mechanisms and conditions	13
1.5	Terminological overview	14
2.1	Significance of governance levels over time (Trade Policy)	23
3.1	Nested EU governance: significance of governance layers over time	40
4.1	Significance of governance layers over time (Food Safety)	60
5.1	Significance of governance layers over time (Competition Policy)	84
6.1	Significance of governance levels over time (Social Policy)	97
6.2	Vertical export/promotion and horizontal diffusion of social standards	99
6.3	The trade-off between policy fit and take-up rate in vertical export/promotion	103
7.1	Significance of governance layers over time (Environmental Policy)	113
8.1	Significance of governance levels over time (Transport Policy)	136
8.2	Overlaps of authority in standard-setting across the levels of governance	137
9.1	Significance of governance levels over time (the field of refugee protection)	156
10.1	Significance of governance layers over time (Nuclear Non-proliferation)	172
10.2	Overview of international non-proliferation institutions	173
11.1	Significance of governance levels over time (Financial Market Regulation)	188
11.2	International standards endorsed by the Financial Stability Board	189
11.3	Global regime for bank capital	193
11.4	Global regime for accounting	198

Contributors

Marco Botta, PhD is an assistant professor at the Institute for European Integration Research (EIF) of the University of Vienna. He holds a LL.M. in European Business Law from Leiden University, as well as a PhD in the field of competition law from the Law Department of the European University Institute.

Marcin Dąbrowski, PhD is an assistant professor at the Institute for European Integration Research (EIF) of the University of Vienna and his research focuses on multi-level governance, Europeanization as well as regional and transport policies. He graduated from Sciences Po Paris and completed his PhD on EU regional policy at the University of the West of Scotland.

Carsten Daugbjerg is a professor in the Crawford School of Public Policy, The Australian National University, Australia, and a part-time professor in the Department of Food and Resource Economics, University of Copenhagen, Denmark.

Dirk De Bièvre is a professor of international relations and international political economy, and a member of the Antwerp Centre for Institutions and Multilevel Politics (ACIM), Department of Political Science, Universiteit Antwerpen, Flanders, Belgium.

Gerda Falkner is Head of the Institute for European Integration Research, a professor of political science at the University of Vienna, and Editor-in-Chief of the refereed journals *Living Reviews in European Governance* and *European Integration Online Papers*. She serves on scientific advisory boards of international institutions such as the European University Institute in Florence and the Wissenschaftszentrum Berlin.

Katharina Holzinger is Chair for International Politics and Conflict Management at the University of Konstanz, Germany. Her research focuses on European Union politics, deliberative democracy and internal conflict in Africa.

Vessela Hristova, PhD is an assistant professor at the Institute for European Integration Research (EIF) of the University of Vienna. She holds a PhD in Political Science from Harvard University.

Zdenek Kudrna, PhD is an assistant professor at the Institute for European Integration Research, University of Vienna. He has been a consultant to the IMF, World Bank, UNDP and the Czech Minister of Finance. He holds a PhD in political economy from Central European University in Budapest.

Patrick Müller, PhD is an assistant professor at the Institute for European Integration Research (EIF) at the University of Vienna. Previously, he worked as a postdoctoral fellow at the German Institute for International and Security Affairs (SWP) in Berlin, the Institut Français des Relations Internationales in Paris and the Johns Hopkins University in Washington.

Arlo Poletti is an assistant professor of international relations and political science in the Department of Political Science at the University GUIDO Carli in Rome, Italy, and FWO postdoctoral research fellow at the University of Antwerp.

Christilla Roederer-Rynning is an associate professor in comparative politics at the Department of Political Science and Public Management, University of Southern Denmark. Her research interests include policy-making in the EU and the parliamentarization of EU politics.

Guido Schwellnus, PhD is an assistant professor at the Institute for European Integration Research (EIF) of the University of Vienna. He holds a Magister Artium in Political Science and History from the Technical University of Braunschweig and a PhD in Political Science from Queen's University Belfast.

Thomas Sommerer is a postdoctoral Research Fellow at the Department of Political Science, Stockholm University. His primary research interests are international organizations, transnational actors, policy diffusion and comparative environmental politics.

Florian Trauner, PhD is an assistant professor at the Institute for European Integration Research (EIF) of the University of Vienna. He wrote his PhD in the framework of the postgraduate programme 'European Integration 2004–2007' offered by the Institute for Advanced Studies in Vienna and was a visiting fellow at the European Union Institute for Security Studies (EU ISS) in Paris (2010).

Abbreviations

ACP	African, Caribbean and Pacific countries
AETR	Accord Européen sur les Transports Routiers (European Agreement concerning the work of crews of vehicles engaged in international road transport)
ASEAN	Association of Southeast Asian Nations
BAC	Banking Advisory Committee
BCBS	Basel Committee on Banking Supervision
BENELUX	Belgium, Netherlands and Luxembourg
BRIC	Brazil, Russia, India and China
CAP	Common Agricultural Policy
CFSP	Common Foreign and Security Policy
CMOs	common market organizations
CO	carbon monoxide
COSCAPs	Cooperative Development of Operational Safety and Continuing Airworthiness Programs
CSDP	Common Security and Defence Policy
CTBT	Comprehensive Test Ban Treaty
DG	Directorate-General
EASA	European Aviation Safety Agency
EASO	European Asylum Support Office
EBA	European Banking Authority
EBA	Everything But Arms
EC	European Community
ECAC	European Civil Aviation Conference
ECB	European Central Bank
ECCAIRS	European Coordination Centre for Accident and Incident Reporting Systems
ECE	Economic Commission for Europe
ECJ	European Court of Justice
ECSC	European Steel and Coal Community
EEA	European Economic Area
EEC	European Economic Community
EFTA	European Free Trade Association

END	European Nuclear Disarmament
ENP	European Neighbourhood Policy
EP	European Parliament
EPC	European Political Cooperation
ESARDA	European Safeguards Research and Development Association
ETS	emissions trading scheme
EU	European Union
Euratom	European Atomic Energy Community
EUROCAE	European Organization for Civil Aviation Equipment
EUROCONTROL	European Organisation for the Safety of Air Navigation
FAO	Food and Agriculture Organization
FSAP	Financial Stability Assessment Program
FSB	Financial Stability Board
FTA	free trade agreement
GATT	General Agreement on Tariffs and Trade
GCIM	Global Commission on International Migration
GDP	gross domestic product
GI	geographical indications
GM	genetically modified
GMOs	genetically modified organisms
GRPE	Group of Rapporteurs on Pollution and Energy
GSP	Generalized System of Preferences
HC	hydrocarbons
IAEA	International Atomic Energy Agency
IASB	International Accounting Standards Board
IATA	International Air Transport Association
ICAO	International Civil Aviation Organization
ICN	International Competition Network
ICPAC	International Competition Policy Advisory Committee
IDP	internally displaced persons
IFRS	International Financial Reporting Standards
ILO	International Labor Organization
IMF	International Monetary Fund
INFCIRCS	IAEA Information Circulars
IOM	International Organization for Migration
IOs	international organizations
IOSCO	International Organization of Securities Commissions
IPCC	Intergovernmental Panel on Climate Change
IPR	Intellectual Property Rights
ISO	International Organization for Standardization
ITO	International Trade Organization
JAA	Joint Aviation Authorities
JHA	Justice and Home Affairs
JRC	Joint Resarch Centre

Abbreviations xiii

LDC	Least Developing Countries
MEPs	members of the European Parliament
Mercosur	Mercado Común del Sur (Southern Common Market)
NAFTA	North American Free Trade Agreement
NAMA	non-agricultural market access
NCA	National Competition Authority
NCAs	National Competition Authorities
NextGen	Next Generation Air Transportation System
NGOs	non-governmental organizations
NOx	nitrogen oxides
NPT	Treaty on the Non-Proliferation of Nuclear Weapons
NSG	Nuclear Suppliers Group
OECD	Organization for Economic Cooperation and Development
PHARE	Poland and Hungary: Aid for Restructuring of the Economies
PM	particulate matter
PN	particulate nitrogen
PTA	preferential trade agreement
REACH	Registration, Evaluation, Authorisation and Restriction of Chemicals
ROSC	Reports on Observance of Standards and Codes
RPP	Regional Protection Programme
SCM	Subsidies and Countervailing Measures
SEA	Single European Act
SESAR	Single European Sky Air Traffic Management Research
SPS Agreement	Agreement on the Application of Sanitary and Phytosanitary Measures
STABEX	Système de Stabilisation des Recettes d'Exportation
TBT Agreement	Agreement of Technical Barriers to Trade
TCNs	third country nationals
TFEU	treaty on the functioning of the European Union
TRIPs	Trade-related Aspects of Intellectual Property
UNCTAD	United Nations Conference on Trade and Development
UNECE	United Nations Economic Commission for Europe
UNEP	United Nations Environment Program
UNHCR	UN High Commissioner for Refugees
URAA	Uruguay Round Agreement on Agriculture
WMD	Weapons of Mass Destruction
WMO	World Meteorological Organization
WTO	World Trade Organization
WWII	World War II

1 The EU as a policy exporter?
The conceptual framework

Patrick Müller and Gerda Falkner

1 Introduction[1]

European integration started off as an internal project centring on the making of the Single Market and the harmonization of Member State policies. Yet, over time, the external dimension of major EU policies gradually gained in importance and the EU became actively involved in shaping governance beyond its borders (Wunderlich and Bailey 2011). At the same time, the EU has progressively strengthened policies designed from the outset for external projection, such as its external trade policy and its foreign and security policy (Hill and Smith 2005a; Bretherton and Vogler 2006; Orbie 2009b; Tèlo 2009; Knodt and Princen 2003). But what has been the EU's policy-specific impact on global governance – has the EU been a policy shaper or a policy taker? And what explains the EU's capacity for policy export? The aim of this book is twofold. First, it seeks to establish the relative importance of selected EU policy regimes in the multi-level global governance system as compared to both national and global activities. Second, it explores the EU's capacity for exporting its domestic rules, norms and standards to the global arena, the mechanisms it uses and the conditions leading to success or failure.

Research comparing the EU's impact on global governance in different EU policy areas is still largely a research desideratum. Much of the existing literature portrays the EU as a regional power whose willingness and ability for external projection weakens as geographical distance away from the EU increases (Börzel and Risse 2012; Lavenex 2011; Schimmelfennig 2010). Others suggest that the EU is emerging as a 'partial' global power, with the capacity to exercise global (regulatory) leadership and shape international regulatory outcomes in at least a few policy areas (Bretherton and Vogler 2006; Tèlo 2009; Wunderlich and Bailey 2011; Vogel 2012). Andrew Moravcsik even went so far as to describe the EU as a 'second superpower' possessing a 'range of effective civilian instruments for projecting international influence that is unmatched by any country' (Moravcsik 2010). The portrayal of the EU's role in global governance in the existing literature thus appears fragmented and even contradictory, with contributors to the debate frequently drawing general conclusions about the EU's global role on the basis of individual case studies.

2 Transgressing the state of the art

Addressing the question of EU policy export (which we understand to cover all kinds of formal and informal norms such as rules, standards, operating practices, etc.) in a comprehensive fashion, this project speaks to several distinct bodies of literature that can inform our understanding of key mechanisms of policy export and the conditions for their success. We will discuss them one by one in this section.

The role played by the EU in promoting its own policies at the international level constitutes an important theme in research on the *EU's external relations*. Different analytical perspectives have contributed to this debate. Prominent among them are conceptions of the EU as a 'civilian power' (Hill 1990; Orbie 2009a; Tèlo 2007) or as a 'normative power' (Manners 2002: 239). The 'civilian power' perspective argues that the EU is a new type of foreign policy actor that has transcended traditional realist power politics based on military strength. Applying its own successful model of regional cooperation to its external relations, the EU's foreign policy relies predominantly on economic means to promote peace and security. Central shortcomings of the civilian power perspective are its reductionist focus on the EU's economic dimension and its indeterminate character that fails to clearly specify whether the concept serves as a description of 'means, ends, and/or impacts' (see Schimmelfennig 2010). The debate on whether the EU may still be considered a 'civilian power' following the developments of military capabilities through the Common Security and Defence Policy (CSDP) or whether a 'civilian power' may rely on military instruments to pursue civilian objectives is indicative of this indeterminacy. The concept of 'normative power' shares the idea that the EU's external behaviour is rooted in its unique identity as a foreign policy actor, emphasizing Europe's particular historical context, hybrid polity and political-legal constitution (Manners 2002: 240). It is concerned with the EU's ideational influence on global politics, with the EU shaping global norms in line with core principles of European integration such as democracy, rule of law, social solidarity and anti-discrimination. Our aim, by contrast, is not to establish whether the EU acts as a normative force for good in international relations, but to explore its capacity for projecting its domestic policies globally. For our study of EU policy export – which transcends the focus on core EU norms and puts forward a systematic conceptualization of policy export – established notions of civilian or normative power in Europe remain both too narrow and imprecise.

A more systematic understanding of the pathways, mechanisms and conditions of EU policy export is provided by the literature on 'external EU governance' (Schimmelfennig and Wagner 2004; Lavenex and Schimmelfennig 2009; Schimmelfennig and Sedelmeier 2005; Lavenex 2004). This body of literature explores the promotion of EU institutions, policies, governance modes and norms in the EU's near abroad. It has focused on institutionalized EU rule transfer to accession and candidate countries or states in the EU's neighbourhood through integration, association and political partnerships. The EU's ambition to shape global regimes and international rules beyond its neighbourhood, in turn, has thus far largely been neglected in the external governance literature.

This neglect of the global dimension is also reflected at the conceptual level. The external governance concept is geared towards situations of institutionalized rule transfer where power and interdependence are highly asymmetrical in favour of the EU (see Lavenex 2011). External EU governance is conceived as a one-directional transfer of policies from the EU to partner countries in which active, power-based mechanisms (see Table 1.4) of EU influence – such as the use of political rewards and sanctions – figure particularly prominently. Global governance, by contrast, takes place in a context of mutual dependence and frequently relies on multilateral frameworks, with the EU functioning both as a shaper as well as a taker of global policy. Here, the process of EU rule transfer is less top-down and less encompassing than in the EU neighbourhood, with passive forms of policy diffusion through emulation and policy externalities playing a greater role. Accordingly, we prefer to speak of 'EU policy export' rather than of 'external EU governance'. At the same time, the role of multilateral institutions as arenas and instruments for EU policy export needs to be considered.

There are large literatures on transnational *policy diffusion* and policy transfer in the field of international relations that can inform our understanding of horizontal patterns of diffusion of EU policies around the world (Holzinger *et al.* 2007; Lütz 2007; Braun and Gilardi 2006; Evans and Davies 1999; Stone 2004; Dussauge-Laguna 2012). The main focus of the policy diffusion and policy transfer literatures is on processes of domestic adaption as a result of rising international interdependence, enhanced international communication and the growing legalization of international relations. Even though the literatures on policy diffusion and transfer are based on distinct terminologies and methodologies, they identify similar mechanisms that drive processes of policy change including coercion, competition, learning and emulation (Gilardi 2012). There is also an emerging literature on the EU's specific role in transnational policy diffusion. A number of authors have described the EU's involvement in global governance as a result of functional pressures arising from globalization, growing interdependence and increasing transnational externalities (Bach and Newman 2007; Drezner 2005; Vogel 2012).[2] Issues like global environmental pollution or climate change represent problems of scale that exceed the domestic problem-solving capacity of even large international players like the EU, demanding coordinated international action. At the same time, the EU benefits from an international environment that mirrors its own standards and norms. Through policy export to the global level the EU reduces domestic adaptation costs, generates competitive advantages, and ensures a 'level playing field' for European firms bound by high domestic regulatory standards (Bach and Newman 2007; see also Drezner 2005). The main analytical focus here is on international regulatory competition and harmonization, generally portrayed as a game of horizontal coordination between the world's great economic powers.

Others have looked at the transfer of institutional arrangements, policy patterns, and norms from the EU *to other regional actors* (e.g. NAFTA, Mercosur, ASEAN), which is often based on softer forms of EU influence such as learning and emulation (De Lombaerde and Schulz 2009; Gaens 2008; Wunderlich and Bailey 2011). Recently, attempts have been made to examine the way in which EU policies and institutions diffuse across different contexts using a single analytical framework, considering EU policy transfer to the neighbourhood in addition to other regions in the world (Börzel and Risse 2012). This project, by contrast, seeks to escape the 'region-to-region' approach that dominates the literature on EU policy transfer. Rather, it is concerned with the EU's role as a global rule-setter, examining EU policy export to formal and informal regimes at the international level.

Finally, there is a growing literature on the EU's role in global governance that can inform our understanding of the EU's *role in multilateral institutions*. Some authors have focused on the EU's performance at the UN (Laatikainen and Smith 2006) and in other international organizations (Jorgensen 2011), as well as the Union's impact on a variety of international organizations in terms of original institutional design, policy-making processes, activities and institutional reforms (Jorgensen 2009a). Our focus, in turn, is on the Union's policy-specific influence. We are interested in international organizations as arenas and instruments for EU policy export. Moreover, works on the EU's role in global governance include insightful collections of essays (Tèlo 2009; Bretherton and Vogler 2006; Wunderlich and Bailey 2011) as well as studies that deal with EU governance in single policy domains (e.g. environmental, social or trade policy) (Meunier and Nicolaidis 2005; Oberthür and Gehring 2006; Orbie and Tortell 2009). Others have looked at the EU's role in international affairs more broadly (Hill and Smith 2005b; Smith 2010). By contrast, we aim to produce a comparative study focusing on several major policies the EU adopted for itself, hence the substantial output of EU decision-making, and on how these EU policies bear intended or unintended effects on a global scale. By bridging between and adding to the separate strands of literatures discussed here, this book promotes a comprehensive and systematic understanding of the EU's role in shaping global policy.

3 Mapping EU policy areas in a multi-level governance system

In an increasingly globalized world, the interactions between global, European and national policy spheres have intensified. The phenomenon of distinct but ever more intertwined policy spheres has been described as 'multi-level governance' (Wessel and Wouters 2008: 11; Hooghe and Marks 2010; Hooghe 1996). The possibility of policy export is closely linked to the density of regulation at different governance levels, i.e. national, European and global. We can expect EU policy export only in areas where the EU has accumulated a certain degree of policy competences and regulation. Conversely, areas in which the EU faces strong international rules in the absence of strong internal policies are more likely to produce policy import. To be sure, the relative significance of individual governance levels may change over time and is itself influenced by processes of policy import and export. To gain a better understanding of the significance of the EU regulatory sphere in the multi-level global governance system, the individual contributors to this book map the relative importance of sectoral EU regimes as compared to both national and global regulatory activities. It is useful to see if the global and/or the EU regulatory levels have increased in importance over time, and if the EU may be considered to be a 'first mover' in a policy area (with the EU's regulatory activities preceding the establishment of the corresponding international regime).[3]

The mapping of governance levels is conducted on the basis of expert judgements by the authors, relying on common criteria for orientation. A number of different indicators have been developed in the literature to capture the intensity of individual EU policy areas (Lindberg and Scheingold 1970; Alesina et al. 2005; Schmitter 1996; Hooghe and Marks 2001). These indicators, however, omit the global dimension. Our project also needs to assess to what extent core aspects of a policy area are governed by regimes beyond the EU.[4] Therefore, we refer to selected criteria developed by Helmut Breitmeier et al. (2006) as part of the International Regimes Database when discussing the respective importance of levels of governance over time. More specifically, our expert judgements centre on the following factors for orientation:

- functional scope of rules;
- depth as measured by density and specificity of rules;
- binding character of the rules for the regime members as opposed to only indicative soft law.

We ask: What is the significance of governance levels during a specified period in terms of the scope and depth of rules and the extent to which the rules are binding and formative for the policy overall? Our scores for significance are 'high', 'medium' and 'low'. We leave it to the authors to aggregate the three above-mentioned scores, based on the understanding that even a non-binding policy can be empirically important if many actors take it up, and that even a regime based on a narrow but crucial policy output may be considered empirically highly significant.[5]

Table 1.1 will end each policy chapter's description of the overall regime. The authors will explain their expert judgements in their respective policy chapters. To ensure the reliability and comparability of the results, the judgements made by the individual authors have, furthermore, been cross-checked multiple times (e.g. in an author workshop held in Vienna in July 2012).

Table 1.1 Significance of governance levels over time (Policy X) (indicative example)

Phase	National level	EU level	Global level
Post-WWII	High	–	Low
1957–late 1980s	High	Low	Low
1990s	High	Medium (increasing relevance after 1991 due to ECJ judgment x)	Low
2000s	Medium (decreasing relevance after 2008 EU Directives)	High	Medium (increasing relevance after 2001 due to Agreement x)
2020 (extrapolation)	Low	High	High

Note
Scale – Significance high, medium, or low.

4 EU policy export: yardsticks, pathways and mechanisms

We understand EU policy export as a process through which the Union actively and passively projects beyond its borders formal and informal norms or policy paradigms, which are first defined and consolidated in the making of EU public policy. Our main focus is on the export of policy content, rather than on the diffusion of political institutions or practices. EU policy export differs from more general phenomena such as EU influence or impact, as it focuses exclusively on the EU's capacity to transfer its own internal policies to the global level.

EU policy export to the global level will be classified according to the three dimensions 'policy fit', 'relevance' and 'take-up rate'. 'Policy fit' relates to the degree that international outcomes reflect core internal policy positions and standards of the EU.[6] It may be assessed by comparing domestic policies and standards adopted by the EU to the outcomes of international negotiations and horizontal coordination. It is important to note, however, that the EU may also formulate positions for external projection that deviate from its domestic policy *acquis*. The EU may do so for strategic reasons, or because it engages in global policy matters that are not regulated at the EU level (e.g. in the realms of CFSP [Common Foreign and Security Policy] or external trade that serve external purposes). In such cases we speak of the promotion of external positions rather than EU policy export. 'Relevance' refers to the functional scope and significance of the exported policies when compared to the scope of the EU's own internal regime and the global regime. The 'take-up rate', in turn, refers to the number of members of a regime that accept a new policy in addition to the EU (we focus on regimes that include the EU). To establish the take-up rate, we rely on what the literature on international institutions has described as formal rule adoption by international actors (e.g. via vote in the legislative assembly), as opposed to behavioural or discursive conceptions of rule adoption (Hasenclever *et al.* 1997: 14–21; Schimmelfennig and Sedelmeier 2005: 8).[7]

From the perspective of the EU, successful export entails that international policy outputs closely resemble core elements of domestic EU policies and are widely shared among international actors (comprehensive EU export). In practice, however, a series of actors will inject their positions in international negotiations and compete with the EU for setting global standards. Accordingly, the EU may only be able to get some of the relevant actors to adjust to certain aspects of its own standards. While our main focus is on the question of EU policy export, the individual chapters will also report on other important modes of EU interaction with global policy regimes, in particular 'EU policy protection' and 'EU policy import'. The EU may face a situation where other important actors, such as the US, succeed in getting positions accepted as global standards that do not fit the EU's policy preferences. The EU's response may range from shielding its domestic policy from external pressures (policy protection) to adjusting its own domestic policy to global standards (EU import).

Two main *pathways* exist through which the EU can project its own policies, norms and standards to the international level: a 'vertical' one via international or global regimes and a 'horizontal' one via other countries.

First, the EU can engage in *vertical policy export* (EU to IOs). Here, the EU relies on its strong representation in international organizations and global transgovernmental networks – which serve as key instruments for global governance – to anchor its policies in international regimes. Often, a strong international regime already existed before the EU became active in a policy space. The existence of such a regime that pre-dates EU activities sets the framework conditions for vertical EU policy export, not least as it confronts the EU with policy precedents that might be difficult to alter or reverse in accordance with its own policy preferences. Yet, there are also instances where the EU enjoys a first-mover advantage, i.e. domestic EU policy was established prior to the formation of the corresponding international regime. In this case, the EU can influence the policy development at the global level from the outset. Moreover, given the complexity of international regimes, the EU often has different focal points to project its policies to the international level (Alter and Meunier 2009; Drezner 2009), allowing the EU to strategically select its venues to effectively advance its policy preferences. The outcomes of vertical export are multilaterally negotiated policies and rules that generally possess a certain degree of institutionalization (i.e. international treaties, conventions and codified obligations) and a high take-up rate (i.e. they generally apply to all the members of the policy regime, with room for mutually agreed opt-outs and withdrawal of individual members).[8]

Second, the EU can shape global outcomes through *horizontal export* (EU to states), using bilateral influence and regional institutions to entice other actors to assume EU policies. When a significant number of countries adopt policies similar to the EU, horizontal coordination can result in de facto international standards and informal regimes. Research has shown that the adoption of a policy by a critical mass of states may trigger a dynamic that makes adoption by the other actors in the system more likely (Kern 2000; Finnemore and Sikkink 1998). By contrast, if no critical mass can be achieved, policy convergence will at best be limited to different nodes.

Moreover, we distinguish different *mechanisms* of EU policy export (understood as ideal-type styles of interaction; see Table 1.5). First, EU policy export can rely either on 'active mechanisms' where the Union pro-actively shapes global outputs, or on 'passive EU export' resulting from the EU's mere 'presence' in international affairs. This distinction is important, since EU policy export should not necessarily result from deliberate EU strategies of regulatory transfer. As a major global economic power and model of peace and prosperity, EU policies also have unintended consequences that make other actors adjust to its domestic standards even without the EU actively promoting them.[9] Passive mechanisms are only at work in the horizontal dimension, as vertical EU policy export is per definition about the active negotiation of global standards. Based on the rationalist–constructivist debate in international relations theory, our second distinction is between mechanisms of EU policy export building on a 'rationalist logic of consequence' and mechanisms that are based on a 'logic of appropriateness' (March and Olsen 1989). The former logic assumes that rational actors base their choices on instrumental calculations of utility, understood in terms of power and welfare gains. The latter logic is rooted in constructivist thinking and assumes that actors are motivated by internalized norms and rules of appropriate or exemplary behaviour. In this view, policy export is driven by processes of persuasion, socialization and learning (rather than by coercion), and by voluntary emulation of the EU model by third countries (rather than by external effects of EU policies). Both logics have been discussed in depth and shown in their detailed workings in various well-known studies. On this basis, our ambition is not to pitch one against the other in the kind of either/or approach that characterized much of political science a while ago, but to use the full scope of mechanisms potentially at work. This presents the most fruitful starting point for an innovative empirical study exploring EU policy export. In other words, our analytical framework assumes that both rationalist and constructivist logics can possibly lead to EU policy export, and that it is a matter of empirical enquiry to establish if so, to what extent, and under which conditions. Table 1.2 displays a typology of this study's main mechanisms for EU policy export.

Table 1.2 Mechanisms of EU policy export

	Active	*Passive*
Rationalist	Bargaining	Policy externalities
Constructivist	Persuasion	Emulation

5 Vertical EU policy export through international institutions: mechanisms and conditions

Through its membership in international regimes the EU can vertically export its policies to the global level. Vertical policy export corresponds with the EU's self-stated goal of 'effective multilateralism', which aims to strengthen international institutions and pursue political objectives through multilateral frameworks (Kissack 2010). Two main mechanisms of vertical EU policy export may be distinguished: bargaining and persuasion.

Bargaining is an active mechanism of policy export that builds on rationalist assumptions. Bargaining involves actors exchanging threats and promises to promote their individual preferences. The EU's bargaining power is central to the promotion of its external preferences. International actors can rely on strategies such as side payments and package deals to induce cooperation from other actors. There is an important difference between bargaining in multilateral negotiations, which is constrained by the rules and procedures of the institutional setting (rule-mediated outcomes), and bilateral bargains that are less constrained by rules (power-based outcomes). International organizations provide rules for membership, decision-making, dispute settlement and the enforcement of agreements which enable and constrain the EU's capacity for policy export.

The membership status of the EU – represented by the European Commission – and its Member States varies in international organizations, treaty bodies and conventions. While the EU enjoys full membership status in some international organizations – including the World Trade Organization (WTO), the UN Framework Convention on Climate Change, and the Food and Agriculture Organization (FAO) – in most cases it only functions as an observer.[10] Yet, even in the cases where the EU has not been granted formal membership, as a block of 27 Member States it often has a considerable share of membership in international organizations. The strong representation of the EU Member States translates into considerable 'voting power'. The EU is also a major financial contributor to the budget of international organizations including the UN, which further increases its standing in international organizations (Jorgensen 2009b: 6).

The EU's ability to use its collective weight in multilateral forums depends on a number of factors. The decision-making procedures of the international setting matter, which differ among international organizations. Majoritarian decision-making and weighted voting rules generally benefit the EU as a large 'voting bloc', while unanimity voting grants veto power to each member. Certain international regimes, moreover, have established independent bodies for dispute settlement through adjudication, such as the dispute settlement mechanism of the WTO, the International Tribunal of the Law of the Sea, or the International Criminal Court (Merrills 2005; Boisson De Chazournes *et al.* 2002). Negotiations – which remain the principal way of dispute settlement – grant states a high degree of control over their dispute. International adjudication, by contrast, takes the ruling on the dispute out of their hands. While international dispute mechanisms lack centralized enforcement powers, their rulings still carry weight, not least because of their precedential significance. It has been argued for the case of the WTO dispute settlement mechanism that negotiations on trade disputes take place in the 'shadow of the law' (Bush and Reinhardt 2001). Defendants of a protectionist policy often seek to negotiate political compromises prior to litigation to avoid legal precedents that might put additional policies at risk, making their position more malleable than it would be in a 'pure' bargaining situation.

The Union's capacity to make effective use of its bargaining power in international negotiations also depends on internal properties of the EU (Jupille and Caporaso 1998; Groenleer and Van Schaik 2007). 'EU unity' is central to the external performance of the EU. It is a common assumption that a centralized voice increases the EU's leverage in international affairs; at least in situations where the EU strives for a change of the status quo as is the case for policy export (see Meunier 2005).[11] EU unity not only requires coordination among the individual foreign policies of its Member States; it also necessitates the reconciliation of potentially conflicting foreign policy priorities represented by EU institutions like the European Commission, for instance, with respect to trade and environmental objectives. Moreover, the format of the EU's external representation matters, as the EU enjoys distinct legal competences to act in different policy areas. The European Commission – representing the EU – enjoys the most substantial authority for external action in areas of exclusive competence (Art. 3, TFEU) and in some areas of shared competence (Art. 4, TFEU). In the area of trade, for instance, the Commission holds far-reaching competences. Very importantly, it has the exclusive power to negotiate trade agreements on behalf of the EU. In the realm of the intergovernmental CFSP, in turn, the EU is represented by the High Representative for the CFSP who remains strongly dependent on the support of the Member States, which makes coherent and unified external action more difficult.

From a constructivist perspective, by contrast, vertical EU policy export depends on the EU's ability to *persuade* others about the legitimacy of the EU model. *Persuasion* is an active mechanism of policy export that is facilitated by socialization and learning processes. In this view, the EU's 'normative capabilities' (i.e. its normative authority, the success and transferability of its domestic policy solutions, and its expertise in a policy area) are key for convincing others to follow EU policies (Schimmelfennig and Sedelmeier 2005; Checkel 2001). The EU can rely on global institutions, including international organizations and global policy networks, to communicate innovative policy solutions and to make normative claims about the legitimacy of its own standards. Here, international institutions are primarily understood as a social environment whose prevailing norms and values structure the choices of actors and provide arenas for routine interactions. Conducive to persuasion strategies are international settings that are little politicized, deal with complex and technical matters, facilitate dense interactions among its members, and are based on consensus-seeking rather than hard political bargains and formal voting (Checkel 2005; Beyers 2005; Alderson 2001).

Internal properties of the EU also matter for effective persuasion strategies. From a constructivist perspective, EU unity is conceived primarily in terms of

Table 1.3 Vertical EU export – mechanisms and conditions

Mechanism	Conditions
Bargaining (active, rationalist)	• INTERNATIONAL SETTING • *First mover/latecomer* • *Formal procedures (membership, decision-making, dispute settlement)* • EU CAPACITY • *Formal capacity (authority delegated to EU institutions)* • *Informal capacity (bargaining power)* • EU UNITY *(shared preferences over strategies and outcomes between Member States, within Commission)*
Persuasion (active, constructivist)	• INTERNATIONAL SETTING • *Informal norms and procedures (e.g. consensus-seeking)* • *Politicization of setting, institutionalization of interactions* • *First mover/latecomer* • EU CAPACITY • *Informal capacity (EU institutions accepted as representatives of common norms and values by Member States; normative EU capabilities in terms of authority, expertise, transferability of domestic solutions* • EU UNITY *(shared norms and values between Member States, within Commission)*

shared values and normative objectives among EU institutions and the Member States (see also Groenleer and Van Schaik 2007). EU unity is important to formulate consistent external positions, to communicate norms and rules in a clear fashion to external actors, and to persuade others about European solutions. The acceptance of EU institutions as the legitimate representative of common European norms and positions by the Member States (which can be facilitated by the formal delegations of external powers) also matters.

6 Horizontal EU policy export through diffusion: mechanisms and conditions

The EU also exports its policies through horizontal diffusion, working through its bilateral relations with third countries and regional institutions. Over time, the horizontal export of EU policies can also lead to convergence around the EU position in multilateral forums and the formal adoption of international rules and standards.

Horizontal EU policy export may be based, first, on active forms of EU influence, with the EU making deliberate efforts to spread its domestic norms and standards globally. Through *bargaining*, the EU can urge other countries to adapt to EU norms and standards, offering rewards and sanctions – including access to the large EU market (Drezner 2005; Bach and Newman 2007; Damro 2012). Bargaining as a form of EU rule transfer enjoys a prominent role in the EU's relations with accession, candidate and neighbourhood countries, and has been extensively studied in the literature on external EU governance (see above). Yet the EU also incorporates specific norms and standards in its trade and association agreements with third countries situated beyond its neighbourhood. As observers have noted, the EU is not only a major power *in* trade but it has also developed into a power *through* trade, using 'market access as a bargaining chip to obtain changes in the domestic arena of its trading partners, from labor standards to development policies' (Meunier and Nicolaidis 2005: 266; Meunier 2006). Its economic importance as the world's largest industrial market gives the EU considerable bargaining power, understood in terms of the relative size and diversity of its internal market, to promote third-party compliance with EU positions. The EU collectively accounts for about 30 per cent of global GDP and is also the world's biggest trading block, accounting for about 20 per cent of global trade flows.[12]

As is the case with bargaining in multilateral settings, the EU's capacity to collectively employ its weight in its bilateral relations depends on important internal properties of the EU. More specifically, the EU benefits from a high degree of internal unity and from the delegation of authority to EU institutions, such as the Commission (see above). The EU can also rely on *persuasion* strategies to actively promote its policy preferences. Horizontal EU policy export through persuasion may involve regional institutions and transgovernmental networks, technical EU assistance programmes, or political dialogue with third countries (Bach and Newman 2007; Stone 2004). As elaborated above, the EU's 'normative capabilities' are key for EU policy export through persuasion strategies.

Second, horizontal EU policy export can also be the outcome of passive forms of EU influence resulting from its mere 'presence' in international affairs (see Allen and Smith 1990). Given the considerable size of the EU's domestic market, internal European decisions often have important external implications. Externalities of EU policies can alter cost/benefit calculations of third countries without deliberate externalization strategies of the Union, at times creating strong pressure to adapt to EU standards. Externalities of EU policies may lead to what has been described as the 'California effect', i.e. a process by which a government's more stringent domestic regulatory standards are diffused to other political jurisdictions. To gain access to the EU's large single market, the products of third countries need to be compliant with European standards. Accordingly, European policies can have a significant impact on industries selling in the EU market. Given the EU's regulatory leadership in important policy domains and its large domestic market, Vogel has even argued that the California effect has become the 'EU effect' (Vogel 2012: 16). Conversely, policy externalities may also lead to downward trends (i.e. 'race to the bottom'), creating pressures for actors with high domestic standards.

The EU's 'presence' in the international system can also lead to passive EU policy export through emulation. As observers have noted, the multi-level EU system of governance constitutes itself a unique experiment in governance beyond the state that can serve as an important reference point for the global governance system and the transformation of the traditional Westphalian model of state sovereignty (see Wunderlich and Bailey 2011: 5). Emulation entails the imitation of the EU as a role model by outside actors without a pro-active role of

Table 1.4 Horizontal EU export – mechanisms and conditions

Mechanism	Conditions
Bargaining (active, rationalist)	• EU CAPACITY • *Formal capacity (authority delegated to EU institutions)* • *Informal capacity (bargaining power)* • EU UNITY *(between Member States, within Commission)*
Persuasion (active, constructivist)	• EU CAPACITY • *Informal capacity (normative acceptance of EU institutions as representatives of common norms and values by Member States); normative EU capabilities in terms of authority, expertise, transferability of domestic solutions* • EU UNITY *(between Member States, within Commission)*
Policy Externalities (passive, rationalist)	• EU PRESENCE *(EU market power)*
Emulation (passive, rationalist)	• EU PRESENCE *(EU as a model)*

the EU, which sets it apart from active forms of rule transfer through persuasion. It assumes that in situations of uncertainty and dissatisfaction with domestic policies, third countries may voluntarily adopt EU standards if they believe in their legitimacy, view them as appropriate solutions to their own problems, and accept the normative authority of the EU (see also Checkel 2001).

7 Outline of the book

This study covers the *major EU policy domains*, providing a comprehensive treatment of EU activities.[13] The following policies (covered in Art. 3, TFEU on exclusive competence, Art. 4, TFEU on shared competence and Art. 24, TEU on special competences in the realm of CFSP) are analysed: competition policy, trade policy, social and anti-discrimination policies, agriculture and fisheries, environment, consumer protection, regulation of financial markets, and nuclear non-proliferation. At the same time, the contributors to this project identify the main corresponding international regimes with respect to their salience in the global governance of the examined policy area.

The individual policy chapters follow a *common analytical framework and text structure*, answering the same questions and using common terminology. The notions used in our conceptual outline aim to depict, in the briefest possible manner, rather complex phenomena. Table 1.5 lists the most important terms and their intended meaning. To avoid potential misunderstandings, we highlight, in particular, that the notion of 'mechanism' is not used to imply a specific causal chain of events (or repetitive patterns of cause and effect) as done in part of the neo-institutionalist literature (see Mayntz 2002: 24), but to refer to distinct ideal-type forms of interaction. Hence, we are using the term in a wider sense, as is common practice in the literatures on Europeanization and external governance.

Table 1.5 Terminological overview

Term	Basic question	Alternatives discussed
'Pathway' of EU export	What is the *direction* of transfer?	Horizontal (EU to state) vs. vertical (EU to IO)
'Mechanism' of EU export	What is the (*ideal-type*) *style* of interaction?	Bargaining; persuasion; Externalities; emulation
'Mode of EU interaction with the global regime'	What is the dominant *mode of policy (non-)diffusion* (either inward-out or outward-in from the EU's perspective)?	Policy export; policy import; policy protection

Each chapter provides a general overview of the EU policy area, its main sub-policies and its historical evolution in terms of institutions (e.g. treaty changes, distribution of competences) and policy development. Further issues that are addressed relate to EU unity, EU capacity and EU presence. One section describes the corresponding international regimes in the particular policy area (e.g. its main organizations, institutions and functions). If relevant, the section also describes important informal regimes and quasi-international standards that govern a policy area. It covers the interface between the EU's domestic policy and the international regime, which matters most for potential policy export. Important issues are the relevance of a regime over time (in terms of the functional scope, depth and binding character of the rules), the timing of EU involvement (did the international regime already exist before the EU became internationally active in that policy area?), and the EU's participation in international regimes (how is the EU represented and what are the rules of decision-making?).

Thereafter, each chapter examines the EU's interaction with the corresponding global regime in the selected policy areas. Focusing on important milestones in the development of each of the major international regimes, the contributions subsequently trace the EU's influence in shaping these policies. As discussed above, the following issues are studied in depth:

- Pathways of EU external projection: Did the EU engage in vertical and/or horizontal export and has it shifted arenas for projection over time?
- Mechanisms of EU export: What were the dominant mechanisms of EU policy export?
- Success of EU policy export: Relying on the dimensions of (1) policy fit, (2) relevance, and (3) take-up rate, how successful has the EU been in shaping global policy outputs?
- EU policy import: How did the EU's involvement in the global governance of a particular policy domain and its participation in the corresponding international regime impact on its domestic policy?
- EU policy protection: Did the EU try to shield its domestic policy against external pressure/unwanted policy import?

To facilitate understanding, each chapter will summarize the findings along the lines of the main pathways, mechanisms and conditions. The book's concluding chapter then compares all policies on the meta-level, developing extensive policy recommendations as well. The comparison follows the cornerstones of our analysis as outlined above, based on the above-mentioned factors, and the resulting tables discussed during the project's author workshops.

Notes

1. The framework was elaborated in a series of workshops with the team of authors. Inputs and feedback regarding the concept by Michael Blauberger, Liesbet Hooghe and Gary Marks are also gratefully acknowledged.
2. For a broad discussion of globalization in general, see Caporaso and Madeira (2012).
3. A regime may be defined as 'sets of implicit and explicit principles, norms, rules, and decision-making procedures around which actors' expectations converge in a given area of international relations' (Krasner 1982: 186). Regimes can be formal and informal and they may include institutions as well as organizations or they may be based on an informal understanding.
4. It would be a major project in its own right to establish the details of formal competence location, let alone the de facto execution of such powers in a more or less authoritative manner. Comprehensive research on the coding of several international governmental organizations is currently being carried out by Gary Marks and Liesbet Hooghe. See: www.polsoz.fu-berlin.de/en/v/transformeurope/team/fellows/Hooghe/hooghecv.pdf.
5. Only a true policy expert can judge this, and hence we trust that our authors will – based on their intense knowledge of the relevant literature – be ideally suited to attribute scores and argue why.
6. A good fit between a EU policy and international outcomes merely shows a correlation and is not necessarily the result of deliberate EU strategies to achieve regulatory transfer, which is an empirical question. The same is true for a policy misfit between international outcomes and internal EU policies, which should not necessarily lead to EU import (the EU can still maintain its distinct standards).
7. In cases where we lack data on formal rule adoption, however, authors will rely on the best available proxy to establish the take-up rate of a policy, such as the number of signatories to an international treaty or convention.
8. It is important to note, however, that international treaties and conventions require ratification by the state parties.
9. Unintended consequences of EU policies do not inevitably facilitate external adjustment to EU policies and may also have undesired implications for the EU.
10. The UN Charter (Chapter I, Art. 4.1) confines membership in its main bodies to states only and the majority of specialized UN agencies have not welcomed the EU as a member.
11. In situations where the EU seeks to defend the status quo, by contrast, a veto power position for the Member State with the most 'conservative view' may strengthen the EU's ability to defend a hardline position.
12. See http://ec.europa.eu/economy_finance/international/index_en.htm.
13. We usually identify policy areas with respect to 'nominal categories' (Windhoff-Héritier 1987: 21), i.e. we distinguish among policy fields as they are generally described in daily language, which is typically also shown in the institutional competences of the specific Directorate General (DG) in the EU Commission (e.g. social policy, agricultural policy).

References

Alderson, K. (2001) 'Making Sense of State Socialization', *Review of International Studies* 27(3): 415–433.

Alesina, A., Angeloni, I. and Schuknecht, L. (2005) 'What does the European Union do?', *Public Choice* 123(3–4): 275–319.

Allen, D. and Smith, M. (1990) 'Western Europe's Presence in the Contemporary International Arena', *Review of International Studies* 16(1): 19–37.

Alter, K.J. and Meunier, S. (2009) 'The Politics of International Regime Complexity', *Perspectives on Politics* 7(1): 13–24.

Bach, D. and Newman, A.L. (2007) 'The European Regulatory State and Global Public Policy: Micro-institutions, Macro-influence', *Journal of European Public Policy* 14(6): 827–846.

Beyers, J. (2005) 'Multiple Embeddedness and Socialization in Europe: The Case of the Council Officials', *International Organization* 59(4): 899–936.

Boisson De Chazournes, L., Romano, C. and Mackenzie, R. (eds) (2002) *International Organizations and International Dispute Settlement: Trends and Prospects*, Ardsley, NY: Transnational Publishers.

Börzel, T.A. and Risse, T. (2012) 'From Europeanisation to Diffusion: Introduction', *West European Politics* 35(1): 1–19.

Braun, D. and Gilardi, F. (2006) 'Taking "Galton's Problem" Seriously – Towards a Theory of Policy Diffusion', *Journal of Theoretical Politics* 18(3): 298–322.

Breitmeier, H., Young, O.R. and Zürn, M. (2006) *Analyzing International Environmental Regimes: From Case Study to Database*, Cambridge, MA: MIT Press.

Bretherton, C. and Vogler, J. (2006) *The European Union as a Global Actor*, 2nd revised edn, London; New York: Routledge.

Bush, M.L. and Reinhardt, E. (2001) 'Bargaining in the Shadow of the Law: Early Dispute Settlement in GATT/WTO Disputes', *Fordham International Law Journal* 24(1): 158–172.

Caporaso, J.A. and Madeira, M.A. (2012) *Globalization, Institutions & Governance*, Sage Series on the Foundations of International Relations, Los Angeles, CA; London: Sage.

Checkel, J. (2001) 'Why Comply? Social Learning and European Identity Change', *International Organization* 55(3): 553–588.

—— (2005) 'International Institutions and Socialisation in Europe: Introduction and Framework', *International Organization* 59(4): 801–826.

Damro, C. (2012) 'Market Power Europe', *Journal of European Public Policy* 19(5): 682–699.

De Lombaerde, P. and Schulz, M. (eds) (2009) *The EU and World Regionalism: The Makability of Regions in the 21st Century*, Farnham: Ashgate.

Drezner, D.W. (2005) 'Globalization, Harmonization, and Competition: The Different Pathways to Policy Convergence', *Journal of European Public Policy* 12(5): 841–859.

—— (2009) 'The Power and Peril of International Regime Complexity', *Perspectives on Politics* 7(1): 65–70.

Dussauge-Laguna, M.I. (2012) 'On The Past and Future of Policy Transfer Research: Benson and Jordan Revisited', *Political Studies Review* 10(3): 313–324.

Evans, M. and Davies, J. (1999) 'Understanding Policy Transfer: A Multi-level, Multi-disciplinary Perspective', *Public Administration* 77(2): 361–385.

Finnemore, M. and Sikkink, K. (1998) 'International Norm Dynamics and Political Change', *International Organization* 52(4): 887–917.

Gaens, B. (ed.) (2008) *Europe–Asia Interregional Relations: A Decade of ASEM*, Aldershot: Ashgate.
Gilardi, F. (2012) 'Transnational Diffusion: Norms, Ideas, and Policies', in W. Carlsnaes, T. Risse and B.A. Simmons (eds) *Handbook of International Relations*, London: Sage.
Goertz, G. and Mahoney, J. (2012): 'Concepts and Measurement: Ontology and Epistemology', *Social Science Information* 51(2): 205–216.
Groenleer, M.L.P. and Van Schaik, L.G. (2007) 'United We Stand? The European Union's International Actorness in the Cases of the International Criminal Court and the Kyoto Protocol', *Journal of Common Market Studies* 45(5): 969–998.
Hasenclever, A., Mayer, P. and Rittberger, V. (1997) *Theories of International Regimes*, Cambridge: Cambridge University Press.
Hill, C. (1990) 'European Foreign Policy: Power Bloc, Civilian Model – or Flop', in R. Rummel (ed.) *The Evolution of an International Actor: Western Europe's New Assertiveness*, Boulder, CO: Westview Press.
Hill, C. and Smith, M. (eds) (2005a) *International Relations and the European Union*, Oxford; New York: Oxford University Press.
Hill, C. and Smith, M. (2005b) 'Acting for Europe: Reassessing the European Union's Place in International Relations', in C. Hill and M. Smith (eds) *International Relations and the European Union*, Oxford; New York: Oxford University Press.
Holzinger, K., Jörgens, H. and Knill, C. (2007) 'Tranfer, Diffusion und Konvergenz: Konzepte und Kausalmechanismen', in K. Holzinger, H. Jörgens and C. Knill (eds) *Transfer, Diffusion und Konvergenz von Politiken*, Wiesbaden: VS Verlag für Sozialwissenschaften.
Hooghe, L. (ed.) (1996) *Cohesion Policy and European Integration: Building Multilevel Governance*, Oxford: Oxford University Press.
Hooghe, L. and Marks, G. (2001) *Multilevel Governance and European Integration*, Lanham, MD: Rowman & Littlefield.
—— (2010) 'Types of Multi-level Governance', in H. Enderlein, S. Wälti and M. Zürn (eds) *Handbook on Multi-level Governance*, Cheltenham: Edward Elgar.
Jorgensen, K.E. (ed.) (2009a) *The European Union and International Organizations*, London; New York: Routledge.
—— (2009b) 'The European Union and International Organizations. A Framework for Analysis', in K.E. Jorgensen (ed.) *The European Union and International Organizations*, London; New York: Routledge.
—— (2011) 'Introduction: Assessing the EU's Performance in International Institutions – Conceptual Framework and Core Findings', *Journal of European Integration* 33(6): 599–620.
Jupille, J. and Caporaso, J.A. (1998) 'States, Agency, and Rules: The European Union in Global Environmental Politics', in C. Rhodes (ed.) *The European Union in the World Community*, Boulder, CO: Lynne Rienner.
Kern, K. (2000) *Die Diffusion von Politikinnovationen. Umweltpolitische Innovationen im Mehrebenensystem der USA*, Opladen: Leske & Budrich.
Kissack, R. (2010) *Pursuing Effective Multilateralism. The European Union, International Organizations and the Politics of Decision Making*, Basingstoke: Palgrave Macmillan.
Knodt, M. and Princen, S. (eds) (2003) *Understanding the European Uion's External Relations*, London, New York: Routledge.
Krasner, S.D. (1982) 'Structural Causes and Regime Consequences: Regimes as Intervening Variables', *International Organization* 36(2): 185–205.

Laatikainen, K.V. and Smith, K.E. (2006) *The European Union at the United Nations: Intersecting Multilateralisms*, Basingstoke: Palgrave.

Lavenex, S. (2004) 'EU External Governance in Wider Europe', *Journal of European Public Policy* 11(4): 680–700.

—— (2011) 'Concentric Circles of Flexible "EUropean" Integration: A Typology of EU External Governance Relations', *Comparative European Politics* 9(4/5): 372–393.

Lavenex, S. and Schimmelfennig, F. (2009) 'EU rules Beyond EU Borders: Theorizing External Governance in European Politics', *Journal of European Public Policy* 16(6): 791–812.

Lindberg, L. and Scheingold, S.A. (1970) *Europe's Would-be Polity: Patterns of Change in the European Community*, Englewood Cliffs, NJ: Prentice-Hall.

Lütz, S. (2007) 'Policy-transfer und Policy Diffusion', in A. Benz, S. Lütz, U. Schimank and G. Simonis (eds) *Handbuch Governance. Theoretische Grundlagen und empirische Anwendungsfelder*, Wiesbaden: VS Verlag für Sozialwissenschaften.

Manners, I. (2002) 'Normative Power Europe: A Contradiction in Terms?', *Journal of Common Market Studies* 40(2): 235–258.

March, J. and Olsen, J. (1989) *Rediscovering Institutions: The Organizational Basis of Politics*, New York: Free Press.

Mayntz, R. (2002) 'Zur Theoriefähigkeit makro-sozialer Analysen', in R. Maynetz (ed.) *Akteure – Mechanismen – Modelle. Zur Theoriefähigkeit makro-sozialer Analysen*, Frankfurt: Campus.

Merrills, J.G. (2005) *International Dispute Settlement*, Cambridge: Cambridge University Press.

Meunier, S. (2006) 'The European Union as a Conflicted Trade Power', *Journal of European Public Policy* 13(6): 906–925.

Meunier, S. and Nicolaidis, K. (2005) 'The European Union as a Trade Power', in C. Hill and M. Smith (eds) *International Relations and the European Union*, Oxford; New York: Oxford University Press.

Moravcsik, A. (2010) 'Europe, the Second Superpower', *Current History* March: 91–98.

Oberthür, S. and Gehring, T. (eds) (2006) *Institutional Interaction in Global Environmental Governance. Synergy and Conflict among International and EU Policies*, Cambridge MA; London: MIT Press.

Orbie, J. (2009a) 'A Civilian Power in the World? Instruments and Objectives in European Union External Policies', in J. Orbie (ed.) *Europe's Global Role. External Policies of the European Union*, Farnham: Ashgate.

—— (2009b) 'The European Union's Role in World Trade: Harnessing Globalisation?', in J. Orbie (ed.) *Europe's Global Role. External Policies of the European Union*, Farnham: Ashgate.

Orbie, J. and Tortell, L. (eds) (2009) *The European Union and the Social Dimension of Globalization*, New York: Routledge.

Schakel, A.H., Hooghe, L. and Marks, G. (forthcoming) 'Multilevel Governance and the State', in S. Leibfried, E. Huber and J. Stephens (eds) *The Oxford Handbook of Transformations of the State*, Oxford: Oxford University Press.

Schimmelfennig, F. (2010) 'Europeanisation Beyond the Member State', *Zeitschrift für Staats- und Europawissenschaften* 8(3): 319–339.

Schimmelfennig, F. and Sedelmeier, U. (eds) (2005) *The Europeanization of Central and Eastern Europe*, Ithaca, NY: Cornell University Press.

Schimmelfennig, F. and Wagner, W. (2004) 'Preface: External Governance in the European Union', *Journal of European Public Policy* 11(4): 657–660.

Schmitter, P.C. (1996) 'Imagining the Future of the Euro-polity with the Help of New Concepts', in G. Marks, F.W. Scharpf, P.C. Schmitter and W. Streeck (eds) *Governance in the European Union*, London;Thousand Oaks, CA: Sage.
Smith, K.E. (2010) 'The European Union in the World: Future Research Agendas', in M. Egan, N. Nugent and W.E. Paterson (eds) *Research Agendas in EU Studies*, Basingstoke: Palgrave Macmillan.
Stone, D. (2004) 'Transfer Agents and Global Networks in the "Transnationalization" of Policy', *Journal of European Public Policy* 11(3): 545–566.
Tèlo, M. (2007) *Europe: A Civilian Power? European Union, Global Governance, World Order*, Basingstoke: Palgrave Macmillian.
—— (ed.) (2009) *The European Union and Global Governance*, London; New York: Routledge.
Vogel, D. (2012) *The Politics of Precaution: Regulating Health, Safety, and Environmental Risks in Europe and the United States*, Princeton, NJ: Princeton University Press.
Wessel, R. and Wouters, J. (2008) 'The Phenomenon of Multilevel Regulation: Interactions between Global, EU and National Regulatory Spheres. Towards a Research Agenda', in A. Follesdal, R.A. Wessel and J. Wouters (eds) *Multilevel Regulation and the EU. The Interplay between Global, European and National Normative Processes*, Leiden; Boston, MA: Martinus Nijhoff.
Windhoff-Héritier, A. (1987) *Policy-Analyse. Eine Einführung*, Frankfurt; New York: Campus Verlag.
Wunderlich, J.-U. and Bailey, D.J. (eds) (2011) *The European Union and Global Governance. A Handbook*, London; New York: Routledge.

2 The EU in trade policy
From regime shaper to status quo power

Dirk De Bièvre and Arlo Poletti

1 Introduction

It is a well-known economic fact that the European Union (EU) is, and has been for decades, one of the world's two largest trading blocs. Accounting for 20 per cent of global trade with only 5 per cent of the world's population, the EU is the second largest importer and the world's largest exporter of goods and services. Somewhat less well known and acknowledged is the EU's historical political power and influence in making the rules governing international trade. The Treaty of Rome establishing the EU (then the European Economic Community (EEC)) not only embodied the creation of a unified European market without obstacles to trade, but this decision triggered multilateral trade liberalization. Since its establishment, the EU has projected some principles of European economic integration externally, contributing to the liberalization, constitutionalization and judicialization of the international trading regime. The EU structural power, due to the attractiveness of its internal market, enabled it to export some of its key regulatory preferences, as well as to protect policy arrangements from outside challenge.

While the European Economic Community had not yet been founded at the time of the creation of the General Agreement on Tariffs and Trade (GATT) in 1947, the European Steel and Coal Community (ECSC) of 1951 and especially the EEC of 1957 turned the EU into a formidable trade power. The creation of the EU's internal market had important external effects on global trade, triggering the first large liberalization within the GATT during the Kennedy Round of multilateral trade negotiations. Since the EC was created, the US adamantly demanded increased market access, and the EEC found itself in a comfortable bargaining position. As a result, it was able to obtain large market access concessions in return. Having imposed most of its preferences on the US during the Kennedy Round, the EC started to export its own policies to third countries with the US and created rules limiting the policy options of other countries by starting to write the rule book of the global GATT trade regime. At the same time, the EU was instrumental in warding off the challenge of newly decolonized members, deflecting a fundamental recast of the GATT to the creation of a new forum, the United Nations Conference on Trade and Development (UNCTAD) in 1964, granting a GATT waiver for the establishment of the Generalized System of Preferences (GSP) for developing countries in 1971, and autonomously structuring its relations with its ex-colonies in the Lomé Conventions as of 1976.

The EU's policy of decisively co-shaping the rules of the world trade regime continued in the results of the Tokyo Round (1979) with an expansion of regulatory rules disciplining GATT members' discretion in applying trade policy instruments, largely in line with the EU's own policies. This successful export saw its epitome in the form of a constitutional export in the outcomes of the Uruguay Round (1994), ushering in the addition of numerous new areas of multilateral rules and the shaping of stronger institutions for the enforcement of extant rules. By exporting some of its own internal policies and promoting multilateral institutions that solidified its preferred policy outcomes, the EU thus played a crucial part as a shaper of the world trade regime throughout the 1958 to 1995 period.

Shortly afterwards however, the European Union started to become far less successful in exporting its domestic regulatory framework or promoting its preferred external policies, and more recently has embarked on the path of preferential trade agreements (PTAs). Indeed, after many years of refusing to engage in bilateral or regional trade agreements in order to try to force its partners to the WTO negotiation table on its own terms, in the mid-2000s the EU embarked on the path of trying to secure better market access for some of its producers as well as to export some of its regulatory policies under preferential trade agreements. By so doing, the EU joined the other key players of the world trade regime: the United States, Southern Asian and Latin American countries, and Japan.

Contributing to this book's overall assessment of the EU's capacity to engage in policy export, this chapter first reconstructs the origins of the Union's historical significance in global trade relations – a cross-temporal comparative perspective often neglected in contemporary political science. Second, it offers a near comprehensive overview of the most important elements in EU external economic policies from its beginnings up until the present. This overview covers European policies within the global trade regime GATT/WTO and European relations with developing countries, while conceiving of trade policy-making in a comprehensive manner by combining the analysis of European trade negotiations (bilateral, regional and multilateral) with an analysis of administrative, unilateral European trade policies.

When throughout this chapter we probe into the origins of the European Union's capacity to protect, export or promote its preferred policies, we direct our view towards changes in the EU's sheer economic attractiveness as an export market, as well as its key institutional characteristic of consensus decision-making, which creates a high decision threshold for any deviation from the status quo to be accepted internally.

2 The emergence of the EU's trade policy

Prior to the creation of the European Economic Community, trade policies were determined by national West European governments, interacting – quite unsuccessfully – within the GATT. Whereas the European states insisted on international liberalization within the GATT, the main trading nation in the world at that time, the US, was entirely uninterested in pursuing liberalization in any meaningful way. Instead, the US concentrated on monetary and financial assistance to post-war Europe, while being unwilling to lower its tariffs on European exports in exchange for increased market access in Europe. European countries being relatively small, they had a far greater interest in re-obtaining foreign market access after the war than did the United States with its large internal market. Contrary to conventional wisdom (Krasner 1976; Keohane 1989), the United States did not use the GATT legal framework to negotiate gradual trade liberalization in rounds of negotiations throughout the late 1940s and the entire 1950s (Dür 2004). Instead, the US maintained its level of protective tariffs in response to constant lobbying by import-competing industries in the US Congress, while exporters failed to mobilize to push for the reduction of foreign tariff levels (Dür 2010).[1]

Meanwhile, in contrast, European states engaged in what was to become a new nucleus in the world trading regime. The smallest West European states moved first when the Belgian–Luxemburg Economic Union and the Netherlands signed the BENELUX customs union as early as 1944. Subsequently, France took the initiative to integrate newly created West Germany (1949), Italy and the BENELUX countries in the ECSC in 1951 (Rittberger 2009). The landmark Treaty of Paris abolished all barriers to trade in steel and coal products and established external tariffs for both sectors. As the ECSC founding member countries had committed to the prohibition of preferential arrangements in the GATT 1947 treaty, they were obliged to ask for a waiver for the two sectors of coal and steel from that GATT obligation and were successful in securing such an agreement from the GATT membership. The ECSC agreement contained the first international anti-cartel rules as well as rules to be followed in the event of overproduction. Since cartel dynamics and overproduction had both been perceived as having nurtured heavy arms production in Germany and France in the two World Wars, this arrangement was believed to make war virtually impossible in the future (Eilstrup-Sangiovanni and Verdier 2005). The enforcement of those rules was placed under a supranational High Authority, raising the relevance of the European governance level as early as 1951, at least in those two sectors of industry.

Next to the creation of the ECSC, Western European countries continued to exchange numerous initiatives to create liberalization among themselves throughout the 1950s. Disappointed by the lack of market opening by the US during the GATT Annecy (France 1949) and Torquay (Great Britain 1950–1951) rounds, and the fact that Congress refused to delegate significant negotiating authority to the US President in 1955, continental European countries decided that regional trade liberalization among themselves would be the best path to pursue (Dür 2004). Negotiated at the conferences of Messina and Val Duchesse in 1956, six Western European states signed the Treaty of the European Economic Community and the Euratom Treaty in Rome in 1957, establishing a customs union, an internal market and a common external commercial policy.

Over time, the EU developed into the most relevant governance level by far in comparison to the national or the global level in the field of international trade. While initially limited to measures restricting trade in goods, it gradually included trade-related regulatory measures covering issues such as technical standards and, later on, even intellectual property rules. The EU's capacity to project some of its regulatory norms and practices is remarkable because the EU is not a state and does not dispose of all conceivable policy instruments that can impact upon trade policy power, and thus impact upon an entity's capacity to protect, export or promote policies. The Union disposes of full authority to levy tariffs and to introduce regulations about market access rights for goods producers and service providers. At the same time, it does not have the exchange rate mechanism at its disposal to promote or restrict trade. By lowering the exchange rate of its currency, a state can temporarily make its exports cheaper, enabling greater foreign market access for its producers while reducing foreign imports to the advantage of its domestic producers. Monetary policy, however, was and remained in purely national hands in 1958, and when the rise of independent central banking in the 1980s and 1990s ushered in the creation of the European Central Bank in 1998, its mandate was limited to inflation-targeting price stability to the exclusion of exchange rate policy.

Table 2.1 provides an overview of this historical evolution of the EU in the global trade regime and the importance of the national, EU and international layers of governance.

3 The rise of the EC/EU as co-shaper of the global trade regime: 1958–1994

The creation of the European Customs Union and its external common commercial policy greatly enhanced the EU's presence in global trade and turned it into a major player in multilateral trade negotiations. Together with the US, the EU was able to greatly influence key developments in the international trade regime consistent with its multilateral liberalization agenda. In the period between 1958 and 1994, the EU successfully engaged in both policy protection and vertical

Table 2.1 Significance of governance levels over time (Trade Policy)

Phase	National level	EU Level	Global level
1947–1957	High	–	Medium (GATT)
1958–1994	Medium	High	Medium (GATT)
1995–2012	Medium	High	High (WTO and PTAs)
2020 (extrapolation)	Medium	High	High

policy export, largely managing to shape the global trade regime to its liking. The reasons for this success lie in its bargaining power vis-à-vis other industrialized countries, such as the US, as well as vis-à-vis developing countries. Moreover, important changes in the global trade system were also triggered as external effects resulting from European economic integration.

3.1 Obtaining multilateral trade liberalization while protecting EC interests: transatlantic trade relations and the Kennedy Round

Although an internal EU policy, the establishment of the single market also had a profound external effect on global trade. Triggering a drastic increase of trade between EC Member States, the set-up of the single market led to trade diversion causing harm to those exporting firms excluded from it (Dür 2010). Among the most harmed were American exporters, seeing how European companies turned to European foreign suppliers that gradually became cheaper as internal European tariffs were all being phased out between 1958 and 1967. As a result, American exports continued to have to jump over the new European common external tariffs – an average of pre-existing national tariffs – and found themselves confronted with losing market shares or the threat thereof. This triggered American exporters to mobilize far more than they had done throughout the 1950s in order to put pressure on the American Congress and the executive branch of government to negotiate a lowering of European tariffs. Therefore, the US suddenly found itself on the taking side in its trade policy-making, while the EC could lean back in its negotiating chair until the US side came along with offers of market access that would be attractive to European export industries. The American side was thus surprised to find the newly created entity of the EEC in the role of co-shaper in the GATT world trade regime.

As a result of this intensified US exporter mobilization, the US Congress delegated trade negotiating powers to the president in its Trade Expansion Act of 1962 on condition that the administration obtain market access for American agricultural exports. However, the US side of the negotiations saw itself obliged to drop this demand as the European side was unwilling to include agricultural trade liberalization in the agenda of the round. Indeed, simultaneously with the Kennedy Round that started in 1963, the six EC Member States were creating the Common Agricultural Policy (CAP) to modernize, subsidize and protect European agricultural producers; guaranteeing minimum prices, cementing quotas for imports, and installing export subsidy arrangements in case of European overproduction – a distant hypothetical scenario at the time. The European side thus benefited from a very comfortable bargaining position, caused by a double advantage. On the one hand, the American side was clearly in the position of the *demandeur*. On the other hand, the European Commission representatives' hands and feet were bound by extremely stringent oversight and effective veto power of every single EC Member State (Putnam 1988; Tsebelis 2002; Dür 2007). The Commission's weakness and lack of negotiating autonomy at the same time amounted to a large bargaining power advantage, as the European side of the negotiations could play on time and refuse to budge to American demands going against European policy preferences.

Thus, the large size of the EU's internal market contributed to the EU becoming an attractive partner for trade liberalization negotiations, in turn enabling the Union to resist demands that were inconsistent with its domestic preferences. Moreover, the trade diversion caused by the Community's very establishment created incentives for those suffering most from (the threat of) exclusion to move away from their preference for the status quo. As the balance between import-competing sectors advocating the maintenance of existing trade barriers on the one hand, and exporters wanting the restoration or even the increase of their market access abroad on the other hand shifted, the US negotiating side saw its bargaining power weakened. As Congress came under ever more pressure to make offers to the Europeans in order to satisfy the demands of exporters, the US State Department saw its negotiating autonomy rise and its bargaining power diminish. This dynamic resulted in a dramatic reduction in trade barriers across the Atlantic, with the US side ending up lowering its tariffs significantly more than the European side.[2]

The bilateral deal between the EEC and the US from the Kennedy Round produced strong external effects on global trade once more; first, all lowering of EEC and US tariffs automatically became applicable for all other trading partners of those two entities and were effectively multilateralized on a non-discriminatory basis by virtue of the Most Favoured Nation principle (GATT Article I). The drastically lower levels of tariffs on the products of the greatest importance for the EU and the US became the bound tariff levels that any exporter from other GATT members would have to pay when shipping goods into Europe or America. Second, the Kennedy Round bound tariff commitments between the EU and the US established the Euro-American tandem as the linchpin of the global GATT trade regime, laying the ground for future policy and even constitutional export by both the US and the EU.

The EC's power in trade negotiations was further enhanced by the set-up of its internal decision rules, allowing European Commission negotiators to always benefit from the strategic advantage of the paradox of weakness (Schelling 1960; Meunier 2005). Since Member States endowed Directorate-General (DG) Trade and DG Agriculture of the European Commission with closely monitored mandates and exerted strict control over their agent-negotiating liberalization (De Bièvre and Dür 2005), the use of consensus decision-making in the Council of Ministers made EU positions in external trade negotiations very rigid – often to the exasperation of the EC's negotiation partners but to the benefit of EC policy preference attainment. The EC's clout in international negotiations became apparent in the results of two important negotiation areas in European external trade policy-making in the 1960s and 1970s: trade relations with developing countries and the creation of new GATT rules disciplining trade policy discretion of GATT members through the Tokyo Round Codes.

3.2 Policy protection against the challenge of developing countries: UNCTAD, GSP and Lomé

The wave of decolonization during the late 1950s and early 1960s created demand for a radical reform of the post-war global economic regime on the part of the newly independent developing countries. However, rather than radically transforming the global trade regime, the EU and Western industrialized countries deflected pressures from it and supported the creation of a parallel organization, the United Nations Conference on Trade and Development (UNCTAD) in 1964, and granted a large GATT waiver from reciprocal non-discriminatory liberalization through the establishment of the Generalized System of Preferences (GSP) for developing countries in 1971. In 1976, the EU added the structuring of its relations with its ex-colonies in the Lomé Conventions.

Although appearing to result from development-motivated largesse on the part of the EU, the details of the EU's Generalized System of Preferences and Lomé Conventions are testimony to its capacity to keep shaping the global trade regime, and its relations with developing countries, to its advantage and at considerable cost for developing countries. First, it is important to appreciate the crucial role of the EC in the installment of the trade-restricting Multi-Fibre Agreement of 1972. This agreement excluded the textiles sector – of potentially great economic importance to developing countries – from the GATT bound tariffs and the GATT prohibition of quota. The agreement effectively enticed developing countries into an agreement on preferential, tariff-free market access to the EC, while at the same time introducing a disincentive for long-term investment in large-scale textile manufacturing. This was so because market access to the EC was contingent on quota ceilings and the imposition of trade restrictions whenever the EC should autonomously decide that its domestic producers were 'unable' to cope with import surges (Underhill 1998). Second, the EC also effectively protected its agricultural policy from any exogenous demands, excluding that second economic sector of potential significance for development country exporters. Third, GSP arrangements were an entirely autonomous policy and not subject to any negotiations. The EC could, and did, implement detailed exclusion arrangements for 'sensitive' products in which developing countries could have acquired a comparative advantage. Fourth, a similar logic undermined the long-term economic development potential of developing countries, while enabling the EC to export some of its own new domestic arrangements to its ex-colonies embodied in the Lomé agreements.

The Lomé Conventions (trade and aid agreements between the EU and 71 African, Caribbean and Pacific countries (ACP) signed in 1975 or later) contained the same type of lure for developing countries – preferential access for primary export products such as cocoa, coffee and tropical fruit, while being equally topped by quantitative restrictions. Although the European Commission had originally proposed a policy that would provide financial assistance to producers of these Third World commodities suffering from the vicissitudes of global price volatility or detrimental terms of trade, EC Member States insisted that no measures should be allowed to harm European producers. They consequently transformed the so-called STABEX scheme from sector-specific assistance, into unconditional, direct budgetary aid to the EU's developing country negotiation partners (Gruhn 1976; Ravenhill 1984). The basic set-up of the Lomé and successor conventions thus eliminated any likely creation of long-term trade, as the EC pursued a policy of buying off the support of mostly autocratic state elites dependent on captive markets in the North.

At the same time, the EC turned these countries and their agricultural sectors into beneficiaries of the European Common Agriculture Policy and its subsidy programmes, and provided large sums of development aid – turning the policy into a form of collective clientelism (Ravenhill 1985). In this manner, the EC effectively exported one of its key domestic regulatory policies horizontally, relying on its bargaining power vis-à-vis developing countries. Unsurprisingly, most developing countries towards which these policies were targeted remained dramatically trapped in a lack of diversification of domestic production, relying on the export of primary products, failing to invest in processing capacity – the economic activity where the largest value added can be realized – and often retaining a monopolistic or oligopolistic reliance on one or only a few of these primary products. These developments ended up cementing rather than transforming the often authoritarian socio-economic governance structures of these countries. The up side for the EC, of course, was that it turned out to be remarkably successful in shielding two key assailed domestic sectors – agriculture and textiles – from global competition, as it possessed the structural economic power to do so.

3.3 Vertical policy export and the expansion of the world trade regime's regulatory reach

Meanwhile, the EC embarked on its policy to write a more detailed international rule book in the GATT global trade regime. The Tokyo Round of GATT multilateral trade negotiations indeed constituted the first round in which the EC and the US drafted and committed to rules that essentially tried to limit the negative externalities of other GATT members' regulatory policies. These rules concern the limitation of anti-dumping policies, the disciplining of subsidy wars, the attempt to forestall protectionist and/or discriminatory abuse of health and safety rules, etc. Cast in the terms of international relations theory, these agreements are typical cases of institutional solutions to cooperation problems among states. If all states engage in levying high so-called anti-dumping duties, they might collectively end up undermining their mutually beneficial adherence to the non-discrimination principle. If all states, however, agree to the same, somewhat restricting conditions under which each is allowed to impose anti-dumping duties they are able to reach an equilibrium, limiting an anti-dumping duty arms race. And if, on top of that, there is monitoring and enforcement in the form of the GATT dispute settlement system to discourage free riding, then the occurrence of suboptimal aggregate outcomes is diminished. Although institutional solutions to cooperation problems may well be beneficial to all, their exact form and content are not necessarily neutral (Gruber 2000). The Tokyo anti-dumping code largely formalized and effectively exported the broad lines of US and EC anti-dumping policy to the other GATT members. The negotiations on the Tokyo anti-dumping code indeed coincided with the drafting of the EC's own nascent anti-dumping policy.[3] The EC and the US thus used their first-mover advantage by setting limits to others' anti-dumping policy that would be permissible under the GATT. While those members already engaging in anti-dumping policy would have to stay within the disciplines imposed by the code, the rules would limit the margin of manoeuvre for others wanting to draft and implement their own anti-dumping policy in the future – something that many countries did in subsequent decades (Zanardi 2004).

Of the same kind were a whole range of plurilateral regulatory codes dating from the end of the Tokyo Round in 1979 that fed into multilateral regulatory agreements at the end of the Uruguay Round in 1994. These concern the Tokyo Standards Code, which was later transformed into the more detailed WTO Agreement on Technical Standards and Trade, the code on import licensing procedures, the government procurement code, the customs valuation code, the agreement on trade in civil aircraft, the bovine meat arrangement, and the international dairy arrangement.

These agreements and the coverage of these agreements were of importance to the main GATT negotiating parties: the 'Quad' of the EC, the US, Canada and Japan. They constituted the basic building blocks for the further regulation of world trade in terms of content, scope and procedures that were to be negotiated and made binding for all WTO members as of 1995.

During the Uruguay Round – the most significant round since the Kennedy Round – the EU shaped both substantial policy outcomes (liberalization in sectors and areas dear to its own) and, most importantly, subscribed or actively promoted agreements that required little or no domestic regulatory changes in the EU, yet created large adaptation costs for other members. The EU and the US jointly managed to have developing countries accept their preference for an expansion of the trade regime's regulatory reach by threatening other GATT members with exclusion from market access benefits already acquired in the GATT. Indeed, rights acquired under the GATT were made conditional upon accession to the to-be-founded new organization the WTO. Moreover, accession to the WTO meant the acceptance of a host of new regulatory agreements that were placed under its umbrella. In other words, the EU and the US were able to force a large package deal on all issues on the negotiating table (Steinberg 2002). This take-it-or-leave-it option was called the 'Single Undertaking' of the Uruguay Round. Thanks to this formula, for the first and arguably the last time, the EU and the US could use the threat of exclusion from existing GATT market access commitments to force recalcitrant GATT members into accepting liberalization and regulatory commitments in services, intellectual property rules, public procurement, technical barriers to trade, rules of origin, food health and safety standards, and trade-related investment measures. The EC – in tandem with, or hiding behind, the US – thus secured the vertical export of policies dear to its own while ensuring that the new international governance level embodied the institutionalization of those policy preferences.

3.4 Vertical policy export and global institutions for trade rules enforcement

As the EU–US bilateral relationship generated the bulk of global trade regulation, these actors acquired an increasing and overarching stake in cementing these rules and procedures more firmly in institutions that would lend them increased stability and predictability. Several reasons can explain the strengthening of enforcement of GATT obligations during the Uruguay Round. The first incentive to strengthen dispute settlement at the end of the Uruguay Round was the aggressive US economic foreign policy throughout the 1980s. The creation of automatic, binding and sanctions-backed enforcement of all WTO commitments was certainly a by-product of the US's push for harsher sanctions in cases of non-compliance. Throughout the course of the 1980s, the US had repeatedly pressured the EC, Japan and others to honour their existing GATT commitments (or other 'obligations' in the eyes of the American administration) by imposing retaliatory sanctions against other products (Bello and Holmer 1994). In reaction, the EC developed the negotiating position whereby retaliatory sanctions in cases of non-compliance with GATT law would only be permissible after a GATT panel had established the non-compliance, and after a panel had authorized such retaliatory 'withdrawal of concessions' (Hudec 2000).

A second key reason for the EU's support for strengthened enforcement was that the regulatory agreements of the Uruguay Round would be severely devalued if they were not enforceable in a credible way. The extension of depth and scope of the global trade regime into matters of regulation was thus intricately linked to the increased bindingness of the rules, due to strengthened enforcement of those rules. Regulatory agreements are more difficult to enforce than simple exchanges of market access concessions (De Bièvre 2006). On the one hand, tariff agreements can be enforced by threatening to withdraw tariff concessions in response to defection from previous agreements, making reciprocal trade liberalization in goods generally quite stable and easy to enforce. The equilibrium can be maintained through simple tit-for-tat, whether cooperative or retaliatory. And, of course, large reductions in bound tariff levels, like those concluded in the Uruguay Round, are valuable exactly because their enforcement is easy and credible. On the other hand, the Uruguay Round package contained many regulatory agreements – agreements that entail higher transaction costs regarding policing, measurement, and especially enforcement (Majone 1996). Furthermore, regulatory agreements might entail little implementation costs for some – like for the EC with regard to the URAA on services on intellectual property, etc. – but large implementation costs for others – like developing countries when they have to establish an entire domestic intellectual property protection regime. For this reason, it is crucial to appreciate the significance of an agreement that GATT countries concluded in 1989 on making jurisdiction automatic whenever a GATT country deems another country to be violating or annihilating the benefits of an agreement (GATT 1990). This agreement codified an emerging practice and made crystal clear that vetoing or threatening to veto the progress of judicial proceedings would no longer be considered legitimate in Geneva. Moreover, the agreement took immediate effect, independent of what would happen further down the road during the ongoing Round, and thus constitutes the only – yet very important – exception to the negotiating rule of the Single Undertaking. The 1989 agreement on strengthened dispute settlement created the very preconditions for far-reaching regulatory agreements to be worth concluding, as it short-circuited the bedevilling 'no future enforcement/no bargain' problem in international cooperation (Fearon 1998).

During the Uruguay Round negotiations on the reform of the GATT dispute settlement system, the EU successfully opposed the unilateral sanctions and retaliation policy of the US, which had frequently bypassed, yet not breached, the GATT. Loath to merely undergo the negative externalities of unilateral American policies, the EC successfully insisted – together with other major GATT members such as Canada and Japan – that these American policies be put under multilateral surveillance, as the EC supported the creation of a permanent appeals court, the so-called WTO Appellate Body. The Canadian delegation to the Uruguay Round brokered a deal between the two elephants in the room, the EU and the US, leading to the major institutional innovation of the Round: the formal instalment of automatic jurisdiction (reiterating the elimination of the defendant's veto contained in the 1989 agreement), the creation of the Appellate Body at the request of the EC, and the multilateral authorization of sanctions in cases of enduring non-compliance at the request of the US (Croome 1999; Hudec 2000).

At the end of 1994, the EU had thus eliminated a source of unpredictability in the transatlantic trading environment by putting an end to unilateral American trade sanctions policy, secured a deal on regulatory issues much in line with its own preferences, and contributed significantly to the creation of a multilateral organization with independent adjudication authority and enforcement capacity. The EU's contribution to the constitutionalization and judicialization of the world trading system therefore resembled its own form of institutionally locking-in economic integration to some extent.

4 Status quo and relative decline of EU regime-shaping capacity: 1995–2012

This pinnacle of EU relevance in the global trade regime would soon dwindle in the subsequent period. In the second half of the 1990s, the EU was still largely influential in two multilateral agreements in the framework of the WTO that were concluded outside of any round. As the WTO member with large stakes in the international telecommunications and financial services sectors, the EU was an important contributor to the successful conclusion of these negotiations in

1997. Yet several developments soon started to undermine the EU's prominence in the global trading system. First, the option of threatening to exclude others from the benefits of liberalization commitments was no longer available, as threatening to leave the WTO was obviously not a feasible card for the EU to play. Second, Article 20 of the Uruguay Round Agreement on Agriculture (URAA) mandated WTO members to start a new round of negotiations on agriculture by the end of 1999. This seemingly minor Uruguay Round concession of playing on time forced the EU to start negotiations from a defensive position. Third, the rise of China (admitted to the WTO in 2003), Brazil and India in the global trading system significantly curtailed the EU's ability to shape policy outcomes in the WTO to its liking.

While still a hugely important importer, the EU could no longer co-dictate the agenda of WTO trade rounds. Whereas so far the EU had been the courted actor, for the first time in its existence the EU was the one demanding a new Round, what the European Commissioner for Trade at that time, Leon Brittan, intended to be a 'Millennium Round'. Decision-makers in the EU consistently made clear that extending the scope of negotiations beyond agriculture was a key priority, however (Poletti 2012). When WTO members started to seriously discuss among themselves how to proceed with the built-in agenda on agriculture, the EU made its support for an ambitious agenda on agriculture contingent upon the acceptance by other members of broad-based negotiations, including services, further Intellectual Property Rights (IPR) commitments, trade-and-environment, and the so-called Singapore issues. The Singapore issues refer to the four subject matters for which permanent WTO working groups had been set up at the instigation of the EU, Japan and Korea at the first WTO Ministerial Conference held in 1996 in Singapore: transparency in government procurement, trade facilitation (customs valuation), trade and investment rules, and trade and competition policy.

The EU was so keen to submerge agricultural negotiations into a comprehensive package that in February 2001, it unilaterally decided to grant duty- and quota-free access to imports from least developed countries through the 'Everything But Arms (EBA)' initiative with the aim of gaining support for its strategy among a group of recalcitrant developing countries (Ahnlid 2005). The EU thus started a trade round from the position of the *demandeur*, the one that would have to offer something first in order to achieve its policy objectives.

Several other reasons contributed to this change in structure and initiative in the global trade regime. The prospect of having to play on the defensive in agricultural trade negotiations was certainly a key factor. In order to minimize concessions in this sensitive field, the EU sought to widen the negotiating package as much as possible to increase the potential for trade-off deals (Poletti 2010). Second, and differently from the past, the EU found itself incapable of shaping negotiating dynamics in line with its preferences. While continuing to be one of the key hubs for large-scale intercontinental trade in basic goods, processed and finished manufactures as well as a key provider of services, the European Union had become a mature and saturated market for many goods and services with low to no growth rates. This contrasts starkly with emerging economies such as

Southeast Asia and Latin America where demand was and is growing. The sheer economic attractiveness of the EU's internal market has thus dwindled relative to other markets.

Furthermore, the very bindingness of WTO commitments through the increased judicialization of the world trade regime caused the EU, just like any other WTO member, to be vulnerable to legal challenges. The EU found that its WTO partners were able to force substantial concessions in agricultural negotiations by threatening to resort to WTO dispute settlement against the EU's domestic support schemes incompatible with its WTO commitments in case the EU would not concede – a strategy used especially by Brazil. This, in addition to the impossibility of threatening recalcitrant countries with exclusion, made it easier for developing countries to resist requests for further harmonization of regulatory issues with high adjustment costs for them. Indeed, throughout the Doha Round, developing countries consistently and successfully refused to succumb to EU attempts at policy export, such as new commitments on IPRs, services and the Singapore issues, just as the US had been fatally unsuccessful at including minimum labour standards on the agenda at the Seattle Ministerial Conference.

Even in its relations with other industrialized trading partners, the EU's attempts at regulatory export were no longer crowned with success, for example, in the case of geographical indications (GI) of origin. During the Uruguay Round, the EU had secured the insertion of the global protection of GIs in the WTO Agreement on Trade-related Aspects of Intellectual Property (TRIPs). Section 3 spelled out the conditions under which the names of agricultural products coming from a particular place and with particular characteristics can acquire special protection. GIs in the TRIPs treaty had never received unanimous support among the GATT membership, yet were included through the single package formula. It had been clear to most negotiation participants that Europe stood to gain most from such a form of protection, as Europe is home to household names like champagne, Parma ham or Roquefort cheese (Goldberg 2001; Raustiala and Munzer 2007). During the Doha Round, the EU has tried to go beyond the TRIPs agreement by demanding a multilateral register for wines and spirits and a higher level of protection for other agricultural products. The EU proposal calls for some 'generic' household names to be especially protected, an arrangement that would turn the agricultural producers from particular areas of production into de facto global monopolists. In 2011, the EU proposed a programme to facilitate geographical indications in ACP countries that showed how these countries were home to several agricultural products that would benefit from global protection of their name (Intellectual Property Watch 2011). So far, the EU has managed to enlist a range of developing countries in its camp, now counting 52 WTO members. Yet many other members find existing levels of GI protection sufficient, while the US has not really contemplated going beyond its own domestic system of GI protection through trademarks.

In addition, the negotiation assertiveness of middle-income developing countries such as Brazil, India and, to a lesser extent China further reduced the room for the EU to export its preferred policies in the WTO framework. Immediately after the launch of the Doha Round in 2001, an aggregation process of previously diverging negotiating approaches of a number of developing countries took place (Bjornskov and Lind 2005). This process culminated in the failure of the Cancun WTO Ministerial Conference in 2003, when the so-called G20 group of countries opposed a deal on agriculture jointly proposed by the EU and the US and forced the EU to drop the Singapore issues from the negotiating agenda. The negotiating process leading to Cancun made clear that an EU–US agreement no longer sufficed to provide a breakthrough in negotiations, that middle-income developing countries were ready to exert negotiating power, and, therefore, that their positions were to be fully considered as part of the equation for any future deal in the multilateral trade arena.

Despite being confronted with such difficulties in exporting and even protecting its domestic policies at the multilateral level, for a long time the EU held the official line that it was entirely dedicated to multilateralism and would maintain its moratorium on negotiating preferential trade agreements. In the mid-2000s however, the EU finally admitted defeat and radically reversed course by engaging in the horizontal route. EU policy-makers arguably realized that their multilateral bargaining power had waned and that the deadlock of the Doha Round was unlikely to be resolved any time soon. Moreover, many other prominent WTO members were concluding preferential trade agreements (PTAs) – a process that might well lead the EU to find itself left behind with less market access opportunities than the others. Consequently, the EU initiated so-called free trade agreement (FTA) negotiations with important partners such as South Korea, Japan, Canada and the United States, as well as with a whole host of smaller countries. Many of the regulatory issues that the EU had sought in vain to include into a Doha package thus became the subject of bilateral or regional agreements. Yet most of these regulatory exports in FTAs are quite inconsequential, written in legal inflation language with no rights and obligations specified, while enforceability of EU preferences is weak or mostly entirely absent (Horn *et al.* 2009).

Clearly, the EU is no longer one of the chief regime shapers at the global level and its capacity for policy export as well as policy protection has been significantly curtailed during the first decade of the new millennium. During this period, the EU was successful only in engaging in horizontal policy export mirroring its own regulatory framework in bilateral and regional agreements. While a detailed treatment of these horizontal regulatory exports is beyond the scope of this chapter, it suffices to mention three types of such agreements. First, the EU succeeded in exporting much of its *acquis communautaire*, of course also on trade matters, to future EC members and European Neighbourhood Policy countries in its Association agreements (Schimmelfennig and Lavenex 2009). Second, the EU managed to conclude some Economic Partnership Agreements, including exactly the regulatory trade agenda it had for so long sought to advance at the multilateral WTO level with some of its former ACP developing country partners. Finally, the jury is still out on the exact balance between regulatory policy exports and imports in the EU FTA with South Korea, as well as in such possible future agreements with Canada, Japan and the United States.

5 Conclusion

In this chapter, we have shown the early rise of the EU's capacity to shape the global trade regime and its relative decline into a status quo actor. While Western European states were unable to get real liberalization negotiations off the ground after the start of the GATT in 1947, the EC level of governance was able to enhance its role in global trade politics with the establishment of its unified market and the common commercial policy in 1957. The EC's ability to decisively shape the global trade regime was owed to the external effects of European economic integration giving the EC enhanced bargaining power as a major trade bloc and allowing it to engage in multilateral trade negotiations on an equal footing with the US. Owing to the rising attractiveness of its domestic market and the relatively constant rigidity of its trade policy-making decision rules, the EC successfully engaged in both policy protection and policy export throughout this period. On the one hand, the EC managed to resist demands for far-reaching liberalization in agriculture brought forward by other industrialized countries, such as the US, and was able to deflect developing countries' pressures for a radical reform of the global trade regime, especially in the sectors of textiles and clothing and tropical agriculture. On the other hand, the European Union, in tandem with the US, successfully engaged in the introduction of global regulation that affected the very nature of the trade regime in terms of both content and process. Indeed, parallel to transforming the trade regime into a forum for global regulatory harmonization, the EU and the US also managed to push through the key institutional changes of the regime's system for trade rules enforcement and the *modus operandi* in multilateral trade negotiations.

In the final section we bear witness to how changes in the relative power within the international economic system and the resulting assertiveness of developing countries within the trade regime have led to a gradual decline in the EU's capacity to shape global trade developments. The EU's inability to have developing countries accept further expansions of the WTO's regulatory reach and its decision to cede to the competitive pressures of other international trade actors to engage in preferential instead of multilateral trade and investment agreements show how the EU has lost its prominence as co-shaper of the global trade regime. Since the mid-2000s, the EU has turned into a status quo actor, unable to engage in vertical policy export to the global level, forced instead to turn to seeking enhanced foreign market access, horizontal regulatory export, and the defense of some of its internal arrangements in the context of bilateral and regional agreements.

Notes

1 In 1955, the US even asked other GATT members for and obtained a waiver from its GATT obligations for its agricultural sector.
2 US tariffs on manufactures were cut by 38 per cent, EC tariffs by only 32 pe cent, US tariffs on chemicals by 50 per cent, EC tariffs by only 20 per cent, and US tariffs on machinery and equipment by 47 per cent, and EC tariffs by only 40 per cent (UNCTAD 1968, quoted in Dür 2010: 127).

3 Until 1992, import-competing industries in the EC had the option of filing complaints to their national administration under Article 115 of the EC Treaty. As these national barriers to trade from outside the EC were gradually placed under Commission surveillance, demand for EC external anti-dumping policy among import-competing industries increased (see also Hanson 1998; Schuknecht 1992).

References

Ahnlid, A. (2005) 'Setting the Global Trade Agenda: The European Union and the Launch of the Doha Round', in O. Elgstrom and C. Jonsson (eds) *The European Union Negotiations: Processes, Networks and Institutions*, New York: Routledge.

Barton, J.H., Goldstein, J.L., Josling, T.E. and Steinberg, R.H. (2006) *The Evolution of the Trade Regime: Politics, Law, and Economics of the GATT and the WTO*, Princeton, NJ: Princeton University Press.

Bello, J.H. and Homer, A.F. (1994) 'U.S. Trade Law and Policy Series No. 24: Dispute Resolution in the New World Trade Organization Concerns and Net Benefits Recent Developments', *The International Lawyer* 28(4): 1095–1104.

Bjornskov, C. and Lind, M. (2005) 'Progress or Retreat in the Doha Round? Analysing Underlying Policies in the WTO and Harbinson Proposal', *Revue Economique* 56(6): 1385–1412.

Croome, J. (1999) *Reshaping the World Trading System: A History of the Uruguay Round*, Geneva: World Trade Organization.

De Bièvre, D. (2006) 'The EU Regulatory Trade Agenda and the Quest for WTO Enforcement', *Journal of European Public Policy* 13(6): 105–129.

De Bièvre, D. and Dür, A. (2005) 'Constituency Interests and Delegation in European and American Trade Policy', *Comparative Political Studies* 38(10): 1271–1296.

Dür, A. (2004) *Protecting Exporters. Discrimination and Liberalization in Transatlantic Trade Relations, 1932–2003*, PhD dissertation, Florence: European University Institute.

—— (2007) 'Avoiding Deadlock in European Trade Policy', in D. De Bièvre and C. Neuhold *Dynamics and Obstacles of European Governance*, Cheltenham: Edward Elgar.

—— (2010) *Protection for Exporters. Power and Discrimination in Transatlantic Trade Relations, 1930–2010*, Ithaca and London: Cornell University Press.

Eilstrup-Sangiovanni, M. and Verdier, D. (2005) 'European Integration as a Solution to War', *European Journal of International Relations* 11(1): 99–135.

Evenett, S.J. (2007) 'EU Commercial Policy in a Multipolar Trading System', *Intereconomics* 42(3): 143–155.

Fearon, J.D. (1998) 'Bargaining, Enforcement, and International Cooperation', *International Organization* 52(2): 269–305.

GATT (1990), 'Improvements to the GATT Dispute Settlement Rules and Procedures, Decision of 12 April 1989 (L/6489)', in The Contracting Parties to the GATT (eds) *Basic Instruments and Selected Documents, Thirty-sixth Supplement. Protocols, Decisions, Reports 1988–1989 and Forty-fifth Session*, Geneva: General Agreement on Tariffs and Trade.

Goldberg, S.D. (2001) 'Comment: Who will Raise the White Flag? The Battle between the United States and the European Union over the Protection of Geographical Indications', *Journal of International Economic Law* 22(1): 107–151.

Gruber, L. (2000) *Ruling the World: Power Politics and the Rise of Supranational Institutions*, Princeton, NJ: Princeton University Press.

Gruhn, I.V. (1976) 'The Lomé Convention: Inching Towards Interdependence', *International Organization* 30(2): 241–262.
Hanson, B.T. (1998) 'What Happened to Fortress Europe?: External Trade Policy Liberalization in the European Union', *International Organization* 52(1): 55–85.
Horn, H., Mavroidis, P.C. and Sapir, A. (2009) *Beyond the WTO? An Anatomy of EU and US Preferential Trade Agreements*, Brussels: Brueghel Blueprint Series VII.
Hudec, R.E. (2000) 'Broadening the Scope of Remedies in WTO Dispute Settlement', in F. Weiss (ed.) *Improving WTO Dispute Settlement Procedures – Issues and Lessons from the Practice of other International Courts and Tribunals*, London: Cameron May.
Intellectual Property Watch (2011) 'EU Makes Push to Facilitate Geographical Indications in ACP Countries', Catherine Saez for Intellectual Property Watch, 16 May 2011. Online. Available: www.ip-watch.org/ (accessed 17 May 2012).
Irwin, D.A., Mavroidis, P.C. and Sykes, A.O. (2008) *The Genesis of GATT*, Cambridge: Cambridge University Press.
Keohane, R.O. (1989) *International Institutions and State Power. Essays in International Relation Theory*, Boulder, CO; San Francisco, CA; London: Westview Press.
Krasner, S.D. (1976) 'State Power and the Structure of International Trade', *World Politics* 28(3): 317–343.
Lindner, J. and Rittberger, B. (2003) 'The Creation, Interpretation and Contestation of Institutions – Revisiting Historical Institutionalism', *Journal of Common Market Studies* 41(3): 445–473.
Majone, G. (1996) *Regulating Europe*, London; New York: Routledge.
McGuire, S.M. and Lindeque, J.P. (2010) 'The Diminishing Returns to Trade Policy in the European Union', *Journal of Common Market Studies* 48(5): 1329–1349.
Meunier, S. (2005) *Trading Voices: the European Union in International Commercial Negotiations*, Princeton, NJ: Princeton University Press.
Poletti, A. (2010) 'Drowning Protection in the Multilateral Bath: WTO Judicialisation and European Agriculture in the Doha Round', *British Journal of Politics & International Relations* 12(4): 615–633.
—— (2012) *The European Union and Multilateral Trade Governance. The Politics of the Doha Round*, London and New York: Routledge.
Poletti, A. and De Bièvre, D. (forthcoming) 'The Political Science of European Trade Policy: A Literature Overview with a Research Outlook', *Comparative European Politics*.
Putnam, R. (1988) 'Diplomacy and Domestic Politics: The Logic of Two-level Games', *International Organization* 42(2): 427–460.
Raustiala, K. and Munzer, S. (2007) 'The Global Struggle over Geographic Indications', *European Journal of International Law* 18(2): 337–365.
Ravenhill, J. (1984) 'What is to be Done for Third World Commodity Exporters? An Evaluation of the STABEX Scheme', *International Organization* 38(3): 537–574.
—— (1985) *Collective Clientelism. The Lomé Conventions and North–South Relations*, New York: Columbia University Press.
Rittberger, B. (2009) 'The Historical Origins of the EU's System of Representation', *Journal of European Public Policy* 16(1): 43–61.
Schelling, T. (1960) *The Strategy of Conflict*, Cambridge, MA: Harvard University Press.
Schimmelfennig, F. and Lavenex, S. (2009) 'EU Rules Beyond EU Borders: Theorizing External Governance in European Politics', *Journal of European Public Policy* 16(6): 791–812.
Schuknecht, L. (1992) *Trade Protection in the European Community*, Chur: Harwood Academic Publishers.

Steinberg, R. (2002) 'In the Shadow of Law or Power? Consensus-based Bargaining and Outcomes in the GATT/WTO', *International Organization* 56(2): 339–374.
Tsebelis, G. (2002) *Veto Players: How Political Institutions Work*, New York: Sage.
Underhill, G.R.D. (1998) *Industrial Crisis and the Open Economy: Politics, Global Trade and the Textile Industry in the Advanced Economies*, London and Basingstoke: Macmillan.
Woolcock, S. (2005) 'Trade Policy: From Uruguay to Doha and Beyond', in H. Wallace, W. Wallace and M. Pollack (eds) *Policy-making in the European Union*, Oxford: Oxford University Press.
World Trade Organization (1999) *The Legal Texts. The Results of the Uruguay Round of Multilateral Trade Negotiations*, Cambridge: Cambridge University Press.
Young, A.R. (2011) 'The Rise (and Fall?) of the EU's Performance in the Multilateral Trading System', *Journal of European Integration* 33(6): 715–729.
Zanardi, M. (2004) 'Anti-dumping: What are the Numbers to Discuss at Doha?', *World Economy* 27(3): 403–433.

3 The EU's Common Agricultural Policy

A case of defensive policy import

Carsten Daugbjerg and
Christilla Roederer-Rynning

1 Introduction

Seen from a global perspective, the EU may appear to be a club of rich countries with high regulatory standards that are very difficult to meet and protective legislation that impedes access to the EU market. Under these conditions, the EU may choose to protect its uniqueness, advocate a European model in global governance, or reform to align its regimes along a global line, options that are not mutually incompatible. A combination of global and domestic (EU) factors shapes the global policy or policy mix that the EU will pursue. In this chapter we focus on agriculture, one of the EU's most pivotal regimes in terms of budget and political salience. In this regime the EU has practised 'defensive policy import', a policy aligning EU policy instruments with global practice, all the while preserving the overarching redistributive objectives of EU intervention, epitomized in a generous scheme of public support for European farmers. Much of the EU's global policy has revolved around protecting European farmers' entitlements and EU market interests in the face of growing global pressures, rather than seeking to export a specific model of agricultural policy. Attempts to export the European model have been few and far between, and they have succeeded only at the margins of the agricultural regime.

Defensive policy import reflects the growing enmeshment between EU and international norms. Global norms have become biting as a reflection of a broader turn towards disembedded liberalism and the strengthening of trade multilateralism. However, policy import has fallen short of lowering agricultural subsidization; the EU has succeeded in maintaining its overarching goals of farm redistribution, but has done so with less trade distortion than before. EU resilience reflects the fact that the Common Agricultural Policy (CAP) remains rooted in historical settlements, whose political bases remain strong today, albeit contested by a powerful group of EU Member States. Recently, defensive policy import has been supplemented by greater EU activism in relation to developing countries, in the form of the Everything But Arms (EBA) agreement. In this chapter we provide insights into the EU's global engagement in both core and marginal areas of the GATT/WTO agricultural regime, and show how the Commission forged a compromise between conflicting pressures, navigating in an environment increasingly characterized by political and institutional competition.[1]

2 Agriculture: from national policies to competitive regulation

'Agriculture' is a patchwork of policies that have evolved over time to encompass rather different and heterogeneous domains of regulation; we focus here on the farming component of agriculture, known as the Common Agricultural Policy (CAP). This domain not only represents the bulk of EU activities in agriculture, but also constitutes one of the most developed and institutionalized areas of EU intervention in terms of historical continuity, legal output, as well as administrative and budgetary resources. Table 3.1 traces the varying relevance of different layers of farm governance over time. The extraordinary role and significance of the EU appears readily, although it is also clear that EU intervention has developed under the increasing pressure of global regulation.

It is possible to distinguish between four main periods of agricultural regulation in Europe (Roederer-Rynning forthcoming). The first period stretches from the immediate post-WWII to 1957, the year the European Economic Community was established. It is the *era of national agricultural policies*. Projects to pool agricultural policies flourished but failed to materialize in concrete policies (Tracy 1989). At the international level, the GATT regime on trade liberalization encompassed agriculture but these rules remained inoperative due to a political consensus to embed liberalism in domestic social and political compromises, termed 'embedded liberalism' by scholars of international law and international politics (Ruggie 1982; Steinberg 2006), and reflected by ad hoc concessions to vested interests both in Europe and the US.

The second period stretches from 1957 to the late 1980s. These years marked the *Europeanization of agricultural policy* – understood as the largely unchallenged delegation and pooling of farm competences at the European level (Daugbjerg 2012). The European level of intervention was by far the most significant. Following the Treaty of Rome (1957), a Common Agricultural Policy (CAP) developed around protective common market organizations (CMOs) and the core policy belief of agriculture as an exceptional sector needing special treatment (Skogstad 1998). Although key decision-makers at the European level, national politicians had relinquished the right (with some exceptions) to independently regulate farming at the domestic level. Accordingly, the functional scope of regulatory activities at the European level substantially increased while the regulatory power of national authorities became confined to a few domains not transferred, or transferred on a shared basis, to European Economic Community (EEC) institutions (e.g. land tenure, social security, education, the regulation of working conditions and wages of agricultural workers). The Council of Ministers dominated farm regulation during this period of 'hegemonic policy-making' (Roederer-Rynning 2011). Thus, the CAP unfolded itself as a formidable regime, breaking internal barriers to trade and supporting European farm modernization and production, thanks to the combined application of detailed legal rules enabling transfers through consumer prices and generous budget outlays. At the same time, agricultural trade liberalization within the GATT

Table 3.1 Significance of governance levels over time (Agricultural Policy)

Phase	National level	European level	Global level
Post-WWII to 1957	*High*: National regulation is uncontested and takes various shapes; some initiatives advocate concerted action on the European level	–	*Low*: GATT regulation lacks impact due to permissive consensus and non-enforceable discipline
1957 to mid-1980s	*Medium*: National authorities have power in a few domains not transferred, or transferred on shared basis, to EEC institutions (e.g. land tenure, social security, education, the regulation of working conditions and wages of agricultural workers)	*High*: Treaty of Rome (1957) transfers core domains of agricultural policy to EEC institutions; CAP develops around protective common market organizations (CMOs); agriculture is perceived as an exceptional sector needing special treatment	*Low*: GATT regulation lacks impact due to permissive consensus and unenforceable recourses
Mid-1980s to 2009	*Medium*: Same as above; in addition, renationalization debate illustrates pressures to renationalize CAP expenditure while meeting national diversity	*High*: The CAP goes through a reform momentum: CAP spending is stabilized; CAP instruments change with shift from price support to direct payments; a multifunctional view of agriculture now links direct farm payments to the provision of public goods such as: consumer, environmental and animal welfare concerns	*High*: political interests in favour of farm trade liberalization are mobilized in the GATT and the institutional means of enforcement are strengthened in the WTO
2009 to present	Medium	*High*: The Lisbon Treaty puts the European Parliament on an equal footing with the Council of Ministers: What does this mean for the reform momentum?	*Medium*: Global institutions are strengthened, but is there a political commitment to use them?
2020 extrapolation	High	High	Medium

arena largely failed due to entrenchment of farm interests and the lack of enforceable recourses.

The third period, spanning the 1990s and 2000s, marked the development of *competitive farm regulation* (Roederer-Rynning 2011). While still pivotal, the EU was no longer the unchallenged regulator of European farm affairs. At the global level, the permissive consensus that existed during the previous decades gave way to a determination to fight agricultural exceptionalism. At the same time, budgetary pressure and the diversification of EU membership introduced some degree of CAP renationalization. The CAP went through a reform momentum as a result of these combined sources of pressure. CAP spending was stabilized and support was increasingly channelled through less market-distorting direct payments. Views of agriculture as a special economic sector needing exceptional support expanded to incorporate requirements for public goods provision in the field of environmental protection, animal welfare, and broader consumer concerns. In terms of functional competences, this evolving multifunctional paradigm involved the development of new 'rural development' competences across the subnational, national and EU levels.

A fourth period arguably began with the ratification of the Lisbon Treaty and the *parliamentarization of the CAP*. While the respective significance of the European and global levels does not seem to be very different from that of the previous period, the 'rules for making rules' have changed at the EU level, ending the preferential treatment of the Council of Ministers (Roederer-Rynning and Schimmelfennig 2012). The CAP is now considered a normal domain of policy-making, where decisions have to be jointly approved by the European Parliament and the Council of Ministers. In addition, renationalization is becoming an increasing reality as the overall CAP budget is set to diminish and Member States are seeking to secure ever-more flexibility on implementing future greening requirements, equalizing support among sectors, shifting resources among the two pillars of the CAP (respectively, 'direct payments' and 'rural development'), and contributing additional national money to rural development measures.

3 The CAP: a deeply institutionalized regime of redistribution

The CAP finds its legal roots in the Treaty of Rome of 1957. Title II of the Treaty laid down rather vague provisions for the establishment of a European agricultural policy. It was clear that a European regime of agriculture would include both negative integration (the removal of barriers to intra-community trade in agricultural commodities) and positive integration (the adoption of a common agricultural policy proper). The Treaty also conferred key decision-making powers to Member States, originally the sole legislators in this domain. The actual CAP regime materialized in the 1960s in the aftermath of difficult intergovernmental negotiations. It developed along two axes: a fully Europeanized market policy axis, devoted to the organization and regulation of agricultural commodity markets, and a structural policy axis, with most of the policy competences vested in the Member States, devoted to the organization, rationalization and modernization of farm structures. These two broad orientations of farm regulation persist to this day, with some modifications. In the last decades, EU regulators have sought to institutionalize and broaden the structural policy component into a 'rural development pillar', which is now considered as the second pillar of the CAP, side-by-side with the market policy pillar. This pillar remains second in terms of EU budgetary and administrative resources. As a result of this evolution (and as illustrated in Table 3.1), the CAP reflects a broadened functional scope, leaving only a relatively small number of policy issues in the exclusive hands of national policy-makers. In addition, it is an EU policy regime characterized by a high degree of density and legal bindingness.

The CAP is a deeply institutionalized policy regime. Deep institutionalization, as evidenced by the arsenal of rules, shared understandings and standard procedures means that in agriculture, the EU does not proceed on a *tabula rasa*: it engages a formidable *acquis communautaire* in its dealings with third parties. The depth of the institutionalization is due to the fact that the CAP is one of the oldest common policies in the EU and that the legal provisions transfer significant competences to the supranational level. National intervention is precluded in areas of market policy, where the EU received complete decision-making authority. When national intervention has occurred, it has taken place in concert with EU action in areas of shared competences such as rural development. A legal illustration of the strength and bindingness of EU intervention in agriculture is the pervasive use of regulations (legislative acts binding in their entirety across the EU) as the favoured legal instrument. However, directives have been increasingly employed recently, when a degree of flexibility may be achieved without jeopardizing the single market. Finally, EU involvement in agriculture has not only generated a formidable body of EU legislation and ECJ jurisprudence; it has also underpinned key institutional developments in the EU, such as the comitology system.

The role of the Commission in farm policy is especially important, as the Commission negotiates on behalf of the Member States in all questions of trade with third parties. Until the Lisbon Treaty, the Commission enjoyed the widest array of institutional prerogatives on paper under the Community method; it had the power to initiate and withdraw legislation, to broker agreements within the Council and to execute policy.[2] In reality, the actual role played by the Commission in agricultural affairs has varied over time, depending on political circumstances. An agenda-setter in the aftermath of the signature of the Treaty of Rome, the Commission played a more modest role in the wake of the Luxembourg crisis, becoming little more than a secretariat of the Council. It later enjoyed renewed discretionary powers, exploiting the increased politicization of the CAP and new institutional opportunities to develop a reform agenda. Thus, from the mid-1980s to the Lisbon Treaty, the Commission was more assertive in CAP policy-making and was able to carry out several important CAP reforms. Even so, it had to reckon with an all-powerful Agriculture Council, which adopted legislation alone and preferably through consensus. With the ratification of the Lisbon Treaty in 2009, a new situation materialized where the CAP is subject to the 'normal legislative procedure': the Council of Ministers is no longer the sole legislator in this core Community policy, but must decide jointly and on equal footing with the European Parliament.

Finally, the CAP has an essentially redistributive nature. This characteristic has important implications for the EU's capacity to project its power at the global level. One of the notoriously vague objectives of the CAP laid down in the Treaty of Rome was to 'ensure a fair standard of living for the agricultural community, in particular by increasing the individual earnings of persons engaged in agriculture' (Art. 39, EEC). Whether the architects of the Treaty of Rome had in mind the establishment of a full-scale arsenal of redistributive measures is a moot point. In practice, the redistributive dimension has been an essential component of all blueprints to flesh out the CAP, although the type of policy instruments underpinning the CAP has sometimes obscured this dimension (Knudsen 2009; Daugbjerg and Swinbank 2009).

To simplify, two types of policy regimes for the CAP materialized. From the 1960s to the early 1990s, intervention took place through a cumbersome system of micro-managed *price support*. The CAP stabilized markets and farm incomes by providing floor prices in the markets for almost all agricultural commodities. Variable import levies ensured that imports from the world market could not be sold below minimum import prices (threshold prices) set well above the floor prices. Schemes for stockpiling, destruction and/or export subsidies ensured that when EU internal supplies increased, EU prices would not fall below politically determined floor prices, which were usually substantially higher than world market prices. Measures encouraging the modernization of farm units played a secondary role. This system generated structural over-production capacities because it was geared towards output. At the same time, price support entailed real, though ambiguous, redistributive effects; real because consumers paid a price premium to support farming as they could not reap the advantages of buying typically cheaper non-EEC farm products, ambiguous because policy instruments were overtly regulatory and arguably entailed a regressive form of redistribution.[3] Although real, redistribution was masked by the seemingly regulatory nature of the main policy instruments.

From the early 1990s, EU policy-makers moved away from the system of price support, instead channelling public resources to the farming community through *direct payments* to producers. These payments were introduced in the MacSharry reform in 1992 as compensations for a phasing out of price support and were initially differentiated by types of agricultural commodities. With successive reforms, farm payments took on a permanent character and became the chief instrument of farm support (now called single payment). This development was accomplished through a double movement of decoupling direct payments from specific commodities and coupling them to a range of broader public concerns, and requiring that farmers comply with environmental, animal health and welfare, and food safety regulations to qualify for direct payments (cross-compliance).

The shift to direct payments, financed by large EU budgetary transfers, highlights the redistributive character of the CAP (Daugbjerg and Swinbank 2009). Today, the EU spends a considerable amount of resources on farm policy, total CAP spending (including newer rural development concerns) representing slightly less than 45 per cent of the EU budget. While this has decreased (from 70 per cent in 1980[4]), it still makes the CAP, with its emphasis on redistribution, an anomaly in a EU so dominated by the regulatory logic of intervention that it has been dubbed a 'regulatory state' (Majone 1994).

4 The strenghtening of multilateralism and the erosion of embedded liberalism

At the global level, several fora are relevant for agricultural policy, although the GATT, now the WTO, is clearly the most pertinent and significant international regime. Following the implementation of the agreements forming the WTO's legal framework in 1995, agricultural trade is now an integral part of the WTO regime, albeit with its own agreement – the Uruguay Round Agreement on Agriculture (URAA).

In 1948, 53 countries signed the charter for the International Trade Organization (ITO) in Havana, a charter that was never ratified by the US Congress. In the absence of an international trade organization, one of the agreements, the General Agreement on Tariffs and Trade agreed upon in 1947, survived and underpinned the international trade regime. GATT-1947, as it was dubbed, was conceived as an interim measure until an international trade organization could be established. This happened first in 1995 when the WTO was formed. In the meantime, the GATT gradually developed into an organization, though not formally sanctioned by its Member States, with a secretariat established in Geneva.

It is often incorrectly argued that agricultural trade was exempted from the GATT. Agricultural trade was clearly covered (Table 3.1), and a number of disputes on agricultural trade were put before panels in the GATT. However, the GATT's recourses in cases of agricultural support and protection were weak, allowing domestic trade restrictions and distortion to continue. Two articles of GATT-1947 introduced special provisions for agricultural (and fisheries) trade, meaning that the farm sector had exceptional status within the GATT, as measures prohibited in other economic sectors were allowed in agriculture. These two articles encapsulated embedded liberalism.

Article XI of GATT prohibited the use of quantitative import restrictions, while allowing them for agricultural products provided they were *necessary* to enforce government measures that applied domestic marketing or production quotas, or when measures were introduced to remove temporary surpluses of domestic products. In practice, the GATT had little effect on curbing import restrictions, regardless of domestic production controls. In 1950, the US introduced quantitative restrictions on dairy product imports in the absence of controls on domestic production, and thereby contravened GATT rules. The US applied for and was granted a waiver to the provisions of Article XI for an unlimited duration. As Josling *et al.* (1996: 28) suggest: 'The other member countries had no choice but to accede to this request, for the alternative might have been the withdrawal of the United States from the GATT.' This waiver had a long-lasting impact on the GATT farm trade regimes because it meant that 'no other major country was prepared to abide by the GATT rules' (ibid.). The establishment of the CAP signalled that the EU was not prepared to respect GATT rules. The binding of tariff levels was a basic measure to lower protectionism within the GATT. These bindings would be established as part of a trade round agreement. Since variable import levies were pivotal for the functioning of the CAP, except for oilseeds and soybeans, the EU was not prepared to transform the levies into tariffs and bind them.[5] Subsequently, no other country was willing to bind their tariffs.

The original Article XVI allowed for the use of export subsidies for manufactured and agricultural products. In the mid-1950s, the Article was tightened, prohibiting the use of direct and indirect export subsidies with the exemption of primary products, though members were urged to limit their use so that if subsidies were to be applied this should not result in the country capturing 'more than an equitable share of world export trade in that product' (Art. XVI: 3). This rule proved very difficult to police, with the result that there was virtually no recourse in cases of farm export subsidies. Half of the EU farm budget in 1980, for instance, was spent on export subsidies, causing severe distortions in world farm trade and fuelling trade conflict (Wolfe 1998) between the EU and the US.

It was not until the adoption of the Uruguay Round Agreement on Agriculture, an integral part of the package of trade agreements forming the WTO, that agriculture was fully incorporated into the global trade regime, albeit with its own agreement: the Agricultural Agreement, agreed upon in 1993 and formally adopted in 1994. The Agreement forms the core of the global farm trade regime. It consists of three pillars: market access, domestic support, and export subsidies. A set of commitments to reduce support and protection applies to each pillar, and were to be implemented over a period of five years, i.e. by 2000.

1. For *market access*, countries were requested to convert their existing non-tariff barriers (for example, the EU's variable import levies) into tariffs – a process dubbed 'tariffication' – on the basis of which developed countries were obliged to reduce their tariffs by a simple average of 36 per cent over the implementation period, with no tariff line subject to a reduction of less than 15 per cent, using the 1986 to 1988 average tariff level as the base period from which to reduce.
2. The Uruguay Round Agreement on Agriculture did not do away with domestic support, nor did it aim to phase it out. Rather, the objective was to curb the use of the most trade-distorting types of support. The agreement distinguishes between three different types of support. Support schemes that have 'no, or at most minimal, trade-distorting effects or effects on production' are categorized into the *green box*. Annex 2 of the Agreement specifies the criteria for subsidy schemes to qualify as green box support. Green box

support is decoupled from production and production input, and therefore, though not undisputed, is deemed to have minimal or no impact on the level of farm production. The *blue box* is a support category for direct farm payments under production-limiting programmes. Such payments are often seen as partially decoupled from production, albeit not production-neutral since they serve in practice to subsidize agricultural production that is otherwise unprofitable. All other payments linked to production or to production input are categorized into the *amber box*. Such support is linked to production by either subsidizing farm outputs or farm inputs such as fertilizers. Amber box support is seen as highly trade distorting because it provides incentives for farmers to increase production, which in the 1980s caused major surpluses. On the basis of the overall 1986 to 1988 level of amber box support, the Uruguay Round Agreement on Agriculture commits WTO Member States to reduce amber box support by 20 per cent while blue and green box supports are exempt from reduction commitments.

3   In relation to *export competition*, the Uruguay Round Agreement on Agriculture binds, on a commodity-specific basis, export subsidy expenditure and the volume of subsidized exports based on the 1986 to 1990 average levels of expenditure and volume. Developed countries are committed to a reduction of 36 per cent in the expenditure bindings and 21 per cent in the volume bindings.

By covering market access, domestic support and export competition, the Uruguay Round Agreement on Agriculture had a fairly broad functional scope, but it did not cover all aspects of agricultural trade. Export restraints and export taxes were very weakly disciplined because the agenda of the negotiations focused on addressing depressed world market prices rather than a situation with high prices, which occurred in 2007 to 2008 and in 2011 to 2012. This was not envisaged at the time the negotiations took place in the late 1980s and early 1990s. Disciplines on sanitary and phytosanitary measures were covered by the SPS Agreement. The agricultural trade rules laid down in the Agreement are very specific and detailed, and the structure of its commitments on domestic support made the Agreement unique (Daugbjerg and Swinbank 2009: 59; Josling *et al.* 1996). The level of detail is clearly illustrated by the fact that it includes 20,000 pages of schedules in which the country-level commitments are described for the 117 signatories (Josling *et al.* 1996: 175). The commitments of the Agreement are legally binding and may therefore be characterized as hard law.

The immediate impact of the Agreement's reduction commitments was limited. First, reduction commitments were based on generous references – in the years 1986 to 1988 (1986 to 1990 for export subsidies) world market prices were exceptionally low and import protection and export subsidies correspondingly high. Second, non-tariff barriers were to be converted into tariffs and bound, enabling countries to assign artificially high tariff values (known as 'dirty tariffication'). Third, the creation of a blue box shielded EU area livestock payments and US deficiency payments from reduction commitments (see Tangermann 2004: 39–40).

The wider impact of the Uruguay Round Agreement on Agriculture, however, transcended specific reduction commitments. The Uruguay Round Agreement on Agriculture is more than just an agreement to reduce agricultural support and protection; it is a new institution, or regime, in global agricultural trade underpinned by a liberal market paradigm. This reflected US priorities in the negotiations. In the initial preamble to the Agreement it is explicitly emphasized that the 'long term objective ... is to establish a fair and market-oriented trading system' and that the aim of 'substantial progressive reductions in agricultural support and protection' is to result in 'correcting and preventing restrictions and distortions in world agricultural markets'. Articles XI and XVI of GATT-1947, the legal expressions of agricultural exceptionalism, were overridden by Article XXI of the Agreement. Article XX states that farm trade liberalization is 'an ongoing process' and that 'negotiations for continuing the process will be initiated one year before the end of the implementation process', i.e. before the end of 1999 (the continuation clause). The EU had to accept a WTO farm trade regime pushing for the continual liberalization of agricultural trade throughout the twenty-first century. When negotiations on further farm trade liberalization were initiated in the WTO's Doha Development Agenda Trade Round in 2001, there were high hopes that they would result in continued liberalization. However, the inability of negotiators to agree on a new agreement on agriculture in the still ongoing (2013) round indicates a decreasing importance of the global impacts on domestic agricultural policy-making.

5 Importing policy settings: defending the European paradigm

The EU's attempts to export core features of its model of agricultural policy have been short-lived and have mainly failed. In contrast, the EU has succeeded in preserving a European model of agriculture that continues to redistribute money in favour of farmers and thus remains embedded in domestic social and political arrangements.

5.1 Case 1 – the GATT Uruguay Round: CAP re-instrumentation within the blue box

In the Uruguay Round (1986–1995), the EU could no longer reject attempts to liberalize agricultural trade. In the 1960s and 1970s, the target of the US had been the EU's variable import levy system, which curtailed US exports into the EU. While this was still an important US concern during the Uruguay Round, the mounting surplus production in the EU sold on the world market with significant export subsidization had become a more serious concern for the US. Not only were its exports excluded from the EU market to a considerable extent, it also had to increasingly compete with the EU's directly subsidized exports in its traditional non-EU export markets (Mahler 1991: 35). Pressure on the EU also came from the Cairns Group, a new coalition of 14 farm-exporting developed and developing countries formed in 1986, including the major exporters Brazil and Australia.[6] These countries could not match the level of export subsidies provided by the EU and suffered from declining world market prices caused by the fierce export subsidy competition between the EU and the US. The Cairns Group was led by Australia (Kenyon and Lee 2006).

The US submitted its *Proposal for Negotiations on Agriculture* in July 1987 (GATT 1987), known as the 'zero-2000 proposal'. It was radical and asked for

> [a] complete phase-out overtenyears of all agricultural subsidies which directly or indirectly affect trade ... [a] freeze and phase-out over ten years of the quantities exported with the aid of export subsidies ... [and] a phase-out of import barriers over ten years.
>
> (GATT 1987)

The zero-2000 proposal did not suggest outlawing the use of subsidies, but allowed only those with minimal trade distorting effects (later to be known as green box support). Faced with this radical proposal, the EU adopted a reactive strategy of damage control (Ingersent *et al.* 1994: 61). A major priority of the EU in the round was to defend the CAP and its support mechanisms. The initial proposal of the EU was weak but acknowledged the need for concerted reduction in agricultural support and a readjustment of external protection. It did not advocate phasing out support (Daugbjerg and Swinbank 2009).

As the negotiations proceeded, the differences between the US and the EU turned out to be paradigmatic. The US position reflected the Reagan Administration's neoliberal assault on the very paradigm of agricultural policies in most liberal democracies – agricultural exceptionalism.

The EU, in turn, sought to export its agricultural exceptionalist position that was at the core of the CAP. In its 'Global Proposal' of December 1989 the EU put forward the idea that 'agricultural production has its own [economic] characteristics which explain the special characteristics of current agricultural policies' (Commission of the European Communities 1989: 1). The EU attempted to legitimize its position and to persuade its negotiating partners to accept the EU's desire to shelter its agricultural policy model by basing its position on the idea of exceptional production and market conditions in agriculture, which had underpinned agricultural policies in liberal democracies during the post-war period. However, the EU received very limited support. Its view of the agricultural problem was in stark contrast to that of the US (supported by the Cairns Group), which argued that

> We are on a subsidy treadmill.... The false price signals which result encourage surplus, prices fall, and we have to subsidize more to make up for low prices. It's a vicious cycle. There is a growing recognition that the problem is excessive government support of agriculture.
>
> (Yeutter 1988: 266)

The solution to these problems was to liberalize agricultural trade as outlined in the zero-2000 proposal. While the US was committed to its zero-2000 proposal for the first four years of the negotiations, the Cairns Group was willing to settle for less.

Although the EU initially assumed that the farm trade issue could be dealt with separately, it had to give in to the US and Cairns Group demands that farm trade talks be an integral part of the round; that is, part of a single undertaking (Daugbjerg and Swinbank 2009). After one and a half years of tough negotiations among EU Farm Ministers, Farm Commissioner Ray MacSharry was able to use these exogenous pressures as a means to bring about policy change within the CAP in May 1992 (Coleman and Tangermann 1999). The reform represented a substantial break by transforming the architecture of the CAP through a partial shift from price support to direct payments, enabling a further change of policy direction within the CAP a decade later. The policy changes in 1992 mainly took place in the arable sectors but also affected the beef sector, where minimum prices were reduced and direct livestock payments were increased (see Swinbank (1993) for an overview of the reform).

This reform enabled the EU to maintain a substantive amount of redistribution in favour of the farm sector. Indeed, during the CAP reform process, the EU negotiated bilaterally with the US on a farm trade deal in which a new domestic support category emerged: The so-called 'blue box' (Cunha and Swinbank 2011). The CAP reform enabled the EU to shift a substantial part of its domestic farm support from price support (amber box support) to direct support linked to production-limiting measures (blue box support). While support schemes categorized in the amber box support are seen as very trade-distorting and subject to reduction commitments, blue box support is defined as being less trade-distorting and not subject to reduction commitments. The CAP reform was shaped to comply with the envisaged WTO Agricultural Agreement and this enabled the US and the EU to reach a deal on farm trade. The other negotiating parties accepted this as a *fait accompli*.

5.2 Case 2 – the Doha Development Round: from failure over non-trade concerns to limited success on development concerns

The inclusion of farm trade as an integral part of the GATT and then the WTO trade rounds introduced a strong and lasting exogenous influence on the CAP. EU agricultural policy could no longer be decided in isolation, since it had become linked to the global arena and increasingly needed to take WTO trade rules into consideration. The Uruguay Round Agreement on Agriculture set the scene for continued negotiations on farm trade liberalization. This meant that the EU had to consider how to respond to the agenda of the forthcoming trade round. The Agenda 2000 reform adopted in 1999 attempted to do so. It is generally understood as 'a deepening' of the 1992 reform, as it lowered guaranteed minimum prices further and raised direct payments but, at the end of the day, the reform did not create much leeway for the EU in the WTO.

In November 2001, a new trade round in the WTO began in Doha, Qatar (the Doha Round). The EU was again under pressure as the US and the Cairns Group wanted the blue box domestic support category abolished and payments under this category to be included in the reduction commitments. This would force the EU to undertake substantial cuts in its domestic farm support unless its support system was changed. Decoupling the direct farm payments from production was a potential response to this pressure on the CAP. The Commission believed that by shifting the direct payments into the green box (a support category for minimally trade-distorting domestic support) they would be exempted from reduction commitments. This would relieve the pressure on the EU's domestic farm support scheme and was expected to improve the EU's negotiating position in the Doha Round. The reform, agreed to by the farm ministers in June 2003, decoupled direct payments from production requirements and transformed them into a flat rate, single farm payment. However, Member States were allowed to tie up to 25 per cent of the direct area payments to production and to choose from among various options for coupled payments in the beef cattle and sheep sectors – leading to a considerable renationalization of the CAP and, as a result, 31 different versions of the CAP emerged in EU-27 (two variants in Belgium and four in the UK) (Daugbjerg 2012).

While the 2003 reform affected the large arable sectors (cereals, oil and protein crops), a second phase of reforms brought cotton, tobacco, olive oil, hops (2004), sugar (2005), fruit and vegetables (2007) and wine (2008) into the decoupled framework. The Health Check Reform adopted in November 2008 pushed the CAP back towards the Europeanized track by restricting the freedom of the Member States to retain coupled direct farm payments. This created some extra leeway for the EU in the Doha Round negotiations, but had little impact on the negotiations which stalemated in December 2008 as a result of disagreements between India and the US. Attempts to promote its preference on agriculture policy in the Doha Round have been very limited and failed, with one exception: Duty- and quota-free market access for the Least Developing Countries (LDC). The attempt to place non-trade concerns at the centre of the agricultural negotiations failed.

In the run up to the ill-fated Ministerial in Seattle in 1999 and before the start of the Doha Round, the EU attempted to utilize the Uruguay Round Agreement on Agriculture's reference to non-trade concerns to export its concept of multifunctional agriculture to the global level in defence of blue box support. It was argued that in addition to producing food and fibre, agriculture also provided a number of public goods such as land care, maintenance of the rural economy and conservation of natural resources. Within the EU, this broader view on agriculture has continuously been referred to as multifunctionality. However, this attempt to legitimize EU non-trade concerns by referring to the public goods provided by agriculture largely failed. As Daugbjerg and Swinbank (2009: 159) point out, 'the EU's trading partners in the *New World* were suspicious that, if used in an abstract or blanket fashion, talk of multifunctionality could serve as a smokescreen to deflect attention from the EU's real intent, which was, they believed, protectionist'. This unsuccessful attempt of policy export again demonstrated that the EU faced severe difficulties in persuading its trading partners to accept its view that agriculture was an exceptional economic sector requiring special treatment. As a result of the initial hostile reaction in the WTO, the EU's enthusiasm for defending the concept declined, demonstrated by the fact it has not used it in the WTO since 2001 (Daugbjerg and Swinbank 2009).

The EU was more successful in promoting its policy preferences at the margin of the agricultural negotiations. The political necessity to accommodate the interests of developing countries in the Doha Round became evident following the dramatic failure of the Seattle Ministerial, which was intended to launch the Millennium Round. The EU launched initiatives sympathetic to the trade interests of developing countries in an effort to demonstrate that the EU was increasingly prepared to take their interests into account. After a policy process that was relatively short in the EU context, the EU adopted the EBA initiative in February 2001 well before the launch of the Doha Round in November. The EBA was a trade policy initiative developed by the Trade Commissioner and agreed by the Trade Ministers with little involvement from the Farm Commissioner. It is a preferential trade agreement granting the Least Developing Countries duty- and quota-free access for all goods, with the exception of arms, into the EU internal market by 2001. For rice, bananas and sugar there were longer transition periods with free access delayed until 2009 (van der Hoven 2007). In the WTO, the EU has persistently argued that the developed and advanced developing countries should commit themselves to do likewise and has so far been successful in this endeavour.

The Council adopted the EU's WTO offer on agriculture unanimously in January 2003. The offer emphasized a 'radically better deal for developing countries' and proposed that for products originating within the Least Developing Countries, developed countries and 'all advanced developing countries' should provide duty- and quota-free access, reflecting the EU's own 'Everything But Arms' initiative (European Commission 2003). This proposal first appeared in the July 2004 Framework Agreement on Agriculture, in which it was stated that '[d]eveloped Members, and developing country Members in a position to do so, should provide duty-free and quota-free market access for products originating from least-developed countries'.[7] The statement was confirmed by the WTO Ministerial Conference in Hong Kong in 2005.[8] The word 'should' in the statement urged, rather than committed, WTO members to implement this market-opening measure. A year later there were strong indications that developed countries had become more positive towards providing duty- and quota-free market access for Least Developing Countries.[9] By July 2008 'should' had been replaced by 'shall' in the draft text for the agricultural modalities. However, the EU's success in promoting its policy preferences was much less impressive than it appeared because the US and Japan succeeded in limiting their commitments to provide duty- and quota-free access to Least Developing Countries to only 97 per cent of their tariffs lines, continuing to restrict access for most of the products of major importance to Least Developing Countries. In contrast to the EU's defensive attempts to persuade its trading partners to legitimize the EU's view on agricultural as an exceptional industry, the EU was more successful in gaining support for proposals of opening markets. The EBA initiative agreed to unilaterally among the EU Member States enabled the EU to take the moral high ground when attempting to 'upload' its own policy to the WTO (Wilkinson 2006: 298). Since the Doha Round negotiation stalled in December 2008, the Member States have not yet committed themselves within the WTO to open their markets for exports from the Least Developing Countries.

6 Explaining defensive policy import

'Defensive policy import' encapsulates the phenomenon of the EU reforming its Common Agricultural Policy in order to preserve it. One may speak of 'import' insofar as the EU selectively adopted shared GATT/WTO standards; the import was 'defensive' however, since the core redistributive paradigm underpinning the CAP was preserved, reformulated as 'the multifunctionality of agriculture'. The EU succeeded by and large in preserving its model of agriculture within the context of global trade regulation.

Exogenous factors explain why the EU could no longer insulate its agricultural policy from GATT/WTO developments. These changes were political as well as institutional. Politically, the mobilization of trade liberalization interests eroded the moral base of embedded liberalism, making it increasingly difficult to uphold the view that agriculture is a special sector, to be treated exceptionally. Institutionally, a series of measures strengthened trade multilateralism. Unlike earlier GATT rounds, the Uruguay and Doha rounds were organized as single undertakings, which meant that all Member States had to accept the whole package of agreements before the rounds could be closed. Since the EU had offensive interests in most of the other issues on the negotiating table, it eventually had to accept that agricultural trade needed to become an integral part of the package deal in order to achieve gains in other areas. The Uruguay Round Agreement on Agriculture with its 'continuation clause' was institutionalized as an integral part of the WTO's legal framework, meaning that the EU was committed to comply with and engage in negotiations on further farm trade liberalization. Together, these political and institutional factors provided the impetus for change. The Uruguay Round Agreement on Agriculture introduced specific and enforceable disciplines for agricultural trade. The cotton case launched against the United States by Brazil, and the sugar case against the EU launched by Australia, Brazil and Thailand in 2002 demonstrated that the WTO Dispute Settlement System was able to rule against the major trading powers on politically sensitive policies. The EU lost the sugar case and complied with the ruling by reforming its sugar policy to conform to the Agreement on Agriculture (Ackrill and Kay 2011). Thus, the WTO Dispute Settlement System is yet another exogenous factor that may be used as an instrument to bring about policy import.

Turning to endogenous factors, the EU engaged in the GATT and WTO negotiations with largely defensive interests. This was in response to the fact that a broad range of Member States – Austria, Belgium, Cyprus, France, Greece, Hungary, Ireland, Italy, Lithuania, Poland, Portugal and Spain – formed a conservative coalition defending a relatively high level of import protection and farm subsidization. Germany currently pursues protectionist interests in farm trade but is a major exporter in services and manufactured goods; therefore it has to balance defensive and offensive interests. This implies that Germany sometimes sides with the conservative coalition of Member States and at other times gives higher priority to its manufacturing and services interests. Another group of Member States expresses more liberal interests in agricultural trade. This group includes the Czech Republic, Denmark, Estonia, Finland, Latvia, Luxembourg, Malta, the Netherlands, Slovakia, Slovenia, Sweden, and the United Kingdom – usually the lead member within this group. With the exception of the Netherlands and Denmark, these Member States have relatively small agricultural sectors and offensive interests in trade in manufactured goods and services (Conceicão-Heldt 2011: 83–84).

The responsibility of forging a compromise between these conflicting pressures fell largely upon the European Commission, the official EU negotiator in global trade negotiations. Elsewhere, it has been argued that the CAP reforms taking place from 1992 to 2008 may be referred to as 'enabling change' (Roederer-Rynning 2011), an institutionalist term relating to situations during turbulent times when an 'organization attempt[s] to enhance [its] control over the institutional environment ... and embark on a design strategy ... aimed at either dominating the environment or circumventing the obstacles in the environment' (Peters and Pierre 1998: 577). The European Commission played a pivotal role in 'enabling change' (defensive import), by using its expertise and presence in global negotiations as well as in an increasingly polarized Agriculture Council.

At the global level, the Commission has used a mix of persuasion and bargaining. It has achieved some success in 'uploading' the trade offensive EBA initiative to the global level, but has been much less successful in its defensive strategy of promoting its exceptionalist view on agriculture. Bargaining has been used as a damage control strategy in both the Uruguay and Doha rounds. During the Uruguay Round, the EU Farm Commissioner MacSharry conducted the agricultural negotiations rather autonomously from the rest of the EU's negotiating agenda and was able to block an agreement on the whole package of agreements negotiated in the round. However, there are some indications that the EU's bargaining strategy has become more flexible during the Doha Round. The former Agricultural Commissioner Fischer Boel did not conduct the agricultural negotiations in the Doha Round as unilaterally as her two predecessors. She was unwilling to allow a lack of flexibility in the EU's position to block progress in the negotiations on trade in manufactured products and services.[10]

Meanwhile, within the EU, the Commission used a broad range of techniques to 'enable change', and in practice resulted in a series of CAP reforms among which the MacSharry reform of 1992 and the Fischler reform of 2003 were the most notable (Roederer-Rynning 2011: 25–26). These reforms were initiated by a Commission-led Community debate on the effectiveness and appropriateness of the CAP, in which the Commission insisted that 'the only option that is not viable is the status quo' (Commission of the European Communities 1991:19) (strategic framing). The techniques used by the Commission in order to facilitate change included agenda shielding within the Commission services and adding an international dimension to the debate by linking the reforms to the developments in the GATT/WTO (Daugbjerg and Swinbank 2009: 125–141). In the Fischler reform coalition-building with Members of the European Parliament (MEPs) and with like-minded members in the Council of Ministers was added to the repertoire. During the McSharry reform, the Commission kept traditional farm groups at arm's length and developed reform blueprints within a restricted circle of individuals (agenda shielding). At the same time, it used the political and institutional opportunities provided by the global trade talks by nesting CAP reform in GATT/WTO negotiations (arena shifting). The subsequent reforms revealed how adept the Commission had become at cultivating support for its emerging reform agenda in the other EU institutions. During the Fischler reform, the Commission went to great lengths to cultivate political support from MEPs (Roederer-Rynning 2013). A very good working relationship developed at the highest level, between Commissioner Fischler and MEP Joseph Daul, President of the EP's Agriculture Committee. This fact is not well known, and it may appear trivial given that the EP still lacked formal legislative power in the CAP. However, EP support was important in enabling Commissioner Fischler to organize a 'tour des capitales' and secure progress through bilateral talks with individual heads of states. Working with Daul also helped Fischler win the support of President Chirac. In part thanks to EP support, the Commission was able to prepare a deal and put it through in the Council. The Commission learned on this occasion that, if no revolution may come out of an alliance with the Conservatives in the EP, there was room for reform if the Commission used its leadership (interview with a former member of the Fischler Cabinet, 9 December 2010). In the following years, the Commission was aided by an increasingly polarized Agriculture Council, following the serial enlargement of the EU and the growing salience of redistributive issues among Member States. Growing heterogeneity in the Council has heightened the cost of opposing a Commission proposal (which formally requires unanimity); in turn, this has allowed the Commission to develop a more autonomous agenda, less confined by individual national positions and more geared towards cultivating coalitions. This is what happened during the Doha Round negotiations, as the Commission, leaning on a friendly Council Presidency, agreed to phase out EU farm export subsidies in spite of French resistance.

CAP politics is high politics insofar as it commands a significant share of the EU budget. Political compromises are increasingly poised on the calculus of net budget transfers and vulnerable to negative public opinion in Member States that are net contributors to the EU budget (Ackrill 2005). These enduring conflicts have weakened the cohesion of the Council and made it easier for the Commission to instrumentalize divisions. While clearly responding to global pressure, the European Commission was also inspired by calculations to preserve the CAP and restore the competitiveness of European agriculture.

7 Conclusion

In sum, the EU has been unable to export its core agricultural policy model based on agricultural exceptionalism. In the early days of the GATT era, agriculture was considered an exceptional economic sector and therefore the EU was able to shield the CAP from reforms attempts from within the GATT. In the Uruguay and Doha rounds, it became increasingly difficult to uphold the view that agriculture was exceptional and as a result proposals based on agricultural exceptionalism were met with suspicion by the other major players in the farm trade negotiations. Therefore, the attempts to use the concept of multifunctionality to legitimize exceptional treatment of agriculture have failed.

At the margins of the farm trade negotiations, the EU appears to be more successful by gaining support for a provision committing developed and advanced developing countries to provide duty- and quota-free access for exports from Least Developing Countries. The EU has been an agricultural policy importer rather than exporter. There has been a significant move in the CAP from supporting farmers indirectly through price support to direct and decoupled farm payments which are considered far less trade-distorting. Further, by shifting from price support to direct payments, the variable import levy system could be dismantled and tariffs and export subsidies lowered. In other words, the CAP has become much more WTO-compatible. However, policy import has not involved a subscription to the underlying market liberal paradigm of the WTO farm trade regime. Rather, the EU has maintained its agricultural exceptionalist position, now phrased as multifunctionality, and aligned its agricultural support schemes with WTO developments.

Notes

1 We do not include fisheries in this chapter, as fisheries are included in the non-agricultural market access (NAMA) negotiations in the WTO. These negotiations relate to the Agreement on Subsidies and Countervailing Measures (SCM). A key issue is whether subsidy disciplines for fisheries should be specified in a separate fisheries agreement or should remain within the more general SCM Agreement. Unlike the agricultural negotiations, which focus exclusively on trade distortion caused by subsidies, the WTO agenda for fisheries and trade has a significant environmental dimension in terms of the preservation of fish resources (see Chang (2003) for an overview).
2 Policy implementation is carried out by Member States.
3 Price support rewarded large-scale farming while failing to address the specific problems of smaller and relatively inefficient farm units.
4 This relative decline in the agricultural budgetary share is not caused by a reduction in agricultural support, but by an increase in the total EU budget.
5 This is so because variable import levies were continuously adjusted to prevent imports from entering the EC internal market below a threshold price.
6 The Cairns Group comprised Argentina, Australia, Brazil, Canada, Chile, Colombia, Hungary, Indonesia, Malaysia, New Zealand, the Philippines, Singapore, Thailand and Uruguay.
7 www.wto.org/english/tratop_e/dda_e/ddadraft_31jul04_e.pdf, p. A-7.
8 www.wto.org/english/thewto_e/minist_e/min05_e/final_text_e.pdf, p. A-7.

9 www.wto.org/english/tratop_e/agric_e/mod_ag_12jul_e.pdf, p. 15. The text appears in square brackets indicating that it is not agreed.
10 Fischer Boel, talk given at DIIS Seminar and personal conversation, 12 April 2012, Copenhagen.

References

Ackrill, R. (2005) 'The Common Agricultural Policy', in P. van der Hoek (ed.) *Handbook on Public Administration and Policy in the European Union*, Baco Raton, FL: Taylor & Francis.

Ackrill, R.W. and Kay, A. (2011) 'Multiple Streams Approaches to EU Policy-making: The 2005 Sugar Policy Reform', *Journal of European Public Policy* 18(1): 72–89.

Chang, S.W. (2003) 'WTO Disciplines on Fisheries Subsidies: A Historical Step Towards Sustainability?', *Journal of International Economic Law* 6(4): 879–921.

Coleman, W.D. and Tangermann, S. (1999) 'The 1992 CAP Reform, the Uruguay Round and the Commission', *Journal of Common Market Studies* 37(3): 385–405.

Commission of the European Communities (1989) *Global Proposal of the European Community on the Long-term Objective for the Multilateral Negotiation on Agricultural Questions*. Online. Available http://aei.pitt.edu/3032/ (accessed 17 April 2013).

Commission of the European Communities (1991) *Communication to the Council: The Development and Future of the CAP. Reflections Paper of the Commission*, COM(91)100. Brussels: CEC.

Conceição-Heldt, E. (2011) *Negotiating Trade Liberalization at the WTO: Domestic Politics and Bargaining Dynamics*, Basingstoke: Palgrave Macmillan.

Cunha, A. and Swinbank, A. (2011) *An Inside View of the CAP Reform Process: Explaining the MacSharry, Agenda 2000, and Fischler Reforms*, Oxford: Oxford University Press.

Daugbjerg, C. (2012) 'Globalization and Internal Policy Dynamics in the Reform of the Common Agricultural Policy', in J. Richardson (ed.) *Constructing a Policy-making State? Policy Dynamics in the European Union*, Oxford: Oxford University Press.

Daugbjerg, C. and Swinbank, A. (2009) *Ideas, Institutions and Trade: The WTO and the Curious Role of EU Farm Policy in Trade Liberalization*, Oxford: Oxford University Press.

European Commission (2003) 'WTO and Agriculture: The European Union Takes Steps to Move the Negotiations Forward', Press Release IP/03/126, 27 January, Brussels.

GATT (1987) *United States Proposal for Negotiations on Agriculture*, MTN. GNG/NG5/W/14, Geneva: GATT.

Ingersent, K.A., Rayner, A.J. and Hine, R.C. (1994) 'The EC Perspective', in K.A. Ingersent, A.J. Rayner and R.C. Hine (eds) *Agriculture in the Uruguay Round*, New York: St Martin's Press.

Josling, T., Tangermann, S. and Warley, T.K. (1996) *Agriculture in the GATT*, Basingstoke: Macmillan.

Kenyon, D. and Lee, D. (2006) *The Struggle for Trade Liberalisation in Agriculture: Australia and the Cairns Group in the Uruguay Round*, The Foreign Affairs and Trade Files No. 4, Barton, ACT: Department of Foreign Affairs and Trade.

Knudsen, A.-C.L. (2009) *Farmers on Welfare. The Making of Europe's Common Agricultural Policy*, Ithaca, NY: Cornell University Press.

Mahler, V.A. (1991) 'Domestic & International Sources of Trade Policy: The Case of Agriculture in the European Community & the United States', *Polity* 24(1): 27–47.

Majone, G. (1994) 'The Rise of the Regulatory State in Europe', *West European Politics* 17(3): 77–101.
Peters, B.G. and Pierre, J. (1998) 'Institutions and Time: Problems of Conceptualization and Explanation', *Journal of Public Administration Research and Theory* 8(4): 565–583.
Roederer-Rynning, C. (2010) 'The Common Agricultural Policy', in H. Wallace, M. Pollack and A. Young (eds) *Policy-making in the EU*, Oxford: Oxford University Press.
—— (2011) 'The Paradigmatic Case: Beyond Emergency Exits in the CAP', in G. Falkner (ed.) *The EU's Decision Traps: Comparing Policies*, Oxford: Oxford University Press.
—— (forthcoming) 'Parliamentary Politics Meets Globalization: The Third Era of European Farm Governance', in A.M. Arranz, P. Winand and N. Witzleb (eds) *Contemporary Europe: Political Integration and Global Engagement*.
Roederer-Rynning, C. and Schimmelfennig, F. (2012) 'Bringing Codecision to Agriculture: A Hard Case of Parliamentarization', *Journal of European Public Policy* 19(7): 951–968.
Ruggie, J.G. (1982) 'International Regimes, Transactions, and Change: Embedded Liberalism in the Postwar Economic Order', *International Organization* 36(2): 379–415.
Skogstad, G. (1998) 'Ideas, Paradigms and Institutions: Agricultural Exceptionalism in the European Union and the United States', *Governance* 11(4): 463–490.
Steinberg, R. (2006) 'The Transformation of European Trading States', in J. Levy (ed.) *The State After Statism*, Cambridge, MA: Harvard University Press.
Swinbank, A. (1993) 'CAP Reform, 1992', *Journal of Common Market Studies* 31(3): 359–372.
Tangermann, S. (2004) 'Agricultural Policies in OECD Countries Ten Years After the Uruguay Round: How Much Progress?', in G. Anania, M.E. Bohman, C.A. Carter and A.F. McCalla (eds) *Agricultural Policy Reform and the WTO: Where Are We Heading?*, Cheltenham: Edward Elgar.
Tracy, M. (1989) *Government and Agriculture in Western Europe*, New York: Harvester Wheatsheaf.
van der Hoven, A. (2007) 'Bureaucratic Competition in EU Trade Policy: EBA as a Case of Competing Two-level Games', in G. Faber and J. Orbie (eds) *European Union Trade Politics and Development: 'Everything but Arms' unravelled*, London: Routledge.
Wilkinson, R. (2006) 'The WTO in Hong Kong: What it Really Means for the Doha Development Round', *New Political Economy* 11(2): 291–303.
Wolfe, R. (1998) *Farm Wars: The Political Economy of Agriculture and the International Trade Regime*, New York: St Martin's Press.
Yeutter, C. (1988) 'U.S. Negotiating Proposal on Agriculture in the Uruguay Round', in E.U. Petersmann and M. Hilf (eds) *The New GATT Round of Multilateral Trade Negotiations: Legal and Economic Problems*, Deventer: Kluwer Law and Taxation Publishers.

4 Food safety
The resilient resistance of the EU

Vessela Hristova

1 Introduction

Food safety policy aims to regulate the production and marketing of food in order to protect human health and the consumer. It encompasses a wide variety of issues such as food hygiene, food labelling, the use of additives and flavourings, residues from pesticides and veterinary drugs, food contamination, and others.

Food exports accounted for about 7.5 per cent of total merchandise exports worldwide in 2010, thus making up a substantial part of global trade flows.[1] Divergent national or regional food safety regulations often impede trade in food products. The aim of the international regime for food safety is to harmonize substantive food standards or the procedures according to which they are developed in order to facilitate global trade in food products and simultaneously ensure a level of food safety that is acceptable for most trading regions and countries. Reconciling this dual objective can sometimes be a contested process.

The European Union (EU) has developed a comprehensive body of food safety legislation, constituting one of the highest levels of protection in the world. At the same time, the EU is a net importer of food and the largest food importer in absolute terms. Because the EU relies on the rest of the world for its food supply and is a major market for food imports, it is not only interested in supporting the existence of a functioning international food safety regime, but also in substantively shaping this regime to reflect its own policies. This chapter assesses the extent to which the EU is successful in exporting its food safety policy at the international level, the pathways through which it attempts to do so, and the conditions that facilitate or constrain the EU's policy export. I begin by briefly outlining the development of food safety policy at the national, EU and the international level and then trace the changes in the relevance of these three governance layers over time. Next, I analyse the extent to which the EU is able to export its policies to the international food safety regime. First, I explore the role of the EU in the Codex Alimentarius Commission by looking at how it has influenced major principles of international food safety regulation as well as the EU's ongoing engagement in regular legislative activities. Second, I focus on the EU's interaction with the World Trade Organization. Here again, the analysis is broken down into an examination of the EU's success in the negotiations of the main agreement regarding food safety and a review of its application in the case of two WTO disputes involving EU food safety measures.

2 Mapping the relevance of governance layers over time

2.1 From a common market in food products to EU food safety policy in its own right

Prior to the founding of the European Union,[2] food safety was regulated exclusively at the national level. In some European countries, laws ensuring the safety of food products, such as eggs, cheese and sausages, existed as early as the Middle Ages. More comprehensive and general regulations started to be developed in the nineteenth century as advances in science and technology ushered in the industrial production and processing of food, which brought many advantages but also created new food safety risks (MacMaolain 2007).

The 1957 Treaty of Rome did not explicitly empower the EU to act in the fields of public health and consumer protection, nor specifically in the sub-area of food safety. However, legislative activities indirectly related to food safety commenced as early as the first half of the 1960s. The primary objective of this initial body of EU legislation was the creation of a common market for food products, since they constituted one significant component of intra-EU trade. The preferred approach at the time was the adoption of EU directives harmonizing national food safety measures. The adoption of a single set of European requirements for foodstuffs in order to ensure their free circulation across the borders of Member States had the effect of simultaneously establishing a common level for food safety. This incipient phase in the regulation of food safety was characterized by vertical directives that were narrow in scope but highly detailed and, of course, legally binding. They covered the compositional characteristics of specific groups of food such as jams, chocolate and fruit juices, and began to establish harmonized lists of authorized colouring matters, preservatives and other food additives.

In light of the diverse and deeply ingrained national traditions regarding food, the exhaustive re-regulation of food products at the EU level proved time-consuming and cumbersome. In the wake of the *Cassis* judgment of the European Court of Justice from the mid-1980s, which established the principle of mutual recognition, the Commission came up with a new approach to harmonization, which significantly alleviated the need for spelling out standards in great detail. This second phase is marked by the consolidation of vertical directives into horizontal ones with broader scope laying down general principles and requirements. In sum, the first several post-war decades were marked by a gradual but steady decline in the relevance of the national level and a corresponding increase in the relevance of the EU level. This increase can be attributed to expansion of both the functional scope and depth of EU food safety legislation.

In the mid- to late 1990s a series of food crises erupted in the EU and precipitated the beginning of a third phase that decisively shifted the focus away from the creation of an internal market for food products and placed the regulation of food safety at the centre. Food scares relating to mad cow disease and dioxins in food products shook consumer confidence in the capacity of the EU to ensure the safety of the food chain. This created pressures for reforming the existing patchwork and piecemeal approach to food safety. The European Commission responded with a White Paper on Food Safety in 2000, proposing the overhaul of the existing system and the introduction of a comprehensive and integrated approach to food safety, according to which the EU would regulate all stages of the food production process from feed production to food processing and distribution. Moreover, this comprehensive and integrated approach would be based on scientific risk analysis and an EU agency would be created to provide scientific advice to EU regulators.

Many of the proposals for reform contained in the White Paper were taken up and codified in Regulation EC/178/2002, the watershed framework legislation also known as the General Food Law. This sets out broad, general principles and procedures for regulating food safety with which national- and European-level measures relating to all aspects of food production and distribution have to comply. It mandates the establishment of the European Food Safety Authority, an independent scientific agency at the EU level conducting risk assessment and providing scientific opinions that inform EU food safety measures. Other central principles in the General Food Law include the precautionary principle, traceability of food and food ingredients in the production and distribution chain, better consumer information, transparency of EU food regulations, and improved monitoring and enforcement of compliance. The General Food Law, with its broad horizontal sweep, further increases the scope of legislation at the European level. The legal instrument used takes the form of a regulation rather than a directive, which has been the trend in recent food safety legislation. This has the effect of further centralizing power at the EU level, since it eliminates the need for transposition at the national level.

In short, the regulation of food safety at the EU level underwent a remarkable development. From something epiphenomenal to the creation of an internal

Table 4.1 Significance of governance layers over time (Food Safety)

Phase	National level	EU level	Global level
Post-WWII	High	–	–
1957–late 1980s	High to medium	Low to medium	Low to medium (starting in 1963)
1990s	Medium	Medium	Medium (high since 1995 due to reference of Codex standards in WTO)
post-2000	Low	High	High
2020 (extrapolation)	Low	High (increasing scope)	High (increasing scope)

market for food products, it had turned into a full-fledged policy in its own right by the early 2000s (MacMaolain 2007). The increased centralization and comprehensiveness of food safety regulation resulting from these reforms raised the relevance of the EU as a governance layer to 'high'.

2.2 The international regime for food safety

Currently, two principal organizations at the international level are responsible for setting the global regime on food safety: the Codex Alimentarius Commission and the World Trade Organization.[3] Each is briefly discussed below.

2.2.1 The Codex Alimentarius Commission

The most prominent standard-setting body in the area of food safety at the international level is the Codex Alimentarius Commission (from here on simply the Codex). It was established in 1963 jointly by the World Health Organization and the Food and Agriculture Organization, both agencies of the United Nations (UN). The main objective of the Codex is to protect the health of consumers and ensure fair trade practices. To this end, the Codex develops food standards, codes of practice, recommendations and guidelines in the area of food safety. They are formally adopted by the Codex Alimentarius Commission at annual meetings. The Commission is assisted in its activities by permanent committees that focus on specific topics such as food additives, pesticide and veterinary drug residues, food labelling, food hygiene, animal health, and others. These expert subsidiary bodies work continuously on developing technical standards in their respective subfields. The depth or level of specificity of the Codex standards varies. Some issues are regulated through broad guidelines that leave a lot of space for interpretation, while other standards, such as those on maximum residue levels, contain concrete numerical values that do not allow for much discretion.

Codex standards are formally non-binding and only take effect when transposed in national or EU law. Codex standards may be taken up in their entirety or with reservations. The general trend is that developing countries, whose domestic food safety regulations are less advanced, typically adopt the Codex standards in their entirety whereas developed countries selectively adopt them, often with reservations (Victor 2004; Post 2005). Codex members may also set more stringent standards if they deem that the levels set in the Codex do not foster appropriate health and consumer protection.

In the first decade after its establishment, the Codex quickly gained significance as reflected by its growing membership, which by the mid-1970s comprised about 70 per cent of UN states (Büthe and Harris 2011). However, Codex activities almost came to a halt in the next decade due to the global economic slowdown (Büthe 2009). The importance of the Codex has grown again since 1995, when the 'Agreement on the Application of Sanitary and Phytosanitary Measures' (from here on the SPS Agreement) under the WTO designated the Codex standards as a reference point for international food standards (see the section on WTO below). The Codex currently has 186 members (185 countries and the EU). Over 200 organizations participate as observers without voting rights.

2.2.2 The World Trade Organization

The World Trade Organization is the second major organization that currently influences global food safety standards. The WTO aims to liberalize trade through the removal of both quantitative and non-quantitative barriers to trade. Because national food safety regulations may function as non-quantitative barriers to trade, the WTO members negotiated the Agreement on the Application of Sanitary and Phytosanitary Measures during the Uruguay Round of negotiations to regulate this aspect of trade.[4] The SPS Agreement lays down general principles and criteria for determining when national food safety measures may be allowed to interfere with international trade in food products and when such obstructions are not justified. In other words, it affects national and EU food safety policy by setting procedural constraints or requirements. If they are not met, a possible WTO dispute may arise.

Of particular relevance for the international food safety regime is that the SPS Agreement encourages WTO members to base their SPS measures on harmonized international standards, where such exist, and it refers specifically to the Codex standards in the case of food safety.[5] The designation of the Codex as the primary reference point for food safety standards of WTO members was a pivotal moment in the development of the international food safety regime (Veggeland and Borgen 2005). As subsequently elaborated in the *EC–Meat Hormones*[6] case, countries that implement the Codex food standards are presumed to be in compliance with WTO rules. Thus, while Codex standards remain non-binding, the incentives for countries to adopt them are stronger, as this guarantees fulfilment of their WTO obligations. The fact that decision-making in that forum became much more contentious after 1995 also indirectly confirms the increased relevance of the international governance layer (Matthee 2009; Veggeland and Borgen 2005; Matthee 2009).

Countries that choose to deviate from the Codex standards and implement higher levels of protection can still do so. However, they have to be able to demonstrate that their national measures are based on scientific risk assessment and do not pose disproportionate and discriminatory obstruction to trade. It is important to underline that the SPS Agreement does not prescribe substantive food safety standards per se. Instead it affects the food safety regime in that it imposes a *procedural* obligation that national food safety measures have to fulfil, namely that they be based on scientific assessments regarding risk to health rather than other considerations (e.g. consumer tastes) (Victor 2004).

In contrast to the Codex, the SPS Agreement is, as are all WTO provisions, legally binding, and compliance is enforced through dispute settlement procedures. The referencing of the Codex standards in the SPS Agreement increased their relevance precisely because of the stronger enforcement through the WTO dispute settlement procedures.

In sum, the foundations of an international regime for food safety were laid down in 1963 with the establishment of the Codex Alimentarius Commission. For the next three decades, the relevance of the international level grew gradually with the accumulation of international standards as a result of the Codex functioning. During that time, the relevance of the global level remained lower than that of the EU, primarily owing to the non-binding nature of the Codex standards compared to the legally binding EU directives and regulations. The relevance of the international level increased noticeably in 1995 when the Codex standards became the reference point for resolutions of WTO disputes concerning food safety measures.

2.3 Current relevance of governance layers

The overall trend for the national level has been one of a steady decrease in relevance while the European and the international level have progressively gained significance, albeit at a different pace. Currently, the national level is of low relevance as a locus of food safety policy-making. EU states can legislate in a few remaining areas that are not covered by EU rules and can make use of narrow derogations and safeguard clauses contained in EU rules (Szajkowska 2009). The relevance of both the EU and the international level has increased over time and may be assessed currently as high in absolute terms. In the case of the international level, this evaluation is based mainly on the cross-referencing of the Codex standards in the SPS Agreement and the stronger enforcement procedures of the WTO since 1995. It should be noted, however, that in relative terms the EU level is estimated to be of higher significance than the international level. First, the EU remains the level where most binding policy decisions regarding food safety are formally taken. Second, the collection of EU food safety standards is denser and has a wider scope than the Codex collection. Moreover, even though the bindingness of Codex standards has de facto increased since 1995 by virtue of the WTO enforcement mechanisms, the adoption of Codex standards still formally remains voluntary and Codex members can deviate from the standards when transposing them, especially if those deviations are backed by scientific risk analysis. The extent to which the significance of the international level will remain high or continue to grow in the future depends to some extent on the relevance of the WTO.

3 EU interaction with the international food safety regime

3.1 Features of the EU regime

One distinctive feature of the EU regime on food safety is that it maintains an overall high level of protection in substantive terms, especially compared to other national or regional regimes. In procedural terms, the main characteristics of the EU approach to food safety are its emphasis on the precautionary principle and the inclusion of other legitimate factors beyond science when making food safety policy (Poli 2004; Peel 2010).

The precautionary principle originated in the 1970s in the environmental regulation of Northern European countries (Fisher 2002). From there it was adopted at the European level and was also transferred to other policy areas such as the protection of health and safety. The starting point of the precautionary principle is the understanding that science cannot always provide sufficient and conclusive evidence about harmful substances or processes and their long-term effects. Recognizing this limitation of scientific knowledge, the precautionary principle allows precautionary regulatory measures to be put in place in cases where the potential for harm exists even if it is not yet proven. At the EU level, the precautionary principle was developed through the case law of the European Court of Justice and eventually codified in 2002 in the General Food Law.[7]

The other distinctive feature of the European approach to food safety is a broader conception of the factors that ought to inform the setting of food standards. In particular, this means that other factors beyond scientific considerations about health risks also need to be taken into account. While a clear definition of 'other legitimate factors' is largely missing, these are generally held to include considerations about technological need, consumer attitudes, environmental concerns, socio-economic sustainability, animal welfare, and ethical and religious considerations.

These distinctive features of the EU food safety regime also determine the main lines of contention that the EU faces at the international level. Both the precautionary principle and the concept of other legitimate factors are generally viewed negatively by countries that are major exporters of agricultural products such as the United States, Canada, New Zealand, Australia and some South American states. The suspicion on their side is that these approaches can be used to disguise protectionist practices. These countries insist that food standards be based on narrower grounds, namely *sound* science (rather than precautionary principle based on scientific uncertainty) and *only* sound science (to the exclusion of other factors beyond scientific risk assessment).

These differences in the procedural principles guiding the regulation of food, along with the fact that the EU typically defends more stringent standards in substantive terms, determine the contours of conflict at the international level. There are no permanent alliances as coalitional constellations shift depending on the particular issue. Still, in many cases the EU finds itself up against the US and/or the Cairns Group, made up of 19 agricultural exporting countries that are all interested in liberalizing trade in agricultural products. At other times, the EU meets the opposition of developing countries, for which implementing technologically demanding food safety measures is not always feasible.

Having outlined the distinct features of the European regime, the chapter proceeds to explore how successful the EU is in exporting it to the international level. The main pathway through which the EU engages at the international level is the vertical one, namely through participation in the international organizations described above. To a limited extent, the EU also exports its policies through horizontal pathways, most notably by providing technical assistance to third countries.

3.2 The vertical pathway to export

To arrive at an assessment of whether the EU has been successful or not in exporting its policies, I examine the EU's engagement in the two main organizations that shape food safety standards at the international level: the Codex Alimentarius Commission and the WTO. In both cases, I first focus the analysis on the negotiation of framework texts, specifying the general principles and procedures that determine the content of food safety policy, and ask whether the EU was successful in leaving its mark on those framework documents. In the case of the Codex, such a framework text is the Procedural Manual.[8] It sets out the principles and procedures that the Codex subcommittees follow when working out standards concerning individual substances, groups of foodstuffs or types of processes. With regard to the WTO, the framework text is the SPS Agreement. As a second step, the analysis looks beyond the formulation of general principles into the regular legislative activities of the Codex, and finally discusses two adjudication cases involving the EU and the WTO.

3.2.1 The EU's role in the Codex Alimentarius Commission

3.2.1.1 NEGOTIATING FRAMEWORK PRINCIPLES IN THE CODEX[9]

3.2.1.1.1 Contestation over the precautionary principle In 1997, the Codex Committee on General Principles was tasked with drafting working principles for risk analysis to be included in the Procedural Manual. One of the central questions that arose was how to proceed in cases of scientific uncertainty. In particular, the contention revolved around whether the Codex should adopt food safety measures even in cases of scientific uncertainty or refrain from putting in place standards, leaving it up to each country to decide domestically.

The EU countries held the position that lack of conclusive scientific evidence should not prevent the Codex from adopting international food safety measures. They insisted that a reference to the precautionary principle be included in the Codex approach to risk management. The US, along with some Latin American countries, opposed the inclusion of a reference to the precautionary principle, arguing that it was not recognized or elaborated in international law and that precaution was already included in the risk assessment phase. The debates went on for six years. In 2003 the Codex finally adopted 'The Working Principles for Risk Analysis'. The formulation of the final version was diluted and vague but came closer to the approach favoured by the United States (Poli 2004). Codex standards can be developed only when there is sufficient evidence of harm to human health. In cases of uncertainty, the Codex may adopt the weaker codes of practices. It appeared that in this particular case, European countries did not manage to sway enough allies to join their side and rally support for a stronger formulation of the precautionary principle[10] (Poli 2004: 619–622). This instance marks a failure of the EU to export a procedural standard to the international level.

3.2.1.1.2 Contestation over 'other legitimate factors' In 1998, European countries brought to the fore another divisive and contentious issue, namely whether science should be the sole basis for food safety standards or if other factors, such as consumer preferences or socio-economic and environmental considerations, could be taken into account as well. Discussions were launched for the revision of another part of the Codex's Procedural Manual: 'Statements of Principle on the Role of Science in the Codex Decision-Making Process and the extent to which Other Factors are taken into Account'. The final result, adopted three years later in 2001, was mixed. A reference to 'other legitimate factors' was included in the final text against the wishes of the United States, which insisted on a science-only approach to regulation. However, the formulation remained at a very general level. In particular, no definition of 'other legitimate factors' was elaborated which made future reliance on this notion unlikely. Furthermore, the invocation of additional factors is subject to restrictions; such factors cannot override scientific considerations and should be recognized broadly rather than in just a small number of countries, and should not restrict trade or affect developing countries (Poli 2004). Thus, while including the reference to other legitimate factors was a success for EU countries, in practice argumentation relying on other legitimate factors is unlikely to yield results in the Codex (Interview #1). Therefore, the case seems at best a partial success in policy export if one considers the formal text but amounts to an export failure when taking into account the practical application of the procedural principle.

3.2.1.2 LEGISLATING FOOD STANDARDS IN THE CODEX

The EU had a mandate from the Council to seek membership in the Codex Alimentarius Commission since 1993. It only took concrete steps to apply in 2001, after recognizing the increased significance of the Codex in the international regime on food safety as a result of its cross-referencing in the SPS Agreement. The preamble to the Council Decision on the accession of the European Community to the Codex explicitly states that the Codex standards have increased their legal relevance and it is therefore important that the EU participates as a full member in the adoption of these standards.[11]

The EU's accession to the Codex, however, was not straightforward. It required changes in the Procedural Manual in order to make it possible for an organization rather than a country to join. The US, along with other countries, tried to obstruct EU membership by arguing that this violated the 'one state, one vote' principle and voted against EU accession (Poli 2004: 618). The EU eventually succeeded in becoming an official member of the Codex in 2003. It is represented by the European Commission which votes on agenda items that fall within EU competencies with as many votes as Member States are present during the voting (Codex Procedural Manual).[12]

The accession of the EU as a full member to the Codex increased EU capacity. First, coordination of national positions has improved as a common position is formally agreed upon for the areas in which the EU has the competence to speak and vote. Having a central authority like the European Commission that undertakes the organization of preparatory meetings is easier than transnational coordination. Second, the EU has the capacity to send representatives to more meetings of subcommittees and can rely on a greater pool of experts than single European countries, which often send representatives only to some meetings (Interview #1). This enables the EU to have a more complete and comprehensive view of what is happening in the Codex as a whole. Finally, the EU as a bloc is in a stronger position to informally negotiate with its counterparts. It would be very difficult for a representative of a single European country to speak informally with the US delegation in order to exchange preliminary information on positions. In contrast, the EU can easily arrange informal meetings with other regional blocs and the Chair of the Codex (Interview #1). Thus, the formal accession of the EU as a member of the Codex has improved its capacity and, as a result, the EU is in a better position to shape the Codex food safety standards.

In addition, the EU's capacity is augmented by its large market size, since the EU is the largest importer of food and beverages in the world.[13] Finally, with its system of national and EU laboratories and regulatory agencies, the EU has accrued significant expertise in matters of food safety which improves its persuasion potential. It may be concluded that the EU as a whole possesses high capacity for external action, stemming from its membership in the Codex, its large market size and the scientific expertise at its disposal.

With regard to EU unity, the other internal condition posited in the theoretical framework of this book as relevant for successful policy export, it should be noted that in most cases there are no deep divisions or permanent cleavages among groups of EU states. This is partly because in many cases the EU has its own legislation in place upon which Member States have already agreed and so it is clear what the EU is aiming to export.[14] Unity within the Commission is also relatively high. In principle, there is an intrinsic antagonism between Directorate-General (DG) Sanco and DG Trade. While DG Sanco is interested in protecting human health and the consumer through installing stringent safety measures, DG Trade is interested in removing obstructions to trade such as intrusive regulatory requirements. However, there is an informal division of labour between the Commission's Directorates according to which DG Sanco is responsible for the Codex portfolio and DG Trade deals with the WTO (Interviews #3–4). Because of this distribution of activities, whatever divisions may exist internally within the Commission, they do not play out externally and the EU is capable of speaking with one voice at the Codex and the WTO.

Given the relatively high unity and capacity of the EU, how does the EU fare in exporting its substantive food policies? For the most part, the EU is relatively successful, whereby success is defined in pragmatic terms. A significant proportion of Codex rules do not generate conflicts because they come in the form of guidelines that allow enough space for discretion and interpretation. As a result, the EU can comply with them in a way that coincides with its own policies. In cases where the EU is unable to keep its pre-existing policies, success means the ability to delay or block the adoption of Codex standards. This is often the case with standards that, if adopted, would contain specific numeric values such as maximum residue levels from pesticides or veterinary drugs. Having an international standard for maximum residue level already implies that residues are allowed in food products, which is in contradiction of the EU's ban on residues from some substances. In these cases the EU is very often on the defensive. Its goal is to delay decision-making and keep items on the agenda for as long as possible (Interviews #1–2).[15] As one interviewee explained, it is in the interests of the EU not to have a Codex standard in cases when the EU deems it unrealistic to be able to export its own standards (Interview #1). In such cases, preventing the adoption of an international standard avoids a conflict with the European standard and gives the EU a greater chance of maintaining its own rule should a dispute be launched against it in the WTO. Whenever further postponement is not possible, the EU tries to negotiate opt-outs (Interview #2). Similarly, in the instances when the EU takes up Codex standards to incorporate them into its legislation, it does so selectively and to the extent that they conform to its general food safety principles (Poli 2004: 616; Victor 2004). Finally, in a very limited number of cases, the EU has defied Codex standards and maintained its own without having sufficient scientific evidence to back them up, thus making itself vulnerable to a WTO challenge (Interview #3). Thus, the EU overall seems to be more successful in policy protection than policy export.

This behaviour is underpinned by the food safety legislative framework of the EU. Article 5(3) of the General Food Law, rather than impose the more demanding obligation of basing EU laws on international standards, merely requires that the EU take them into consideration (Matthee 2009). Moreover, Article 13(e) of the same regulation asks the EU to promote consistency between its laws and international standards 'while ensuring that the high level of protection adopted in the Community is not reduced'. It appears that the EU, while acknowledging the importance of international standards in its policy-making, has also reserved some room for manoeuvre for itself that makes policy protection possible.

In terms of mechanisms for export, the EU employs both bargaining and persuasion to assert its policies in the Codex. Bargaining has come to be the dominant mode, especially after 1995 when negotiations became more politicized (Büthe and Harris 2011). Trade-offs are typically negotiated during informal meetings which occur several days before the main annual conference of the Codex Alimentarius Commission or during session breaks. An interviewee gave the example of the EU securing the support of African countries for a certain standard in exchange for the European vote for the African candidate for a leading Codex position (Interview #1). At the same time, the EU also engages in persuasion and argumentation. Although this is admittedly the less effective mechanism, there are countries that can be persuaded in some cases (Interview #2).

3.2.2 The EU's role in the WTO

3.2.2.1 NEGOTIATING THE SPS AGREEMENT

The questions about the role of science and the precautionary principle also arose during the negotiation of the SPS Agreement in the Uruguay Round. Regarding the role of science, the US proposed a requirement that food safety measures interfering with trade should be backed by scientific evidence. It succeeded in inserting this into the final text (Peel 2010). National measures that are based on the Codex standards are presumed to comply with WTO obligations. However, Codex standards are voluntary and countries may choose to go beyond them. In such cases, the SPS Agreement requires that measures deviating from the Codex be based on scientific risk assessment. This essentially places the burden of proof on the deviating country to justify its food safety measures and the levels of protection they afford. This requirement of scientific justification somewhat offsets the EU's success in asserting the right for countries to go beyond the Codex standards and decide on their own what an appropriate level of protection entails (Motaal 2004).

The EU, too, managed to score a win in a different aspect of the negotiations. It secured what may be interpreted today as a reference to the precautionary principle (Article 5.7 of the SPS Agreement) although at the time that issue was relatively uncontroversial (Motaal 2004; Peel 2010). At the end, both sides were accommodated through the overall very general manner in which the text of the SPS Agreement was formulated (Peel 2010). The meaning of the SPS Agreement is subsequently elaborated through the rulings of the WTO dispute settlement bodies. In this respect, the need to base food safety measures on scientific risk assessment, something upon which the US insisted, has been affirmed in WTO rulings. In contrast, the precautionary principle, pushed for by the EU, has been interpreted in restrictive ways (Prevost 2005). This decreases the policy fit between the EU's approach to food safety and this component of the international regime.

3.2.2.2 WTO DISPUTES AND EU FOOD SAFETY MEASURES

The EU was a defendant in two WTO disputes that were decided based on the SPS Agreement and entailed food safety issues: the *EC–Beef Hormones* case and the *EC–Biotechnology*[16] case.[17] In both cases, the WTO ruled against the European Union and struck down the EU measures that were at stake.

The *Beef Hormones* case focused on the EU measure banning the use of six growth-promoting substances in beef. The final ruling of the Appellate Body was based on the fact that the EU could not justify its ban on growth promoters with scientific risk assessment and could not show that these substances were actually harmful to human health. In the case of the *EC–Biotech* dispute there were two main issues at stake. The first was the suspension of genetically modified organisms (GMO) authorizations that was in place in the EU at the time. This so-called moratorium was causing undue delays in authorizations, which was considered a barrier to trade. The second issue was several safeguard bans on the cultivation of certain genetically modified (GM) varieties, which were authorized in the EU as a whole but nonetheless banned in the territories of several EU countries. On this point, the Appellate Body found again that these national bans were not based on proper risk assessment. Thus both rulings involved, at least in part, the role of science in regulatory policy-making and reinforced the procedural requirement inserted by the US in the SPS Agreement that measures should be based on scientific evidence.

Despite the unfavourable WTO rulings, the EU has not altered its specific policies and thus its behaviour may be characterized again as policy protection. With regard to the *Beef Hormones* case, to this day the EU continues to keep its policy prohibiting growth promoters in beef and hence bans imports of such meat. Because of the EU's non-compliance with the WTO ruling to lift its ban, Canada and the United States were authorized to impose retaliatory sanctions on EU exports in 1999. An end to the 20-year trade war was finally worked out in 2012. The EU would increase its quotas for high-quality hormone-free meat from the US and Canada in exchange for continuing to keep its ban.

In the *EC–Biotech* case, the EU again did not comply fully. Authorizations of GMOs resumed but not so much as a result of the WTO ruling as because the EU had already completed the reform of its regulatory framework around the time the final WTO ruling came out. However, EU Member States continue to maintain their national bans despite some attempts by the Commission to lift them. Thus, again the EU as a whole is not complying with the WTO ruling and has not changed its policies as a result of pressures from the international regime. In both cases, the EU did not alter its policies and therefore one cannot speak of import from the international level, even though the EU lost in both of these instances.

3.3 The horizontal pathway

Vertical export through participation in international organizations is the main pathway for the EU to shape food policy, as discussed above. However, to some extent, the EU also engages in horizontal export through bilateral initiatives with third countries, although in general this pathway is of smaller relevance. One obvious channel for export of the EU's food safety policy is bilateral agreements, whose relevance has been on the rise as a result of the lack of progress in the multilateral Doha Round. However, the impact of exporting food policies through this instrument is limited (Interview #4). Bilateral trade agreements are package deals that involve multiple sectors with the food sector typically not ranking very high on the agenda. It takes a back seat on issues of higher political priority or to sectors with greater economic consequence for the EU, such as manufacturing goods or raw materials (Interview #4). It may be reasonably assumed that due to its relatively greater bargaining weight in bilateral agreements as opposed to multilateral fora, the EU would be more successful in exporting food standards in bilateral negotiations. However, this is often not the case with food safety policy in particular because the EU prioritizes the achievement of other goals. Another mechanism for EU policy export is through programmes that provide technological assistance or training. One such example is the EU initiative 'Better Training for Safer Food'. Its main goal is to train competent national authorities in the EU involved in the monitoring and control of food imports. However, funding is also available for 'on-the-spot' training of third country experts.

Finally, it may also be said that the EU engages in passive horizontal export. This is due to the fact that the EU food safety standards are regarded as espousing a high level of protection. What facilitates this type of export is that EU food safety legislation is transparent and easily accessible. It is made public online, which is not always the case with the policies of other major food-importing countries (Interview #3). The transparency of the EU legislation makes it easier for countries to consult it and to voluntarily and unilaterally incorporate it into their own legislation.

Conclusions

The EU and the international level have gained importance over time in the multi-level governance of food safety at the expense of the national level. While both the EU and the international level are highly relevant today, the EU remains the level at which most binding policy decisions for EU Member States are taken. Therefore, the EU is the most significant governance layer in the area of food safety, when compared to the national and the global level. The EU is interested in the existence of a credible international regime for food safety. As a net importer of food, the EU is not entirely self-sufficient and relies on other countries for its food supply. A functioning international regime helps to ensure that food produced in the rest of the world does not harm human health or the consumer and is safe for import into the EU.

At the same time, the EU's own food safety policy has one of the highest levels of public health protection in the world. Naturally, it faces difficulties to rally the support of developing countries, which find the technologically demanding EU standards costly to implement. The EU is also faced with the opposition of big blocs of agricultural-exporting countries, which prefer to shield their agricultural sectors from cumbersome or restrictive regulations.

In sum, the EU is in a position where it supports the existence of international food safety standards but is simultaneously in a minority position and cannot always export its stringent policies to the international level in the context of multilateral settings and an increasingly multipolar world. As a result, the EU has adopted a pragmatic approach of policy protection. It complies with Codex standards whenever they are in line with its own policies. It tries to delay or block the adoption of agenda items or negotiate exemptions when Codex standards do not reflect EU rules. As a last measure of policy protection, the EU sometimes deviates from the Codex standards, making sure that the deviations can be justified scientifically whenever possible. In a very limited number of cases, the EU has resisted the import of Codex standards even without scientific risk assessment at hand (Interview #3). That the EU has deviated from the general WTO principle of science-based SPS measures on some issues is evident from the WTO cases that the EU lost. In those instances, the EU engaged in resilient policy protection and did not comply even in the face of retaliatory sanctions, as seen specifically in the *Beef Hormones* case. Still, it should be noted that in the context of the overall body of international food safety standards, these two cases cover very narrow issues and constitute the exception rather than the rule. For the most part, the EU is a cooperative player that tries to work within the international regime rather than undermine it, which sometimes results in policy import of individual food safety standards. At the same time, in a very limited number of extreme cases, the EU is prepared to protect the policies that it deems important even if that means non-compliance with case law or entails a potential for a future legal challenge in front of the WTO. While the large market size of the EU is not a sufficient condition for policy export at the international level, it certainly facilitates policy protection.

The EU engages with the international food safety regime primarily through the vertical pathway of participation in international organizations (the Codex Alimentarius Commission and the WTO). It attempts *active* export both through bargaining as well as argumentation and persuasion, with the former being the more effective of the two mechanisms. To a limited extent, the EU exports its policy horizontally through initiatives such as technical assistance and training of third countries. There is also the possibility for *passive* horizontal export due to the fact that the EU food safety policy is easily accessible and transparent, so it is often a 'go-to' resource and reference point for developing countries.

The EU fulfils most internal conditions that are expected to enable it to successfully export its food safety policies. The EU can be evaluated to have both high unity and high capacity on most issues in the field of food safety. In terms of unity, there are no significant cleavages among Member States or within the Commission. The relationship between the Commission and EU countries is also harmonious, with Member States appreciating the leading role that the EU has taken since it formally joined the Codex as a voting member. Thus, the EU is able to speak with one voice both in the Codex and the WTO. In terms of capacity, the EU has the advantage of its large market size (the world's biggest importer of food and drinks) as well as a sophisticated scientific and legislative machine for food safety regulation that equips the EU with significant food safety expertise.

Yet, despite these favourable internal conditions, the EU is often unable to successfully export and has to resort to defensive strategies of policy protection. This outcome may be attributed to external conditions, namely the international setting in which the EU finds itself. In the case of the Codex, the EU is often outnumbered by some combination of developing countries and/or agricultural exporters and finds it difficult to sway enough countries to support its strict food safety regulations. The odds are further against the EU in the context of WTO, particularly owing to the adjudicative nature of the proceedings, which forecloses the use of mechanisms such as bargaining. Given the high standards of the EU food safety policy, it is perhaps unrealistic to expect that the EU would be able to export them to the international level. The EU market size, while significant, is not enough to override other large blocs of countries in a multilateral setting. It does, however, increase the capacity of the EU to engage in policy protection and defy pressures for policy import. The judicialization of the WTO is also a constraining factor for the EU as the shadow of another WTO case is always present in the background of EU policy-making. However, given that the first and foremost objective of the EU's food policy is to ensure that food products put on the European market are safe, the pragmatic approach of policy protection may be considered a success in itself.

Notes

1 International Trade Statistics 2011. World Trade Organization. Available at: www.wto.org/english/res_e/statis_e/its2011_e/its2011_e.pdf (accessed 24 September 2012).
2 For simplicity, 'European Union' is used throughout the text to also refer to its predecessor, the European Community.
3 Other organizations that are involved with food standard-setting, among other policies, are the United Nations Economic Commission for Europe, the Organization of Economic Cooperation and Development, and the International Organization for Standardization. However, the role and significance of these organizations were eclipsed by the Codex Alimentarius Commission, which established itself as the leading body for food safety standards, especially after 1995 (Büthe 2009). For a detailed account of how the Codex was chosen among the above organizations as a reference point for the SPS Agreement and thus grew to dominate food safety standard-setting, see Büthe (2009).
4 The Agreement of Technical Barriers to Trade (TBT Agreement) may also sometimes be referred to in relation to food products but it is of a more general nature and therefore excluded from this analysis.
5 'SPS measures' is a broader category that includes not only measures affecting human but also animal and plant health. For animal health the SPS Agreement refers to the standards of the International Office of Epizootics and for plant health the reference point is the International Plant Protection Convention.
6 European Communities – Measures Concerning Meat and Meat Products (Hormones). (WT/DS26/AB/R) 16 January 1998. Available at www.wto.org/english/tratop_e/dispu_e/cases_e/ds26_e.htm (accessed 24 September 2012).
7 Regulation (EC) No 178/2002 of the European Parliament and of the Council of 28 January 2002 laying down the general principles and requirements of food law, establishing the European Food Safety Authority and laying down procedures in matters of food safety (OJ L 31, 1.2.2002, pp. 1–24).
8 Codex Alimentarius Commission. Procedural Manual. 20th edition. Issued by the Secretariat of the Joint FAO/WHO Food Standards Programme, FAO, Rome. Available at ftp://ftp.fao.org/codex/Publications/ProcManuals/Manual_20e.pdf (accessed 24 September 2012).
9 Poli (2004) has documented the negotiations of two framework texts (parts of the Codex Procedural Manual) that concern the precautionary principle and the notion of other legitimate factors and this section draws extensively on her account.

10 It is important to note that if one tracks the EU's export record of the precautionary principle across multiple policy fields rather than just in the area of food safety, the picture that emerges is one where the EU also has instances of successful policy export of the precautionary principle. For example, the EU was more successful in implementing the precautionary principle in another international agreement, the Cartagena Protocol on Biosafety, which is a Protocol to the 1992 Convention for the Protection of Biological Diversity.

11 Council Decision of 17 November 2003 on the accession of the European Community to the Codex Alimentarius Commission (OJ L 309/14 from 26.11.2003).

12 This arrangement has been noted as unsatisfactory for the EU on the grounds that EU Member States have conferred general powers on the EU through a legal agreement and not by virtue of their presence in a room (Hoffmeister 2007). EU membership in the Codex was a considerable success however and, at the time, rather exceptional in light of the general resistance of international organizations in the UN family to accept a regional organization as a full member.

13 Eurostat, 'EU-27 consistent world leader in trade of food and drinks', Statistics in Focus 78/2009. Available at http://epp.eurostat.ec.europa.eu/cache/ITY_OFFPUB/KS-SF-09-078/EN/KS-SF-09-078-EN (accessed 24 September 2012).

14 One interviewee noted that what can become more contentious and difficult to agree upon are the fall-back positions of the EU. But even in those cases, EU states typically follow the Commission's proposals as they have learned to trust its expertise. At any rate, fall-back positions are a case of policy promotion rather than policy export, since most of the time they do not reflect actual EU policies (Interview #3).

15 Maximum residue level for growth-promoting substances seems to be an area where one of the biggest clashes between the EU and the US occur. The EU has zero-tolerance policy for such substances whereas the US has allegedly vowed to put all six growth promoters in the Codex standards. The EU tries to avoid this by using various procedural tricks. In one of the last Codex meetings, the EU called a vote on whether there should be a vote on this agenda item (decisions are typically taken by consensus). Since most countries wanted to avoid a precedent deviating from the consensus decision-making norm, the vote on the maximum residue level did not take place and the item remained on the agenda (Interview #1).

16 European Communities – Measures Affecting the Approval and Marketing of Biotech Products (WT/DS/291–293). Reports of the Panel, 29 September 2006. Available at www.wto.org/english/tratop_e/dispu_e/cases_e/ds291_e.htm (accessed 24 September 2012).

17 A third WTO case concerning an EU ban on the import of poultry treated with pathogen reduction substances such as chlorine solutions initiated by the US has been suspended.

References

Büthe, T. (2009) 'The Politics of Food Safety in the Age of Global Trade: The Codex Alimentarius Commission in the SPS-Agreement of the WTO', in C. Coglianese, A. Finkel and D. Zaring (eds) *Import Safety: Regulatory Governance in the Global Economy*, Philadelphia, PA: University of Pennsylvania Press.

Büthe, T. and Harris, N. (2011) 'The Codex Alimentarius Commission: A Hybrid Public–Private Regulator', in T. Hale and D. Held (eds) *Handbook on Transnational Governance: Institutions and Innovations*, Cambridge: Polity Press.

Fisher, E. (2002) 'Precaution, Precaution Everywhere: Developing a "Common Understanding" of the Precautionary Principle in the European Community', *Maastricht Journal of European and Comparative Law* 9(1): 7–28.

Hoffmeister, F. (2007) 'Outsider or Frontrunner? Recent Developments under International and European Law on the Status of the European Union in International Organizations and Treaty Bodies', *Common Market Law Review* 44(1): 41–68.

MacMaolain, C. (2007) *EU Food Law: Protecting Consumers and Health in a Common Market*, Oxford: Hart Publishing.

Matthee, M. (2009) 'The Codex Alimentarius Commission and its Food Safety Measures in the Light of their New Status', in M. Everson and E. Vos (eds) *Uncertain Risks Regulated*, New York: Routledge-Cavendish.

Motaal, D.A. (2004) 'The "Multilateral Scientific Consensus" and the World Trade Organization', *Journal of World Trade* 38(5): 855–876.

Peel, J. (2010) *Science and Risk Regulation in International Law*, Cambridge: Cambridge University Press.

Peel, J., Nelson, R. and Godden, L. (2005) 'GMO Trade Wars: The Submissions in the EC–GMO Dispute in the WTO', *Melbourne Journal of International Law* 6(1): 141–166.

Poli, S. (2004) 'The European Community and the Adoption of International Food Standards within the Codex Alimentarius Commission', *European Law Journal* 10(5): 613–630.

Post, D. (2005) 'Standards and Regulatory Capitalism: The Diffusion of Food Safety Standards in Developing Countries', *The Annals of the American Academy of Political and Social Science* 598(1): 168–183.

Prevost, D. (2005) 'What Role for the Precautionary Principle in WTO Law after Japan-apples?', *EcoLomic Policy and Law: Journal of Trade and Environment Studies* 2(4): 1–14.

Szajkowska, A. (2009) 'From Mutual Recognition to Mutual Scientific Opinion? Constitutional Framework for Risk Analysis in EU Food Safety Law', *Food Policy* 34(6): 529–538.

Veggeland, F. and Borgen, S.O. (2005) 'Negotiating International Food Standards: The World Trade Organization's Impact on the Codex Alimentarius Commission', *Governance* 18(4): 675–708.

Victor, D. (2004) 'WTO Efforts to Manage Differences in National Sanitary and Phytosanitary Policies', in D. Vogel and R. Kagan (eds) *Dynamics of Regulatory Change: How Globalization Affects National Regulatory Policies*, Berkeley, CA: University of California Press.

Wüger, D. (2002) 'The Never Ending Story: The Implementation Phase in the Dispute between the EC and the United States on Hormone-Treated Beef', *Law and Policy in International Business* 33(4): 777–825.

Interviews

Interview #1: Official from Federal Ministry of Agriculture, May 2012, Austria.
Interview #2: Official from Federal Ministry of Health, May 2012, Austria.
Interview #3: Official from European Commission, DG Sanco, June 2012, Belgium.
Interview #4: Official from European Commission, DG Trade, June 2012, Belgium.

5 Competition policy
The EU and global networks

Marco Botta

1 Introduction

Competition policy is one of the oldest exclusive competences of the EU; the wording of its 'core' legal provisions (i.e. Art. 101 and 102, TFEU) has not changed since the Treaty of Rome. The European Community (EC) founding fathers were well aware that in order to establish the common market, free movement rules had to be complemented by competition rules. The latter sanction certain types of anti-competitive agreements (i.e. cartels) and the abusive conducts by dominant undertakings which could represent an entry barrier into a national market for a foreign competitor, thus jeopardizing the establishment of the common market.

The past two decades witnessed a growing debate in many international organizations (IOs) on the need to harmonize competition standards. According to Damtoft and Flanagan, the harmonization of competition standards at the global level would be justified by two intertwined reasons (Damtoft and Flanagan 2009). On the one hand, the globalization of the economy has increased the number of cross-border, anti-competitive behaviours; and on the other hand, a growing number of developing countries have adopted competition laws under the pressure of international donors. These two phenomena have led to a growing risk of diverging national decisions by the National Competition Authorities (NCAs) in charge of enforcing the competition law to sanction the same cross-border, anti-competitive behaviour.

After a brief description of the historical evolution of the EU competition policy, this chapter will focus on the EU's attempts to export its competition model to the IOs and transnational networks active in this sector. In view of the proliferation of competition law jurisdictions in several developing countries, the convergence of regulatory standards in this sector has been high on the agenda of a number of IOs – including the World Trade Organization (WTO), the United Nations Conference on Trade and Development (UNCTAD), the Organization for Economic Cooperation and Development (OECD) and the International Competition Network (ICN). During the past decade, these institutions have adopted a number of guidelines to achieve the convergence of regulatory standards in the field of competition policy. This chapter discusses the process through which these IOs adopt soft law aimed at achieving the convergence of competition standards, as well as the role played by the EU (i.e. Directorate-General (DG) Competition of the European Commission and the National Competition Authorities of the EU Member States) in the process of forming these guidelines. In particular, the chapter relies on a number of interviews conducted by the author in April 2012 on the occasion of the eleventh ICN annual conference.[1]

The main finding of the chapter is that the role played by the EU in exporting its *acquis* has been quite different at the vertical and horizontal levels. At the vertical level, the EU failed to export its preference for a harmonization of core competition principles in the context of the WTO. Through the establishment of the ICN, the US has been more successful than the EU in terms of institution-building in this policy area. Nevertheless, by actively participating in the work of the ICN, OECD and UNCTAD over the past decade, the EU has ensured that the soft law elaborated by these IOs was in compliance with the EU competition model, thus reducing the import of these international standards to the EU. At the horizontal level, by contrast, the EU has successfully exported its core competition provisions to candidate and neighbouring countries by including a competition chapter on bilateral trade/association agreements.

2 EU competition policy

Unlike other policy areas, EU competition policy is characterized by few core binding provisions: Article 101, prohibiting anti-competitive agreements, and Article 102 TFEU, sanctioning the abuse of dominant position. The latter are broad principles which grant a margin of discretion to the 'enforcers' of the competition policy, namely the National Competition Authority (NCA) and the national courts (Cini and McGowan 2009). While the NCA enforces the competition policy through the adoption of administrative decisions which sanction anti-competitive conducts, the national courts review the NCA's decisions. At the EU level, the function of the NCA is played by DG Competition of the EU Commission, while the function of judicial review is played by the EU General Court and by the Court of Justice.[2] In order to provide legal certainty to economic operators, the NCA adopts internal guidelines to explain its enforcement priorities and its interpretation of the core competition principles, while the courts refer to their previous case law in their judgments. Even though the core competition principles are rarely amended (e.g. the wording of Art 101 and 102, TFEU has not changed since the Treaty of Rome), the degree of enforcement for competition policy is strongly influenced by the guidelines adopted by the NCA and by the court case law. The distinction between core competition provisions and NCA guidelines is essential in the context of this chapter; as we will see in the following pages, while the EU Commission proposed to harmonize core competition provisions through a binding WTO agreement, UNCTAD, OECD and ICN have pursued convergence among the NCA's internal guidelines through the adoption of soft law in different areas of competition policy.

The enforcement degree of EU competition policy has only substantially increased during the past two decades in the context of the EU single market project (Cini and McGowan 2009). One important development was the adoption of the Merger Control Regulation 4064/1989, later revised by Regulation 139/2004. By introducing a duty of notification for all the mergers and acquisitions which had a Community dimension, the Merger Control Regulation substantially increased the authority of DG Competition among the Directorates General of the European Commission. Parallel to the increased relevance of competition policy at the EU level, the EU Member States have adopted national competition law. It is worth noting that at the moment of the signature of the Treaty of Rome, only Germany and the UK had a national competition policy in force, while today all 27 EU Member States have a national competition policy. The spread of competition policy in the EU Member States was accelerated by the adoption of the Regulation 1/2003. The latter 'decentralized' the enforcement of EU competition policy by requiring every Member State to establish an NCA in charge of enforcing national, as well as EU, competition rules. National competition rules today are broadly in line with the EU standards in this field. In fact, even with the lack of a legal basis in the TFEU to harmonize national competition law, a 'spontaneous harmonization' of the national competition rules has taken place during the past decade (Vedder 2004). In particular, the 'old' Member States have harmonized their national competition law towards the EU standards in view of the obligations arising from Regulation 1/2003, while the candidate EU Member States were 'encouraged' by the EU Commission to adopt national competition law in line with the EU standards in the context of the enlargement process (Cseres 2007). Furthermore, parallel to the adoption of Regulation 1/2003, the EU Commission supported the establishment of a European Competition Network, a platform chaired by DG Competition which allows NCAs to coordinate their work in cross-border cases by exchanging relevant information. The decentralization of competition policy has thus led to the establishment of a complex regulatory scenario; a 'multi-layered legal order' in which the EU Commission exercises a substantial influence (Ottow 2011).

In conclusion, the past two decades have witnessed a substantial increase in the significance of competition policy, both at the EU and the national level. Competition policy enforcement has been 'decentralized'; but this has not hampered the unity of this policy. By linking the idea of decentralization to the rhetoric of subsidiarity favoured by the EU Member States, the EU Commission has actually achieved a higher degree of consistency throughout the EU as Member States have harmonized their national legislation in light of the EU competition policy (Budzinski and Christiansen 2005).

3 Global competition regimes: harmonization vs. convergence

3.1 WTO: the attempt to harmonize core competition provisions

At the beginning of the 1990s, DG Competition played an important role in initiating the debate concerning a possible harmonization of global competition standards. In 1995, a group of experts appointed by Competition Commissioner Van Miert delivered a report analysing the different possible scenarios to achieve an international harmonization of competition standards (the so-called Van Miert Report).[3] The main conclusions of the Report were included one year later in a EU Commission's Communication; supported both by Commissioner Van Miert and by Trade Commissioner Sir Leon Brittan, the Communication identified a long-term strategy to achieve an international harmonization of competition standards (Commission 1996). The Communication stressed that the wave of trade liberalization which followed the conclusion of the Uruguay Round could be effective only through the adoption of a basic set of competition standards in the context of the WTO. Harmonization of competition standards was therefore justified by trade considerations, as a tool ensuring fair and non-discriminatory access for European companies to the markets of developing countries.

In 1996, competition policy was included among the 'Singapore issues',[4] and a working group was established to analyse the interaction between trade and competition policy. In 2001, the EU Commission successfully managed to include competition policy within the Doha Development Agenda of negotiations.[5] In the context of the Doha negotiations, the EU Commission initially proposed the adoption of a minimum set of binding WTO rules in the field of competition policy. Such rules included the obligation for each WTO Member State to adopt an internal law prohibiting cartel agreements among economic operators and to establish an NCA in charge of enforcing such a rule; the NCA was required to comply with the principles of transparency, procedural fairness, and non-discrimination between foreign and national companies (Van Den Hoven 2006). The latter were 'core principles' which aimed to guide the enforcement activities of the NCA. However, in view of the persisting differences among the competition regimes of the WTO Member States, the proposal did not include the harmonization of the internal guidelines adopted by every NCA to clarify the enforcement of such core principles.

In spite of its long tradition of 'anti-trust' enforcement (i.e. the US equivalent expression of EU competition policy), the US adopted a sceptical approach vis-à-vis the EU's proposal to introduce minimum WTO competition rules. Fox noted that the US did not participate 'in the post-war Western European tradition of community building' (Fox 1997); consequently, the 'natural' EU policy preference for a multilateral harmonization of competition rules was not an 'obvious' solution for the US. The US's sceptical approach vis-à-vis a WTO competition agreement became more evident in 2000, when the International Competition Policy Advisory Committee (ICPAC) delivered its report to the US Attorney

General of the Department of Justice (ICPAC 2000). The departure point of the US group of experts was quite different in comparison to the European academics who had drafted the Van Miert Report a few years before: the justification for an international harmonization of competition standards was not related to market access concerns, but rather to the 'costs' and the 'uncertainty' caused to multinational companies by the growing number of competition law jurisdictions in the world. In particular, the Report showed concerns over the growing number of mergers subject to multiple notifications in the new competition law jurisdictions of the developing countries (i.e. multi-jurisdictional mergers) (ICPAC 2000). The report concluded that the possibility of introducing binding core competition rules within the WTO framework was 'unrealistic and unwise' (ICPAC 2000: ch. 6); unrealistic due to the difficulties in achieving a common consensus among the WTO Member States and unwise since the proposed binding WTO rules would be general principles which would leave a broad margin of discretion for their enforcement to the NCAs of the developing countries. Consequently, a WTO agreement on competition policy would have reduced neither the 'costs' nor the 'uncertainties' caused by the proliferation of competition law jurisdictions in developing countries. On the other hand, the US report supported the establishment of a new 'Global Competition Initiative', a global network of NCAs where competition standards would have been discussed by competition experts (i.e. the officers of the NCAs), rather than by the representatives of the Ministries of Trade (ICPAC 2000: ch. 6). In addition, unlike the WTO, the new network would focus on the adoption of soft law, aiming to achieve a 'convergence' of the internal guidelines of the NCAs rather than supporting the harmonization of the general core competition principles.

Following the failure of the Cancùn WTO Ministerial Conference in 2003, competition policy was dropped from the Doha agenda along with the other Singapore issues (Kerremans 2004). Even though competition policy was less controversial than other Singapore issues (i.e. investment protection), several developing countries were not ready to accept a commitment in this field without any concession from the side of the US and the EU in the field of agriculture. Finally, in view of the ICPAC report adopted a few years before, the US delegation did not regret the fact that competition policy was dropped from the agenda of the negotiations (Damro 2004).

3.2 Convergence through the adoption of soft law

Following the failure to conclude a multilateral competition agreement within the WTO, the debate has progressively shifted from the need to 'harmonize' competition standards to the need to achieve their 'convergence'. Unlike harmonization, convergence does not imply a complete uniformity of regulatory standards; rather it means the broad acceptance of shared substantive and procedural principles (Hollman and Kovacic 2011). While harmonization proceeds through the adoption of binding international agreements, convergence relies on the adoption of guidelines, recommendations, best practices, etc. Regardless of the specific terminology used, these documents share the common feature of being soft law under public international law. The lack of ratification requirements and the lack of a dispute settlement system facilitate the achievement of consensus, and thus the adoption of guidelines which are progressively more detailed. While the EU Commission's proposal to conclude a WTO competition agreement referred only to basic general principles, soft law can achieve a convergence of more detailed substantive and procedural standards (Hollman and Kovacic 2011). The challenge is to understand the dynamics of the implementation of soft law in national competition policy regimes. According to Cheng, a number of peculiarities which characterize competition policy have facilitated convergence in this area as opposed to other regulatory policies (Cheng 2011–2012). First of all, the growing number of competition law jurisdictions has created a demand for globally accepted guidelines explaining how competition policy should be properly enforced; the technical and interdisciplinary character of competition policy makes the recently established NCAs of developing countries eager to implement up-to-date best practices in this field. Second, due to the administrative character of competition policy enforcement, NCAs which participate in the IOs where best practices are discussed are also the main actors in charge of enforcing these guidelines. Due to the fact that NCAs' internal guidelines are not legislative acts, the latter institutions are free to update their guidelines without the intervention of the legislative and executive powers. To sum up, due to the margin of discretion enjoyed by NCAs in enforcing competition rules, these institutions can quickly implement the latest best practices recommended by these IOs.

3.3 *The role played by UNCTAD and OECD in the convergence of competition standards*

UNCTAD and OECD have traditionally pursued an international convergence of competition standards since the 1970s. These two IOs have a different membership. While UNCTAD has a quasi-universal membership since it includes most of the Member States of the United Nations,[6] OECD is usually considered the 'club of the rich nations', since it includes the 34 most industrialized economies in the world.[7] Despite their different membership, UNCTAD and OECD share several similarities in relation to the types of activities carried out: both IOs pursue the logic of the convergence of competition standards through the adoption of soft law and also provide mechanisms of peer review to assess the enforcement of national competition law in accordance with international standards in this field. The peer review often supports the process of convergence towards common international standards and is a useful mechanism for the newly established NCA of a developing country, argues former US Federal Trade Commissioner William Kovacic, since the latter institution can rely on the IO's report to lobby the government of its country to amend the competition law.[8]

Besides the similar approach to achieve convergence, UNCTAD and OECD share a number of common institutional features. In particular, they are both full-fledged IOs established on the basis of an international agreement and both have permanent secretariats based in Geneva and Paris. The structure of these IOs is sometimes seen as an obstacle to the activities pursued by these organizations; in particular, UNCTAD and OECD are sometimes considered as 'bureaucratic' institutions, subject to multi-language translation requirements. Furthermore, since they are established on the basis of an international agreement, the NCAs of their Member States have to coordinate their participation in these IOs along with the permanent diplomatic missions of their countries in Paris and Geneva. As argued by Damtoft and Flanagan, the meetings of UNCTAD and OECD 'are heavily populated by resident diplomats who are not well-versed in competition issues' (Damtoft and Flanagan 2009). Consequently, considerations of national interest might filter into the work of these IOs, making achieving a consensus on technical competition standards more difficult.

3.4 The international competition network: the 'virtual' competition network

The limits of UNCTAD and OECD were the main reasons which led the US group of experts who had drafted the ICPAC report in 2000 to establish a new 'Global Competition Initiative'. In particular, stressing the difference to UNCTAD and OECD, the report pointed out that the new initiative:

> should be inclusive in its membership, open to developed and developing nations, and comprehensive, or at least open to the possibility of breadth, in its coverage of issue areas; it should also allow room for the private sector, NGOs and other interested parties to play a role.
>
> (ICPAC 2000)

The proposal was accepted in 2000 by both the US Federal Trade Commission and by the US Department of Justice under the new Republican administration (Janow and James 2011), and was also strongly supported by the Antitrust Committee of the International Bar Association.[9] In addition, former EU Competition Commissioner Monti favoured the new initiative since its early stage and publicly stated the support of the EU's DG Competition in a number of public events.[10] In the first annual conference in Naples in September 2002, the Global Competition Initiative was renamed the International Competition Network (ICN). The support of Commissioner Monti for the establishment of the ICN signalled a clear change of strategy in comparison to his predecessor, Karl Van Miert, who in the absence of the ICN had supported the harmonization of competition standards within the WTO (Damro 2007). This choice may be partly explained in terms of venue preference. Within intergovernmental IOs like UNCTAD and OECD, DG Competition occupies only an observatory status, while it is a full member and the exclusive representative of the EU Commission within the International Competition Network, where it has always been a member of the Steering Board and co-chaired a number of working groups.

Since the first annual conference of the International Competition Network (ICN) in Naples in September 2002, the ICN has substantially increased its number of members and expanded the scope of its activities. However, the ICN has preserved the 'virtues of a virtual network' (Fox 2009). The lack of a permanent secretariat and the lack of involvement from the national Ministries of Foreign Affairs are substantial differences in comparison to OECD and UNCTAD. The work of the ICN is carried out through an impressive number of teleconferences and email exchanges among the representatives of the NCAs which have joined the network. Since the ICN does not have a permanent secretariat, its output strongly depends on the resources that each NCA invests in the network.[11] Consequently, even though all NCAs are formally equal members of the ICN, in practice only the NCAs from developed economies have sufficient human resources to devote to the ICN's activities. Most of the NCAs from developing countries, on the other hand, are rather 'passive' members of the ICN. They attend the annual conference and other occasional workshops, but they rarely provide an input to the ICN activities. As recognized by Fox, even though the ICN works on the basis of consensus rule, 'the ICN agenda is principally set and norms principally forged by the developed world' (Fox 2009).

Similar to UNCTAD and OECD, the ICN guidelines aim at achieving a convergence of the internal guidelines of the NCAs in different areas of competition policy. The terminology of the guidelines is usually sufficiently 'broad' to accommodate both the EU competition as well as the US anti-trust models. Although the ICN does not have a system of peer review and does not provide forms of technical assistance, its soft law is highly valuable for the NCAs, especially for the newly established NCAs of the developing countries. These NCAs rely particularly on the ICN recommendations to update their enforcement guidelines, and to convince the government and legislative bodies to amend controversial aspects of the national competition law.[12] In sum, while not an exporter of its domestic model, the EU was still successful in policy protection, ensuring that international negotiation outcomes did not conflict with key aspects of its domestic model.

In the literature, the ICN is generally considered a success story due to two main reasons (Fox 2009). First of all, the ICN has increased its members from the initial 15 NCAs which attended the first conference in 2002 to the current 123 NCAs.[13] The second aspect of ICN's success is usually connected with the broad output of soft law that ICN has produced over a single decade. This result has arguably been achieved due to the lack of involvement of the national Ministries of Foreign Affairs. Consensus has been achieved at the level of ICN where like-minded competition experts from different countries in the world discuss common best practices with little interference from national interests (Jenny 2011).

Table 5.1 Significance of governance layers over time (Competition Policy)

Phase	National level	EU level	Global level
Post-WWII	–	–	–
1957–late 1980s	Low	Medium (i.e. inclusion of competition rules in Treaty of Rome)	Low
1990s	Medium (i.e. competition law adopted by EU candidate countries)	High (i.e. DG Competition broadens its tasks after the adoption of Merger Control Regulation in 1989)	Low
Post-2000	High (i.e. decentralization of competition law enforcement through Regulation 1/2003)	High	Medium (i.e. establishment of the International Competition Network in 2002)
2020 (extrapolation)	High	High	Medium

4 The EU and US in global competition networks

4.1 EU unity in global competition networks

As mentioned in the previous section, former Competition Commissioner Monti was one of the first supporters of the US proposal for the establishment of a Global Competition Initiative, which later became the ICN. However, besides DG Competition, all the NCAs of the EU Member States participate in the activities of the ICN, OECD and UNCTAD. The size of each NCA directly determines its degree of involvement in the activities of these IOs. This is especially the case of the ICN, where the lack of a secretariat leads to a direct correlation between the output in terms of soft law production and the resources invested by each NCA in the network. In particular, only the NCAs of the 'big' EU Member States (i.e. the UK, France, Germany and Italy) have been constant members of the Steering Board and have chaired ICN working groups since the ICN establishment in 2002.[14]

In the context of the OECD, UNCTAD and ICN there is no formal system of coordination between DG Competition and the NCAs of the EU Member States; these agencies are all equal members of these global competition networks.[15] Nevertheless, the high degree of harmonization achieved during the past decade between the EU and the national competition law of the EU Member States minimizes the risk of diverging positions within global competition networks.[16] Consequently, even though both DG Competition and the NCAs of the major EU Member States try separately to influence the process of drafting the soft law elaborated by these IOs, they all try to shape global standards in light of the same reference model, namely the EU competition model. In conclusion, despite the lack of formal mechanisms of coordination, the EU has a moderate level of unity within the global competition networks, due mainly to the high degree of consistency in its competition policy at the internal level.

4.2 The EU and US: shapers or takers within global competition networks?

Due to the fact that the soft law elaborated by global networks is adopted by consensus, its language is often sufficiently broad to include different national specificities.[17] In particular, since DG Competition and the NCAs of the 'big' EU Member States are usually actively involved in the process of drafting new soft law, it is unlikely that an IO would adopt a new standard clearly in opposition to the EU competition model. In relation to the ICN soft law, there are only 'anecdotal' cases where the EU amended its competition *acquis* to take into consideration ICN's best practices.[18] Similarly, in view of the high degree of uniformity of national competition law with the EU competition model, few EU Member States have amended their national competition law in order to implement the ICN recommendations.[19] This was especially the case with aspects of national competition law which had a low degree of harmonization with the EU competition model. Similarly, US anti-trust authorities have modified only some aspects of their anti-trust system in line with the ICN principles of transparency of the activities of the NCAs.[20] As mentioned in the previous section, the terminology of the ICN guidelines is usually sufficiently 'broad' to satisfy both the EU competition and the US anti-trust model. Consequently, neither the EU nor the US has substantially imported the soft law of the global competition networks.

While neither the EU nor the US were clear 'takers' of the standards elaborated by global competition networks, the NCAs of these competition jurisdictions had a different role in 'shaping' global competition standards. In particular, the US Federal Trade Commission and the Department of Justice were more successful than the EU Commission in shaping global competition networks in line with their policy preferences. The fact that the EU Commission's proposal to harmonize core competition principles at the WTO level failed while the US proposal to establish a Global Competition Initiative has developed during the past decade into the most successful competition network (i.e. the ICN) is a clear sign that the US preference constellation has prevailed. The US was not only successful in terms of forum choice, but also in setting the agenda of the global competition networks and, in particular, the ICN's agenda. For instance, the initial focus of the ICN's activities on 'multi-jurisdictional mergers'[21] was clearly connected to the concerns expressed by the ICPAC report in relation to this type of transaction (ICPAC 2000). In addition, US Competition Authorities were successful in promoting their enforcement priority against cartels in global competition networks. In particular, in 1998, the US delegation convinced the OECD Competition Committee to adopt a Recommendation against cartels (OECD 1998). At the time when DG Competition was still reviewing hundreds of notifications every year concerning 'vertical' agreements which seldom harmed competition in the market,[22] the OECD Recommendation indicated a clear change in the priorities of competition policy enforcement at the global level. During the past decade, most Competition Authorities of the world have prioritized the fight against cartels in their enforcement agenda and have adopted a system of leniency which resembles the US system.

A number of reasons may explain why the EU was less successful than the US in shaping global competition networks. First of all, the EU was a latecomer in the debate on convergence. The EU initially promoted the idea of the harmonization of core competition principles, an approach influenced by its history of supranational institutions which was incompatible with the cultural and legal background of other regions of the world. Second, the ICN and the other global competition networks emerged at the time when the EU was undertaking a radical internal change of its competition policy. In fact, during the early stages of the ICN establishment in the early 2000s, a 'row' of judgments by the EU courts undermined the credibility of DG Competition. The EU General Court annulled a number of decisions adopted by the EU Commission in controversial merger cases contesting the poor quality of evidence analysis carried out by DG Competition (Morgan and McGuire 2004). These judgments led DG Competition to 'modernize' the EU competition policy. The modernization went beyond the adoption of the merger control Regulation 139/2004, and affected different areas of competition policy enforcement (McGowan 2005). In particular, by employing new economists and by appointing a Chief Economist, DG Competition shifted from the traditional 'legalistic' approach of competition enforcement based on a mechanical enforcement of the Treaty provisions to a 'more economic' approach in which each case should be subject to a review in light of the relevant theories in economics (Neven 2006). As a consequence of the 'more economic approach', the EU Commission shifted its enforcement priorities from vertical agreements which usually had a marginal impact on competition in the market to the detection of hard-core cartels which have the explicit object of harming competition (McGowan 2005). In improving its economic analysis and by prioritizing cartel enforcement, DG Competition 'borrowed' some aspects of the US anti-trust model (Kunzlik 2003). Even though the assessment of the effective impact of the US anti-trust model on the EU competition model goes beyond the scope of this chapter, it could be argued that the process of internal reforms undertaken by DG Competition at the beginning of the 2000s temporarily undermined the external credibility of the EU competition model, thus allowing the US to be more successful in terms of the institutional building of global competition networks.

To sum up, in the vertical contest, the EU has followed an approach of 'policy protection'. Even though the EU failed to export its venue preference for the WTO, it has managed to be actively involved in global competition networks. In particular, the EU has secured that such soft law was in compliance with its competition model, thereby reducing the need to import similar soft law at the internal level.

4.3 The vertical vs. horizontal export of competition standards

While the role of the EU has been mixed in the vertical contest, the EU has clearly acted as an exporter of its core competition provisions at the horizontal level. Unlike the US, the EU has usually included a competition chapter in association and trade agreements concluded with third countries.[23] The latter usually requires third countries to establish an NCA and to introduce a competition law which includes provisions that mirror the core EU competition provisions (i.e. Art. 101 and Art. 102, TFEU). The EU's capacity for policy export has clearly been more profound in its relations with accession and neighbouring countries, with different export mechanisms being at play. Membership conditionality exercised by the EU vis-à-vis its candidate countries has played a prominent role (Fingleton *et al.* 1997). In fact, the transposition and effective enforcement of the EU competition *acquis* was constantly monitored by the EU Commission for the countries of Central and Eastern Europe during the previous enlargement wave, and is currently one of the factors annually monitored by the EU Commission for the countries of Southeast Europe (Efremova 2012). Still, even in the absence of prospective EU membership, neighbouring countries have adopted national competition laws which closely resemble the EU competition model (Shahein 2012). Although the EU Commission does not constantly monitor the implementation of the competition policy in these countries, other mechanisms like the programmes of technical assistance provided by the NCAs of the EU Member States to the NCAs of the EU's neighbouring countries ensure that the latter progressively align their competition policy with EU standards (Jaros 2012). Finally, a number of developing countries have spontaneously introduced a competition law inspired by the EU competition model.

Through the inclusion of almost identical competition chapters in the bilateral agreements, the EU also aimed towards the horizontal export of its 'core' competition *acquis* beyond its neighbourhood. However, the effective degree of implementation concerning the competition chapters of the agreements varies from country to country. In particular, conditionality as formulated in trade chapters does not seem a credible and effective strategy for policy export. Despite the legally binding nature of the agreements under public international law, there is no record of any bilateral trade and association agreement having been suspended by the EU due to the fact that the third country had not introduced a competition law at the internal level. Second, the EU is apparently not ready to suspend trade with third countries due simply to the fact that the latter country does not have a competition law in force.

It is thus predominantly through the soft mechanisms of persuasion and emulation that vertical export develops an effect even beyond the EU's neighbourhood. As pointed out by an officer of DG Competition interviewed by the author, the fact that the EU has 23 official languages facilitates the adoption of the EU competition model by third countries.[24] Most of the legislation, guidelines and notices adopted by the EU are translated and freely available on the website of DG Competition in the majority of the spoken languages of the world. The accessibility of these documents and the degree of persuasion exercised by one of the most 'mature' competition law jurisdictions in the world favour the spontaneous adoption of the EU competition model by third countries, even with the lack of any element of conditionality. In contrast, the US has failed to export the core aspects of its anti-trust model to third countries. This is particularly due to the judicial system of enforcement of the US anti-trust system, which relies heavily on the enforcement of the anti-trust law by private parties before state and federal courts.[25] Due to the ineffectiveness of the judicial system, developing countries usually find it 'easier' to enforce the EU administrative system of competition policy enforcement. The latter relies primarily on a public enforcement conducted by an NCA, which carries out investigations and adopts administrative decisions; at the same time, the role of courts is usually limited to cases of appeals against the decisions of the NCA.

To sum up, by including competition chapters in its bilateral trade/association agreements, the EU has been more successful than the US in exporting its core competition provisions at the horizontal level. Most of the developing countries in the world have adopted a competition law that includes substantive provisions which mirror Art. 101 and Art. 102, TFEU, and have established an NCA taking DG Competition as an example of administrative authority. However, it is important to bear in mind that the NCAs of the developing countries have interpreted and enforced these core competition provisions in light of the guidelines and best practices adopted by global competition networks, especially the ICN.

5 Conclusions

This chapter has shown that during the past two decades, the globalization of the economy and the 'bloom' of new competition law jurisdictions in several emerging economies have pushed a number of IOs to start talks concerning the possible harmonization of national competition standards. The initial EU proposal to adopt minimum binding rules at the WTO level was quickly abandoned. By contrast, the past decade has witnessed the development of global competition networks as leading players in the process of convergence of competition standards. In particular, IOs like UNCTAD and OECD have broadened the scope of their activities, while the International Competition Network has emerged as a 'new' form of global governance in this policy field. The 'virtual' nature of ICN has allowed for its rapid development in terms of membership and output of soft law.

The EU has played an active role in UNCTAD, OECD and ICN. Nevertheless, the US was more successful in terms of institution-building by leading this debate in terms of venue preference and by setting the agenda of the global competition networks. The chapter has identified a number of reasons which prevented the EU from successfully offering its proposal to harmonize competition standards within the WTO. In particular, the internal division between DG Trade and DG Competition concerning venue preference and the internal transformation of the EU competition model at the time when the discussions on the establishment of the ICN began undermined the ability of the EU to shape global competition networks. On the other hand, import by the EU of the soft law elaborated by these IOs has been quite limited. Benefiting from the internal cohesion between the EU and national competition policy, DG Competition and the NCAs of the EU Member States have played an active role within the global competition networks, ensuring that the 'broad' language of the soft law adopted in these fora was in compliance with the EU competition model.

If the EU success in the vertical contest was mixed, the opposite is true in relation to the horizontal export of its core competition provisions. Even though the focus of this chapter was the role played by the EU in IOs active in competition policy, it is worth stressing that during the past decade the EU has successfully exported its competition model through competition chapters included in the trade and association agreements concluded with several developing countries. While EU membership conditionality was the main factor relied upon by the EU to actively export its competition model to its future Member States, a number of endogenous factors have allowed the passive export of the EU competition model to countries of different regions of the world. The 'emulation' of the EU competition model has been favoured both due to its 'authority' resulting from the long history of EU competition policy enforcement over several decades, and because of its 'availability' due to the multiple EU official languages in which each competition legislation and soft law is systematically translated. Furthermore, the administrative system of competition policy enforcement which characterizes the EU regime is usually perceived as most suitable to the features of emerging economies in comparison to the US judicial system of anti-trust enforcement. To sum up, even though the US was more successful than the EU in establishing and shaping the agenda of global competition networks, members of these networks have been increasingly influenced at the bilateral level by the EU competition model. This creates a complex scenario which may lead to a shift in the balance of power in the IOs dealing with competition policy over the coming decades.

It is a 'daunting task' predicting the future development of global competition networks (Lugard 2011). The flexibility which has allowed their rapid development may also lead to their rapid disappearance if stakeholders lose interest in the networks. During the next decade, global competition networks will continue to pursue the convergence of national competition standards. It is difficult to predict whether such a result will ever be fully achieved. On the contrary, it is clear that the EU will continue being an active member of global competition networks, as it will continue with the effort of exporting its competition model through its network of bilateral trade and association agreements.

Notes

1 The eleventh ICN annual conference was hosted in Rio de Janeiro between 17 and 20 April 2012 (http://icn-rio.org/annual.html (9 May 2012)).
2 For further information concerning the functioning of DG Competition see http://ec.europa.eu/competition/index_en.html (accessed 22 January 2013).

3. http://eur-lex.europa.eu/LexUriServ/LexUriServ.do?uri=COM:1995:0359:FIN:EN:PDF (9 May 2012).
4. www.wto.org/english/thewto_e/whatis_e/tif_e/bey3_e.htm (9 May 2012).
5. www.wto.org/english/thewto_e/minist_e/min01_e/mindecl_e.htm#interaction (9 May 2012).
6. http://unctad.org/en/Pages/DITC/CompetitionLaw/Competition-Law-and-Policy.aspx (accessed 22 January 2013).
7. www.oecd.org/competition/ (accessed 22 January 2013).
8. Interview with William Kovacic on 18 April 2012.
9. www.ibanet.org/LPD/Antitrust_Trade_Law_Section/Antitrust/Default.aspx (10 May 2012).
10. www.globalcompetitionforum.org/regions/Ditchley%20Final%20Report.pdf (10 May 2012).
11. Interview with an officer from DG Competition on 19 April 2012.
12. Interview with an officer from the US Federal Trade Commission on 20 April 2012.
13. www.justice.gov/atr/public/press_releases/2012/282485.htm (14 May 2012).
14. www.internationalcompetitionnetwork.org/about/steering-group/members.aspx (10 May 2012).
15. Interview with an officer from the German Competition Authority on 19 April 2012.
16. Interview with an officer from DG Competition on 19 April 2012.
17. Interview with an officer from DG Competition on 19 April 2012.
18. This was the case, for instance, of the introduction of a pre-merger notification in Regulation 139/2004. According to Michael Reynolds, Art. 4 was directly influenced by the ICN recommendation on the timing of merger notification, included in the ICN. Interview by the author with Michael Reynolds, vice-president of IBA, on 18 April 2012.
19. For instance, Germany has modified the threshold of its system of merger control in order to comply with the ICN recommendation with the proper 'local nexus' introduced in the ICN Recommended Practices on Merger Notification in September 2002. Interview with an officer of the German Competition Authority on 19 April 2012.
20. Interview with two officers of the US FTC on 20 April 2012.
21. A merger is 'multi-jurisdiction' when it is has to be notified to the competition authorities of different countries, creating a problem of coordination among the different national institutions.
22. The expression 'vertical agreements' indicates the distribution agreement between a producer and a distributor. A vertical agreement partially restricts competition. However, contrary to cartels, vertical agreements also generate efficiencies which counterbalance their potential anti-competitive effect.
23. http://ec.europa.eu/competition/international/bilateral/index.html (16 May 2012).
24. Interview with an officer from DG Competition on 19 April 2012.
25. Interview with Michael Reynolds on 18 April 2012.

References

Budzinski, O. and Christiansen, A. (2005) 'Competence Allocation in the EU Competition Policy System as an Interest-driven Process', *Journal of Public Policy* 25(3): 313–337.

Cheng, T. (2011–2012) 'Convergence and Its Discontents: A Reconsideration of the Merits of Convergence of Global Competition Law', *Chicago Journal of International Law* 12(1): 433–490.

Cini, M. and McGowan, L. (2009) *Competition Policy in the European Union*, Basingstoke: Palgrave Macmillan.

Commission of the European Communities (1996) *Towards an International Framework of Competition Rules.* Online. Available: http://aei.pitt.edu/3971/ (accessed 22 January 2013).

Cseres, K. (2007) 'Multi-jurisdictional Competition Law Enforcement: The Interface between European Competition Law and the Competition Laws of the New Member States', *European Competition Law Review* 3(2): 465–502.

Damro, C. (2004) 'Multilateral Competition Policy and Transatlantic Compromise', *European Foreign Affairs Review* 9(1): 269–287.

—— (2006) 'The New Trade Politics and EU Competition Policy: Shopping for Convergence and Co-operation', *Journal of European Public Policy* 13(6): 867–886.

Damro, C. (2007) 'EU Delegation and Agency in International Trade Negotiations: A Cautionary Comparison', *Journal of Common Market Studies* 45(4): 883–903.

Damtoft, R. and Flanagan, R. (2009) 'The Development of International Networks in Antitrust', *The International Lawyer* 43(1): 138–150.

Efremova, V. (2012) 'Evolution of Competition Law in South-Eastern European Countries on the Way Towards EU Membership', *Mediterranean Competition Bulletin* 6(1): 23–43.

Fingleton, J., Fritsch, M. and Hansen, H. (eds) (1997) *Rules of Competition and East–West Integration,* The Hague: Kluwer Law International.

Fox, E. (1997) 'Towards World Antitrust and Market Access', *The American Journal of International Law* 91(1): 1–25.

—— (2009) 'Linked-in: Antitrust and the Virtues of a Virtual Network', Law and Economics Research Paper Series No. 27/2009, Law School of New York University. Online. Available at: http://papers.ssrn.com/sol3/papers.cfm?abstract_id=1431560 (accessed 22 January 2013).

Hollman, H. and Kovacic, W. (2011) 'The ICN: Its Past, Current and Future Role', in P. Lugard (ed.) *The International Competition Network at Ten,* Antwerp: Intersetia.

ICN (2005) *Implementation of the ICN Recommended Practices for Merger Notification and Review Procedures.* Online. Available at: www.internationalcompetitionnetwork. org/uploads/library/doc324.pdf (accessed 22 January 2013).

ICN Merger Working Group (2011) *Comprehensive Assessment 2010–2011.* Online. Available: www.internationalcompetitionnetwork.org/uploads/library/doc767.pdf (accessed 22 January 2013).

ICN Steering Body (2012) *International Competition Network Operational Framework.* Online. Available at: www.internationalcompetitionnetwork.org/about/operational-framework.aspx (accessed 22 January 2013).

International Competition Policy Advisory Committee (ICPAC) (2000) *Final Report.* Online. Available at: www.justice.gov/atr/icpac/finalreport.html (accessed 22 January 2013).

Janow, M. and James, R. (2011) 'The Origins of the ICN', in P. Lugard *The International Competition Network at Ten,* Antwerp: Intersetia.

Jaros, K. (2012) 'Developing Competition Policy in Morocco – A Model for the MENA-Region?', *Mediterranean Competition Bulletin* 6(1): 6–22.

Jenny, F. (2011) 'The International Competition Network and the OECD Competition Committee: Differences, Similarities and Complementarities', in P. Lugard *The International Competition Network at Ten,* Antwerp: Intersentia.

Kerremans, B. (2004) 'What Went Wrong in Cancun? A Principal-agent View on the EU's Rationale Towards the Doha Development Round', *European Foreign Affairs Review* 9(1): 363–393.

Kunzlik, P. (2003) 'Globalization and Hybridization in Antitrust Enforcement: European "Borrowings" from the US Approach', *The Antitrust Bulletin* 48(spring/summer): 319–353.

Lugard, P. (2011) 'The ICN at Ten', in: P. Lugard *The International Competition Network at Ten*, Antwerp: Intersentia.

McGowan, L. (2005) 'Europeanization Unleashed and Rebounding: Assessing the Modernization of EU Cartel Policy', *Journal of European Public Policy* 12(6): 986–1004.

Morgan, E. and McGuire, S. (2004). 'Transatlantic Divergence: GE-Honeywell and the EU's Merger Policy,' *Journal of European Public Policy* 11(1): 39–56.

Neven, D. (2006) *Competition Economics and Antitrust in Europe*. Online. Available at: http://ec.europa.eu/dgs/competition/economist/economic_policy.pdf (accessed 22 January 2013).

OECD (1998) *Recommendation Concerning Effective Action against Hard Core Cartels*. Online. Available at: www.oecd.org/competition/cartelsandanti-competitive agreements/2350130.pdf (accessed 22 January 2013).

Ottow, A. (2011) 'Europeanisation of Market Supervision', unpublished paper presented on 14 February 2011 in the context of the SCORE series of seminars at the Florence School of Regulation, Florence (Italy).

Shahein, H. (2012) 'How Is the EU Seeking to Influence Competition Law in Egypt?', *Mediterranean Competition Bulletin* 6(1): 54–64.

Shenefield, J. (2004) 'Coherence or Confusion: The Future of the Global Antitrust Conversation', *Antitrust Bulletin* 49(spring/summer): 385–434.

United Nations, General Assembly (1980) *United Nations Set of Multilaterally Agreed Equitable Principles and Rules for the Control of Restrictive Business Practices*. Online. Available at: http://unctad.org/en/docs/tdrbpconf10r2.en.pdf (accessed 22 January 2013).

Van Den Hoven, A. (2006) 'Assuming Leadership in Multilateral Economic Institutions: The EU's "Development Round" Discourse Strategy', *West European Politics* 27(2): 256–283.

Vedder, H. (2004) 'Spontaneous Harmonization of National Competition Laws in the Wake of the Modernization of the EC Competition Law', *The Competition Law Reviewer* 1(1): 5–21.

6 Social rights
The EU and the International Labour Organization (ILO)

Guido Schwellnus

1 Introduction

It has become customary for EU officials to refer to the 'European Social Model', characterized as a market economy providing high levels of social protection and adhering to fundamental social rights, as a central element of the integration project. Thus, it may be plausible to assume that the EU should be a driving force in developing social standards on the global level. High levels of social regulation on the European level are, however, a comparatively recent phenomenon, and 'implementation of ILO norms within the Union was initially minimal and is still far from comprehensive' (Novitz 2005: 216). Only since the mid-1980s has the EU shown significant levels of social standards in certain areas such as occupational health and safety, working conditions, and non-discrimination. Since then it has also begun to actively promote social standards internationally, both within the ILO and – following a failed attempt to include a 'social clause' in the World Trade Organization (WTO) – in trade relations with third countries. Therefore, the question is: to what extent has the role changed from a policy importer to a policy exporter?

Moreover, a significant measure of international rules in the social sphere can only be found in regulatory areas. For instance, social rights are created as flanking measures to correct or mitigate the effects of market failure within liberal economies, whereas distributive policies such as wages, pensions or social security schemes remain firmly under national competence.[1] This is not only true on the global level, where the focus has always been on the provision of fundamental rights and minimum standards, but also for the EU. As Majone observed directly after the adoption of the Maastricht Treaty:

> [T]he Community remains, and will very possibly remain, a 'welfare laggard'. In the field of social regulation, however, the progress has been so remarkable that some recent EC directives exceed the most advanced national measures in the level of protection they afford.
>
> (Majone 1993: 155–156)

Although further significant developments have since taken place within the EU, Majone's verdict is still valid today. For this reason, this chapter focuses on social rights when comparing EU and international rules, and assessing the export or import of such rules by the EU. However, it should always be kept in mind that the national level remains highly relevant for the provision of social policies.

The chapter is structured as follows. Section 2 presents the development of social regulation within the EU, mainly covering the issues of occupational health and safety, working conditions, and non-discrimination. Section 3 turns towards the global level, with the ILO as the main organization devoted to social and labour standards. While the ILO traditionally relies on a wide array of conventions, it has more recently focused on so-called 'core labour standards' which include four areas: freedom of association and the right to collective bargaining, elimination of forced labour, abolition of child labour, and the elimination of discrimination in employment. Section 4 analyses the relationship between the two organizations and their standards. Possibilities for EU export are assessed along two dimensions: first, whether the EU pursues vertical 'uploading' of its standards or preferences within the ILO, or whether it promotes them horizontally towards other states or regions; second, whether the EU tries to export its own social *acquis* or the ILO's core labour standards. Section 5 concludes and summarizes the findings.

2 The development of social rights in the European Union

For a long time, social matters in the EU were left almost entirely to the Member States. Although the preamble to the Treaty of Rome stated a commitment to 'the economic and social progress' of Member States and 'the constant improvement of the living and working conditions of their peoples', social rights were initially not included in the Treaties. The main contribution which the newly founded Community was expected to make in social development was to foster economic growth in Europe. Even ILO experts consulted during the negotiation period did not see any need to include social provisions in the Treaties (Novitz 2005: 216). Notable exceptions were rules enabling the free movement of workers irrespective of nationality, which were directly connected to the functioning of the proposed common market, and provisions on equal pay and gender equality, which were mainly inserted to alleviate French fears of social dumping. During the 1970s, these rather rudimentary anti-discrimination rules were first elaborated through European Court of Justice (ECJ) case law, determining them to have direct effect.[2] Subsequently, they were formalized into several directives, namely the Equal Pay Directive[3] and the Equal Treatment Directive (Bell 2002: 45).[4] Apart from this, social rights – unlike fundamental human rights – did not find their way into the *acquis communautaire* as general principles of Community law (Schimmelfennig *et al.* 2006: 28–29).

This attitude of dismissing social protection as a matter for European-level governance changed during the 1980s, when the Single Market project took shape and the introduction of flanking measures to the liberalization of the common market became a salient topic. Although a parallel guarding of social rights may not be functionally necessary for the working of a single market, it was increasingly evident that European integration undermined national social rights protection systems (Giubboni 2003: 5). A first explicit mention of social rights in the Treaties may be found in the preamble of the Single European Act, which lists the Council of Europe's European Social Charter together with the European Convention on Human Rights as sources of fundamental rights for the Community. Although the Member States were generally still not willing to delegate social policy competences to the European level, a notable exception was made in the field of occupational health and safety, deemed to be closely linked to the internal market and allowed to be decided by Qualified Majority Voting. Eventually, the Commission began to use an extensive interpretation of the provision to encourage improvements, 'especially in the working environment, as regards the health and safety of workers' (Art. 118a) to adopt legal acts such as the Working Time Directive (Falkner *et al.* 2005: 43–44).[5]

Shortly after the adoption of the Single European Act, it was decided that the European Community should develop its own instrument to ensure that the liberalizing thrust of the single market programme was balanced by social rights, instead of simply referring to the Council of Europe's Social Charter. The Rhodes Summit in December 1988 emphasized that the '[c]ompletion of the Single Market cannot be regarded as an end in itself' (European Council 1988: 5), and that '[a]s regards implementation of social rights, the European Council awaits such proposals as the Commission might consider useful to submit having drawn inspiration from the social charter of the Council of Europe' (ibid.: 6). This led to the adoption of a Community Charter of Fundamental Social Rights for Workers, which was proclaimed at the Strasbourg summit in December 1989, albeit with the abstention of the United Kingdom, which also opposed introducing a social chapter into the Maastricht Treaty. Instead, a Protocol on Social Policy was annexed to the Treaty, stating that the other 11 Member States 'wish to continue along the path laid down in the 1989 Social Charter' (Falkner 1996).[6] However, the social chapter was only fully incorporated into the Amsterdam Treaty with the end of the British opt-out under the Blair government in 1997 (Schimmelfennig *et al.* 2006: 28–29).

Still, the Maastricht Treaty further extended competences in important areas that already had some footing in Community law, especially in the fields of working conditions and equal treatment. On the other hand, central areas of internationally guaranteed social rights were explicitly left out: freedom of association (which, even as a fundamental human right, was interpreted restrictively by the ECJ), the right of workers to bargain collectively, and the right to strike and impose lock-outs. The Amsterdam Treaty, in addition to ending the British opt-out, extended the anti-discrimination *acquis* to other areas than gender. In addition, soft mechanisms such as guidelines and benchmarking were introduced in the employment chapter under the newly established Open Method of Coordination.

Despite these limitations, the 1990s became the 'most active decade' (Falkner *et al.* 2005: 47) in terms of social regulation on the EU level and it saw a large number of directives being adopted. However, this expansion has so far focused largely on three core domains, which correspond to 'focal points' created by an initially very limited transfer of competences, later expanded by legal acts proposed by a pro-active Commission on the basis of a maximalist interpretation of these competences:

- health and safety at the workplace;
- working conditions;
- gender equality and non-discrimination.

This rather short list indicates that despite the impressive development over the past 25 years, not only the distributive parts of social policy, but also core areas of social rights such as the right of association, the right to strike or the right to impose lock-outs (cf. Art. 153/5, Lisbon Treaty), remain explicitly outside Community competence. Even the otherwise very pro-active Commission has deemed these areas to be 'an inappropriate matter for EC intervention' (Novitz 2005: 218) due to differing systems in the Member States. In principle, the EU Charter of Fundamental Rights, adopted in 2000, breaks with this imbalance and follows the idea of the indivisibility of fundamental rights, meaning that social rights, including freedom of assembly and association (Art. 12) and the right to collective bargaining and action (Art. 28), feature in the same document and on the same level as the 'classical' civil and human rights (Schwellnus 2006). The Charter, however, only became binding with the Lisbon Treaty in 2009; the United Kingdom and Poland have opted out of it, and the ECJ also has yet to make clear reference to it in its rulings. The full impact of this document in the field of social rights therefore remains to be seen.

3 The global regime regarding social rights: ILO conventions and core labour standards

On the international level, the ILO is the main global organization for social and labour standards. Founded in 1919 under the League of Nations system, the ILO became a specialized agency within the United Nations after World War II. After 1945, the ILO has constantly expanded both its membership (from 53 to 185 states by 2012) and its normative basis of adopted conventions (from 67 to 189 by 2011). Originally, the ILO relied on a wide array of conventions that were binding only to Member States that ratified them.

However, with one of its objectives being to set minimum labour standards for the liberal Western states in order to counter communism, the relevance of the ILO has declined significantly with the end of the Cold War and the dominance of neoliberal policies (Novitz 2005: 237). This crisis manifested itself in a sharp decline of ratifications for newly adopted conventions since the mid-1980s (Langille 2005: 425). In addition, as will be discussed below, the 1990s saw the – ultimately failed – attempt to 'push for a labour dimension in the WTO ... to get some "teeth" into the system' (ibid.: 413). In order to counteract its decreasing relevance, the ILO adopted the Declaration on Fundamental Principles and Rights at Work in 1998, which defines four issues, based on eight fundamental ILO conventions, as core labour standards whose principles are assumed to be binding to all ILO members irrespective of their ratification record:

1 Freedom of association and the right to collective bargaining (C 87/1947 and C 98/1949).
2 Elimination of all forms of forced labour (C 29/1930 and C 105/1957).
3 Abolition of child labour (C 138/1973 and C 182/1999).
4 Elimination of discrimination in employment (C 100/1951 and C 111/1958).

This move has been hailed by some commentators as a 'constitutional moment' (Langille 1999: 232) in the ILO's history, while others condemned it as:

> playing a central role in efforts to replace the broader labour rights agenda with a narrow focus on a much more limited corpus of four core labour standards and to move towards an approach that is fundamentally promotional, rather than grounded in firm legal obligations.
> (Alston and Heenan 2004: 223)[7]

In any case, the declaration has induced a significant boost in the ratification of the eight fundamental conventions; within only a few years after the declaration was adopted, the average percentage of ILO Member States having ratified the core conventions increased from approximately 70 per cent, where it had stagnated for 30 years, to 90 per cent. By comparison, the ratification rate of 'technical' conventions remained constant at a much lower level (below 20 per cent).

4 The EU's interaction with the ILO

If we compare the EU's main areas of regulation in the field of social rights with ILO standards, we observe only a partial overlap between the two organizations. With regard to the *functional scope* of issues covered by regulations of the respective organizations, the EU's social agenda is significantly narrower than the ILO's broad set of conventions. Even among the much narrower list of core standards, only non-discrimination is an area covered by EU rules, and only directives passed after 2000 extend anti-discrimination rules beyond gender

Table 6.1 Significance of governance levels over time (Social Policy)

Phase	National level	EU level	Global level
1945–1957	High	–	Medium
1957–1985	High	Low	Medium
1986–2000	High	Medium	Medium
since 2000	High	Medium	Medium
2020 (extrapolation)	High	Medium	Medium

equality to the broader grounds covered by the ILO conventions. Of the other three core areas, the classic social right to strike and collective bargaining has been deliberately left out of the EU's social policy, and forced and child labour are regarded as irrelevant for the EU internally, since they are assumed to be observed by all Member States. But although the Member States have a nearly perfect ratification record for the core ILO conventions, this is no substitution for regulation on the European level. Without clear competence, the Commission has been unwilling to supervise and enforce compliance with these rules, and at least some EU Member States have been criticized by the ILO for breaching core labour standards (Novitz 2005: 216).

In terms of the *depth* of regulations, the EU has long trailed behind ILO standards, but since the 1990s the EU has developed a dense net of rules surpassing ILO standards in the three main areas of social regulation addressed in the EU context: anti-discrimination, working conditions, and occupational health and safety. Finally, the *legally binding character* of the rules needs to be considered in a differentiated manner: ILO conventions are legally binding for signatories, but ratification is optional, giving states a rather easy possibility to opt out. In terms of enforcement, the record is mixed. The ILO has no judicialized system of enforcement and relies on measures such as technical assistance and 'shaming' non-compliant states, which makes it a 'decidedly soft law system' (Langille 2005: 413). At least the supervisory procedures of the ILO are reported to be much more robust than other mechanisms in the UN (Kissack 2010: 31). By comparison, EU rules in areas regulated by 'hard' legislative instruments are binding for all Member States and supported by the supremacy and direct effect of EU law, although the transposition of directives into domestic law allows for some flexibility in domestic adaptation. Still, if Member States fail to transpose directives correctly and in time, they may face infringement procedures before the ECJ. Other areas such as the employment chapter rely on 'soft' measures such as guidelines and benchmarking, but there is 'no indication so far that voluntary measures actually replace binding ones' (Falkner *et al.* 2005: 54).

One important factor when assessing the prospects of policy import or export is, of course, *timing*. Basically all social rights regulated by ILO conventions clearly pre-date any rule-making on the EU level in the respective area. Hence, it is no surprise that the EU has most often been a 'policy-taker', with ILO norms acting as inspiration for the development of EU rules. Even early social policy provisions may be seen as being inspired by the respective ILO standards. For example, the 'equal pay' provision introduced in the Treaty of Rome, although triggered by the existence of such a standard in the French domestic system in contrast to other founding Member States, closely resembled the definitions of 'equal remuneration' offered by the ILO. Moreover, the ECJ explicitly referred to ILO conventions in its judgments on the first landmark cases involving gender discrimination. 'In the *Defrenne (No. 2)* Case the ECJ referred to ILO Convention No. 111 as part of the general principles of law that the Court respects where there is a gap in EU written law' (Landau and Beigbeder 2008: 54), and the Court's interpretation of the Equal Pay Directive closely followed the concept of equal pay for work of equal value as formulated in ILO Convention No. 100 (Novitz 2005: 221 fn. 34).[8] Global norms also provided inspiration for more policy-oriented tools, such as the concept of 'gender mainstreaming', which was first proposed in the UN context at the Third World Conference on Women in Nairobi 1985 and formally adopted at the follow-up conference ten years later, before the EU included it as an official aim of gender equality policy into the Amsterdam Treaty in 1997.

However, since the role of the ILO is to set globally applicable minimum standards, national rules in developed EU Member States often provide higher levels of protection, and areas of dense EU regulation, such as anti-discrimination, working conditions, and occupational health and safety, have surpassed ILO rules. One example of 'catching up' and then expanding EU rules compared to ILO standards may be observed in the non-discrimination field. Whereas the first generation of directives in the 1970s was considered inadequate, the new or amended anti-discrimination directives adopted after 2000 offer a higher and more specific standard than the ILO conventions (Novitz 2005: 222).[9] In the field of occupational health and safety, the EU has strongly engaged in developing ILO conventions since the 1980s.[10]

For the assessment of EU export, two conceptual dimensions are of relevance. On the one hand, we can distinguish between areas of dense EU regulation in the social field (anti-discrimination, working conditions, occupational health and safety) and core labour standards, which are promoted by the EU externally without being regulated on the EU level (forced labour, freedom of association, and the right to collective bargaining and action). On the other hand, a distinction can be made between the direct vertical promotion of EU standards or preferences during the negotiation of international standards and the horizontal diffusion of such rules through policies vis-à-vis third countries. Based on this differentiation, four potential pathways of EU influence on the international regulation of social rights may be formulated. First, vertical policy export occurs when the EU develops high and specific standards in certain areas and becomes active in trying to 'upload' these maximal standards to the ILO system. Second, the EU can also diffuse its social *acquis communautaire* horizontally. This is mainly achieved through '*acquis* conditionality' (Schimmelfennig and Sedelmeier 2004) during enlargement rounds and within the neighbourhood policy. Third, the promotion of non-EU standards – most prominently the core labour

Table 6.2 Vertical export/promotion and horizontal diffusion of social standards

	Vertical	*Horizontal*
Export of EU standards	ILO conventions in areas with high EU regulation	Conditionality to transpose the *acquis*
Promotion of non-EU standards	ILO conventions on core labour standards that are outside the *aqcuis*	Core labour standards in preferential trade rules

standards defined in 1998 – may occur directly within the ILO, in case EU Member States press for high standards in new conventions falling within those three of the four core areas that are not part of EU regulation. Finally, the same standards may also be subject to horizontal diffusion by being included in trade agreements signed by the EU with third countries.

4.1 Vertical export or promotion

Vertical export means the direct 'uploading' of EU standards into global norms, mainly achieved through negotiations within international organizations, finally leading to the adoption of new standards. In order to achieve this within the ILO, EU Member States have coordinated their positions since 1973 (Kissack 2010: 32). Parallel to the rapid expansion of internal social regulation, actively coordinated involvement of EU Member States in the drafting of new ILO conventions peaked during the 1980s and early 1990s (see Kissack 2009). In 1994, a Council Resolution identified the external promotion of labour standards as an important task for the EU. The resolution states that in order to strengthen the Union's international competitiveness,

> discussions should be conducted constructively in the relevant fora, such as the ILO, GATT, or subsequently the WTO, for the future organization of international trade and above all for combating forced and child labour and securing freedom of association and free collective bargaining.[11]

Thus, the EU began to promote social rights beyond the areas regulated under EU law. As the ILO was seen to be in crisis at this time because the ratification rates of new conventions were declining, attention shifted temporarily to including a social clause in the WTO. After this attempt failed and the ILO used the designation of core labour standards as an instrument to enhance their take-up rate, the EU again turned towards the ILO as the main multilateral venue for promoting its social agenda.

4.1.1 Decision-making in the ILO: EU agency and unity

Standard-setting within the ILO takes place during the annual International Labour Conferences, where new conventions are drafted and then adopted by simple majority in a final vote. One institutional specificity of the ILO is its tripartite structure: not only state governments, but also representatives of the social partners are involved and have voting rights. For each country, two votes are cast by the government and one vote by each representative of employer organizations and trade unions (Delarue 2006: 97). Dating back to 1919, however, the ILO Constitution does not foresee membership of international organizations. The European Commission was granted observer status in 1989, but not the exclusive right to represent the EU. Hence, the *capacity* of the EU for joint action rests on the ability of EU Member States to coordinate their

Social rights 101

positions. Attempts by the Commission to gain a stronger role have been curbed by the Member States, and the ECJ has confirmed that EU positions must be formulated and presented through the Member States even in areas of Community competence for external action (Delarue 2006: 107).[12] For this reason, the Presidency takes responsibility for coordinating and presenting common EU positions during the conferences, whereas the Commission plays an important informal role in the preparation phase. But even without elaborate coordination, existing EU standards often provide a focal point for a position that can be supported by most, if not all, EU Member States (Kissack 2010: 82).

EU *unity* within the ILO can be assessed as being quite high, despite the observation that in roughly one-third of the votes since the start of EU coordination there were cases of Member States voting against proposals on which there was a common position (ibid.: 34). This record is qualified by two factors. First, dissenting votes are mostly due to single countries voting against proposals otherwise widely supported among EU Member States. Second, voting in the ILO is highly predictable, since the vast majority of proposals that reach the voting stage are adopted. This gives countries the opportunity to signal discontent to domestic audiences, while at the same time running no risk of blocking collectively desirable decisions that are negotiated in the consensual drafting stage.

> The side payment made for acquiescence at the upstream negotiation is a 'free vote' in the plenary session, where a national government may voice dissent on ideological or political grounds to satisfy their domestic audience, free riding on an expectation that the majority of ILO delegates will pass the vote.
>
> (Kissack 2010: 37)

4.1.2 Mechanisms and success of EU policy export

Kissack identifies two strategies of promoting EU norms in negotiations for new labour standards at the ILO, linked to a rationalist bargaining and a constructivist arguing mechanism, respectively. The rationalist bargaining mechanism involves 'using threats to ensure that ILO conventions are congruent with existing EU law' (Kissack 2010: 83), mostly to limit the costs of adaptation for EU Member States, but also to create similar standards outside the EU and thus mitigate competitive disadvantages. The constructivist arguing mechanism is 'to appeal to reason and offer EU law as an example of best practice' (ibid.) and is, in fact, not only limited to EU Member States but is used by other states or social partners with similar interests (ibid.: 85). A complementary relationship between interest- and norms-based reasoning may also be found in the motivation and justification for promoting high standards. On the one hand, it serves the EU's commercial interests by raising labour standards in lesser developed competitor states and mitigates competitive disadvantages in global trade; on the other hand, it has also been found that the EU even promotes norms that are costly to comply with for its Member States, and whose adoption outside of the EU is not beneficial to its economic interests (Riddervold 2010).

In order to assess the success of these export strategies, two examples will be presented. The first concerns 'technical' ILO conventions in areas where EU directives provide a high level of protection, and the second relates to a convention from the set of core labour standards where the EU has pressed for high standards that are not covered by the *acquis*. Due to the fact that the principles enshrined in the eight conventions designated as core labour standards are binding for all ILO members irrespective of ratification, there is also a significant difference in the salience of the conventions, especially to those states that are unwilling to accept high standards. 'Technical' ILO conventions provide states with an opt-out alternative that may lower their resistance to the adoption of unfavourable rules.

The Health and Safety in Agriculture Convention (C 184), adopted in 2001, and the Promotional Framework for Occupational Safety and Health Convention (C 187), adopted in 2006, are examples of 'technical' conventions falling into an area of high EU regulation. Both conventions 'share a high level of EU member state input in the drafting process, yet none have received much support from *any* ILO members' (Kissack 2010: 84). In both cases, EU Member States successfully used references to EU directives as well as threats of non-ratification to achieve a high degree of compatibility between the adopted ILO standard and the *acquis communautaire*, but failed to foster widespread ratification. This seems to reflect a broader trend. The more input the EU puts into drafting ILO conventions, the less states sign up for ratification afterwards (Kissack 2009). It may even be concluded that those states that were opposed to the high standards promoted by the EU only acquiesced to their adoption because it was virtually cost-free; without ratification ILO conventions are not binding. In the end, the assertive position of EU Member States could prevail because resistance was unnecessary.

The 1999 Convention Concerning the Prohibition and Immediate Action for the Elimination of the Worst Forms of Child Labour (C 182) is the only ILO convention that is part of the core labour standards negotiated both after the EU began to coordinate and actively promote its positions and after the ILO declaration of 1998 designated the core standards. High standards in this area were supported by EU Member States not only for normative reasons, but also in order to alleviate competitive disadvantages due to social dumping in lesser developed countries, which opposed what they perceived as excessively high standards. The Child Labour Convention is therefore not only an example of attempts by EU Member States to promote high standards in an area not regulated by Community law, but is also a test case for the EU's success in influencing the outcome of a negotiation of high salience for all ILO members, because they were under strong moral pressure to ratify the 'constitutional' convention and hence could not simply opt out of compliance as in the case of 'technical' conventions. In addition, the EU Member States did not have the usual strategies at their disposal. They could neither present the *acquis communautaire* as best practice, nor could they threaten non-ratification themselves. EU Member States, together with the group of industrialized countries, were not able to successfully push through their preferences (e.g. with regard to addressing problems of child soldiers or preventing the use of poverty as a possible justification for child labour). Instead, they had to settle for a compromise in order to gain acceptance for the convention to be included in the list of core labour standards (International Labour Organization 1999: §395–413; Dennis 1999). 'The result, while acceptable to all, fell short of what many European states wanted' (Kissack 2010: 81).

In summary, the EU seems to face a dilemma when it comes to 'uploading' its rules within the ILO. There is a trade-off between being highly successful on the dimension of *policy fit* to the detriment of the *take-up rate* – and the ability to opt out from ratification may well be the main reason for EU success with regard to the content. There are two caveats against over-interpreting the clear correlation between high EU input into drafting a convention and low ratification numbers (Kissack 2009). First, this pattern also applies to EU Member States, who are no more likely than other states to ratify the conventions into which they allegedly 'uploaded' their own standards. Second, the heyday of EU influence coincides with the general crisis of the ILO during the 1980s and 1990s; thus ratification may have dropped for other reasons, and high EU involvement in drafting the conventions at that time was just a coincidence. It is, however, plausible to assume that the EU contributed to the downturn in the ratification of 'technical' ILO conventions, as one criticism of the ILO system is that its regulations have become 'too detailed, too complex and unratifiable' (Langille 2005: 426), and most of the conventions featuring strong EU input fall under the area of occupational health and safety, which is highly regulated within the EU.

4.2 Horizontal diffusion

Horizontal effects (i.e. pressure exerted by the EU on other states in a bilateral manner) can mainly be observed in two areas. First, the incentive to adopt the EU's *acquis communautaire* in general and its directives related to social standards in particular, mainly applies to candidate states striving to become EU members. Through conditionality, these states are obliged to transpose the entire *acquis* prior to accession. Second, core labour standards have been promoted by the EU in trade agreements and have been included in its general trade rules.

Table 6.3 The trade-off between policy fit and take-up rate in vertical export/promotion

Policy fit	Take-up rate	
	High	*Low*
High		Export of high EU standards into 'technical' ILO conventions
Low	Promotion of high core labour standards	

4.2.1 The mechanisms and success of policy diffusion by conditionality

The effectiveness of conditionality as a mechanism to induce compliance with EU rules has been studied intensely by enlargement scholars. In general, research has corroborated a predominantly rationalist view on how the EU has been able to induce compliance by candidate states, whereas more 'constructivist' mechanisms such as social learning and persuasion have been found to be less effective. Within a rationalist framework, those faced with conditionality are seen as utility maximizers calculating the material as well as political costs and benefits of rule adoption. Conditionality can induce rule adoption in candidate states, 'if the benefits of EU rewards exceed the domestic adoption costs' (Schimmelfennig and Sedelmeier 2004: 664). Consequently, rule adoption depends on the presence of EU demands linked to positive incentives for compliance, or negative sanctions in the case of non-compliance. Prior to accession, the EU gives candidate states positive incentives in the form of a membership perspective. Several factors determine the effectiveness of conditionality, provided political adoption costs are not prohibitively high: the size of the reward, the credibility of delivering or withholding it, the strength of conditionality in terms of how explicit and urgent the demands are voiced, and the determinacy of conditions. The requirement to transpose the entire *acquis communautaire* prior to accession theoretically offers good prospects for inducing compliance; 'hard' EU law is more determinate than often vague political conditions and external incentives remain in place even after accession as conditionality is replaced by the internal sanctioning mechanism, so that non-compliance can be punished by opening infringement procedures.

In areas related to social regulation such as anti-discrimination, working time and occupational health and safety (Sissenich 2005; Falkner *et al.* 2008; Schwellnus 2009; Sedelmeier 2009), empirical findings largely confirm the prediction of the rationalist model, at least with regard to the formal transposition of directives. New Member States after Eastern enlargement show a very good transposition record, although a lack of implementation often relegates them to 'dead letters' (Falkner *et al.* 2008) at least in the short term, and success is mostly limited to 'hard' legislation, with far less positive results in 'softer' areas such as social dialogue (Sissenich 2005). Interpreting these results from compliance research related to enlargement in terms of horizontal policy diffusion, it may be concluded that the EU's accession conditionality has clearly contributed to broadening the number of states with EU-compatible social standards. However, the fact that these states became EU members transforms the diffusion of EU standards beyond its borders into the task of upholding high social standards in view of growing membership, thus increasing the risk of preference heterogeneity among EU Member States.

Since the social *acquis* has, to a large degree, been included in the European Economic Area (EEA) agreement, the horizontal export of EU rules at least includes some permanent EU non-members, namely the states of the European Free Trade Association (EFTA), while export to the states within the European

Neighbourhood Policy is less evident (Gstöhl 2009: 76). This also highlights a further limitation of this horizontal effect; it exclusively features developed industrial states within Europe – already with a good record of ratifying ILO conventions independent of EU accession – while having no impact on the opponents of strong and binding labour standards, especially developing countries. The territorial restriction of the horizontal diffusion of EU social standards to the nearer neighbourhood thus strongly limits the effect it may have on raising support for these standards at the global level.

4.2.2 The promotion of core labour standards in EU trade rules

Beyond the scope of prospective members and the immediate neighbourhood, the EU as a significant trading bloc is exerting 'power *through* trade, using access to its huge market as a bargaining chip to obtain changes in the domestic policies of its trading partners, from labour standards to human rights' (Meunier and Nicolaïdis 2006: 907).

Since the ILO – traditionally the main venue for international standard-setting with regard to social rights – was perceived to be in crisis due to decreasing ratification rates before the turn to 'constitutionalize' core labour standards, the mid-1990s saw a temporary venue-shifting towards the international trade regime during the negotiations leading to the establishment of the WTO. In this context, the 1994 Council Resolution 'was the precursor to Commission attempts to persuade WTO members of the merits of linking compliance with ILO standards to trade access under the General Agreement on Tariffs and Trade (GATT)' (Novitz 2005: 230). The EU thus joined the US under the Clinton Administration in its attempt to include a social clause in international trade rules. Still, this vertical promotion of labour standards in the global trade regime failed. On the one hand, developing countries strongly opposed the social clause, fearing protectionism and losing their competitive advantage vis-à-vis developed countries. On the other hand, unity within the EU was mixed:

> France, Belgium and the European Parliament were the most enthusiastic supporters, followed by the Commission.... At the same time, the Council Presidency was more wary.... This cautious stance results from opposition by some member states, notably Germany and the UK.
> (Orbie and Tortell 2009: 6)

Following the failure of including a social clause vertically in the WTO, the EU shifted towards a horizontal approach, which was much easier to establish unilaterally without involving developing countries in the negotiation. Core labour standards (although without a reference to specific ILO conventions) were included in the 2000 Partnership Agreement with the African, Caribbean and Pacific states (the so-called Cotonou Agreement).[13] The EU's Generalized System of Preferences (GSP), a system of preferential trade rules for developing countries, went further and represents 'one of the best examples of the introduction of social rights concerns into the external relations of the EU' (Gatto 2005: 356). In existence since 1971, labour standards were introduced into the GSP in the form of 'social conditionality' in 1998 (Novitz 2005: 230).[14] In order to benefit from reduced tariffs, third countries

> had to demonstrate that they had adopted and implemented in their national legislation the ILO Conventions on the freedom of association (Convention 87), on the rights to organize and bargain collectively (Convention 98), and on the minimum age for admission to employment (Convention 138). On the other hand, withdrawal from GSP benefits was envisaged where any form of forced labour or export of goods made by prison labour was possible.
>
> (Gatto 2005: 356–357)

In 2001,[15] the ILO Conventions on forced labour and non-discrimination were added, completing the set of all conventions constituting core labour standards (Novitz 2005: 231). Notably, the GSP does not refer to EU-specific social rights but directly to ILO standards and the respective conventions.

In terms of effectiveness, the horizontal promotion of core labour standards has, at best, a mixed record. 'The EU has clearly made some effort to promote respect for labour standards through its bilateral and unilateral trade instruments. Whether it has been successful is debatable' (Orbie *et al.* 2009: 152). In any case, the instruments were rarely used. For example, within the context of the Cotonou Agreement, only one declaration regarding Zimbabwe made reference to core labour standards, and under the GSP only three cases of 'social conditionality' are reported: Burma/Myanmar, Moldova and Sri Lanka (ibid.: 153). Moreover, developing countries often already enjoy preferential conditions under other bilateral agreements, providing few incentives to sign up for the social clauses under GSP (ibid.: 157). On the other hand, sanction threats can be effective even when not executed. In 1995, concerns about forced child labour in Pakistan were raised by the European Trade Union Confederation and investigated upon request by the European Parliament. Although the Commission ultimately decided against applying sanctions under the preferential trade agreement and instead opted for a 'softer' approach within the ILO, EU pressure nevertheless contributed to inducing Pakistan to adopt national legislation banning child labour (Hafner-Burton 2005: 610–611).

5 Conclusion

This chapter has scrutinized the occurrence of both vertical 'uploading' and horizontal diffusion of social standards by the EU. As a latecomer, the Community initially had hardly any social provisions. Over time, the density and scope of social regulation increased, mainly by importing standards already existing within the ILO, the main global body devoted to the development of social rights. While surpassing ILO standards in some areas, the scope addressed by

EU rules is considerably narrower than the areas covered by ILO standards, and excludes some core labour standards such as child and forced labour and the right to association, collective bargaining and action. On the other hand, the EU has promoted these core labour standards externally since the mid-1990s.

Following this differentiation, four potential pathways of EU policy export or promotion have been highlighted: First, the EU has quite successfully attempted to 'upload' its internal standards into ILO conventions in areas with highly developed Community rules, such as working conditions or occupational health and safety. However, success with regard to policy content has been bought with an extremely low take-up rate, as other countries chose not to ratify ILO conventions with excessively high standards. Second, when the EU promoted high standards in areas such as child labour, part of the ILO's core labour standards and thus binding irrespective of ratification, EU Member States have encountered stronger resistance and were forced to settle for compromised results. Hence, with regard to vertical export and promotion in the ILO context, the EU faces a trade-off between policy fit and take-up rate. Third, horizontal policy export has mainly been limited to candidate states for EU accession and – to a much lesser degree – states in the European neighbourhood. While membership conditionality was effective, its impact on the take-up rate on the global level is small due to territorial restriction. Fourth, following a failed vertical attempt to include a social clause in the trade rules of the WTO, core labour standards have been promoted horizontally through the EU's preferential trade rules with developing countries, albeit to a limited degree. In sum, the EU's impact on policy content is most pronounced in the vertical export of a narrow set of Community rules, whereas the ability of the EU to broaden the take-up rate of social standards is generally small.

Notes

1 For the distinction see e.g. Majone 1997: 140–141.
2 ECJ Cases 80/70 *Defrenne vs. Belgian State (I)* [1971] ECR 445 and 43/76 *Defrenne vs. Sabena* [1976] ECR 455.
3 Council Directive 75/117/EEC of 10 February 1975 on the approximation of the laws of the Member States relating to the application of the principle of equal pay for men and women. OJ L 045, 19–20.
4 Council Directive 76/207/EEC of 9 February 1976 on the implementation of the principle of equal treatment for men and women with regard to access to employment, vocational training and promotion, and working conditions. OJ L 039, 40–42.
5 Council Directive 93/104/EC of 23 November 1993 concerning certain aspects of the organization of working time. OJ L 307, 18–24.
6 Treaty on European Union signed at Maaastricht on 7 February 1992, Protocol on Social Policy. OJ C 191, 90.
7 For a controversial debate on this issue see also Alston 2004, 2005; Langille 2005; Maupain 2005.
8 See ECJ Case 61/81 *Commission vs. UK* [1982] ECR 2601.
9 Council Directive 2000/43/EC of 29 June 2000 implementing the principle of equal treatment between persons irrespective of racial or ethnic origin. OJ L 180, 22–26; Council Directive 2000/78/EC of 27 November 2000 establishing a general framework

for equal treatment in employment and occupation. OJ L 303, 16–22; Directive 2002/73/EC of the European Parliament and of the Council of 23 September 2002 amending Council Directive 76/207/EEC on the implementation of the principle of equal treatment for men and women with regard to access to employment, vocational training and promotion, and working conditions. OJ L 269, 15–20.
10 Most ILO directives that were drafted with high EU input belong to this issue area: C155/1981, C161/1985, C164/1987, C167/1988, C174/1993, C176/1995, C184/2001 (see Kissack 2009: 106).
11 Council Resolution of 6 December 1994 on certain aspects pf a European social policy: a contribution to economic and social convergence in the Union. OJ C 368, 8.
12 ECJ Opinion 2/91 [1993], *ECR* I-1061, 1077–1080. See also Delarue 2006: 107; Nedergaard 2009.
13 Partnership Agreement between the members of the African, Caribbean and Pacific Group of states (ACP) of the one part, and the European Community and its Member States, of the other part, signed in Cotonou on 23 June 2000. 2000/483/EC, OJ 2000 L 317, 3.
14 Council Regulations 3281/94. OJ L 348, 1 and 1256/96. OJ L 160, 1; 2820/98. OJ L 348, 1.
15 Council Regulation 2501/2001. OJ L 346, 1.

References

Alston, P. (2004) '"Core Labor Standards" and the Transformation of the International Labour Rights Regime', *European Journal of International Law* 15(3): 457–521.
—— (2005) 'Facing the Complexities of the ILO's Core Labour Standards Agenda', *European Journal of International Law* 16(3): 467–480.
Alston, P. and Heenan, J. (2004) 'Shrinking the International Labor Code: An Unintended Consquence of the 1998 ILO Declaration on Fundamental Principles and Rights at Work?', *NYU Journal of International Law and Politics* 36(2–3): 221–264.
Bell, M. (2002) *Anti-discrimination Law and the European Union*, Oxford: Oxford University Press.
Caume, H., Jacquot, S. and Paliet, B. (2011) 'Social Europe in Action: The Evolution of EU Policies and Resources', in P.R. Graziano, S. Jacquot and B. Palier (eds) *The EU and the Domestic Policies of Welfare State Reforms*, Basingstoke: Palgrave Macmillan.
Delarue, R. (2006) 'ILO–EU Cooperation on Employment and Social Affairs', in J. Wouters, F. Hoffmeister and T. Ruys (eds) *The United Nations and the European Union: An Ever Stronger Relationship*, The Hague: TMC Asser Press.
Dennis, M.J. (1999) 'The ILO Convention on the Worst Forms of Child Labor', *The American Journal of International Law* 93(4): 943–948.
European Council (1988) *Conclusions of the Presidency, European Council Rhodes*, 2 and 3 December 1988, SN 4443/1/88, www.europarl.europa.eu/summits/rhodes/rh1_en.pdf (accessed 4 September 2012).
Falkner, G. (1996) 'The Maastricht Protocol On Social Policy: Theory and Practice', *Journal of European Social Policy* 6(1): 1–16.
Falkner, G., Treib, O., Hartlapp, M. and Leiber, S (eds) (2005) *Complying with Europe. EU Harmonization and Soft Law in the Member States*, Cambridge: Cambridge University Press.
Falkner, G., Treib, O. and Holzleithner, E. (2008) *Compliance in the Enlarged European Union: Living Rights or Dead Letters?*, Aldershot: Ashgate.
Gatto, A. (2005) 'The Integration of Social Rights Concerns in the External Relations of

the European Union', in G. de Búrca and B. de Witte (eds) *Social Rights in Europe*, Oxford: Oxford University Press.

Giubboni, S. (2003) 'Fundamental Social Rights in the European Union: Problems of Protection and Enforcement', *Italian Labor Law eJournal* 5(1), www.labourlawjournal.it (accessed 4 September 2012).

Gstöhl, S. (2009) 'The Social Dimension of EU Neighbourhood Policies', in J. Orbie and L. Tortell (eds) *The European Union and the Social Dimension of Globalization: How the EU Influences the World*, London: Routledge.

Hafner-Burton, E.M. (2005) 'Trading Human Rights: How Preferential Trade Agreements Influence Government Repression', *International Organization* 59(3): 593–629.

International Labour Organization (1999) *Report of the Committee on Child Labour*, International Labour Conference, 87th Session, Geneva, June, www.ilo.org/public/english/standards/relm/ilc/ilc87/com-chil.htm (accessed 4 September 2012).

Kissack, R. (2009) 'Writing a New Normative Standard? EU Member States and ILO Conventions', in J. Orbie and L. Tortell (eds) *The European Union and the Social Dimension of Globalization: How the EU Influences the World*, London: Routledge.

—— (2010) *Pursuing Effective Multilateralism. The European Union, International Organizations and the Politics of Decision Making*, Basingstoke: Palgrave Macmillan.

Landau, E.C. and Beigbeder, Y. (2008) *From ILO Standards to EU Law*, Leiden: Martinus Nijhoff.

Langille, B.A. (1999) 'The ILO and the New Economy: Recent Developments', *International Journal of Comparative Labour Law and Industrial Relations* 15(3): 229–258.

—— (2005) 'Core Labor Rights – The True Story (Reply to Alston)', *European Journal of International Law* 16(3): 409–437.

Majone, G. (1993) 'The European Community Between Social Policy and Social Regulation', *Journal of Common Market Studies* 31(2): 153–170.

—— (1997) 'From the Positive to the Regulatory State: Causes and Consequences of Changes in the Mode of Governance', *Journal of Public Policy* 17(2): 139–167.

Maupain, F. (2005) 'Revitalization Not Retreat: The Real Potential of the 1998 ILO Declaration for the Universal Protection of Workers' Rights', *European Journal of International Law* 16(3): 439–465.

Meunier, S. and Nicolaïdis, K. (2006) 'The European Union as a Conflicted Trade Power', *Journal of European Public Policy* 13(6): 906–925.

Nedergaard, P. (2009) 'The European Union at the ILO's International Labour Conferences: A "Double" Principal-agent Analysis', in K.E. Jørgensen (ed.) *The European Union and International Organizations*, London; New York: Routledge.

Novitz, T. (2002) 'Promoting Core Labour Standards and Improving Global Social Governance: An Assessment of EU Competence to Implement Commission Proposals', EUI Working Papers RSC No. 59/2002, San Domenico: European University Institute.

—— (2005) 'The European Union and International Labour Standards: The Dynamics of Dialogue between the EU and the ILO', in P. Alston (ed.) *Labour Rights as Human Rights*, Oxford: Oxford University Press.

—— (2009) 'In Search of a Coherent Social Policy: EU Import and Export of ILO Labour Standards?', in J. Orbie and L. Tortell (eds) *The European Union and the Social Dimension of Globalization: How the EU Influences the World*, London: Routledge.

Orbie, J. and Tortell, L. (2009) 'From the Social Clause to the Social Dimension of Globalization', in J. Orbie and L. Tortell (eds) *The European Union and the Social Dimension of Globalization: How the EU Influences the World*, London: Routledge.

Orbie, J., Gistelinck, M. and Kerremans, B. (2009) 'The Social Dimension of EU Trade Policies', in J. Orbie and L. Tortell (eds) *The European Union and the Social Dimension of Globalization: How the EU Influences the World*, London: Routledge.

Riddervold, M. (2010) '"A Matter of Principle?" EU Foreign Policy in the International Labour Organization', *Journal of European Public Policy* 17(4): 581–598.

Schimmelfennig, F. and Sedelmeier, U. (2004) 'Governance by Conditionality: EU Rule Transfer to the Candidate Countries of Central and Eastern Europe', *Journal of European Public Policy* 11(4): 661–679.

Schimmelfennig, F., Rittberger, B., Bürgin, A. and Schwellnus, G. (2006) 'Conditions for EU Constitutionalization: A Qualitative Comparative Analysis', *Journal of European Public Policy* 13(8): 1168–1189.

Schwellnus, G. (2006) 'Reasons for Constitutionalization: Non-discrimination, Minority Rights and Social Rights in the Convention on the EU Charter of Fundamental Rights', *Journal of European Public Policy* 13(8): 1265–1283.

—— (2009) 'Anti-discrimination Legislation', in B. Rechel (ed.) *Minority Rights in Central and Eastern Europe*, London: Routledge.

Sedelmeier, U. (2009) 'Post-accession Compliance with EU Gender Equality Legislation in Post-communist New Member States', in F. Schimmelfennig and F. Trauner (eds) 'Post-accession Compliance in the EU's New Member States', *European Integration online Papers* (EIoP), Special Issue 2, Vol. 13, Art. 23, http://eiop.or.at/eiop/texte/2009-023a.htm (accessed 4 September 2012).

Sissenich, B. (2005) 'The Transfer of EU Social Policy to Poland and Hungary', in F. Schimmelfennig and U. Sedelmeier (eds) *The Europeanization of Central and Eastern Europe*, Ithaca, NY: Cornell University Press.

7 EU environmental policy
Greening the world?

Katharina Holzinger and Thomas Sommerer

1 Introduction

Despite some precursors in the late nineteenth century, environmental policy developed as a distinct field only after 1970. Environmental policy emerged simultaneously within the developed Western countries and at the international and European levels. During the first two decades, either single countries, such as the US, Japan, Scandinavia or Germany, took the lead in shaping a certain policy, or problems were first tackled at the international level. In general, the determination of who was a pioneer and who was a follower, who introduced strict and encompassing regulations and who acted more hesitatingly, depended very much on the subfield of environmental policy. The EU usually acted in response to demands from its Member States; however, it also imported rules in reaction to international processes. It became signatory of many international environmental treaties, but it was only after 1990 that the Commission acted as a supranational institution representing the EU in international environmental treaty negotiations and beginning to promote its own policy models at the international level. More often, however, the active export of EU environmental policies to other countries took place in the context of pre-enlargement negotiations and its neighbourhood policy. To a certain extent, EU policies were also voluntarily emulated by non-Member States.

In this chapter we offer an overview of policy export and import, and analyse two examples representing the most important mechanisms. We start with a brief history of EU environmental policy and then describe its interaction with the international level for important subfields of environmental policy. Thereafter, we present the mechanisms of policy export that played a role in the environmental field. In the fourth and fifth sections we use two cases to illustrate the causal mechanisms of active and passive, horizontal and vertical export of EU policies.

2 The development of EU and international environmental policy

At the European Council in Paris in 1972, the European heads of states and governments decided to establish the first environmental action programme.

This event marked the official beginning of a European environmental policy (Holzinger 2011; Andersen and Liefferink 1997). Since then, the EU's environmental policy has developed into a comprehensive and complex regime.

Although the Treaty of Rome did not contain any environmental provisions, a limited number of product standards on vehicle emissions and hazardous substances had already been adopted before 1972. As these policies were not motivated by environmental concerns, the period from 1957 to 1972 has been described as a phase of 'incidental environmental measures' (Hildebrand 2005). In the wake of the first three environmental action programmes (1973–1976, 1977–1981, 1982–1986), environmentally motivated policies were adopted in all subfields of this area and amounted to approximately 150 regulations, directives and decisions (Holzinger 2011). In this second, 'responsive' phase (Hildebrand 2005), the scope of European environment policy grew, but was still rather scattered and dealt only with acute pollution problems (e.g. acidification). The beginning of a third phase was marked by the adoption of the Single European Act (SEA) in 1987, which added a chapter on environmental policy to the Treaty. In the following decade, environmental policy was closely linked to the project of the Single Market. The field developed at an unexpected speed (Andersen and Liefferink 1997), such that 96 legal acts were adopted before the ratification of the Maastricht Treaty, as well as about 160 acts before the Nice Treaty in 2000 (Holzinger 2011). Density and specificity of the regime grew constantly, while new integrative policies broadened the functional scope. It is less clear if we can speak of a distinct fourth phase of European environmental policy since 2000, although we still observe the adoption of over 120 legal acts by 2008. Over the past 25 years, environmental policies have surely been undergoing a process of Europeanization, with a clear shift of competences to Brussels (Siebenhüner 2011: 109).

International environmental regimes emerged simultaneously with European environmental policy. The UN Conference on the Human Environment in Stockholm in July 1972 marked the beginning of a period of international cooperation. The United Nations, its Environment Programme (UNEP) and its specialized agencies are the most important but not the only fora for environmental cooperation. Overall, the international environmental regime is broad in scope with more than 2700 multilateral agreements (Mitchell 2012). Important variations may be observed across the subfields of environmental regulation. Most treaties are concerned with nature, habitat and species, followed by agreements dealing with water problems: the oceans and marine pollution on the one hand, and freshwater resources on the other. The European regime has a similar scope, with a total of 528 legal acts prior to 2008 (Holzinger 2011). However, the distribution across the subfields differs from the international level: air pollution, waste management and the regulation of chemicals dominate.

Table 7.1 gives a summary of the relevance of environmental policy at the national, European and international level. The early 1970s marked an important change in the development of environmental policy, since it was recognized at all levels as a pressing issue. The pioneers of modern environmental policy at the domestic level were Japan, the United States and Sweden (Jänicke 2005:

Table 7.1 Significance of governance layers over time (Environmental Policy)

Period	National level	EU level	Global level
Post WWII	Low	–	–
1957–1971	Low (some subfields medium)	Low	Low
1972–1986	Medium	Medium	Medium
1987–1999	Medium (some subfields high, varies across subfields and countries)	Medium (some subfields high, varies across subfields)	Medium (some subfields high, varies across subfields)
Post-2000	Medium (some subfields high, varies across subfields and countries)	High	High
2020 (extrapolation)	High	High	High

136), followed by some European countries, the EU and the international level. Environmental policy became more significant over time at the EU and the international level, although varying in terms of the regulated objects and bindingness. At the national level there is still high variance with respect to the political significance attributed to environmental problems both across the world and in Europe (Jänicke 2005).

3 From an importer to an exporter of environmental policy

Establishing the main areas of overlap between EU and international environmental policy is crucial when examining the interaction between the two governance layers in this policy domain. To outline the overall potential of the export and import of EU policies, we thus compare the scope, timing and depth of the international and the European regime in the most important subfields of environmental policy: air pollution, noise protection, chemicals policy, water protection, waste management, nature protection and horizontal environmental policies with cross-cutting scope, such as environmental impact assessment.

Policy measures against air pollution have a long tradition in the EU. Starting with product standards for vehicle emissions (70/220/EEC), different aspects of air pollution were regulated in the 1970s (e.g. sulphur and lead in fuels), but progress occurred only slowly. Policies were specific and highly binding, but the regime was not dense. In 1996, a more integrated approach led to the adoption of the air quality framework directive (96/62/EC). Before the mid-1990s, however, the initiative on air policy was mainly left to the international level (Siebenhüner 2011: 107). The 1979 UNECE Convention on Long Range Transboundary Air Pollution was the first international legally binding instrument to deal with problems of transnational air pollution. The EU was among the first signatories of the equally narrow but highly binding international regimes of the Vienna

Convention (1985) and the Montreal Protocol (1987) on the Protection of the Ozone Layer. Although there are other international agreements, the European air pollution policy today is broader, deeper and stricter than the global regime, especially for product-related policies. Today, the EU has a large number of binding standards and has achieved a high level of regulation (Siebenhüner 2011).

European noise policy started in 1970 with the motor vehicle noise directive (70/157/EEC). This subfield was limited in scope and depth until 2000, however, with only a few highly binding vehicle and aircraft noise standards. In substance, the early noise directives followed closely what had been agreed upon in international conventions. Since the 1960s, product standards for emissions from aircraft and motor vehicles had been an important element of the noise regime of the WHO, the ISO and the OECD. However, the global noise policy was limited to a few transboundary issues. A major change in the scope of the European noise regime was achieved in 2002 with the adoption of the environmental noise directive END (2002/49/EC). With this, the EU established a broader and more stringent approach than international organizations.

The earliest European legislation on chemicals policy dates back to the 1967 directive on dangerous substances (67/548/EEC). Over time, European chemicals policy became broader and more binding. A first step towards an integrative approach was the classification directive in 1979, followed by the regulation on chemicals and their safe use 25 years later (REACH, 2006/1907EC). At the global level, chemicals policy started with the OECD Environment, Health and Safety Programme in 1971. The International Programme on Chemical Safety of WHO, UNEP and ILO (1980) represents a second important international project (Garrod 2006: 13). Since the late 1990s, the global trend followed the increasing regulatory activity of the EU with the ratification of conventions on chemicals and pesticides (1998) and persistent organic pollutants (2001). Today, both the European and the global regime have a broad functional scope but the EU policies are much more binding.

In a first phase from 1973 to 1988, EU water policies were directed towards the protection of human health (e.g. by directives on the quality of drinking and bathing water (76/160/EEC) and on dangerous substances released into surface water (76/464/EEC)). A second stage from 1988 to 1995 brought more comprehensive measures which widened the scope of regulation (e.g. with the urban wastewater directive (91/271/EEC)). This development culminated in the adoption of the water framework directive (2000/60/EC) (Kissling-Näf and Kuks 2004). Overall, ambient quality standards and process standards were dominant, which are less binding than product standards. International cooperation on water policy grew faster than the European policy from the early 1970s onward, and led to institutions such as the Convention on the Prevention of Marine Pollution (1972), the Helsinki Convention (1974), the Barcelona Convention (1976), and various river basin commissions. The integrated management approach of river basin regimes inspired the development of the EU water framework directive (Aubin and Varone 2002: 54). Collaboration in the context of the UNEP included the Regional Seas Programme and, since 1992, freshwater resource management. Since 2000, however, the European regime has become broader, whereas the global regime has lost its initial dynamic. The EU is now considered an international policy leader in water policy and influences water programmes outside its geographic boundaries (Vogel and Swinnen 2011).

European waste policy is an extensive and evolving system (Mazzanti and Montini 2009). Framework regulations were adopted earlier than in other subfields, most notably with the waste framework directive (75/442/EEC) and the hazardous waste directive (91/689/EEC). More specific directives followed, such as one on incineration (94/67/EC). For waste management, we find fewer regulations at the global level, with the shipments of waste being the only aspect that is highly internationalized. The most important international regime is the UNEP Basel Convention on Transboundary Movements of Hazardous Waste of 1989. The OECD introduced a comprehensive but voluntary waste management policy back in 1976, which became more binding after 1992. EU directives implement international agreements on the shipment of waste; however, European waste policy affects Member States significantly more than international regimes (O'Neill 2004: 166).

Nature protection is less important at the European level than internationally. Policy-making started late and resulted in a few specific measures, such as the directive on wild birds (79/409/EEC). At the global level, nature protection policies appeared much earlier. The world's first global nature protection organization was created in 1948. In the 1970s, Conventions on Trade in Endangered Species (1973), on Migratory Species (1979), as well as the Bern Convention on the Conservation of European Wildlife (1979), were pioneering policies in this field. EU policy on nature protection caught up in only one area, when in 1992 the Habitats Directive (92/43/EEC) was adopted at the same time as the UN Convention on Biological Diversity.

Finally, horizontal policies were not on the agenda until the mid-1980s and remained limited in numbers. Horizontal regulation in European environmental policy began with the directive on Environmental Impact Assessment (85/337/EEC). Other policies followed, for example, on public access to information (2003/35/EC). Important elements of the global regime are the Espoo Convention on Environmental Impact Assessment (1991) and the UNECE Aarhus Convention on Access to Information (1998). The EU is a signatory to both agreements. Climate policy may also be seen as a horizontal issue. Here, the UN Framework Convention on Climate Change from 1992 and the Kyoto Protocol from 1997 are the main building blocks of the global regime, where all EU Member States and the EU are contracting parties. The Commission plays an active role in climate policy (Vogler and Stephan 2007; Damro and Mendez 2003). Kelemen (2010) considers the EU to also be a leader in GMO regulation and in 'greening' the world trade regime.

On the basis of this review, we highlight four important aspects. First, environmental policy started in the late 1960s at the national level in some pioneer states, and later developed into an area where the main regulatory activity takes place at the European or international level. The US influenced international negotiations from Stockholm to Montreal, whereas some EU Member States followed only reluctantly and thus hampered EU progress (Kelemen 2010). Today, however, the EU has become the most important actor in international environmental policy. As Kelemen (2010: 341) puts it,

> by the early 1990s, the EU had strong incentives to try to export its environmental standards and an increasing capacity to do so. The EU deployed the strategies of 'exercising regulatory influence' and 'empowering international institutions' ... to spread its environmental standards to other jurisdictions.

Second, we find interesting differences in the relative strength of the EU regime vis-à-vis the global level between subfields of environmental policy. In waste management and chemicals policies the EU played a leading role from the beginning. The same seems true for most horizontal policies. In the fields of air, noise and water policies, import from the international level was more common in the first phase, but the EU turned to become an exporter after 1990. Only for nature protection is the EU still a laggard.

Third, there is variation in the formal involvement of the EU at the global level that might be related to the import and export of environmental policies. While the EU has always been a signatory of international treaties it became an active player in international negotiations from the 1990s onwards. The 1992 Rio Conference was a turning point, since for the first time the Commission President was given a status equivalent to a head of state (Vogler and Stephan 2007).

Fourth, there seems to be some division of labour between the EU and the international level. European environmental policy is particularly strong when it comes to trade-related policies and product standards. Evidence from the literature on environmental policy convergence has shown that these policies are more likely to diffuse horizontally (Holzinger et al. 2008), seemingly driven by harmonization demand (Holzinger and Sommerer 2011) and market externalities.

In sum, there have been parallel and complementary developments of environmental policy at the European and international level, but also interactions. The two levels seem to have inspired each other in many instances. To some degree, the response of the respective level follows the geographical reach of the environmental problem or the associated economic processes. Over time, we observe a development towards more comprehensive approaches at both levels. The European regulation was always more stringent in terms of bindingness. Meanwhile, the EU has also become the leader in terms of scope and comprehensiveness.

4 Typical mechanisms of environmental policy export

Based on the empirical findings of the relevant literature, we give a brief account of the main mechanisms of horizontal and vertical policy export. Horizontal export plays an important role in the environmental field. We learn from the literature on environmental policy convergence that EU policies have been adopted by non-members to notable degrees. Holzinger *et al.* (2008) studied the adoption of 40 environmental policies from 1970 to 2000 in 24 countries. For 19 of these measures, an obligatory EU regulation had been introduced during the observation period. A closer look at the adoption pattern (Holzinger *et al.* 2008: 107) shows that most old EU members had already adoptedtento 15 policies in 1980, and had come close to 40 policies by 2000. Non-EU environmental pioneers showed similar numbers until 1980, but then split in their development. The EFTA countries joining the EU quickly caught up with the old members, whereas non-EU members lagged behind. However, the US, Mexico, Norway and Switzerland also adopted at least some of the EU policies.

In terms of policy export, we find active horizontal export by conditionality. EU accession candidates of the Southern enlargement show some increase in the adoption of EU environmental policies following their accession, but still lag behind for non-EU-related policies. The Eastern enlargement accession candidates started with very low numbers in 1980, expanded after 1990, and arrived at above 25 policies in 2000. For the latter two groups we can clearly see that conditionality had its effect: in preparation for the accession, or shortly thereafter, candidate countries introduced the obligatory EU policies. However, we also observe passive horizontal export by emulation, as is shown in the examples of the US, Mexico, Norway and Switzerland.

Finally, product standards spread much wider and quicker than other kinds of standards. This seems due to the positive externalities of a large market, in which harmonized standards provide an advantage. Further evidence is provided by Knill and Tosun (2009), who analyse the spread of three policies (nitrogen oxides from large combustion plants, the eco-label and environmental impact assessment) across 33 countries between 1980 and 2006. They find that non-Member States did indeed adopt the EU policies to some degree. The effect of hierarchical governance on adoption, including membership and quasi-membership in EEA and conditionality towards accession candidates, is most robust (active export). However, information exchange with neighbouring countries also shows a positive and significant effect on the adoption of the eco-label and large combustion plant regulation. This may be interpreted as indicative of the effect of persuasion as a channel of passive horizontal export.

While we observe passive and active horizontal export on a broader scale – which is due to enlargements and the attractiveness of the EU market and its economic power – cases of vertical export seem comparatively rare during the period before 1990. Although the EU participated in many international environmental agreements, it must be seen as an importer of policies – ratifying international treaties but not shaping them. In the period after 1990, however, the EU became an active exporter, promoting its own models and being able to exert substantial influence in several cases of international negotiations. Examples include the policies on chemicals, pesticides and organic pollutants, GMO regulation, 'greening' of the world trade regime (Kelemen 2010), water protection (Vogel and Swinnen 2011), car emissions regulation and climate policy.

Having presented some evidence for the mechanisms of exporting EU environmental policies, we turn to studying them in more depth by presenting two illustrative case studies. We select car emissions regulation and climate policy because of their significance in environmental and economic terms, and because they show that the various mechanisms of import and export, and successes and failures, may appear in the very same policy over time. This way, only two examples serve to present all mechanisms. The regulation of emissions from motor vehicles provides examples for both import and export of policies, active vertical export, active horizontal export by conditionality, and passive horizontal export by externalities and emulation. Climate policy serves as an example of the active and vertical mechanism of export by bargaining and persuasion, including a failed and a successful attempt.

5 Car emissions standards: active and passive, vertical and horizontal export

The regulation of car exhaust emissions in Europe dates back to the 1950s. The whole field encompasses many types of vehicles and an increasing number of substances emitted: carbon monoxide (CO), hydrocarbons (HC), nitrogen oxides (NO_x), particulate matter (PM) from diesel engines, and particulate nitrogen (PN). In order to reduce complexity, we concentrate in the following on the most relevant sector: the regulation of passenger cars and light duty vehicles, both gasoline and diesel engines, which are usually included in the same legal acts.

The first organization to regulate car emissions at the international level was the UN Economic Commission for Europe (UNECE). The aim of all ECE vehicle regulation is the enhancement of trade by technical harmonization across countries. Harmonization of technical standards for cars started in 1958 with the Geneva Agreement. A special group dealing with car emissions, the Group of Rapporteurs on Pollution and Energy (GRPE), was founded at the end of the 1960s. Representatives of industry and administration from the then six EEC Member States were present in this group, among those from other European countries. Nowadays, ECE car emissions regulation is usually implemented by about 50 European and non-European countries.

5.1 The EEC as importer of car emissions regulation

CO emissions, which are lethal in higher concentrations, have been regulated at the national level in Europe since the mid-1950s. The first comprehensive approach to emissions was achieved by ECE R 15, which regulated CO and HC emissions and defined the first European test cycle for measuring emissions. The development of the limit values by the GRPE was informally coordinated with the EU Commission's Motor Vehicle Emissions Group, a technical committee. R 15 was taken over by the EEC in its Directive 70/220/EEC, the basic legal act for EEC passenger car emissions regulation. In the following years, limit values were tightened several times, and NO_x was included in the regulation in 1977

(R 15/01 to R 15/04). Until 1983, the EEC merely followed the UNECE regulation. Whereas the ECE rules were voluntary for car producers, the EEC standards had a more obligatory character. In substance, the limit values adopted by the R 15 regulations and the EEC counterparts were rather lax. Only for CO did they have a limiting effect; for HC and NOx they could be achieved with simple technical measures (Holzinger 1994: 190ff.). Thus, in its first phase of car emissions regulation, the EU imported standards from an international organization.

From 1983 onwards, EC legislation on car exhaust emissions became independent of the ECE. In May 1983, the Council of Environmental Ministers adopted directive 83/351/EEC implementing R 15/04. At the same Council meeting, the German government took an initiative to amend the car emissions directive. The political background was the growing public awareness of forest decline in Germany; 'Waldsterben' turned out to become a major topic in the 1983 general election campaign. As exhaust emissions, especially NO_x, were accused of playing a decisive role in damaging forests, the German government requested that limit values be lowered drastically. The terms of reference were the so-called US-83 standards: the US Clean Air Act Amendment of 1970 which had formulated the ambitious goals of a 90 per cent reduction in exhaust emissions (Heaton and Maxwell 1984: 18ff.). American experience clearly showed that, with the closed-loop three-way catalyst, technology was available that permitted the US-83 standards to be met. Moreover, Japan had also decided to introduce standards comparable to the US-83 in 1972, and was able to successfully implement them as early as 1976 (Shibata 1989: 102ff.).

After two years of contentious negotiation, a first agreement among EC Member States was concluded in June 1985. The main element was a division of passenger cars into three classes according to engine capacity, different limit values for the three classes, and a respective timetable for compliance. The standards for large cars came close to the US-83 standards, those for medium-sized cars did not require a catalyst, and the decision for the most contentious class of small cars was postponed. This was due to the fierce resistance of France and Italy, the greatest producers of small and medium-sized cars (Holzinger 1995). The directive 88/76/EEC was finally adopted in 1988.

A decision on the small cars was only possible in June 1989 against the opposition of some Member States. After the Single European Act, car emissions regulation as part of the common market legislation was subject to the Cooperation procedure; that is, it was no longer to be decided by unanimity but by qualified majority in the Council, and the European Parliament had a say. The Parliament was in favour of introducing US-83 standards for small cars as well. Since the Member States could not reach a unanimous decision against such a position, the Commission sided with the Parliament and those Member States demanding US-83 standards. The small car directive 89/458/EEC provided for US-83 standards for small cars, whereas the medium class still had to comply with more lax limit values. Since this was inconsistent, a consolidated directive 91/441/EEC was adopted by the Council in June 1991, which provided for uniform limit values for all cars, measured by a new European test cycle.

To sum up, during the 1980s the EU imported the US model of car exhaust gases regulation following a tedious conflict between the Member States (Holzinger 1995).

From then on, however, the EU set the pace in car emissions regulation. The 1991 directive became the new worldwide reference point as the so-called Euro 1 norm. The limit values were gradually tightened over a series of revisions and two additional harmful substances were included in the regulatory scheme: particulate matter (dust) and particulate nitrogen. Currently valid is Euro 5, with Euro 6 to be implemented in the EU Member States by 2014.

5.2 The EU as a policy exporter of car emissions regulation

From 1991 onwards, the EU became an active and passive exporter of its car exhaust emissions policy (for details see Delphi 2012/2013; Timilsina and Dulal 2009). First of all, the EU succeeded in vertically exporting its directive 91/441/EEC to the UNECE, which incorporated the EU standards into its new exhaust emissions regulation R 83/01. By that time, all European car-producing countries were members of the EU. An agreement found between these countries within the EU legal framework could easily (i.e. without further conflict) be transferred to the UNECE. For the same reason, all subsequent changes to the EU regulation have been emulated by respective ECE regulations. This implies that the non-EU-member signatories of the UNECE agreement on car regulation also usually apply the EU rules, albeit on a voluntary basis on the side of the car manufacturers. Currently, 51 states (including EU members) have signed ECE R 83/06 (equivalent to Euro 5, EU Regulation 715/2007). Not all of these states accept the Euro norm as the only standard. In New Zealand, for example, cars may conform to either European, US or Japanese standards. Export from the EU to the UNECE may be judged as active export, as there is active coordination between the EU Commission and the ECE committee responsible (GRPE), and vertical export to an international organization with wider membership than the EU.

Second, during the 1990s the EU was also an active horizontal exporter of its car emissions policies towards candidate countries. As the *acquis communautaire* is a precondition for access, the car emissions directives had to be transposed into national law during the EFTA enlargement by Austria, Finland and Sweden (which had been using US standards in the years before joining the EU) and during the Eastern enlargements by 12 Central and Eastern European candidates. Although many of these states were signatories of the UNECE regulations R 15 and R 83, preparation for EU accession made the standards binding law in these countries. For all these cases, we can talk of active export by conditionality.

Third, we observe passive horizontal export. The Euro norm has been emulated by countries which became neither EU members nor signatories of the UNECE Geneva agreement, such as China, India, Indonesia, certain other Asian countries, Argentina, Brazil, Chile, Israel and Saudi Arabia. In these countries the Euro norms were often introduced later than in the EU or they were only partly implemented (e.g. not for all vehicles classes). Chile, for example, employs US standards for gasoline cars and the Euro norm for diesel engines. However, most countries claim that they are striving for full compliance with the Euro norm in the future. There are two reasons for the prevailing of the Euro norm over the US standards. First, the European driving cycle fits conditions in most countries better. Second, car-producing countries outside Europe, such as Japan, have a large market in Europe and thus have to produce cars according to the Euro norm anyway. Car-importing countries outside the EU and UNECE import cars from Europe or Japan to a large degree and from the US to a lesser degree. Furthermore, emulation is supported by externality, as the harmonization of standards in a worldwide product market is a positive externality. The sheer size of the area and number of states in which the Euro norm is now applied draws more and more countries towards it.

It may thus truly be said that the Euro norm has become the leading standard in the world for passenger car exhaust emissions. Even countries that had been using the US standards for some time, such as Switzerland (1982 to 1995), Norway, Brazil, Chile and Hong Kong, changed their policies to emulate the Euro norm. The Asian Development Bank recommends the introduction of the Euro norms for Asian countries (ADB 2003). There are still two other standards, however, namely the US federal standards and the stricter California standards (emulated by a number of other US states), which are also applied in Canada, several Latin American states, Taiwan and South Korea. Japan uses its own limit values and driving cycle but accepts vehicles licensed according to EU/ECE standards.

The case of the regulation of car exhaust emissions shows that the role of the EU has changed over time from an importer of a policy to an active and passive exporter. The change occurred at the beginning of the 1990s, which coincided with the institutional change towards majority voting in the Council, new and environmentally friendly members, a general 'greening' in the EU Member States (Holzinger 1997) and a growing ambition on the side of the Commission. In this respect the case is representative for the field of environmental policy. Second, the case is also typical when it comes to export by conditionality. Accession candidates had to take over the EU directives on car emissions as part of the *acquis*. Third, the active role the EU assumed after 1990 made it a vertical exporter of its car exhaust policies to the UNECE. Finally, we observe also passive export through emulation of EU regulation by further countries.

The case shows that various types of export can appear together within the same policy and can even mutually reinforce each other. The vertical export of the Euro norm to the UNECE almost doubled the number of countries applying this model. The growing number of states using the Euro norm made it, in turn, more attractive for UNECE outsiders to emulate. The active horizontal export by conditionality before the Eastern enlargement had a comparatively minor effect, since it affected only 12 countries. Earlier enlargements, however, brought all significant European car manufacturers, and thus the important players, into the

EU. This explains why the EU became the major negotiation arena for car emissions standards and was able to vertically export to the UNECE.

6 Climate policy: a case of vertical export

Climate policy entered the agenda of EU policy-making shortly after the beginning of a global regime on this issue. In 1988, the World Meteorological Organization (WMO) and the UNEP established the Intergovernmental Panel on Climate Change (IPCC) as a scientific body to assess the risk of climate change (Agrawala 1998: 606). In parallel to first commitments to CO_2 reductions by some of the 'greener' Member States in 1989 and 1990 – most notably Denmark, the Netherlands and Germany (Porter and Brown 1991: 95) – the EU became engaged in climate policy. The first step consisted of the establishment of an ad hoc committee on global warming that involved representatives of three European Commission General Directorates: Energy, Environment and Indirect Taxation in 1989 (Sjöstedt 1998: 239).The first resolution of the Energy and Environment Council followed during the same year, justifying climate policy by ongoing attempts of international cooperation, such as the conference in Montreal (Council Resolution 89/C 183/03). In 1992, the European Commission drafted its first comprehensive climate strategy (COM(92) 246).

This early action marked a change in the development of EU environmental policy vis-à-vis global regimes. Before, the EU had been a latecomer in some important international negotiations. An important manifestation of the 'greening' of the EU environmental policy was the Dublin declaration in 1990. The EU officially expressed its ambition to become a leading actor in international environmental politics, 'already then seeing itself as having an enormous capacity to provide leadership' (Kilian and Elgström 2010: 257). The commitment to leadership, in that sense, may be seen as a prerequisite for the active export of EU policies in this field.

6.1 Lack of unity: the EU initiative on a global energy tax

In contrast to the explicit claim for leadership, early attempts by the EU to influence international climate policy failed. In October 1990, the Joint Council of Environment and Energy Ministers agreed to undertake measures to stabilize CO_2 emissions in the Community at 1990 levels by the year 2000 (EC Press Release 9482/90). This decision was a response to similar commitments by some Member States and other countries, for example, Norway (Andresen and Agrawala 2002: 45). When the EU tried to find support for its targets during the negotiations of the UN Framework Convention on Climate Change, the US and many non-OECD countries were opposed to early action and binding targets (Oberthür and Roche 2008). The EU stabilization goal was complemented by a set of policy instruments, the centre-piece being an energy tax (Yamin 2000). During the period prior to the UN summit in Rio, the European Commission pushed other OECD countries to adopt similar energy taxes, but they refused to do so (Kelemen 2010).

One major reason for this failure was lack of EU unity. There was a strong internal disagreement over CO_2 taxation between Member States, but also within the Commission (Wettestad 2000: 27). A coherent internal policy was prohibited by concerns about loss of competitiveness of European industries, put forward by some key Member States. The British and French governments were strongly opposed, but also less developed Member States, such as Spain and Greece, expressed concerns about their growth perspective (Klok 2002: 111). An energy tax would have required international harmonization to avoid EU loss of competitiveness, and because there was no support from other key countries, important Member States were opposed to unilateral action (Yamin 2000: 53). As a compromise, a clause was added that made the EU tax conditional upon similar measures being taken by other OECD countries, particularly the US and Japan (Klok 2002: 111). An institutional hurdle for EU unity on this issue was the fact that a CO_2 tax as a financial measure had to be adopted unanimously in the Council of Financial Ministers.

In addition to low coherence, the EU lacked the reputation and experience of a green leader. The failure has been particularly assigned to the actions of the Commission and led to the resignation of Commissioner Ripa de Meana. It was claimed that the Commissioner generated a lot of attention, but was 'playing to the gallery rather than trying to build workable compromises' (Andresen and Wettestad 1990). With a disharmonious Council, even an engaged and active Commission faced severe difficulties in becoming a successful exporter of a European model. This credibility gap of the EU was used by other industrialized countries as an argument against EU claims for leadership and ambitious goals before the first Conference of Parties of the UN Framework Convention on Climate Change (Yamin 2000: 49). In the following, we will contrast the export of emission targets in Kyoto with this previous failure and illustrate how changes in EU unity and capacity made a difference.

6.2 The EU export of a reduction target in the Kyoto Protocol

The Kyoto Protocol is a major achievement of global environmental politics, setting binding reduction targets for CO_2 emissions in OECD countries (Gupta and Ringius 2001: 281). The influence of the EU on the Kyoto Protocol may be viewed as the export of core elements of its common climate policy. Following the Rio summit, the EU put a stronger focus on its internal climate policy (Gupta and Ringius 2001). This strategy contributed to the successful export in Kyoto, since it allowed for a unified position of the EU-15 prior to the negotiations. In March 1997, six months before the negotiations started, the Council of Environmental Ministers agreed on a common climate policy that involved an internal burden-sharing of greenhouse gas emissions (Sjöstedt 1998: 236; European Council C/97/60). Burden-sharing meant that the commitments of Member States varied, with the most developed states promising more substantial cuts than others (Oberthür and Roche 2008). This agreement facilitated and strengthened the commitments agreed to in Kyoto (Oberthür and Ott

1999). EU unity on emissions reduction put significant pressure on more reluctant parties.

Prior to the negotiations in Kyoto in the autumn of 1997, the EU pushed for binding targets and a reduction of greenhouse gas emissions. The Council of Environmental Ministers demanded that all OECD countries 'shall reduce emission levels for CO_2, CH_4 and N_2O together by 15 percent by 2010, compared to 1990' (European Council C/97/60). Despite resistance from the US, Japan, Canada and some other OECD countries, the negotiations at the third conference led to quantified commitments in a legally binding protocol (Gupta and Ringius 2001). Although the original EU goal of a 15 per cent reduction was not achieved, an overall cut of more than 5 per cent may be seen as a transfer of the EU position. The Kyoto target came closer to the EU's position than that of the United States although the EU was not successful on other important aspects of the agreement, such as an implementation mechanism (Gupta and Ringius 2001: 288f.; Yamin 2000: 65). Even though the overall story of the EU's influence on the international climate regime is one of failure and success, the negotiations that led to the Kyoto Protocol have been described as the biggest international achievement of EU environmental policy (Karlsson *et al.* 2011).

A difference between the pre-negotiation phase of the Kyoto and the Rio Round was the role of the Council and the Commission. The level of conflict among the General Directorates was considerably lower than with the energy tax. The leadership of green Member States after 1992 was an important factor for the ambitious internal goal and for the export of a reduction target. It has been argued that the Dutch presidency in the first half of 1997 was influential in this regard (Yamin 2000; Schreurs and Tiberghien 2007: 25), but Germany and the United Kingdom also strongly supported the common policy. Different explanations have been given for the support of Germany and the United Kingdom. One reason was that both countries strongly benefited from using the year 1990 as the point of reference for an emissions reduction target, thanks to the restructuring of energy supplies from coal to gas in the UK and the shutdown of many heavily polluting sites in Eastern Germany in the early 1990s (Kelemen 2010). The fear of a loss of competitiveness was replaced by the desire to create 'a more level competitive playing field' for the EU, since an agreement could lead to higher energy taxes in the US (Kelemen 2010: 344; Yandle and Buck 2002: 197).

Beyond this economic dimension, the motivation to actively export an ambitious climate policy was also driven by increasing ecological concerns within the EU. Not only did three 'green' states join the EU in 1995, but general support for green parties was also on the rise in many other countries. Within a five-year span, the presence of green parties in Member State parliaments had grown from six in 1992 to 11 by 1997, and their presence in national governments had increased from zero in 1992 to three in 1997 (Heichel *et al.* 2008: 94f.).

Another factor that influenced the export was the broader political relevance of climate talks. A leadership role in the global climate regime was a stepping stone for the development of a strong 'green' reputation (Andresen 2000: 45).

Neither the US nor Japan (both major economic powers and pioneers in the field of environmental regulation) assumed leadership in the global climate regime. The EU filled this power vacuum and the export of its own policy provided the opportunity to build a common foreign identity, while the lack of challenge from another major power made the EU position more acceptable for other countries. The ambitious internal goal was a signal towards other OECD countries and found the support of environmental NGOs, which also gave the EU a 'moral upper hand' in Kyoto (Andersen 2000). It is generally acknowledged that the figure of a 15 per cent emissions reduction worked both to improve the bargaining position with regard to major economic competitors and to convince other actors of the necessity of an effective policy against climate change (Yamin 2000).

Following Kyoto, the EU continued to play an important role in the global climate regime, for example, in bilateral negotiations with Russia (Kelemen 2010: 19). Major summits, such as Johannesburg in 2002 and Copenhagen in 2010, raised the expectations on the EU. These expectations were fuelled by the EU's explicit commitment to leadership (Falkner 2007) and its growing institutional capacity to live up to this role, to which a new General Directorate on Climate Action was added (EC Press release IP/10/164). However, the results were modest and Copenhagen was described as a 'substantial blow to [the EU's] leadership aspirations' (Karlsson *et al.* 2011).

An analysis of EU climate policy after Kyoto corroborates the role of EU unity, Member State leadership, a power vacuum and reputation-building for a successful policy export. First, the EU also prepared a common policy prior to the Copenhagen summit, but a division was obvious within the EU on how far new emissions targets should go (Karlsson *et al.* 2011). More generally, EU unity was also affected by the institutional crisis of the EU following the rejection of the constitutional treaty in 2005. Second, the influence of the group of green Member States was weakened following the accession of 12 new Member States between 2004 and 2007. Third, the leadership of the EU was challenged by an increasing influence of the BRIC states in international negotiations. Finally, climate change is still a prestigious topic in international politics, but it is less central than in the mid-1990s, and has been sidelined by other issues, such as security. Therefore, it is a less attractive field to gain strength in foreign policy by successful exports.

7 Conclusion

Environmental policy started developing contemporaneously around 1970 at the national, international and EU levels. Policies at the EU and international level developed in parallel; both levels reacted to pressing problems first and developed more encompassing policies later. Between the levels we observe variation in the relative strength across the subfields of environmental policy and some division of labour, according to the spatial reach of the environmental problems and their connection with the common market. However, both levels also inspired each other. From 1970 to 1990, the EU was more often a follower than a leader in environmental policy; it imported regulation from international agreements. Generally, the substance of regulation was not very ambitious at the international level; however, import into EU regulation made the policies at least more binding for EU members. Only after 1990 did the EU take the lead in several subfields; it developed more ambitious goals and became a pioneer and active exporter of regulation.

There are two reasons for this change. First, we observe a general process of 'greening' in the EU. In most Member States, the demand for more progressive environmental policies increased owing to the electoral success of green parties. The EFTA enlargement brought three more environmentally friendly countries that formed a green coalition with the former pioneers from 1995 to 2004. This made for more ambitious goals at the EU level. Second, a number of institutional changes supported a more progressive environmental policy of the EU. Environmental policy had been given a basis in the EU treaty with the SEA and had been expanded with the treaties of Maastricht and Amsterdam. The green coalition became effective owing to a shift towards Council majority voting in environmental matters. Even if they could not always form a majority for their position, they could now veto the position of the environmental laggards together. Moreover, the transition from the consultation procedure to the cooperation procedure, and later the co-decision procedure, gave the European Parliament the right to influence legislation. The Parliament turned out to support strict and pioneering environmental policies. Finally, the Commission was permitted to represent the EU directly in international treaty negotiations.

We found indications and examples for all kinds of export and all mechanisms. Passive export by externalities, as in the case of car emissions standards, can lead to a high policy fit and the adoption of EU environmental policies in a large number of countries. However, the relevance of this mechanism is limited due to its focus on market-related policies. Voluntary emulation does not have such a limitation and often leads to a high policy fit, but existing research shows that emulation only affects a limited number of countries. Active export by conditionality and persuasion at the horizontal level takes place in the context of accession negotiations and the EU's neighbourhood policy. Similar to emulation, this mechanism has driven the convergence of a broader set of environmental regulations. It is thus relevant and leads to a high policy fit, but the geographical scope is limited to the EU's periphery. Finally, there are also examples of active vertical export, two of which occurred in our case studies. In cases of success, the take-up rate is high; whereas the policy fit of the outcome with the EU's internal policy position varies from case to case. Since vertical export typically focuses on narrowly defined policies, the relevance of this mechanism for the European environmental regime is low.

The car emissions case shows how import turned into export and how various forms of export appear in parallel. The climate policy case shows that active vertical export seems rather difficult to achieve and that a number of conditions must be fulfilled in order for it to occur. The turn from import to export and from failure to success occurred in the late 1980s and early 1990s. In both cases it was driven by the factors mentioned above: a greening of EU members and institutional changes. Thus, the cases are typical considering the context and the timing.

To sum up, the EU has developed the capacity and the necessary reputation to export environmental policies over time. The EU exported environmental policies with varying degrees of success across the subfields. The case of climate change shows, however, that contextual factors played a major role in the successful bargaining with and persuasion of other powers by the EU. Since those conditions change, it remains unclear whether, to which degree and for how long the EU can keep its position as an active and vertical exporter of environmental regulation.

References

Agrawala, S. (1998) 'Context and Early Origins of the Intergovernmental Panel on Climate Change', *Climatic Change* 39(4): 605–620.

Andersen, M. and Liefferink, D. (1997) *European Environmental Policy: The Pioneers*, Manchester: Manchester University Press.

Andresen, S.S. (2000) *EU Energy Policy: Interest Interaction and Supranational Authority*, Oslo: Arena Working Paper No. 5/2000. Online. Available at: www.sv.uio.no/arena/english/research/publications/arena-publications/workingpapers/workingpapers2000/wp00_5.htm (accessed 12 April 2013).

Andresen, S. and Agrawala, S. (2002) 'Leaders, Pushers and Laggards in the Making of the Climate Regime', *Global Environmental Change* 12(1): 41–51.

Andresen, S. and Wettestad, J. (1990) 'Climate Failure at the Bergen Conference?', *International Challenges* 10(2): 17–24.

Asian Development Bank (2003) *Vehicle Emissions Standards and Inspection and Maintenance. Policy Guidelines for Reducing Vehicle Emissions in Asia*, Manila, Philippines: ADB. Online. Available at: www.adb.org/publications/reducing-vehicle-emissions-asia (accessed 12 April 2013).

Aubin, D. and Varone, F. (2002) European Water Policy: A Path Toward an Integrated Resource Management? EUWARENESS. AURAP-UCL, Louvain-La-Neuve. Online. Available at: www.ucl.be/cps/ucl/doc/espo/documents/Chap_EU_watpol_final.pdf (accessed 12 April 2013).

Damro, C. and Méndez, P.L. (2003) 'Emissions Trading at Kyoto: From EU Resistance to Union Innovation', *Environmental Politics* 12(1): 71–94.

Delphi (2012/2013) *Worldwide Emission Standards. Passenger Cars and Light Duty Vehicles*. Online. Available at: http://delphi.com/pdf/emissions/Delphi-Passenger-Car-Light-Duty-Truck-Emissions-Brochure-2012–2013.pdf (accessed 12 April 2013).

Falkner, R. (2007) *Business Power and Conflict in International Environmental Politics*, Basingstoke: Palgrave Macmillan.

Garrod, J. (2006) 'The Current Regulation of Environmental Chemicals', in R.E. Hester and R.M. Harrison (eds) *Chemicals in the Environment: Assessing and Managing Risk*, Cambridge: Royal Society of Chemistry.

Gupta, J. and Ringius, L. (2001) 'The EU's Climate Leadership: Reconciling Ambition and Reality', *International Environmental Agreements: Politics, Law and Economics* 1(2): 281–299.

Heaton, G.R. and Maxwell, J. (1984) 'Patterns of Automobile Regulation: An International Comparison', *Zeitschrift für Umweltpolitik und Umweltrecht* 7(1): 15–40.
Heichel, S., Holzinger, K., Sommerer, T., Liefferink, D., Pape, J. and Veenman, S. (2008) 'Research Design, Variables and Data', in K. Holzinger, C. Knill and B. Arts (eds) *Environmental Policy Convergence in Europe: The Impact of international institutions and trade*. Cambridge: Cambridge University Press, 64–97.
Hildebrand, P. (2005) 'The European Community's Environmental Policy, 1957 to "1992": From Incidental Measures to an International Regime?', in A. Jordan (ed.) *Environmental Policy in the European Union*, London: Earthscan.
Holzinger, K. (1994) *Politik des kleinsten Nenners? Umweltpolitische Entscheidungsprozesse in der EG am Beispiel der Einführung des Katalysatorautos*, Berlin: Edition Sigma.
—— (1995) 'A Surprising Success in EC Environmental Policy: The Small Car Exhaust Emission Directive of 1989', in M. Jänicke and H. Weidner (eds) *Successful Environmental Policy. A Critical Evaluation of 24 Cases*, Berlin: Edition Sigma.
—— (1997) 'The Influence of the New Member States on EU Environmental Policymaking. A Game-theoretic Approach', in M.S. Andersen and D. Liefferink (eds) *The Innovation of European Environmental Policy*, Copenhagen: Scandinavian University Press.
—— (2011) 'Environmental Policy in the Joint-decision Trap? The Critical Balance between "Market Making" and "Market Correcting"', in G. Falkner (ed.) *Exits from the Joint-decision Trap: Comparing EU Policies*, Oxford: Oxford University Press.
Holzinger, K. and Sommerer, T. (2011) 'Race to the Bottom" or "Race to Brussels"? Environmental Competition in Europe', *Journal of Common Market Studies* 49(2): 315–339.
Holzinger, K., Knill, C. and Arts, B. (eds) (2008) *Environmental Policy Convergence in Europe: The Impact of International Institutions and Trade*, Cambridge: Cambridge University Press.
Jänicke, M. (2005) 'Trend-setters in Environmental Policy: The Character and Role of Pioneer Countries', *European Environment* 15(2): 129–142.
Karlsson, C., Parker, C., Hjerpe, M. and Linnér, B-O. (2011) 'Looking for Leaders: Perceptions of Climate Change Leadership among Climate Change Negotiation Participants', *Global Environmental Politics* 11(1): 89–107.
Kelemen, R. (2010) 'Globalizing European Union Environmental Policy', *Journal of European Public Policy* 17(3): 335–349.
Kilian, B. and Elgström, O. (2010) 'Still a Green Leader? The European Union's Role in International Climate Negotiations', *Cooperation and Conflict* 45(3): 255–273.
Kissling-Näf, I. and Kuks, S. (2004) *The Evolution of National Water Regimes in Europe: Transitions in Water Rights and Water Policies*, New York: Springer.
Klok, J. (2002) *Negotiating EU CO2/Energy Taxation. Political Economic Driving Forces and Barriers*, Copenhagen: AKF Forlaget.
Knill, C. and Liefferink, D. (2007) *Environmental Politics in the European Union: Policy-making, Implementation and Patterns of Multilevel Governance*, Manchester: Manchester University Press.
Knill, C. and Tosun, J. (2009) 'Hierarchy, Networks, or Markets: How Does the EU Shape Environmental Policy Adoptions within and beyond its Borders?', *Journal of European Public Policy* 16(6): 873–894.
Mazzanti, M. and Montini, A. (2009) *Waste and Environmental Policy*, London: Routledge.

Mitchell, R.B. (2012) *International Environmental Agreements Database Project, 2002–2012*. Online. Available at: http://iea.uoregon.edu/ (accessed 27 May 2012).
Oberthür, S. and Ott, H. (1999) *The Kyoto Protocol: International Climate Policy for the 21st Century*, New York: Springer.
Oberthür, S. and Roche, C. (2008) 'EU Leadership in International Climate Policy: Achievements and Challenges', *The International Spectator* 43(3): 35–50.
O'Neill, K. (2004) 'Globalization and Hazardous Waste Management: From Brown to Green?', in D. Vogel and R. Kagan (eds) *Dynamics of Regulatory Change: How Globalization Affects National Regulatory Policies*, Berkeley: University of California Press.
Porter, G. and Brown, J.W. (1991) *Global Environmental Politics*, Boulder, CO: Westview Press.
Schreurs, M. and Tiberghien, Y. (2007) 'Multi-level Reinforcement: Explaining European Union Leadership in Climate Change Mitigation', *Global Environmental Politics* 7(4): 19–46.
Shibata, T. (1989) 'The Influence of Big Industries on Environmental Policies: The Case of Car Exhaust Standards', in S. Tsuru and H. Weidner (eds) *Environmental Policy in Japan*, Berlin: Edition Sigma.
Siebenhüner, B. (2011) 'Transboundary Science for Transnational Air Pollution Policies in Europe', in R. Lidskog and G. Sundqvist (eds) *Governing the Air. Science–Policy–Citizens Dynamics in International Environmental Governance*, Cambridge: MIT Press.
Sjöstedt, G. (1998) 'The EU Negotiates Climate Change', *Cooperation and Conflict* 33(3): 227–256.
Timilsina, G. and Dulal, H. (2009) 'Regulatory Instruments to Control Environmental Externalities from the Transport Sector', *European Transport* 41: 80–112.
Vogel, D. and Swinnen, J. (2011) *Transatlantic Regulatory Cooperation: The Shifting Roles of the EU, the US and California*, Cheltenham: Edward Elgar.
Vogler, J. and Stephan, H. (2007) 'The European Union in Global Environmental Governance', *International Environmental Agreements* 7(4): 389–413.
Wettestad, J. (2000) 'The Complicated Development of EU Climate Policy', in J. Gupta and M. Grubb (eds) *Climate Change and European Leadership: A Sustainable Role for Europe?*, Dordrecht: Kluwer Academic.
Yamin, F. (2000) 'The Role of the EU in Climate Negotiations', in J. Gupta and M. Grubb (eds) *Climate Change and European Leadership: A Sustainable Role for Europe?*, Dordrecht: Kluwer Academic.
Yandle, B. and Buck, S. (2002) 'Bootleggers, Baptists, and the Global Warming Battle', *The Harvard Environmental Law Review* 26(1): 177–229.

8 Transport policy
EU as a taker, shaper or shaker of the global civil aviation regime?

Marcin Dąbrowski

1 Introduction

Transport policy was mentioned as a community policy already in the Treaty of Rome, announcing the creation of a common transport market to complement economic integration (Dempsey 2004). However, the development of this policy stalled until the mid-1980s. This was due to the fact that integration was hampered by the national governments' divergent philosophies of transport policy (harmonization vs. liberalization, state-led vs. market-led), especially with successive enlargements of the Community. In the wake of the acceleration of the process of European integration with the launch of the Single Market and also in response to the increase in international transport intensity, the policy started developing rapidly from the mid-1980s onwards (Stevens 2004; Kerwer and Teutsch 2001).

For the purpose of this chapter, we shall focus on the air transport subfield of the EU transport policy which is particularly relevant from the global perspective owing to the international implications of civil aviation and the significant overlap between the international and EU norms. While the EU maritime transport policy may have similar properties, other subfields of EU transport policy – such as inland transport or Trans-European Networks – are essentially inward-focused and irrelevant from the global governance perspective. By contrast, most of the continuously increasing air traffic is international, which implies the need for the coordination of aviation policies through an international regime. The interactions among the EU and the international organizations dealing with aviation illustrate well the complexity of the patterns of cross-level dynamics of norm export and import. Moreover, what makes air transport a particularly relevant and interesting case for examining these dynamics is the recent rapid expansion of the functional scope of the EU air transport policy, despite the existence of a well-developed international system of norms and standards. This results in an intensification of the interactions between the air transport international organizations and the EU, as the EU is becoming an increasingly important international player and is keen to exert an influence on the global aviation policy regime.

EU air transport policy, like other subfields of the common transport policy, remained dormant until the mid-1980s when it gained considerable impetus, leading to the establishment of a single air transport market, legislation on issues such as air traffic management, safety, security and environment protection, and climate change mitigation, and the development of the external dimension of this policy with the ambition to export the EU norms to third countries and the international arena. The EU is a latecomer when it comes to aviation policy, with the national and international regimes having developed several decades earlier; however, the recent rapid development of the community rules on aviation and the increase of its activeness at the international level have been remarkable. The EU remains an importer of international norms into its air transport policy, but at the same time it attempts to shape their development and export its own standards. While the EU's considerable market power and reputation for expertise in the technical aspects of aviation policy are important assets, the capacity for export of EU norms to the international level is hampered by several obstacles. These include the lack of membership in the main international organization in the field of aviation – the International Civil Aviation Organization (ICAO); cleavages with the major international players (e.g. the United States); and reluctance on the part of the EU Member States for greater involvement of the European Commission at the international level. Trying to overcome these obstacles, the EU strives to export its rules to ICAO using various mechanisms, from bold attempts at shaping the global rules through the use of its market power, tough bargaining and conditionality, to the discreet export of technical standards through persuasion. Even though to date the vertical export of EU aviation norms has been moderate, the EU has used conditionality to shake up the status quo concerning the global approach to tackling aviation emissions and there is some evidence of successful vertical export of the less politically controversial technical aspects of the EU aviation *acquis*. The conditions for horizontal export are more favourable. Since 2002 the European Commission can represent the EU in relations with third countries and the lack of membership in ICAO is irrelevant. Thus, the EU has been successfully exporting its norms to the wider European neighbourhood, taking advantage of its authority and market power while encouraging countries in other parts of the world to adopt EU aviation norms through a combination of conditionalities and 'soft' mechanisms of influence.

The chapter is structured as follows. The next section will outline the development and characteristics of the EU air transport policy. Subsequently, the chapter will map the corresponding international regime over which the EU strives to exert an influence. Finally, drawing on the data from interviews[1] conducted with the key informants in the EU and international institutions as well as from secondary sources, the chapter will analyse the interactions between the EU and the international regime. That section will shed light on the mechanisms of and conditions for the export of EU rules and will assess the outcomes of the EU's attempts at exporting its approaches and standards. The chapter will close with an assessment of the EU's capacity to shape the global aviation policy regime.

2 EU air transport policy: late start and rapid development

It is puzzling that the EU did not develop its transport policy until the mid-1980s, despite the fact that transport had been assigned a high priority in the Treaty of Rome (Kerwer and Teutsch 2001; Dempsey 2004; Stevens 2004). This peculiar trajectory of the EU transport policy may be explained to a large extent by 'the contrasting regulatory approaches and conflicting economic interests of the member states' that resulted in conflicts hampering decision-making on concrete policy issues, thwarting integration within this policy area (Kerwer and Teutsch 2001: 25). Countries such as France, Germany and Italy favoured a more interventionist approach to transport policy, seen as one of the means to achieve the goals of their regional, industrial and social policies. This led them to oppose liberalization of transport policy and defend their own approaches to regulating transport markets by promoting harmonization along their own preferences. By contrast, the Netherlands and the United Kingdom preferred a more liberal approach to transport policy, making it difficult to reach a compromise on a common transport regime, particularly given that decisions had to be taken through unanimity voting within the Council of Ministers. Under those circumstances the Member States were not keen to precisely define the objectives and substance of the common transport policy. A further factor that facilitated non-cooperation and hampered progress in the development of a common transport policy was the possibility of using bilateral or multilateral agreements as a 'fallback solution' instead of pursuing integration (Kerwer and Teutsch 2001: 27–28). Finally, a related problem was the failure of the Commission to broker compromise between the two opposed camps (Kerwer and Teutsch 2001). As a result of this failure, the Commission opted for a pragmatic approach in the 1970s and pursued several transport policy issues separately in order to develop a common transport policy incrementally; however, this shift did not help some of the Member States to overcome their reluctance to open up and liberalize their transport markets.

Nonetheless, a constellation of factors made it possible to break the deadlock and spur the rapid development of the common transport policy from the mid-1980s onwards (Kerwer and Teutsch 2001; Young and Wallace 2000). First, the paradigm shift in Europe away from Keynesianism towards neoliberalism called interventionism into question, preparing the ground for the compromise and making the more liberal 'Anglo-Saxon' model more acceptable to the major continental Member States. The second factor was the introduction of qualified majority voting within the Council of the EU when deciding on transport issues, which facilitated the development of the common transport policy despite the reservations of certain Member States. In addition, the jurisprudence of the European Court of Justice (ECJ) during the 1970s and 1980s established the foundations for the development of the transport *acquis* (Stevens 2004; Dempsey 2004; Young and Wallace 2000).[2] First, the AETR case in 1971 (Case 22/70) established the principle that the Community had competences for external relations whenever it started establishing a common policy, which meant that it was responsible for negotiating and concluding agreements on international road transport. Second, in 1974 the ECJ ruled that the general provisions of the Treaty apply to air and sea transport (*French Seamen*, Case 167/73) and that in the absence of more specific Council regulations they may be directly applied (Case 2/74). Finally, in 1985 the *Parliament vs. Council* ECJ ruling (Case 13/83) supported the European Parliament in its criticism of the Council for its failure to develop a common transport policy, despite it being mentioned in the Treaty. While the practical effects of this judgment were not particularly important (the Council was given no penalties or deadlines), it had considerable political effects providing the impetus for the development of the policy.

The development of aviation policy, in particular, followed a similar path to that of the entire common transport policy. The stage was set by the deregulation reforms in the United States and the United Kingdom in the late 1970s, which enacted a paradigm shift towards the 'Open Skies' policy involving the creation of a free market for civil aviation services (Kassim and Stevens 2010). By 1980, the United States had concluded several Air Service Agreements based on this paradigm with a number of European states (e.g. the Netherlands, Belgium and West Germany). These developments contributed to an awakening of the 'members of the EC to the rigors and opportunities of competition' which in turn fed the 'home-grown desires for reform in Britain and the Netherlands and generally produced a more favourable environment for change' (Dobson 2010: 1132). Subsequently, in 1986 the ECJ ruled against the national control of prices for air services (Nouvelles Frontieres, Cases 209–213/84), arguing that the Treaty of Rome's competition rules did apply to air transport, which opened the way for the development of EU aviation policy and liberalization of air traffic in Europe (Kassim and Stevens 2010; Stevens 2004; Dobson 2010).

Between 1987 and 1997 one could observe the gradual emergence of EU air transport policy (O'Reilly and Stone Sweet 1998; Kassim and Stevens 2010; Dempsey 2004). During this first stage of the rapid development of EU aviation policy, several legislative packages were introduced leading to the creation of the internal air market. Nevertheless, the governments of the Member States, traditionally seeing aviation as their exclusive area of competence, remained reluctant to let the European Commission develop a community policy in this area (Delreux 2011). With the introduction of these packages they saw their weight diminish; however, they continued to play an important role within the bilateral agreements and remained attached to 'patriotic interventionism'. A further major milestone was the 'Open Skies' judgments by the European Court of Justice on 5 November 2002, which reinforced the role of the European Commission as the regulator of external air transport services by giving it a mandate to negotiate with the third countries on behalf of the Member States (Woll 2006; Kassim and Stevens 2010).

The second stage of advancement of the EU aviation policy involved the growing importance of the European Commission and an emphasis on safety, security and air traffic management rules. In these domains the EU has become increasingly active if not a leading actor, despite the fact that 'establishing a role for the EC in the more technical aspects of aviation was altogether more problematic, since here the regulatory space had long been occupied by other international bodies' (Kassim and Stevens 2010: 130). In 2002 the European Aviation Safety Agency (EASA) was established, and entrusted with regulatory and executive tasks in the field of civilian aviation safety within the EU, replacing the pre-existing Joint Aviation Authorities and becoming one of the most important players both in the EU and the global aviation policy arenas. Finally, Single European Sky, an initiative intended to organize air traffic management at the European level, was established through two legislative packages in 2004 and 2009. In addition, the EU developed regulations on issues such as airport charges, protection of air passengers' rights, and environment protection, including measures to tackle greenhouse gas emissions and noise pollution.

Moreover, the external dimension of EU air transport policy has gained importance in the 2000s. The process of the establishment of the European Common Aviation Area, initiated in 2004, extends the EU influence beyond its borders, as it encompasses the neighbouring countries. In order to gain access to the EU air market, they need to comply with the entire *acquis* on aviation. The first multilateral agreement on joining the European Common Aviation Area was signed in 2005, bringing eight Southeastern European countries under the EU aviation regime. Further bilateral agreements were later signed with Georgia, Jordan, Moldova and Morocco, and plans were made to negotiate similar agreements with further countries such as Ukraine, Lebanon, Israel, Tunisia or Azerbaijan.

Last but not least, EU air transport policy has recently focused on environmental issues to a greater extent, in particular on the mitigation of climate change through the introduction of the Emissions Trading System for civil aviation in 2012. As will be argued in section 4 below, this policy has had profound international implications and has spurred vociferous opposition from the major players in global aviation. All in all, it may be argued that EU aviation policy has developed extensively, acquiring a broad functional scope ranging from air traffic management, safety issues and passenger rights to economic issues such as market access, air fares and airport regulation. The depth of the rules within this regime may be considered to be significant; the norms are detailed and specific while being legally binding. The EU aviation norms are specified in directives and regulations, and the Member States have to comply with them or face an infringement procedure.

3 The international aviation regime

The Chicago Convention,[3] signed in 1944, established a framework for bilateral agreements as a method for exchanging traffic rights, which corresponds to the principle of sovereignty. The convention put the ICAO in place as a multilateral, standard-setting body responsible for comprehensively regulating technical, safety, security and environmental issues. The norms set by the ICAO are supposed to be implemented and enforced by the national authorities of its 190 members. The ICAO Assembly comprises all the Member States and meets at least once every three years. The Assembly approves the budget of the organization and the amendments to the Chicago Convention which are then subject to ratification by Member States. The Council, elected for three-year terms and composed of 36 Member States, is elected by the Assembly and runs the daily business of the organization. Finally, the ICAO's Air Navigation Commission is the permanent expert body where the technical standards are drafted and prepared for adoption by the Council.

The functional scope of the regime governed by the Chicago Convention is broad. The Convention and its 18 Annexes cover the core of internationally accepted technical standards in such areas as safety, airworthiness, noise, emissions, and the professional qualifications of pilots and other crew members. The regime does not cover the modalities of access to foreign air transport markets, however, which are determined in bilateral or multilateral agreements. The depth of the rules set by the ICAO may be considered significant. The organization sets precise, specific and universally accepted standards, although, as will be argued below, they are developed as 'minimum standards' and in some cases are not stringent enough from the EU perspective.

Regarding enforcement, the ICAO rules are not legally binding – the signatory states have to observe the rules outlined in the Convention and its annexes, and to implement these in their national regulatory systems to make them legally binding. The ICAO plays the role of watchdog to make sure they are respected (audit programmes were introduced in 1996). Nonetheless, in practice, the 'ICAO doesn't have the teeth or the legal powers to ensure compliance' with its rules.[4] There are several other organizations that are part of the global aviation policy regime and which deserve a mention. The International Air Transport Association (IATA) brings together the vast majority of the world's airlines and has been an important player since the emergence of the global aviation regime in 1945. It represents the interests of the airlines and one of its main roles is to ensure fair competition between them while providing other services such as safety audits.

In the European regional context, EUROCONTROL, founded in 1963, gathers together 39 Member States and deals mainly with issues of organization in civil and military airspace, air navigation and air traffic management. The European Civil Aviation Conference (ECAC) is the regional forum of ICAO, established in cooperation with the Council of Europe in 1955. It comprises 44 members, including all the members of the EU and EUROCONTROL. Its purpose is to facilitate dialogue on the harmonization of civil aviation policies and it also includes an associated standard-setting body, the Joint Aviation Authorities (JAA). The latter gathered together the European civil aviation regulatory authorities cooperating on the development and implementation of common non-binding standards. Finally, the European Organization for Civil Aviation Equipment (EUROCAE), founded in 1963, is a non-profit organization providing a forum for voluntary cooperation between the European aviation stakeholders, such as producers of aircrafts and navigation equipment, air navigation service providers, airlines and airports. The organization develops standardization documents on the basis of the ICAO standards.

As a result of the rapid development of Community regulations on air transport, the EU has gradually overshadowed or changed the role of the regional organizations mentioned above. Thus, the EU has de facto replaced the European Civil Aviation Conference as the main European forum for dealing with aviation issues, while the functions of the Joint Aviation Authorities, operating under the auspices of the latter, have been taken over by the European Aviation Safety Agency (Kassim and Stevens 2010: 152). In a similar way, the development of the Single European Sky has profoundly transformed the role played by EUROCONTROL, which was drawn into the creation and implementation of the EU air traffic management system. Currently, EUROCONTROL provides the European Commission with technical support for the operation of the Single European Sky and other tasks, while being involved as a partner in the EU aviation research programme.

Table 8.1 summarizes the evolution of governance layers in air transport policy. In the decades following World War II, the nation-states were the principal shapers and movers of the global air transport regime. With the Chicago Convention and the establishment of ICAO, the basis for a global policy regime for civil aviation was put in place. This regime provides a framework for bilateral agreements between the signatory states and regulates a wide range of technical issues. By 1953, 15 Annexes had been added to the Chicago Convention, while an additional three Annexes, focused on the issues of environmental protection, security and transport of dangerous goods, were introduced between 1971 and 1984. In early 2013 the ICAO Council approved the new Annex 19 concerning safety, which is expected to be developed further in the coming years.

Table 8.1 Significance of governance levels over time (Transport Policy)

Phase	National level	EU level	Global level
Post-WWII	*High*	–	*Medium* (increasing: Chicago Convention signed in 1944 followed by 15 Annexes adopted by 1953)
1957–mid-1980s	*High*	*Low*	*Medium*
1990s	*High*	*Medium*	*Medium*
post-2000	*Medium* (2002 ECJ 'Open Skies' ruling)	*Medium* (increasing: creation of the European Aviation Safety Agency, the Single Sky, and the European Common Aviation Area agreement with the US in 2007)	*Medium*
2020 (extrapolation)	*Medium*	*High*	*Medium*

The EU was therefore a latecomer in this area. However, over time the situation evolved with a growing importance of the European institutions at the expense of the national governments since the 1980s. Through the introduction of liberalization and an increasing number of aviation safety and air traffic management rules, as well as the mandate for negotiating air service agreements on behalf of its Member States, the EU has become an increasingly relevant governance layer for air transport, eroding the relevance of the national governments. Moreover, the EU continues to expand its air transport *acquis* and is increasingly involved in cooperation with ICAO and third countries, while striving to become an exporter of aviation norms.

4 EU interaction with the corresponding global regime

As the aviation subfield in the common transport policy has developed swiftly since the mid-1980s, the EU has become increasingly involved in the global arena with its areas of competences overlapping those of the ICAO (see Table 8.2). While continuing to strategically import international norms into its legislation, it actively seeks to export its policy both through vertical and horizontal channels.

4.1 Importing ICAO norms to strengthen enforcement and harmonization in the EU

Historically, the EU has been an importer of international rules on air transport. The ideas for a common aviation policy have 'trickled down' from ICAO to the European Commission (Stevens 2004), while EU legislation on the liberalization of air transport services has been inspired to a large extent by the liberalization reforms in the US and the UK. Thus, the bulk of EU legislation on aviation is based on the Annexes to the Chicago Convention.

One example of the import of the ICAO's norms to the EU legislation is in the domain of air traffic services (navigation, air traffic management, flight information, etc.). Thus, the EU has transposed Annex 2 (Rules of the Air) as well as parts of Annex 11 (Air Traffic Services) of the Chicago Convention, and there are plans for the future transposition of Annexes 3 (Meteorological Service for International Air Navigation), parts of Annex 10, and Annex 15 (Aeronautical Information Services).[5] The EU is eager to transpose the international legislation because it allows for ensuring greater harmonization across Europe.[6]

Table 8.2 Overlaps of authority in standard-setting across the levels of governanc

Issue area	International level	EU level	National level
Market access	–	+	+
Technical standards	+	+	–
Safety and security	+	+	–
Environment protection	+	+	–

When transposed into EU directives, the EU Member States have a very strong incentive to comply in order to avoid breaching EU law which could involve opening a case in the European Court of Justice. Thus, the EU is in effect the enforcer of ICAO rules among its Member States, even though in practice the transposition of EU air transport *acquis* into domestic legislation has tended to be laborious (Keading 2008). In addition, since the signing of the EU–ICAO Memorandum of Cooperation in 2010, the European Aviation Safety Agency has been conducting inspections of the implementation of international safety standards in the EU Member States of behalf of the ICAO.

As a result of this import of ICAO norms, the policy fit between the international aviation standards and the EU *acquis* in this matter may be qualified as generally high, albeit in some cases the pattern is different. The EU judges some of the ICAO rules as too lax, as illustrated by the case of the Aeronautical Data Quality, and decides to use those rules as a baseline for defining its own more stringent standards to be applied in the EU and European Common Aviation Area. In fact, the ICAO rules have to be acceptable and enforceable across its 191 Member States, whose capacity to comply with high-level standards varies dramatically. By contrast, in the case of climate change mitigation, the position of the EU differs substantially from that of the ICAO and most of the main national players in international air transport, which pushes the EU to attempt to protect its policy by exporting its norms using both vertical and horizontal pathways, as will be discussed in one of the following sections.

4.2 The mechanisms of export of EU rules: the EU as a shaker or discreet shaper of the international aviation policy?

4.2.1 Conditions for vertical export

The EU's technical expertise on aviation matters and its considerable market size place it in a strong position in the international air transport regime; however, its status as a latecomer and the lack of full membership in the ICAO constrain its capacity for the vertical export of its aviation norms. As Kassim and Stevens argued, 'The EU's relationship with ICAO is marked by a pronounced mismatch between the Community's importance as a regulatory authority and its formal standing' (Kassim and Stevens 2010: 159).

Since 1989, the European Community has had the status of observer at the ICAO Assembly, its committees, technical panels and study groups. The status of observer implies the right to speak only in certain circumstances. When invited by the ICAO Council, the observers may participate in the Council meetings in areas where they have a special interest. The Commission argues that the EU's powers and responsibilities in the field of air transport correspond to practically all the issues within the ICAO's remit and that it is a major financial contributor to ICAO technical cooperation programmes.[7] Gaining the status of member by a regional integration organization such as the EU would require revision of the Chicago Convention which limits the membership to states. This in turn would require a two-thirds majority vote in the Assembly, and is therefore difficult to achieve.

A further obstacle for vertical export is the reluctance of the EU Member States to delegate external competences to the European Commission, resulting in tensions (Delreux 2011: 115). In fact, they remain important players in the external dimension of aviation policy, being members of the ICAO, having bilateral Air Service Agreements with a range of third countries[8] and supporting their national air transport operators. The EU Member States also resist the idea of EU membership in the ICAO. In 2002, the Commission issued a recommendation to be authorized to open and conduct negotiations with the ICAO; however, to date, the Member States have not taken any action in that direction. In addition, even as the EU progressively achieved a greater level of domestic harmonization of its transport policy, certain divisions among the EU Member States remained.[9] Accordingly, a lack of unity can weaken the position of the EU in bilateral and multilateral negotiations. As an interviewee from DG Move maintained, 'the lack of cohesiveness is a handicap and on external front we still have difficulties in punching in our weight, which economically is very high'.[10] By contrast, the EU's main competitor in shaping the global aviation norms, the United States, is far more unified and does not face internal coordination issues.

That being said, the Commission de facto ensures coordination of positions of the EU Member States for the purpose of ICAO dealings.[11] This requires tough intra-EU bargaining through which the Commission seeks to foster a common EU position.[12] As EU legislation on aviation developed, the Member States gradually accepted the idea to concede competence to the Community at the international level (Stevens 2004: 168). Thus, a consensus emerged among the EU Member States to strengthen the position of the EU in the ICAO via informal arrangements and the activity of the EU Representative to the ICAO established in Montreal in 2005. The Representative plays a crucial role in promoting the interests of the EU through informal consultations with the ICAO's Council and expert bodies.

Therefore, while the chances for the EU to become a fully fledged ICAO member remain slim given the said reluctance of the Member States to support the EU in its efforts in this respect, the EU does manage to overcome this limitation and exert a certain degree of influence within the ICAO, thanks to effective internal coordination and informal interactions.

4.2.2 Shaking up the status quo: the case of the emissions trading system

The EU has also employed its bargaining and market power in an attempt to export its norms both vertically to the international level and horizontally to third countries, as illustrated by its bold unilateral decision to extend the EU Emissions Trading System to the aviation sector.

In 2005 the EU introduced a 'cap and trade' system aimed at reducing greenhouse gas emissions that contribute to climate change. This involved putting a 'cap' on the total amount of emissions by various branches of the industry, while granting companies a certain number of emission allowances that they can then sell or, if needed, buy from another company. If a company exceeds the total emissions as defined in its allowances for a given year, it faces heavy fines. By contrast, if a company emits fewer greenhouse gases than it was allotted, it can sell its spare allowances to another company. Over time, the amount of allowances granted is set to be reduced to favour of a gradual decrease in emissions.

The extension of the system to aviation has been justified by the fact that the growing air traffic increasingly contributes to greenhouse gas emissions. As of 1 January 2012, all domestic and international passenger, cargo and non-commercial flights that arrive at or depart from an EU airport are covered by the Emissions Trading System, regardless of the country of origin of the airline. The operators that do not comply face hefty fines and, ultimately, they may be banned from operating within the EU.

Although since 2001 ICAO has endorsed the development of open emissions trading for international aviation, little progress has been achieved in developing the relevant legislation on this issue beyond 'symbolic' measures (Oberthür 2006). This has resulted in a growing frustration of the EU, which has committed itself to an ambitious programme of reduction of its greenhouse gas emissions to at least 20 per cent below 1990 levels by 2020. Since the EU's efforts to stimulate the work on the global aviation emissions trading system within the ICAO through persuasion have failed – not least due to the lack of international appeal of the EU Emmission Trading Scheme as a successful policy model – it decided to 'go it alone'. The EU unilaterally extended the controversial Emissions Trading System, which aimed at providing a model for the use of emissions trading worldwide and thus to form the basis for wider global action,[13] while creating a strong incentive for the third countries to adopt measures to reduce climate change impacts.

At the same time, however, the EU declared openness for negotiation and flexibility by leaving the possibility of exemption from the scheme for countries that adopt similar or equivalent measures to reduce emissions (Euractiv 2012a), therefore encouraging them to take action and follow the EU's example. In addition, the Commission declared readiness to amend its legislation on the Emissions Trading System should an international multilateral agreement on curbing aviation emissions emerge within the ICAO.[14]

The measure created internal tensions within the European Commission, with the Directorate-General for Mobility and Transport (DG Move) opposing it and fearing that such a bold action would disrupt bilateral relations with the major players in the global aviation market and complicate negotiations within ICAO.[15] Nonetheless, the position of the Directorate-General for Climate Action, who championed the Emissions Trading System, prevailed.

The EU's move towards the extension of the Emissions Trading System to aviation indeed stirred discontent among third countries whose operators were forced into the system (Euractiv 2011) and altered the global preference constellations, as an alliance of several countries – including the United States, India,

China, Russia and Brazil – emerged to jointly protest against the EU's unilateral action. Given this strong opposition from the major air transport players as well as criticism from the ICAO Council,[16] it remains to be seen whether the imposition of Emissions Trading System aviation will result in a successful export of the EU model. However, by doing so, the EU has clearly managed to put this issue on the global agenda and stimulated the ICAO to take action.[17] The issue was put on the agenda of the 2013 ICAO Assembly session[18] and the organization has committed itself to speeding up progress on the development of a global solution for tackling aviation emissions.[19] In order to mitigate the widespread discontent about the EU Emissions Trading System and offer a gesture of goodwill in support of fostering a consensus on a global solution via the ICAO, the European Commission announced in November 2012 that it would defer the application of the scheme to third country operators until after the ICAO Assembly session in autumn 2013. At the same time, however, the Commission uses conditionality to put pressure on the ICAO and the United States that oppose Europe's proposals (Euractiv 2012b), by stressing that in case of a lack of progress towards the global aviation emissions solution, the EU scheme would again be applied in full to third country airlines, thus complementing the 'carrot' with a 'stick'. For the EU, a satisfactory agreement within the ICAO should include caps on emissions similar to or greater than those imposed under the EU scheme, to be non-discriminatory for all airlines and to include target measures for ICAO members.[20]

4.2.3 Using persuasion and technical expertise for the discreet vertical export of the EU rules

The EU has developed top-level technical expertise in issues of safety or air traffic management and 'is listened to on technical issues when preparing standards'.[21] This enables it to play the role of a discreet shaper of the international technical standards through persuasion. Thus, ICAO relies on the expertise of the European Aviation Safety Agency and EUROCONTROL. Since its establishment in 2002, the European Aviation Safety Agency has become a widely recognized authority in matters of aviation safety and actively involved in the design of international norms. The Agency provides the ICAO with recommendations on safety issues on behalf of the EU and exerts an influence on its regulations indirectly through coordination of the EU Member States' replies to the State Letters, in which feedback on regulations in development is requested. Thus, while it is difficult to point to a concrete example of a norm put forward by the European Aviation Safety Agency that was later adopted by the ICAO, a number of ICAO standards were based on the input from the EU Member States, which in turn reflected the recommendations of the Agency.[22] Moreover, the Agency actively participated in the ICAO's work on the new Annex to the Chicago Convention on safety (Annex 19).[23]

In addition, the Memorandum of Cooperation between the ICAO and the EU, signed in 2010, enabled the European Commission to reply to the State Letters, a right previously reserved for the nation-states being party to the Chicago Convention. However, in practice, replies to technical issues are delegated to the European Aviation Safety Agency. As part of a working arrangement accompanying the Memorandum of Cooperation, the ICAO also committed itself to promoting the use of European Coordination Centre for Accident and Incident Reporting Systems (ECCAIRS) among its Member States.[24] This software was designed for collecting, sharing and analysing transport safety information developed by the European Commission, yet another example of the export of EU technical solutions to the global level.

Further examples include the vertical export of EU air traffic management standards through persuasion on the basis of working-level cooperation within the ICAO. The EU pushed for changes in Annex 15 to the Chicago Convention that would accommodate its preferences concerning Aeronautical Data Quality.[25] This involved using EUROCONTROL for exerting an indirect EU influence on the work on the amendments to Annex 15. As a result, some of the provisions of the European Commission's Regulation[26] on the requirements for the quality of aeronautical data and aeronautical information for the Single European Sky became the basis for changes in ICAO regulations in this field.[27] Another example of the vertical export of EU technical standards through cooperation and persuasion concerns the Single European Sky Air Traffic Management Research (SESAR), an EU research and development project implemented as part of the Single European Sky initiative. SESAR aims at fostering interoperability between air traffic management systems that could provide the basis for the creation of a 'single global sky'. This is where the interests of the EU and ICAO converge: the EU has a stake in exporting SESAR, while the ICAO welcomes the technical input from the EU and the opportunity to draw on its experience to develop global interoperability in air traffic management.[28] Furthermore, the EU cooperates closely with the US on aviation research in order to align SESAR and its American equivalent, NextGen. The ICAO invited both SESAR and NextGen to help modernize its Global Air Navigation Plan and the so-called Aviation System Block Upgrade, which was discussed at the 12th ICAO Air Navigation Conference in November 2012.

In sum, while there is no evidence of a widespread export of EU rules to the international level, the EU is capable of shaping the technical aspects of the global aviation standards through cooperation on the working level and informal influence on the process of elaboration of international norms. This influence is possible despite the unfavourable conditions for vertical export because of the recognition of European expertise in the technical matters of safety and air traffic management.[29]

4.2.4 The dynamics of horizontal export

The conditions for the horizontal export of the EU air transport norms are more favourable than for vertical export where the EU's capacity is limited by the lack of ICAO membership. Horizontal export of EU norms is supported by its strong normative capabilities underpinned by its widely recognized technical expertise in matters of safety and air traffic management, which favours the export of its aviation norms to the third countries. It is also facilitated by the considerable bargaining power the EU has vis-à-vis third countries wanting their airlines to operate in the European market. Thanks to these two assets and to the use of different strategies for export and influence, the EU has positioned itself as a successful exporter of aviation standards to the countries of the wider European area and beyond, even though globally it has a powerful competitor – the United States.

4.2.4.1 COMPETING WITH THE UNITED STATES

Ever since the EU emerged as a major player in aviation policy, it has been competing with the US international influence and export of policy norms and technical standards,[30] as illustrated, for instance, by the cleavages concerning the norms on noise pollution (Stevens 2004: 168). This competition is also underpinned by the rivalry between European and American businesses,[31] epitomized by the rivalry between Airbus and Boeing, but also affecting airlines and a range of subsectors of the aerospace industry. Both the EU and the United States have their 'zones of influence' where they manage to export their aviation norms. For example, Israel has adopted United States safety rules owing to its special strategic relationship with the United States, while the Mediterranean countries or India, for instance, tend to opt for the EU safety standards.[32] Nonetheless, aside from these clashes of interests there is also ongoing cooperation between the EU and the US aviation authorities, chiefly in the fields of air traffic management and safety, aimed at fostering interoperability and devising common technical solutions.

4.2.4.2 HORIZONTAL EXPORT THROUGH CONDITIONALITY: THE EUROPEAN COMMON AVIATION AREA AND THE 'AVIATION SAFETY LIST'

One of the strategies for promoting the adoption of EU aviation norms by third countries is conditionality upon access to the EU air transport market. The European Common Aviation Area has proven to be a particularly effective means of direct horizontal export of the aviation regulations and standards to the neighbouring countries. In order to become a member of the European Common Aviation Area, the third countries have to transpose the entire *acquis communautaire* concerning aviation into their domestic legislation. The European Common Aviation Area agreement includes Southeastern (Albania, Bosnia and Herzegovina, Croatia, the former Yugoslav Republic of Macedonia, Montenegro, Serbia, Kosovo) and Northern European countries (Norway and Iceland), for which operations in the EU market are of prime economic importance. The EU plans to further expand the European Common Aviation Area to the Mediterranean as well as Eastern Europe, Black Sea countries, the Middle East and Central Asia

(DG Move 2011). For instance, in 2010 an agreement providing for gradual integration within the area had been signed with Jordan.[33] At the time of writing, initial agreements have been signed with Moldova, Georgia and Morocco, while negotiations were ongoing with countries such as Ukraine or Turkey.[34]

The EU also promotes alignment with its safety standards through the 'Aviation Safety List'.[35] The list is based on a periodic review of the international carriers for their compliance with the European Aviation Safety Agency's standards. In case of non-compliance an airline cannot operate flights into EU airports. The list is a political instrument creating a strong incentive for adopting EU norms in order to gain access to the lucrative European market.[36]

4.2.4.3 HORIZONTAL EXPORT THROUGH TECHNICAL ASSISTANCE PROGRAMMES

Apart from using conditionalities, the EU also resorts to persuasion and specific incentives to promote the adoption of its norms and standards in countries in other parts of the world, where it has less leverage than in its immediate neighbourhood. The European Aviation Safety Agency builds up an increasing international presence, with representation offices being set up in Beijing, Washington and Montreal. The Agency's representations are instrumental in promoting the harmonization of safety and air traffic management systems based on EU standards through soft mechanisms of persuasion.[37] Furthermore, these efforts are actively supported by the 'behind the scenes' activity of the European aviation industry. This may be illustrated by the support of the European Organization for Civil Aviation Equipment (EUROCAE) in promoting the standardization of aviation systems.[38] Another example is the activity of Airbus intensely lobbying for harmonization according to European standards, competing with its rival, Boeing, which favours instead the diffusion of American standards. Airbus has, for instance, been actively involved in negotiations with China, where it has established production plants and sees opportunities stemming from the rapidly developing air market.[39]

The technical assistance programmes funded by the European Commission play a key role in the horizontal export of EU standards.[40] They involve the provision of funding for administrative capacity-building within the administration dealing with aviation and deployment of EU experts providing guidance and training. This assistance is offered mainly to neighbouring countries, but also to developing countries in other regions. For example, the EU–Asia Civil Aviation Cooperation Project, totalling €30 million and including 15 countries of the region, provided training and assistance for the regional harmonization of legislation with a view to supporting regulatory convergence based on European standards. Similar projects were also undertaken in collaboration with China and India. For instance, EU–India cooperation has developed incrementally since 1999 (Wülbers 2011). The first initiative was a civil aviation cooperation project running between 1999 and 2006, covering issues such as safety, environmental protection, industrial cooperation and air traffic management. Building on the success of this project, a further technical assistance programme started in 2007, enhancing the capacity of the Indian aviation authority and paving the way for a horizontal agreement between the EU and India in 2008.

EU norms are also exported horizontally through passive mechanisms. In fact, the widespread recognition of the European expertise in aviation matters pushes many third countries to emulate EU standards even without specific EU pressure to do so. This is illustrated by the strong interest of India or sub-Saharan African countries in adopting the European Aviation Safety Agency's technical norms for the purpose of the modernization of their aviation regulations.[41] Likewise, Singapore has expressed interest in copying the elements of the SESAR system and making its system interoperable with the European one.[42]

5 Conclusion

Historically, the EU has been a latecomer when it comes to aviation policy and has been importing international standards. Nonetheless, this has changed dramatically over time. Since the mid-1980s, the EU has been rapidly developing its aviation policy to establish a comprehensive regime covering practically all aspects of air transport. The ICAO norms are still being imported into the European policy and are the baseline for the development of EU regulations; however, the European Commission used this import strategically to enforce compliance and harmonization across the EU and, in some cases, developed the ICAO rules further to foster higher standards. Despite the unfavourable conditions for the vertical export of European aviation norms, such as lack of full membership in the ICAO or the tensions between the European Commission and the Member States, the EU has undeniably been able to influence the global aviation policy regime at least in its technical dimension. While there is no evidence of a widespread vertical export of EU aviation norms to the ICAO, the EU has managed to export some of its technical standards and tools through expert input into the preparation of ICAO norms, persuasion and diplomacy.

The EU has been more successful at exporting its aviation policy horizontally, particularly within the wider European neighbourhood through conditionality mechanisms, but also to other countries through soft mechanisms of influence. Finally, as illustrated by the case of the EU's Emission Trading Scheme, the EU does not hesitate to shake up the global policy regime through bold unilateral action to promote its vision and policy solutions, even if this method of export antagonizes many of the key global aviation players, and its outcome remains unclear.

The EU is as much a taker as a shaper and even a shaker of the global air transport policy. It continues to import the ICAO standards for the purpose of their effective enforcement and harmonization among its Member States, but it also plays an increasingly important role in the global governance of air transport. It has shown a growing capability for the vertical export of its technical norms to the ICAO, while making use of its considerable market power and normative capabilities to effectively export its aviation policy horizontally.

Notes

1. Semi-structured interviews were conducted in the European Commission's Directorate General Move and EUROCONTROL in Brussels in April 2012.
2. For a more detailed discussion of the role of the ECJ rulings for the development of the common transport policy, see Chapter 3 in the monograph by Stevens (2004: 47–65) or Chapter IV in that by Dempsey (2001: 29–36).
3. The text of the Chicago Convention is available at: www.icao.int/publications/pages/doc7300.aspx (accessed 24 July 2012).
4. Interview 5, DG Move, 25 April 2012.
5. Interview 2, EUROCONTROL, 24 April 2012.
6. Interview 1, DG Move, 23 April 2012.
7. For example, since 2001, the European Commission has allocated €3.7 million to ICAO-led Cooperative Development of Operational Safety and Continuing Airworthiness Programs (COSCAPs).
8. Interview 4, DG Move, 25 April 2012.
9. Interview 5, DG Move, 25 April 2012.
10. Interview 5, DG Move, 25 April 2012.
11. Interview 5, DG Move, 25 April 2012.
12. Interview 5, DG Move, 25 April 2012.
13. Directive 2008/101/EC of the European Parliament and of the Council of 19 November 2008 amending Directive 2003/87/EC so as to include aviation activities in the scheme for greenhouse gas emission allowance trading within the Community.
14. See: http://ec.europa.eu/clima/policies/transport/aviation/index_en.htm (accessed 16 November 2012).
15. Interview 1, DG Move, 24 April 2012.
16. See the ICAO's working paper on the EU ETS scheme, C-WP/13790, 17 October 2011: www.ainalerts.com/ainalerts/alertimages/ICAO.pdf (accessed 24 July 2012).
17. Interview 3, EUROCONTROL, 24 April 2012.
18. Ibid.
19. See, for example, www.ainonline.com/aviation-news/aviation-international-news/2011-09-30/icao-moves-forward-global-co2-emissions (accessed 24 July 2012).
20. See: http://ec.europa.eu/clima/policies/transport/aviation/index_en.htm (accessed 16 November 2007).
21. Interview 3, EUROCONTROL, 24 April 2012.
22. Interview 1, DG Move, 23 April 2012.
23. Interview 1, DG Move, 23 April 2012.
24. For more information see: http://ec.europa.eu/transport/air/single_european_sky/doc/2011-09-21-icao-memorandum.pdf (accessed 24 July 2012).
25. Interview 2, EUROCONTROL, 24 April 2012.
26. EC 73/2010.
27. Interview 2, EUROCONTROL, 24 April 2012.
28. Interview 1, DG Move, 23 April 2012; Interview 3, EUROCONTROL, 24 April 2012. See also the Address by the President of the Council of the ICAO to the European Civil Aviation Conference (Strasbourg, 10 July 2012): http://legacy.icao.int/icao/en/pres/kobeh/20120710_pres_speech_2012_ecac_en.pdf (accessed 31 July 2012).
29. Interview 3, EUROCONTROL, 24 April 2012.
30. Interview 1, DG Move, 23 April 2012.
31. Interview 1, EUROCONTROL, 24 April 2012.
32. Interview 4, DG Move, 24 April 2012.
33. See: http://europa.eu/rapid/pressReleasesAction.do?reference=IP/10/292&format=HTML&aged=0&language=EN (accessed 16 November 2012).
34. Interview 1, DG Move, 23 April 2012.

35 For an up-to-date Aviation Safety List see: http://ec.europa.eu/transport/air-ban/list_en.htm.
36 Interview 4, DG Move, 25 April 2012.
37 Interview 4, DG Move, 24 April 2012.
38 Interview 2, EUROCONTROL, 24 April 2012.
39 Interview 4, DG Move, 24 April 2012.
40 Interview 4, DG Move, 24 April 2012.
41 Interview 1, DG Move, 23 April 2012.
42 Interview 1, DG Move, 23 April 2012; Interview 4, DG Move, 24 April 2012.

References

Delreux, T. (2011) 'The Relation between the European Commission and the EU Member States in the Transatlantic Open Skies Negotiations: An Analysis of their Opportunities and Constraints', *Journal of Transatlantic Studies* 9(2): 113–135.

Dempsey, P.S. (2004) *European Aviation Law*, The Hague: Kluwer.

DG Move (2011) *The EU and its Neighbouring Regions: A Renewed Approach to Transport Cooperation. COM(2011) 415*. Brussels: European Commission (7 July 2011). Online. Available at: http://eur-lex.europa.eu/LexUriServ/LexUriServ.do?uri=COM:2011:0415:FIN:EN:PDF (accessed 9 April 2013).

Dobson, A. (2010) 'Civil Aviation and European Integration: Creating the Seemingly Impossible SEAM', *Journal of Common Market Studies* 48(4): 1127–1147.

Euractiv (2011) *Airline Emissions Row Escalates Ahead of EU Ruling*, 31 July 2012. Online. Available at: www.euractiv.com/transport/airline-emissions-row-escalates-news-509852 (accessed 9 April 2013).

—— (2012a) *EU–Chinese Carbon Market Contacts Intensifying*, 4 March 2013. Online. Available at: www.euractiv.com/climate-environment/eu-chinese-carbon-market-contact-news-513120 (accessed 9 April 2013).

—— (2012b) *Hedegaard Stops Clock on Aviation Emissions Law*, 16 November 2012. Online. Available at: www.euractiv.com/climate-environment/hedegaard-stops-clock-airlines-e-news-515994 (accessed 9 April 2013).

Kassim, H. and Stevens, H. (2010) *Air Transport and the European Union. Europeanization and its Limits*, Basingstoke: Palgrave Macmillan.

Keading, M. (2008) 'Lost in Translation or Full Steam Ahead. The Transposition of EU Transport Directives across Member States', *European Union Politics* 9(1): 115–143.

Kerwer, D. and Teutsch, M. (2001) 'Transport Policy in the European Union', in A. Héritier, C. Knill, D. Lehmkuhl, M. Teutsch and A-C. Douillet (eds) *Differential Europe. The European Union Impact on National Policymaking*, Lanham, MD: Rowman & Littlefield.

O'Reilly, D. and Stone Sweet, A. (1998) 'The Liberalization and Reregulation of Air Transport', *Journal of European Public Policy* 5(3): 447–466.

Oberthür, S. (2006) 'The Climate Change Regime: Interactions with ICAO, IMO, and the EU Burden-Sharing Agreement', in S. Oberthür and T. Gehring (eds) *Institutional Interaction in Global Environmental Governance. Synergy and Conflict among International and EU Policies*, Cambridge, MA: MIT Press.

Stevens, H. (2004) *Transport Policy in the European Union*, Basingstoke: Palgrave Macmillan.

Woll, C. (2006) 'The Road to External Representation: The European Commission's Activism in International Air Transport', *Journal of European Public Policy* 13(1): 52–69.

Wülbers, S.A. (2011) *The Paradox of EU–India Relations Missed Opportunities in Politics, Economics, Development Cooperation, and Culture*, Plymouth: Lexington Books.

Young, A.R. and Wallace, H.S. (2000) *Regulatory Politics in the European Union: Weighing Civic and Producer Interests*, Manchester: Manchester University Press.

9 Migration policy
An ambiguous EU role in specifying and spreading international refugee protection norms

Florian Trauner

1 Introduction

This chapter explores the EU's role as a global policy exporter in the field of migration. Policy-making in the area seeks to find answers to questions that are among the most polarized and disputed ones in contemporary Europe. It comes therefore as no surprise that the nature and extent of European involvement has been contested both among practitioners and in academic circles (see e.g. Geddes and Boswell 2011; Guiraudon 2000; Guild and van Selm 2005).

EU migration policy consists of three constituting elements (Geddes 2000: 28). The first category includes laws regulating the free movement of EU citizens within the single market. The second concerns immigration and asylum, and outlines the rights and duties of non-EU citizens – referred to as third country nationals (TCNs) – when entering and staying in the EU. Finally, there is a range of immigrant and integration provisions that seek to improve the integration of migrants in their new environments and societies. The latter category also includes the combating of discrimination based on race, ethnicity and religion – a policy of relevance for both EU citizens and third country nationals.

This chapter starts by giving an overview of the development and key features of the EU migration policy. This is followed by an elaboration of the international governance layer in the field and the EU's interactions with it. In the immigration field the EU has become a relevant rule exporter, yet this rule export has had a strong regional focus and implication due to the fact that there is no corresponding 'global' regime (Fargues 2011; Aleinikoff 2007; Hollifield 1998). Accordingly, the research on the role of the EU as a global policy exporter focuses on the asylum subfield, where such a regime exists in the form of the global refugee protection regime.

2 Overview of EU migration policy and corresponding international regimes

In EU terminology and law, the migratory movement of EU citizens within Europe is no longer considered as 'migration' but as 'free movement of persons' – a fundamental right guaranteed by EU treaties. In the founding treaties of the

European Economic Community (EEC), this right was meant to be given only to a particular sector of the population – namely workers able to sustain themselves in their destination countries. Since the 1970s, the rulings of the European Court of Justice have played a decisive rule in broadening the 'free movement of workers' to a 'free movement of persons' (Koikkalainen 2011). In addition, European politicians displayed a will to deepen the possibilities for free movement and reduce travel restrictions within Europe. This was most clearly reflected by the Schengen free-border project, launched as an intergovernmental cooperation project in 1985. This project provided an important 'blueprint' (Ucarer 2002) for European cooperation in immigration and asylum – subfields that deal with non-EU citizens having entered or who are seeking to enter the EU's territory.

2.1 The development of EU immigration and asylum policy

In the Schengen cooperation, political actors linked the downgrading of internal frontiers control to the necessity of strengthening the external border control policies. Cooperation on immigration and asylum, policies hitherto strictly reserved for the national governance layer, started to enter the European level. The 'compensatory measures' of the 1990 Schengen Implementing Convention entailed common screening mechanisms at the external borders for third country nationals and included rules on how to deal with asylum seekers and refugees arriving in or moving around the Community territory. In 1990, the Member States adopted the 'Convention determining the state responsible for examining the application for asylum lodged in one of the Member States of the European Community'. This Convention laid the basis for the EU's Dublin system that determines the state responsible for assessing an asylum application in the Union and allows for the transfer of the applicant to that state (Kaunert and Léonard 2011).

The Amsterdam Treaty (1999) provided the EU with legal competences by incorporating the Schengen rules and regulations into the EU's legislative framework and transferring immigration and asylum, together with visa, external border controls and civil law matters, from the intergovernmental 'Justice and Home Affairs' pillar to the 'European Community' pillar. With these new competences in mind, the European Council quickly called for the development of 'a common EU asylum and migration policy', including measures aimed at establishing a 'partnership' with countries of origin, ensuring fair treatment of third country nationals legally residing in the EU, creating common asylum procedures and rules, and improved control of irregular migration (European Council 1999). Measures on legal migration did not feature high on this agenda given that the heads of state and governments had been reluctant to give away any decision-making power in this field. Until the Lisbon Treaty, decisions on legal migration required unanimity.

In the field of asylum, development was scheduled to occur in two phases; a first phase was dedicated to the development of common *minimum* standards on issues such as the reception and qualification of asylum seekers (1999–2004). In the second phase initially scheduled for the time period from 2005 to 2010 (then prolonged to 2013), these directives were to be evaluated and a *Common* European Asylum System developed, in particular with regard to asylum procedures and a uniform asylum status (Council of the European Union 2004: 8). The EU has struggled to meet these objectives.[1] Even the minimum standards adopted in the first phase provide Member States with large room for manoeuvre and flexibility. EU asylum laws have been difficult to adopt, as there is an important cleavage between Member States at the EU external border that are exposed to receiving and dealing with great numbers of asylum seekers and Member States with no such borders. Regardless of the fact that some policy instruments such as the European Refugee Fund have been established to mitigate this challenge, the issue of solidarity and fair burden-sharing within the EU has remained salient (Thielemann 2005).

In the immigration field, the Council initially focused strongly on the 'fight against illegal migration', in particular in the wake of the 9/11 terrorist attacks (Wolff and Trauner 2011: 66–68). In legal terms, the major achievements of the Tampere era ranging from 1999 to 2004 were the adoption of two directives which determined the conditions for the right of family reunification of third country nationals and of free movement to long-term residents in the Member States.[2] In the Hague Programme for 2005 to 2010, the Council sought to deal with migration in a more comprehensive manner and also underlined the need to have an open debate on economic immigration at the EU level (Council of the European Union 2004). There has been some progress in terms of adopting common laws and, as Rainer Bauböck (Bauböck 2010: 9–10) put it, the EU 'has indeed cautiously inched forward from a harmonisation of external border control towards a common European immigration policy'. The EU adopted directives on issues such as the admission of (non-EU) students, researchers and highly skilled migrants, and the return of irregular migrants and rejected asylum seekers. Member States, however, have been reluctant to substitute national policies with EU ones. The challenge has been similar to that of the asylum field. 'The harmonisation measures are a little ambitious, confined to defining minimum standards and frequently provide member states with exceptions and/or broad room for discretion' (Wolff and Trauner 2011: 71). In some areas such as migrants' integration, the EU has refrained almost entirely from adopting legally binding rules and has experimented with 'soft law', including the Open Method of Coordination.

2.2 International regimes in the migration field

'Migration has become global but there is no global regime to govern the international movement of persons.' This statement by Philippe Fargues (2011: 18) refers to the fact that there is no migration law that may be considered of global reach. The existing regime is complex, multilayered, and consists of international, regional and transnational treaties as well as bilateral arrangements

(Kunz et al. 2011b). According to Alexander Aleinikoff (2007), the codification of international migration law is not accompanied by a corresponding international architecture. This does not imply that international organizations (IOs) have not dealt with migration-related issues. On the contrary, many IOs such as the International Organization for Migration (IOM) and the International Labor Organization (ILO) have dealt exclusively or partially with aspects of migration governance. These organizations, however, have primarily provided their Member States with services and advice. Regardless of the many international initiatives in the migration field, the willingness of nation-states to subscribe to legally binding international norms has been limited. As the Global Commission on International Migration (GCIM) noted in its final report:

> the very nature of transnational migration demands international cooperation and shared responsibility. Yet the reality is that most states have been unwilling to commit fully to the principle of international cooperation in the area of international migration, because migration policy is still mainly formulated at the national level.
>
> (GCIM, quoted in Kunz et al. 2011a: 1)

There is a lack of an international consensus about how to 'manage' key aspects of migration. Migrants' sending countries often perceive the phenomenon of migration from a very different angle than migrants' receiving countries. In Africa, for instance, migration has a positive connotation and is seen as a way to support family in an often difficult economic situation. The remittances of migrants are of the utmost importance for the economy of poor and developing countries (World Bank 2011). In Europe and other OECD countries, by contrast, migration has been transformed into a law and order issue and has become 'securitized' (Huysmans 2000).

This divide between migrants' source and migrants' receiving countries is difficult to bridge. It has contributed to the failure of a major international attempt to improve the rights of all migrant workers and other migrants, including irregular ones. The 1990 UN Convention on the Protection of the Rights of All Migrant Workers and Members of their Family has been signed almost exclusively by migrants' sending countries. No migrants' receiving state in Europe, North America, the Arab Gulf, East Asia or Oceania has accepted this text due to concerns that this would imply more rights for irregular migrants and constrained possibilities to control legal migration (Fargues 2011: 19).

International migration management often takes place in a regional context or in bilateral relations. Labor migration, in particular, has remained a field that is regulated in bilateral relations or in a unilateral form (meaning that migrant receiving states choose who they admit on to their territory, with little or no influence from the migrant sending countries). In relation to irregular migration and, to some extent, labour migration, a new governance mode has gained prominence in the last decade or so, namely that of 'trans-regionalism' (Betts 2011). This implies that migrants' receiving states, in particular in Europe, the US and

Australia, have stopped to wait (passively) until a migrant has reached the borders of their territory. 'Rather, they have increasingly sought to exert extraterritorial authority in order to shape the movement of people within or from other regions in the world' (Betts 2011: 32). This approach relies on transgovernmental policy networks (with Regional Consultative Processes being a case in point) and on hierarchical modes of governance, where an actor capitalizes on its superior bargaining power to induce rule compliance in another country (Lavenex and Wichmann 2009; Thouez and Channac 2006).

The EU has incorporated this logic of externalization; its strategy to reinforce the external cooperation includes the signing of EC readmission agreements with third countries, the strengthening of border controls and migration management systems in neighbouring countries, and a closer link between development aid and migration policies. In 2005, the EU launched the 'Global Approach to Migration', which should help in developing a more 'comprehensive' approach to migration, opening channels for circular and temporary migration in exchange for comprehensive cooperation in the prevention and combat of irregular migration and trafficking in human beings (Council of the European Union 2005).

The creation and constitution of the 'external dimension' of EU migration policy has received a great deal of scholarly attention (see e.g. Boswell 2003; Lavenex and Uçarer 2002; Trauner and Kruse 2008). It will not, however, be the focus of this chapter as the research interest here is on the EU's policy export to the *global* level. The EU's external migration cooperation has a strong regional focus and implication. Regardless of its label, even the EU's 'Global Approach to Migration' has placed the emphasis on some countries and regions in Africa, Eastern and South Eastern Europe (Commission of the European Communities 2007).

The most institutionalized migration regime at the global level exists in the field of refugee protection. Although the phenomenon of refugees (i.e. people forced to quit their native land) has always existed, the origins of the global refugee protection regime may be located in the early twentieth century. In 1921, the League of Nations set up the High Commissioner for Refugees, headed by Fridthof Nansen, to deal with the one million Russian refugees fleeing the Bolshevik regime (Barnett 2002: 242). It was considered to be a temporary agency but the atrocities of the Second World War and the large number of refugees in Europe demonstrated the need to base the refugee protection regime on a firmer basis.

In December 1950, the United Nations General Assembly founded the office of the UN High Commissioner for Refugees (UNHCR) to deal with the European refugees and displaced persons. The office was given a mandate for three years, the time span believed necessary to solve the European refugee issue. In July 1951, the UN Convention relating to the Status of Refugees was adopted, laying down core international refugee protection norms such as the principle of 'non-refoulement', which states that a refugee should not be expelled or returned if his or her life or freedom is threatened. The 'universal' refugee protection regime was hence 'European in origin and nature' (van Selm 2005: 6). It was not until 1967 that a Protocol to the Geneva Convention removed the geographical constraint on Europe as well as the three-year time limit and expanded the scope of the refugee regime to a global level.

3 The EU's interactions with the global refugee protection regime

The 1951 Convention and its 1967 Protocol are the 'baseline' of the international refugee protection regime, with most of its 'basics' defined by the UNHCR as the regime's guardian and nation-states as implementing partners (Feller 2001; Loescher 2001). The EU's policies have developed following and partly *in response* to the global refugee protection regime. However, the EU has not only been on the reactive end of the regime. It has also exerted an impact on the way the UNHCR has tackled new issues in the refugee protection realm and has sought to increase the take-up rate of the global regime by encouraging the adoption of and compliance with the 1951 Convention in its external relations.

3.1 Refugee protection: the significance of governance layers

States have established the global refugee protection regime to improve international cooperation and coordination with regard to sharing the costs of asylum protection and in the dealings with refugees. The UNHCR has played an essential, albeit not easy, role to achieve these objectives:

> UNHCR has ... been in an ambiguous position of, on the one hand, representing states' interests and being dependent upon donor state funding, and, on the other hand, needing to influence states in order to persuade them to fulfill their humanitarian obligations towards refugees.
>
> (Loescher *et al.* 2008: 3)

In the 1960s and 1970s, European values and actors dominated the UNHCR (Loescher 2001: 176). During the first stages of the Cold War, refugees fleeing from communist rule were welcomed in the democratic West, publicly considered as a sign of attractiveness and superiority of the own system vis-à-vis the ideological competitor. The Soviet Union never signed the 1951 Convention on the grounds that it would contribute to protect people associated with 'fascist and anti-democratic regimes' (Spijkerboer 2000: 197). While refugees were warmly welcomed during the peak of the Cold War, the perception of Western European states towards the global refugee protection regime was altered as the conflict came to an end and the European states started to focus increasingly on the costs of refugee protection. Western European countries began to register significant increases in asylum applications in the mid-1980s, which created a sense of urgency. It was in this altered context that the cooperation on asylum started at the European level (see above). The EU provided Member States with an additional layer to specify and implement the (vaguely formulated) international refugee protection norms. This additional layer, however, was not meant – at least in its beginnings – to install a truly supranational asylum policy that would take away decision-making competences from the national level. Rather, this additional layer was designed to shield an epistemic community (namely security-oriented actors from ministries of the interior of Member States) from constraints exerted by constitutions, jurisprudence and laws at the national level. The EU provided these actors with 'venues of decision-making' in which they were protected from actors with other preferences (Guiraudon 2000). The Europeanization of refugee policies took place in a contested way, marked by tensions between security-oriented considerations and human rights issues (Lavenex 2001). Many policies adopted at the EU level were of a restrictive nature and aimed at reducing the number of (bogus) asylum seekers. The security-oriented nature of asylum cooperation became more accentuated by linking it to the Schengen border-free project. 'The linkage of the asylum question with the foundational norm of free movement in the EU ... justified limitations on the post-war refugee regime in the name of European integration' (Lavenex 2001: 860).

The governance layer of the EU was strengthened by the Amsterdam Treaty's *communitarization* of the policy and the deeper involvement of supranational institutions. The EU asylum regime became denser by adopting a range of regulations and directives to achieve the objective of a Common European Asylum System. However, the EU has not yet managed to reduce the actual differences in the asylum procedures and standards of Member States. The European Council on Refugees and Exiles (2009: 1) spoke of a 'lottery' for refugees within the EU given that, for instance, an asylum seeker from Iraq had a very different prospect of being granted asylum in the EU, ranging from 0 per cent in Greece to 100 per cent in Finland. The Dublin system has been unfair not only to asylum seekers but also to certain Member States at the EU's external southern and eastern borders. In particular Greece has been overstrained. On 22 December 2011, the Court of Justice of the EU maintained that an asylum seeker subject to a transfer back to Greece according to the Dublin rules would 'face a real risk of being subjected to inhuman and degrading treatment' (Court of Justice of the European Union 2011). This ruling confirmed a similar ruling of the Strasbourg-based European Court of Human Rights earlier in January 2011 (*M.S.S. vs. Belgium and Greece*) which found Belgium and Greece in violation of the European Convention of Human Rights. These cases were just the tip of the iceberg. By the end of 2011, more than 600 cases were pending before the European Court of Human Rights concerning the suspension of Dublin transfers to Greece, in addition to a range of preliminary ruling cases brought by higher courts of different Member States to the Court of Justice of the EU (UNHCR 2011).

The court rulings that some EU practices have been in breach of international refugee and human rights norms resulted in a de facto suspension of Dublin transfers to Greece. The Dublin system as a whole, however, was not called into question. To meet the standards set in international and European law again, the European Commission proposed to 'reinforce intra-EU solidarity', for example,

Table 9.1 Significance of governance levels over time (the field of refugee protection)

Phase	National level	EU level	International level
Post-WWII	High	–	Medium (focus on refugees in post-war Europe; 1951 adoption of UN Refugee Convention)
Post-1967	High	–	High (1967 Protocol removed geographical and temporal constraints)
Mid-1980s–1990s	High	Low (intergovernmental cooperation among national law enforcement authorities)	High
Late 1990s–2010	High	Medium (Dublin Convention in force since 1997; EU asylum competence with 1999 Treaty of Amsterdam)	High
2020 (extrapolation)	Medium	High (provided that a *Common* European Asylum Policy is implemented)	High

by providing more financial, technical and operational support to countries in distress and installing an early warning mechanism for problems in the Dublin system (European Commission 2011).

3.2 The vertical dimension: EU–UNHCR interactions

Regardless of the fact that the EU is very important to the UNHCR in terms of financial contributions, it has not been an effective policy exporter within the institutional structures of the UNHCR. Close to half of the UNHCR's annual budget is provided by the European Commission and the 27 Member States. The European Commission's contribution was the third largest in 2010 (and second largest in 2009). However, the EU's financial impact is not as strong, since a look at the sheer numbers would suggest that the contributions are made on a country-by-country basis. Moreover, in the UNHCR Executive Committee – the subcommittee of the UN General Assembly specializing in refugee issues – the EU is a weak institutional actor. Members of this committee are elected by the Economic and Social Council 'on the widest possible geographic basis from those States with a demonstrated interest in and devotion to the solution of refugee problems' (UNHCR 2010: 3). The Executive Committee, comprising 85 members, approves the UNHCR's biannual programmes and its budget. Not all EU Member States participate in the Committee, with weak coordination mechanisms among the participating states. The European Commission has only observer status. The discussions in the UNHCR Executive Committee often take up issues that are salient in European debates, yet the conclusions are usually more refugee-friendly due to the presence of non-European states and the office of the High Commissioner for Refugees:

> The refugee regime by nature is grounded in high moral values, and the restrictive approach of European states towards refugees and asylum seekers in the last two decades means most European states, and Europe as a general region, have lost some of their humanitarian moral clout.
> (van Selm 2005: 6)

This has resulted in declining EU influence and reduced possibilities to export EU policy objectives and rules through persuasion and principled arguments.

The EU and its Member States, however, have influenced the UNHCR and the global refugee protection regime in a different way. When dealing with refugee issues that have not been subject to the 1951 Convention, such as the protection of internally displaced persons (IDP) or mixed migration flows (involving not only refugees but also migrants), the EU Council of Ministers has increasingly referred to inter-state dialogues instead of using UNHCR's Executive Committee. This 'regime shifting' has been problematic for the UNHCR given that 'new mechanisms for addressing asylum and refugee protection get decided without UNHCR involvement' (Betts 2009: 55). In the inter-state settings, these new refugee issues have been discussed in a wider context of migration and security. This has exerted pressure on the UNHCR to adapt its agenda and become more responsive to the security concerns of European governments. According to Betts (2009: 57),

> the danger for UNHCR is that, as it enters new policy arenas and takes on a greater role in areas such as migration and IDP protection, it risks diluting or undermining its original refugee protection mandate and its ostensibly 'non-political character.' However, the danger of not engaging with the new competitive institutional environment is that the organization and the refugee regime risk irrelevance.

A certain ambiguity in EU–UNHCR relations is also reflected in the way in which the UNHCR has followed the development of EU asylum law. According to Johannes van der Klaauw (2002: 35), the former head of the UNHCR office to the European Communities, 'UNHCR considers the developing common asylum and migration policy of the EU as both an opportunity for and a danger to the preservation and strengthening of the international protection regime'. The opportunity would be that harmonized and consistent asylum rules in the EU might allow for raising the protection standards in the continent and elsewhere. At the same time, there is a danger that the harmonization process leads to lowest common denominator policies and an overemphasis on restrictive policy objectives. This would have the adverse effects of curtailing asylum rights and of 'a collective undermining of the international protection framework' (ibid.).

Given these high stakes, the UNHCR has actively sought to influence the EU asylum regime and has systematically commented on EU legislative initiatives in the field. The UNHCR's influence has been strong with the European Commission but the EU Council of Ministers has been more critical towards these (often refugee-friendly) ideas and implemented a more restrictive approach towards asylum-seekers (van der Klaauw 2002: 37). In addition, the UNHCR has cooperated on more operational aspects of the European asylum cooperation. It is represented by a non-voting member in the Management Board of the European Asylum Support Office (EASO) and is involved in the work of the EU's border management agency Frontex (Trauner 2012).

3.3 The horizontal dimension: the EU and asylum policy export in its external relations

The EU has sought to transfer its asylum rules and practices to third countries and to ensure their compliance with international refugee protection norms outlined in the 1951 Convention and 1967 Protocol. The beginnings of the EU's horizontal policy export date back to the Eastern enlargement. The asylum field was part of the accession conditionality (Chapter 24, 'Justice and Home Affairs') with which the (then) candidate countries were required to comply in order to advance in the step-by-step process towards EU accession. The EU encouraged these countries to harmonize their asylum legislation with the *acquis*, and provided equipment, software and advisory support, as well as strengthening the capacity of refugee agencies' staff and improved reception centres. The UNHCR was closely involved in this policy export by advising the governments of the candidate states and contributing to the implementation of the twinning projects financed by the PHARE programme (UNHCR 2003a: 145).

Regardless of its comprehensive involvement, the UNHCR followed the EU's activities again in an ambiguous way. The advantage from the UNHCR's point of view was that the 'political leverage of the accession strategy' helped the office to develop asylum systems in these candidate countries (van der Klaauw 2002: 40). The flip-side of this policy, however, was that the applicant states also introduced changes in their asylum systems and procedures that contributed to a downgrading of existing standards. The UNHCR expressed public concerns when the Central and Eastern European states developed accelerated asylum procedures and increasingly involved security-oriented border guards in decision-making on asylum (ibid.). The UNHCR has not been alone in pinpointing the negative side effects of the EU's enlargement policies. Scholars highlighted that the transformation of the Central and Eastern European countries into safe third countries for receiving and dealing with asylum seekers has had a downgrading effect on international refugee protection standards:

The extension of the current EU refugee regime, coupled with the general goal of combating illegal immigration, weakens the principles, norms and rules of international refugee protection by impeding the entry of asylum seekers and establishing a system of negative re-distribution for handling asylum claims.
(Lavenex 1999: 3)

The experiences acquired in the Eastern enlargement provided the EU with a model case to be applied to other third countries. The Stabilisation and Association Agreements, which the EU signed with Western Balkan countries, and the ENP (European Neighbourhood Policy) Action Plans with neighbouring countries contain substantial Justice and Home Affairs (JHA) components that provide for intense cooperation on asylum-related issues. The UNHCR is again closely involved in the implementation of the EU objectives. In a way, the UNHCR has even become a 'subcontractor to the EU and its member states' (Lavenex 2007: 253) in EU enlargement and neighbourhood policy. Compared to the Eastern enlargement, the EU's possibility to rely on accession conditionality has been more limited for the Western Balkans and Turkey (due to the distant accession horizon of most of these states) and has been lacking for the ENP states. The EU has hence refined its external governance approaches, moving away from purely conditionality-inspired approaches to an expansion of its transgovernmental networks 'as a vehicle for policy transfer through 'softer' means' (Lavenex and Wichmann 2009: 99). While this strategy has contributed to an increase in the take-up rate of the EU's policy export, the challenges have remained the same; this includes the shifting of responsibility for refugee protection to countries whose institutions remain ill equipped to fulfil such a task.

4 Policy export/import: the case of extra-territorial approaches to refugee protection

New global approaches to today's refugee challenges are rarely based exclusively on an EU template (with the EU acting as policy exporter). More often, they are developed in complex interactions between the national, the European and the international level. The case study on the development of extra-territorial approaches to refugee protection and asylum processing is a case in point for such a process; it traces the European and global reverberations of a proposal put forward by the UK. In conceptual terms, extra-territorial protection implies that temporary protection and the processing of asylum claims become separated from the territory of a nation-state. The two distinct approaches of extra-territorial protection are: first, 'third country processing centres'; and second, 'regional protection areas' (Betts 2004: 59).

Ideas for extra-territorial approaches have been put forward at regular intervals by individual Member States at the EU level, first by Austria in 1998 and, most pronounced, by the UK government in 2003. In March 2003, the UK government under Prime Minister Tony Blair searched for venues to decrease the political pressure in the asylum domain domestically:

> The proposed new vision for refugees is a global vision that meets both our international obligations and is response to domestic political and economic concerns.... There may now be a rare opportunity for the UK to truly set the global agenda on this issue.
>
> (UK Government 2003: 1–2)

The central idea was to process all asylum seekers' claims closer to their source regions. Even those who had already managed to come to the British territory should be returned to these regions. In subsequent specifications, the UK Prime Minister explained the role the EU played in his approach (Blair 2003). The processing of asylum claims could take place in both 'regions of origin' and in 'transit processing centres' in nearby third countries such as Croatia. Applications for asylum seekers in Britain would be assessed in this transit processing centre with the EU funding the facility. Successful applicants would then be resettled in the UK or another EU country, while rejected cases would be returned to their countries of origin (*Observer* 2003).

The UK did not intend to develop its concept outside the EU framework, on the one side, and the UNHCR, on the other. It first sought to use the international level to give legitimacy to its ideas. 'The UK has attempted to work *with* UNHCR to negotiate its extraterritorial policies rather than abandon UNHCR involvement' (Betts 2004: 65). At that time, the UNHCR Executive Committee discussed an initiative known as 'Convention Plus', which aimed at modernizing the international refugee protection regime. In response to the UK proposal, the UNHCR published a proposal for a three-pronged approach to refugee protection which incorporated several of the suggested ideas (UNHCR 2003b). In the public perception, this proposal was quickly intermingled with the Convention Plus initiative. It included ideas for a stronger protection in the region of origin and closed processing centres for 'manifestly unfounded' asylum cases. In contrast to the UK proposal, these processing centres should be located in EU territory. In the eyes of many observers, the UNHCR had nevertheless made too many concessions. 'The UNHCR agreed to a policy that departs from the fundamental pillar of the Second-World War refugee regime, that is, the individual commitment and responsibility of liberal democratic countries, under international law, to give access to domestic asylum procedures' (Lavenex 2007: 252). Faced with strong criticism, the UNHCR distanced itself from the UK proposal and highlighted the differences of its own ideas (Betts 2004: 59). The final flaw in the UK proposal was a lack of consensus at the EU level. The idea of extra-territorial processing of asylum claims became an item on the agenda of the European Council summit in Thessaloniki in June 2003. Some states, notably Denmark, Italy, Spain and the Netherlands, supported the idea, but Sweden and (initially) Germany opposed it (Maurer and Parkes 2007: 199). While the decision was postponed at the summit, the idea continues to be discussed up until the present.[3]

EU policy, however, moved in the direction of the second dimension of the extra-territorial approaches, namely that of regional protection areas. This direction was set by a Commission communication (2003) responding to the UK proposal, which highlighted the need to improve the EU asylum system at large and to provide enhanced protection capacities in regions with strong refugee populations. With the European Council (2004) endorsing this approach in the Hague Programme, the Commission (2005) therefore established Regional Protection Programmes (RPPs). Their objective has been to enhance the protection capacities of third countries and to better protect the refugees by providing 'durable solutions', namely repatriation, local integration or resettlement in a third country. The idea of strengthening the protection in third countries corresponded to UNHCR plans of developing supplementary policies for current refugee challenges. According to António Guterres, the UN High Commissioner for Refugees,

> I welcome ... the commitment of the Commission and Council to improving refugee protection capacity and durable solutions. These are indeed UNHCR's *raison d'être* and therefore we offer our full support and are ready to cooperate in the identification of target regions and in programme implementation, including resettlement.
>
> (UNHCR 2005a)

The UNHCR emphasized that these policies 'must be additional to, and not in substitution for' a functioning asylum policy in the EU (UNHCR 2005b).

The first Regional Protection Programmes were carried out in neighbouring countries (Ukraine, Belarus and Moldova) and in Tanzania. In 2010, the time span of these first programmes was prolonged and the concept extended to two new regions: the Horn of Africa (including Kenya, Yemen and Djibouti) and Eastern North Africa (Egypt, Libya and Tunisia). While the EU has promoted these programmes as a success, a central dimension has remained underdeveloped: the resettlement of refugees outside and within the EU territory. The EU's share on global resettlement has remained 'modest' (UNHCR 2009). In 2008, out of 65,596 refugees who were resettled worldwide, only 6.7 per cent (4,378) were relocated in one of the EU Member States (ibid.). In 2009, the Commission proposed to set up a joint EU resettlement programme based on UNHCR forecasts (Commission of the European Communities 2009). The participation for Member States remains voluntary, begging the question to what extent this programme will change the practices of Member States. The unwillingness of Member States to commit to resettlement seems to confirm what NGOs had warned about: that the Regional Protection Programmes would mainly be about keeping refugees out of the EU's territory. According to an expert of Amnesty International, 'keeping refugees close to their regions of origin is seen as a panacea from the perspective of European governments that are keen to limit the numbers of migrants and asylum seekers' (Bouteillet-Pacquet 2005: 2–3).

Overall, the case study shows the dynamics of exporting/importing a new concept in the refugee domain. In the first phase, an EU Member State, the UK, failed to export its ideas for a new policy approach, mainly due to a lack of EU consensus. Aspects of this initial approach, however, corresponded to the preferences of the global actor (UNHCR) and the regional policy entrepreneur (European Commission). Jointly they managed to compel EU Member States to participate in a new policy scheme developing this aspect. The participation of the Member States was fostered by a (perceived or real) interest overlap (possibility to reduce asylum pressure in Europe) and the non-binding nature of cooperation.

5 Conclusion

This chapter has elaborated the EU's potential for global policy export in the migration field. After investigating the scope and nature of EU migration policy and the corresponding international regimes, the analysis has focused on the EU's interactions with the global refugee protection regime – the most institutionalized international migration regime.

By and large, the EU has been an importer of the global refugee protection regime. European states accepted the legal foundation of this regime – the 1951 Convention relating to the Status of Refugees and its 1967 Protocol removing time limits and geographical constraints – long before EU cooperation started in the asylum domain. Viewed from the three-layered perspective of this volume (national, EU, international), it may be argued that Member States used the cooperation at the EU level primarily to specify the vaguely formulated international refugee protection norms. Against the background of a perceived asylum crisis in Europe, this process of 'rule specification' has often implied the adoption of restrictive and security-oriented measures. Recent court rulings have shown that some EU practices, particularly Dublin transfers to Greece regardless of the human rights situation in the country, have become too refugee-hostile and have been in breach of international law.

In the case of refugee protection, the EU is a weak policy exporter at the vertical dimension (from the EU to the UNHCR) in terms of international negotiations and bargaining. Not all EU Member States participate in the UNHCR Executive Committee, the main governing body, and those who do so only have weakly institutionalized coordination mechanisms. The European Commission has observer status. Moreover, the EU's restrictive approach to asylum has made the EU lose normative ground in the UNHCR Executive Committee. Many (non-European) states and the office of the High Commissioner participating in this body have traditionally preferred more refugee-friendly approaches (van Selm 2005). However, the picture is slightly different if one looks at how the EU manages to set standards (albeit often in a weakly legalized form) regarding new refugee issues that are either not included or are poorly regulated in the 1951 Convention and its 1967 Protocol. The EU has exerted pressure on the UNHCR by increasingly tackling new refugee issues in inter-state dialogues outside the UNHCR framework (Betts 2009). The office of the UN High Commissioner has had to engage with these new (often security-driven) approaches and arenas in order to remain the key actor in the realm of international refugee protection.

However, as the case study on the development of extra-territorial approaches to refugee protection has shown, this engagement can also imply the attempt of the UNHCR to alter the initial meaning of an approach developed within the EU. The interactions at the vertical dimension are complex and operate in both directions. The UNHCR actively influences EU policy-making, for example, by commenting on legislative proposals and participating in the Management Board of the European Asylum Support Office.

At a horizontal level, the EU has become a moderate policy exporter, especially in the wider European region. The EU's objective has been to ensure the compliance of third countries with international refugee protection norms by bringing their asylum systems and legislation closer to EU standards. In practice, this has implied the transfer of existing EU asylum rules and practices based on the experiences gained in the Eastern enlargement. The UNHCR has been a close partner in the EU's external strategy and has implemented a series of EU-funded projects in third countries; however, the EU's rule export has had ambiguous results. While the EU has helped develop asylum systems in states that previously had no or only basic systems, the policy has also contributed to effectively shifting the responsibility for dealing with asylum seekers to countries whose institutions have remained ill equipped to fulfil such a task.

Notes

1 In June 2013, the EU agreed on the asylum package that consists of five texts (two on the Dublin regulation, one on the qualification of asylum seekers, one on the Eurodac database and one on the conditions of hosting asylum seekers).
2 Council Directive 2003/86/EC of 22 September 2003 on the right to family reunification and Council Directive 2003/109/EC of 25 November 2003 concerning the status of third country nationals who are long-term residents.
3 In 2004, Germany and Italy relaunched the UK proposal; both the 2004 The Hague and the 2009 Stockholm JHA annual work programme refer to the possibility of joint processing centres (the Stockholm programme, however, does not give any geographical indication).

References

Aleinikoff, T.A. (2007) 'International Legal Norms on Migration: Substance without Architecture', in R. Cholewinski, R. Perruchoud and E. MacDonald (eds) *International Migration Law: Developing Paradigms and Key Challenges*, The Hague: TMC Asser Press.
Barnett, L. (2002) 'Global Governance and the Evolution of the International Refugee Regime', *International Journal of Refugee Law* 14(2–3): 238–263.
Bauböck, R. (2010) 'Regulating the Gates to European Citizenship', in P. Fargues (ed.) *Understanding Human Migration*, Florence: European University Institute.
Betts, A. (2004) 'The International Relations of the "New" Extraterritorial Approaches to Refugee Protection: Explaining the Policy Initiatives of the UK Government and UNHCR', *Refuge* 22(1): 58–70.
—— (2009) 'Institutional Proliferation and the Global Refugee Regime', *Perspectives on Politics* 7(1): 53–58.

—— (2011) 'The Global Governance of Migration and the Role of Trans-regionalism', in R. Kunz, S. Lavenex and M. Panizzon (eds) *Multilayered Migration Governance. The Promise of Partnership*, Abingdon: Routledge.

Blair, T. (2003) *Letter to His Excellency Mr Costas Simitis: New International Approaches to Asylum Processing and Protection*, 10 March 2003. Online. Available: www.statewatch.org/news/2003/apr/blair-simitis-asile.pdf (accessed 14 December 2012).

Boswell, C. (2003) 'The "External Dimension" of EU Immigration and Asylum Policy', *International Affairs* 79(3): 619–638.

Bouteillet-Pacquet, D. (2005) *EU Regional Protection Programs: Enhancing Protection in the Region or Barring Access to the EU Territory?* Amnesty International EU Office. Online. Available: www.amnesty.eu/static/documents/2005/05_09_22_protection_programs_EPC.pdf (accessed 29 November 2012).

Commission of the European Communities (2003) *Towards more Accessible, Equitable and Managed Asylum Systems*, COM(2003) 315 final (3 June).

—— (2005) *Communication on Regional Protection Programmes*, COM(2005) 388 final (1 September).

—— (2007) *Communication from the Commission to the European Parliament, the Council, the European Economic and Social Committee and the Committee of the Regions. Applying the Global Approach to Migration to the Eastern and South-Eastern Regions Neighbouring the European Union*, COM(2007) 247 final (16 May).

—— (2009) *Communication on the Establishment of a Joint EU Resettlement Programme*, COM(2009) 447 final (2 September).

Council of the European Union (2004) *The Hague Programme: Strengthening Freedom, Security and Justice in the European Union*, Brussels, 16054/04 (13 December).

—— (2005) *Global Approach to Migration: Priority Actions Focusing on Africa and the Mediterranean*, Brussels, 15451/05 (6 December).

Court of Justice of the European Union (2011) *Press Release No 140/11*, Luxembourg (21 December).

ECRE (2009) *Comments on the Proposal for a Regulation of the European Parliament and of the Council Establishing a European Asylum Support Office*, European Council on Refugees and Exiles, Brussels. Online. Available: www.ecre.org/component/content/article/57-policy-papers/128-comments-on-the-proposal-for-a-regulation-establishing-a-european-asylum-support-office.html (accessed 3 December 2012).

European Commission (2011) *Communication on Enhanced Intra-EU Solidarity in the Field of Asylum. An EU Agenda for Better Responsibility-sharing and more Mutual Trust*, Brussels, COM(2011) 835 final (2 December).

European Council (1999) *Presidency Conclusions*, Tampere (15 and 16 October).

—— (2004) *Presidency Conclusions*, 14292/1/04 (4/5 November).

Fargues, P. (2011) 'Migration on the Global Governance Agenda', in M. Poiares Maduro (ed.) *An EU Agenda for Global Goverance*, RSCAS Policy Papers 2011/01, Florence: European University Institute.

Feller, E. (2001) 'The Evolution of the International Refugee Protection Regime', *Journal of Law and Policy* 5: 129–139.

Geddes, A. (2000) *Immigration and European Integration: Towards Fortress Europe*, Manchester: Manchester University Press.

Geddes, A. and Boswell, C. (2011) *Migration and Mobility in the European Union*, Basingstoke: Palgrave.

Guild, E. and van Selm, J. (eds) (2005) *International Migration and Security: Opportunities and Challenges*, London; New York: Routledge.

Guiraudon, V. (2000) 'European Integration and Migration Policy: Vertical Policy-making as Venue Shopping', *Journal of Common Market Studies* 38(2): 251–271.

Hollifield, J.F. (1998) 'Migration, Trade and the Nation-state: The Myth of Globalization', *UCLA Journal of International Law and Foreign Affairs* 3(2): 595–636.

Huysmans, J. (2000) 'The European Union and the Securitization of Migration', *Journal of Common Market Studies* 38(5): 751–777.

Kaunert, C. and Léonard, S. (2011) 'The EU Asylum Policy: Towards a Common Area of Protection and Solidarity', in S. Wolff, F. Goudappel and J. de Zwaan (eds) *Freedom, Security and Justice after Lisbon and Stockholm*, The Hague: TMC Asser Press.

Koikkalainen, S. (2011) 'Free Movement in Europe: Past and Present', Migration Information Source: Washington. Online. Available: www.migrationinformation.org/Feature/display.cfm?ID=836 (accessed 12 December 2012).

Kunz, R., Lavenex, S. and Panizzon, M. (2011a) 'Introduction: Governance through Partnerships in International Migration', in R. Kunz, S. Lavenex and M. Panizzon (eds) *Multilayered Migration Governance: The Promise of Partnership*, London: Routledge.

—— (eds) (2011b) *Multilayered Migration Management: The Promise of Partnership*, London: Routledge.

Lavenex, S. (1999) *Safe Third Countries. Extending the EU Asylum and Immigration Policies to Central and Eastern Europe*, Budapest: Central European University Press.

—— (2001) 'The Europeanization of Refugee Policies: Normative Challenge and Institutional Legacies', *Journal of Common Market Studies* 39(5): 851–874.

—— (2007) 'The External Face of Europeanization: Third Countries and International Organizations', in F. Thomas and E. Andreas (eds) *The Europeanization of National Politics and Politics of Immigration*, Basingstoke: Palgrave Macmillan.

Lavenex, S. and Uçarer, E.M. (2002) *Migration and the Externalities of European Integration*, Lanham, MD; Boulder, CO; New York; Oxford: Lexington Books.

Lavenex, S. and Wichmann, N. (2009) 'The External Governance of EU Internal Security', *Journal of European Integration* 31(1): 83–102.

Loescher, G. (2001) *The UNHCR and World Politics: A Perilous Path*, Oxford: Oxford University Press.

Loescher, G., Betts, A. and Milner, J. (2008) *The United Nations High Commissioner for Refugees (UNHCR): The Politics and Practice of Refugee Protection into the Twenty-first Century*, London: Routledge.

Maurer, A. and Parkes, R. (2007) 'The Prospects for Policy-change in EU Asylum Policy: Venue and Image at the European Level', *European Journal of Migration and Law* 9(2): 173–205.

Observer (2003) 'Secret Balkan Camp Built to Hold UK Asylum Seekers' (15 June).

Spijkerboer, T. (2000) *Gender and Refugee Status*, London: Ashgate.

Thielemann, E. (2005) 'Symbolic Politics or Effective Burden-sharing? Redistribution, Side-Payments and the European Refugee Funds', *Journal of Common Market Studies* 43(4): 807–824.

Thouez, C. and Channac, F. (2006) 'Shaping International Migration Policy: The Role of Regional Consultative Processes', *West European Politics* 29(2): 370–387.

Trauner, F. (2012) 'The European Parliament and Agency Control in the Area of Freedom, Security and Justice', *West European Politics* 35(4): 784–802.

Trauner, F. and Kruse, I. (2008) 'EC Visa Facilitation and Readmission Agreements: A New Standard EU Foreign Policy Tool?', *European Journal of Migration and Law* 10(4): 411–438.

Ucarer, E.M. (2002) 'Guarding the Borders of the European Union: Paths, Portals, and Prerogatives', in S. Lavenex and E.M. Ucarer (eds) *Migration and the Externalities of European Integration*, Lanham, MD: Boulder, CO; New York; Oxford: Lexington Books.

UK Government (2003) *New Vision for Refugees* (7 March). Online. Available: www.proasyl.de/texte/europe/union/2003/UK_NewVision.pdf (accessed 21 October 2012).

UNHCR (2003a) *The EU Enlargement Process and the External Dimension of the EU JHA Policy*, Geneva: United Nations High Commissioner for Refugees.

—— (2003b) *UNHCR's Three-pronged Proposal*, Geneva: United Nations Commissioner for Refugee Protection.

—— (2005a) *Remarks by Mr. António Guterres, United Nations High Commissioner for Refugees, on the Occasion of the European Union Council of Ministers of Justice and Home Affairs*. Luxembourg (12 October).

—— (2005b) *UNHCR Observations on the Communication from the European Commission to the Council and the European Parliament on Regional Protection Programmes*, Geneva: United Nations High Commissioner for Refugees.

—— (2009) *Comments on the European Commission Communication on the Establishment of a Joint EU Resettlement Programme and the European Commission Proposal for the Amendment of Decision No. 573/2007/EC Establishing the European Refugee Fund for the Period 2008 to 2013*, Geneva: United Nations High Commissioner for Refugees.

—— (2010) *Statute of the Office of the United Nations High Commissioner for Refugees*, Geneva: United Nations High Commissioner for Refugees.

—— (2011) *Updated UNHCR Information Note on National Practice in the Application of Article 3(2) of the Dublin II Regulation in Particular in the Context of Intendend Transfer To Greece*, Geneva: United Nations High Commissioner for Refugees (31 January).

van der Klaauw, J. (2002) 'European Asylum Policy and the Global Protection Regime: Challenges for UNHCR', in S. Lavenex and E.M. Ucarer (eds) *Migration and the Externalities of European Integration*, Lanham, MD: Lexington Books.

van Selm, J. (2005) 'European Refugee Policy: Is There Such a Thing?', New Issues in Refugee Research, Working Paper No. 115, Geneva: United Nations High Commissioner for Refugees.

Wolff, S. and Trauner, F. (2011) 'A European Migration Policy Fit for Future Challenges', in S. Wolff, F. Goudappel and J. de Zwaan (eds) *Freedom, Security and Justice after the Lisbon Treaty and the Stockholm Programme*, The Hague: TMC Asser Press.

World Bank (2011) *Migration and Remittances Factbook 2011*, Washington, DC: World Bank.

10 Nuclear non-proliferation
The EU as an emerging international actor?

Patrick Müller

1 Introduction

Since the end of the Cold War, preventing the proliferation of nuclear weapons has become an increasingly important priority on the external agenda of the EU (Portela 2003). The European Security Strategy of 2003 described the proliferation of weapons of mass destruction as potentially the greatest threat to European security (European Council 2003). To combat the nuclear proliferation risk, the EU aims for an effective multilateral response based on the universalization of international treaties, the strengthening of the global non-proliferation regime, and the promotion of compliance with international non-proliferation commitments (Council of the European Union 2003). Evidently, the EU's non-proliferation policy displays a strong commitment to international non-proliferation norms, international treaties and multilateral cooperation. But to what extent has the EU shaped global non-proliferation policy in accordance with its domestic standards and solutions?

Studying the EU's interaction with the international non-proliferation system is a complex undertaking. Non-proliferation matters cut through different EU policy domains, emanating from distinct institutional frameworks (see also Grip 2011). The EU's Common Foreign and Security Policy (CFSP) serves as the principal mechanism through which the EU addresses proliferation issues. The core of CFSP activities concerns the promotion of external EU preferences in the global arena, rather than policy export in a strict sense (i.e. the 'uploading' of domestic EU policies and standards to the global non-proliferation regime). This reflects the general nature of the CFSP, which is per definition a policy for external projection. At the same time, the EU's non-proliferation policy is also related to important internal EU policy domains. Core areas of intersection between domestic EU activities and the global non-proliferation regime are export controls for 'dual-use goods', which fall under the EU's common commercial policy, and the field of nuclear safeguards standards established under the framework of the European Atomic Energy Community (Euratom). To study the interplay between EU and global rule-making which is at the centre of this research project, these two subfields of non-proliferation policy thus deserve special attention.

The chapter proceeds as follows. It first gives a brief overview of the evolution of the EU's nuclear non-proliferation policy and the main institutions of the global non-proliferation system. Subsequently, it examines the EU's role in the global non-proliferation system, providing detailed case studies on the issues of nuclear safeguards and export controls for nuclear and dual-use goods. The conclusion summarizes the main findings of the chapter.

2 The EU's non-proliferation policy

The development of the EU's non-proliferation policy began within the framework of the European Atomic Energy Community (Euratom) established in 1957. Designed to deal with civil nuclear energy cooperation in Western Europe, the Euratom Treaty also established a regional system of nuclear safeguards. Nuclear safeguards refer to a set of measures designed to prevent the diversion of fissile nuclear materials and technologies from their intended uses. Developing a nuclear safeguards system was important for the success of Euratom above all, as it was essential to satisfy US policy requirements for nuclear cooperation (Fischer 2000).[1] Under the Euratom Treaty, the European Commission was charged with ensuring, through inspections and related nuclear material accountancy, that source materials and nuclear products were used exclusively for the purposes declared by their Community users.[2]

An important characteristic of the Euratom safeguards system is the direct applicability of Community law. Together with its derived legislation on nuclear safeguards, the Euratom Treaty is binding law in the Member States of the EU, allowing for sanctions against non-compliant Member States. The negotiation of the international Treaty on the Non-Proliferation of Nuclear Weapons (NPT), which entered into force in 1970, raised the question of whether and how global safeguards administered by the International Atomic Energy Agency (IAEA) should apply to Western Europe (see Lindroos 1997; Bunn 2007). In difficult negotiations, a solution was worked out that integrated important aspects of the Euratom safeguards system as an additional layer in the global safeguards regime (see below), with the NPT providing for 'groups of states' to conclude verification agreements with the IAEA. Although Euratom was not made a party to the NPT, which today includes all 27 EU Member States, the European Commission gained observer status in the IAEA in 1975.

In the early 1980s, the EU also began to coordinate external non-proliferation objectives through the intergovernmental framework of the European Political Cooperation (EPC), the forerunner of today's Common Foreign and Security Policy (CFSP). A working party on non-proliferation was set up in the Council that produced common statements at UN forums and the Nuclear Suppliers Group (NSG) (Schmitt 2001). In the 1990s, the EU began to further define its strategic approach to the (nuclear) proliferation risk through a series of declarations, joint statements and concrete proposals on non-proliferation, establishing 'a policy *aquis* around which national policies were expected to converge' (van Ham 2011: 5).[3] The European Council issued its first statements on non-proliferation at the European summits in Dublin (1990) and Luxembourg (1991). In the 2000s, the 9/11 terrorist attacks and the threat of terrorists using weapons of mass destruction as well as concerns generated by the nuclear policies of North Korea and Iran led the EU to further step up its non-proliferation efforts. At its 2003 summit in Thessaloniki, the European Council adopted a declaration that led to the establishment of the EU's 'Strategy against the Proliferation of Weapons of Mass Destruction' (Council of the European Union 2003). In December 2008, the EU agreed on new 'lines for action' for combating the proliferation of weapons of mass destruction (Council of the European Union 2008). The EU's strategic approach relied on three core principles: the strengthening of the global non-proliferation regime, resolute action to resolve proliferation crisis, and cooperation with key international partners to obstruct sensitive transfers.

With the completion of the single market – which necessitated effective control measures based on common standards for EU exports to third countries (Leslie 1994) – export controls for 'dual-use goods' became another important area of European non-proliferation activities. Dual-use goods are items intended for civil applications that may also be used for military equipment. They comprise as much as 10 per cent of EU exports (Commission 2011). Experiences such as the discovery of Iraq's secret nuclear activities following the Gulf War of 1991 to 1992, which was facilitated by the import of dual-use goods, highlighted the important role of effective export controls in combating nuclear proliferation (see Joyner 2009: 30).

Until the 1990s, EU Member States had addressed the proliferation risk through national export controls and international agreements with other exporting countries.[4] It was only in 1994 that a EU regime for coordinating the control of dual-use goods exports was finally established, in an attempt to ensure that dual-use goods could move freely within the internal market (Schmitt 2001; Micara 2012). As dual-use goods exports concern trade matters with important security implications, the EU's export control policy initially sat uneasily between the competences of the CFSP and the EU's common commercial policy. The EU's regime for dual-use goods exports was established based on a Council regulation adopted as part of the common commercial policy (Regulation 3381/94) as well as on a CFSP decision (94/942/CFSP). Soon after the introduction of the EU's export control system, the Court of Justice of the EU ruled in two separate cases that exports of dual-use goods fall within the scope of the common commercial policy (see Micara 2012), which lies within the exclusive competence of the EU. As a result, the Council adopted Regulation 1334/2000 that overruled the previous CFSP decision, basing the dual-use goods control regime exclusively on Art. 133, TEC. This meant that the Commission now had the exclusive right to initiate modifications of the EU's export control policy, requiring a qualified majority in the Council, and infringements were subject to the jurisdiction of the Court of Justice of the EU.

The EU's export control regime for dual-use goods includes, among other things, a common list of goods requiring licensing if exported from the

Community – which implements the lists decided in global export control bodies – and mutual recognition of export licences granted by competent national authorities in the Member States. EU efforts to improve the efficiency of the system and to achieve a greater harmonization of national approaches led to the establishment of Regulation 428/2009. Among other things, the new regulation enhanced consultation among the Member States, which were required to examine valid export denials granted by other Member States for similar cases (even though their final decision could still deviate), and further harmonized the system of EU export licences. While the EU developed its domestic export control system in close reference to global standards, the binding character of EU legislation also encouraged Member States to comply with international non-proliferation obligations. The legal bindingness, broad functional scope and density of EU non-proliferation rules – covering export controls as well as nuclear safeguards in a detailed manner – progressively turned the European level into a highly significant governance layer in the non-proliferation field.

3 The international non-proliferation system

The multifaceted global non-proliferation regime consists of a number of multilateral and regional agreements including, *inter alia*, agreements on nuclear safeguards and export controls, the Comprehensive Test Ban Treaty, and nuclear weapons-free zones. The Nuclear Non-Proliferation Treaty (NPT) of 1970 forms the cornerstone of the global nuclear non-proliferation system. The NPT has three main pillars: stopping a further spread of nuclear weapons, disarmament, and cooperation on the peaceful use of nuclear energy. Essentially, it rests on a basic bargain: the non-nuclear weapons states agree to not develop or otherwise acquire nuclear weapons and, in return, the five nuclear weapons states recognized by the treaty (the US, Russia, the United Kingdom, France and China) agree to pursue 'good faith' negotiations for nuclear disarmament.

Accession to the NPT became nearly universal after the end of the Cold War, with China and France signing the treaty in 1992.[5] All 27 EU Member States are parties to the NPT. The NPT had an initial term of 25 years but was made permanent at the NPT Review and Extension Conference in May 1995. Conferences to review the Treaty (known as review conferences) are held at five-year intervals. Up until this point, eight multilateral review conferences have taken place since the establishment of the NPT, out of which four (1975, 1985, 2000 and 2010) produced common declarations (see Stoiber 2003). While not legally binding, the results of review conferences are considered as political commitments that should govern the behaviour of the regime members (Meyer 2011). The 2000 NPT review conference arguably produced the most substantive final declaration that has been adopted so far, proposing important steps for nuclear disarmament including bringing the Comprehensive Test Ban Treaty (CTBT) into force.

The entry into force of the NPT in 1970 also strengthened the role of the International Atomic Energy Agency (IAEA), assigning it the role of a 'nuclear watchdog' of the global non-proliferation regime. Established in 1957, the IAEA's safeguards function had initially been limited to small research and experimental reactors (see IAEA 1998). The NPT placed new obligations on non-nuclear weapons state parties, including the requirement to accept IAEA safeguards on all nuclear materials. A new system of so-called 'comprehensive' safeguards (INFCIRC/153) was developed that became the model for individual safeguards agreements concluded between the IAEA and parties to the NPT.[6] Constituting one of the most broadly supported international treaties, the NPT is legally binding for all state parties but it does not possess an automatic enforcement mechanism to deal with violations. Concerning the verification provision, the IAEA board of governors reports cases of non-compliance with NPT safeguards to the UN. The responsibility for developing an appropriate response to safeguards violations, which may include measures such as economic sanctions or the use of force (Chapter VII, UN Charta), falls largely on the UN Security Council.[7]

Important developments in the 1990s, such as the discovery of a clandestine nuclear weapons programme in Iraq, triggered significant reforms of the international safeguards system. Whereas the traditional safeguards approach had focused on verifying that there was no diversion of nuclear materials declared by state parties, the reform process aimed for a system that would additionally provide credible detection of illicit undeclared activities of state parties. In May 1997, the IAEA approved a model protocol (the so-called 'additional protocol') that was to be added to the safeguards agreements previously subscribed by state parties with the IAEA. The additional protocol (INFCIRC/540) advanced the functional scope of issues dealt with by the IAEA, providing it with new tools and authority to verify the completeness (rather than solely the correctness) of state party declarations.[8] To combine the new verification measures in an efficient manner with existing safeguards, the board of IAEA governors approved a 'Conceptual Framework for Integrated Safeguards' in March 2002. A further step in strengthening the global non-proliferation system was UN Security Council Resolution 1540, established on the initiative of the United States and the United Kingdom in 2004. Adopted under Chapter VII of the UN Charta, the resolution established binding obligations for all states aimed at preventing and deterring non-state actors from assessing weapons of mass destruction and related material (Council of the European Union 2006).

International safeguards are backed by nuclear export controls that regulate the transfer of sensitive materials and technologies across borders, including items designed for nuclear use as well as dual-use goods. The NPT prohibits state parties from transferring nuclear material, unless it serves peaceful purposes and is subject to IAEA safeguards. Key institutions of the global export control regime are the Nuclear Suppliers Group (1975), the Zangger Committee (1971) and the Wassenaar Arrangement (1996). Among other things, the global export control regime governs a coordinated system of export licences for dual-use goods and promotes the harmonization of national export controls between technology exporting states.

172 P. Müller

Table 10.1 Significance of governance layers over time (Nuclear Non-proliferation)

Phase	National level	EU level	Global level
Post-WWII	Medium (national export control policies)	–	–
1957–1970	Medium	Medium (establishment of Euratom nuclear safeguards system)	Low
1970–90	Medium	Medium	High (NPT establishes a global nuclear safeguards system administrated by IAEA; set-up of a global export control system for nuclear and dual-use goods)
post-1990	Low	High (establishment of binding EU export controls for dual-use goods)	High
2020 (extrapolation)	Low (decreasing)	High	High

A series of meetings of the Nuclear Suppliers Group in the mid-1970s produced agreement on detailed international export guidelines published as an IAEA document (INFCIRC/254) in 1978, which drew on an earlier list of items subject to export controls established by the Zangger Committee (so-called 'Trigger List'). While the NSG was relatively inactive in the period between 1978 and 1991, the Zangger Committee met on a regular basis to review and amend its 'Trigger List'. Following the discovery of Iraq's clandestine nuclear weapons programme, the NSG decided in 1992 to establish guidelines for the transfer of nuclear-related dual-use items that could make a significant contribution to an unsafeguarded nuclear fuel cycle or nuclear explosive activity. These guidelines were published as Part 2 of INFCIRC/254 in July 1992, further extending the functional scope and density of the rules of the global export control regime. At the same time, the international control regime for nuclear and dual-use goods exports remains based on non-binding guidelines and voluntary regulations.[9]

4 The vertical dimension: the EU's interaction with the global non-proliferation system

The EU's impact on global non-proliferation policy has differed over time and between issue areas. In the Cold War era, the EU's political influence as a non-proliferation actor was constrained by the dominant role of the world's two superpowers, the US and the Soviet Union. It was only in the 1990s that the EU

Table 10.2 Overview of international non-proliferation institutions

International institution	Main objectives	Non-proliferation standards
Non-Proliferation Treaty (NPT)	• Pillar one: non-proliferation; • Pillar two: nuclear disarmament; • Pillar three: encourage peaceful use of nuclear energy	Core principles on nuclear non-proliferation: • Five recognized nuclear weapons states must not transfer nuclear weapons nor assist non-nuclear weapons states in manufacturing them; • Non-nuclear weapons states must not acquire nuclear weapons and agree to accept IAEA safeguards to verify peaceful use of nuclear energy
International Atomic Energy Agency (IAEA)	• Support of cooperation in civilian nuclear field; • Verifying (declared) nuclear material and activities through application of safeguards under the NPT; • Strengthening the effectiveness of safeguards	• Establishment of nuclear safeguards standards/techniques as basis for IAEA agreements with third countries; • Safeguard model is primarily defined in IAEA statute and in INFCIRC/66 (applied to any state with safeguards agreement); INFCIRC/153 (basis for agreement with parties to NPT), INFCIRC/540 (model additional protocol); as well as in agreements with groupings of states
Nuclear Suppliers Group	• Development, implementation and review of guidelines for nuclear (related) exports	• Guidelines for nuclear transfers for peaceful purposes (published as IAEA document (INFCIRC/254); • Guidelines for transfer of nuclear-related dual-use goods (published as part 2 of INFCIRC/254)
Waasenaar Arrangement	• Promotes transparency and responsibility in transfer of conventional arms and dual-use goods technologies	• Guidelines, including control list, for export of dual-use goods and technologies
Zangger Committee	• Implementation of NPT requirement to apply IAEA safeguards to nuclear exports	• Maintenance of list of equipment whose export requires safeguards at recipient facility ('trigger list')

emerged as a more active player in the nuclear non-proliferation field, making more systematic efforts to shape global policy outcomes (Müller and van Dassen 1997; Grip 2011). To advance its external non-proliferation objectives, the EU has relied on both its influence in key bodies of the international non-proliferation regime as well as its bilateral relations with third countries. While this section reports on various aspects of the EU's non-proliferation policy, including its various activities that aim at the strengthening and universalization of global non-proliferation norms, special attention will be paid to the question of policy export and other forms of EU–global-level interaction.

4.1 The EU's fragmented agency in global non-proliferation institutions

As a Union of 27 Member States – including several technologically advanced producers of nuclear energy and two nuclear weapons states – the EU as a bloc enjoys considerable weight in global non-proliferation affairs. Yet, while the EU has assumed an increasingly active role in the global nuclear non-proliferation regime over time, its external non-proliferation policy has continued to face important internal constraints. The intergovernmental CFSP remains the core institutional framework for the EU's non-proliferation policy, which also involves Euratom and the EU's common commercial policy (see above). And traditionally, the EU's fragmented agency as an external actor in non-proliferation has raised problems for unified external representation and internal coordination.

The EU's Lisbon Treaty of 2009 sought to address these challenges. Among other things, staff members from the Commission, the Council and Member States were integrated into the newly established European External Action Service.[10] Further reforms included the creation of a permanent President within the European Council, a new High Representative for Foreign Affairs (double-hatting as Vice-president of the Commission) and a legal personality of the EU as an international actor. The High Representative and the President of the European Council share the role of representing the EU's CFSP in key non-proliferation institutions and conferences, with High Representative Catherine Ashton representing the EU in the 2010 NPT Review Conference and the President of the European Council Herman van Rompuy representing it at the Nuclear Security Summit in April 2010 (see Grip 2011). Still, important limitations remained, not least as external representation in the realm of the CFSP still requires effective coordination of common positions among Member States with diverse interests and traditions on nuclear policy (van Ham 2011; Müller and van Dassen 1997).[11] EU states have traditionally lacked unity on several important issues, including the role of nuclear weapons and nuclear energy, the course of disarmament, and the use of (military) force in enforcing compliance with international non-proliferation commitments (see van Ham 2011).

Even in areas of non-proliferation policy where the European treaties grant the Commission important external competences – as is the case in the realm of nuclear safeguards (representing Euratom) and export controls of dual-use goods (representing the common commercial policy) – the Member States still play a leading role in the formulation and representation of EU positions. While almost all EU countries are members of the main international non-proliferation bodies, Commission participation in international institutions is more limited.[12] The Commission is an observer – and not a full member – in the IAEA as well as in key export control institutions like the Nuclear Suppliers Group and the Zangger Committee, and it is not represented at all in the Waasenaar Arrangement.

What is more, initiatives to upgrade the EU's status, such as its request for full membership in the IAEA, have made little inroads thus far, not least as such moves have enjoyed little support by the EU's own Member States. As an observer has noted, this translated into a situation where:

> Community proposals do not automatically mirror a Community position within international regimes; on the contrary, Commission participation is limited and, notwithstanding the co-ordination of members through the Council Presidency, there are cases of divergent positions of EU Member States.
>
> (Micara 2012: 7–8)

Despite its fragmented agency as a non-proliferation actor, the EU has become engaged in a series of diplomatic initiatives and interventions to promote common EU objectives in global non-proliferation bodies. Notable achievements for the EU were its campaign for the indefinite extension of the NPT Treaty at the 1995 review and extension conference and its initiative for the entry into force of the Comprehensive Test Ban Treaty (CTBT), opened for signature in 1996 (Portela 2004). By and large, the EU Member States established common positions on a broad set of issues debated at NPT review conferences. At the latest NPT review conference in 2010, 34 out of 56 specific objectives adopted by the EU prior to the conference (Council Decision 2010/12/CFSP) made it in some form into the conference's final declaration, albeit several of them in a weakened form (Müller 2010). When acting as a block, the EU can thus act as an effective promoter of common positions, given that it succeeds in building support around EU initiatives in global level institutions.

4.2 The EU and the global export control regime: importing international rules into binding EU legislation

An important objective of the EU's non-proliferation policy is to strengthen the international export control system for nuclear and dual-use goods. Overall, the EU's domestic export control policies have followed developments of the global level, with the EU importing international commitments into binding EU legislation. Historically, international cooperation has preceded EU efforts to set up a European system on export controls for dual-use goods (see above). While the EU's export control system that emerged in the 1990s became stricter, more strongly harmonized and more binding than the global export control regime over time, the EU still aimed at developing its national policy with close reference to decisions taken in international control bodies. Very importantly, the EU's export control list for dual-use goods – which forms the core of its export control policy – was based on the lists established by international control bodies, i.e. by the Nuclear Suppliers Group, the Wassenaar Arrangement and the Missile Technology Control Regime (Schmitt 2001). Moreover, the relevant EU legislation on dual-use goods states that decisions to update the EU's common list of items subject to export controls 'must be in conformity with the relevant obligations and commitments, and any modification ... that Member States have accepted as members of the international non-proliferation regimes' (Council Regulation 428/2009, Art. 15).

Developing its domestic export control regime on dual-use goods with close reference to the global level not only allows the EU to promote Member State compliance with international non-proliferation obligations, it is also a strategy to balance its security and commercial interests. Given the technical nature of dual-use goods, the most sophisticated items are only available from a limited number of supplying countries – including most EU Member States as well as several other highly industrialized countries that cooperate in global export control institutions. International cooperation is crucial for the success of non-proliferation efforts, which demands global action covering all major supplier countries. At the same time, the EU's system for export controls clearly impacts on the international competitiveness of its industry, with dual-use goods covering a substantial portion of EU exports (see above). Export controls can result in considerable losses for an exporter (if an export licence is not granted) as well as in significant gains (if a licence is granted more quickly or easily than to competitors) (see COM 2011: 6). Harmonization at the global level is thus not only in the EU's best security interest, it is also crucial to ensure a level playing field for EU exporters, placing a similar bureaucratic burden on all regime members. Accordingly, cooperation on international export control measures for dual-use goods may be expected to remain high on the European agenda, particularly as modernization and technological progress leads to a situation where an increasing number of countries will be able to supply controlled items.

4.3 The EU and nuclear safeguards – from policy protection to the vertical export of technical standards

The field of nuclear safeguards constitutes another interesting case for studying the EU's interaction with the global non-proliferation regime. During the Cold War era, the dominance of the US and the Soviet Union in non-proliferation policy posed clear limits for the EU in terms of exporting domestic solutions to the global level. The EU – which had already established a regional nuclear safeguards system when the safeguards article of the NPT was negotiated in the late 1960s – thus tried primarily to protect its domestic policy regime from external pressure. A key issue in drafting the nuclear safeguards article of the NPT was whether and how it would apply to the non-nuclear weapons states of Euratom that possessed nuclear reactors. The IAEA wanted a universal system based on the uniform treatment of all its members. The EU's regional safeguards approach was also opposed by the Soviet Union. To avoid a situation where Euratom members would inspect themselves, the Soviet Union was eager to bring the nuclear activities of these countries under international control. The EU, in turn, aimed at policy protection, trying to preserve its successful regional safeguards system that constituted an important element of Euratom's activities. In particular the EU's non-nuclear weapon states understood IAEA inspections as intrusive measures that exposed them to the risk of industrial espionage, potentially putting their nuclear industries at a disadvantage with their competitors in nuclear weapon states (which are not subject to IAEA verifications). In the context of the Cold War, accepting IAEA inspectors from non-Euratom countries, including the Soviet Union, raised additional concerns on the part of Euratom members.

To promote their interests, Euratom's non-nuclear weapon states (Belgium, the Federal Republic of Germany, Italy, Luxembourg and the Netherlands) signed the NPT in 1968/1969, which allowed them to participate in subsequent IAEA negotiations on inspection standards but simultaneously made their ratification dependent on negotiating a satisfactory agreement on the implementation of IAEA safeguards (Bunn 2007). The threat of non-ratification put the Euratom countries in a strong bargaining position – not least as a possible German nuclear armament was a strong Soviet concern. As a result, it was agreed that IAEA safeguards in Euratom countries were largely based on IAEA observation of Euratom inspections or on 'joint operations' of both safeguards institutions (INFCIRC/193). At the same time, the Euratom–IAEA safeguards agreement enabled the IAEA to observe Euratom measures and to perform all the required activities in EU Member States to meet its safeguards criteria and to draw independent conclusions (Schleicher 1980). The EU's protection of its regional policy approach also had implications for the global policy regime. The integration of Euratom's regional verification system as an additional layer in the global safeguards regime challenged the IAEA's universal approach, not least as it created a precedent that allowed other groupings of states to make similar demands (Lindroos 1997: 335). It should also be mentioned that the Euratom system led to a duplication of verification measures in a geographical area where the actual nuclear proliferation risk had substantially decreased since the time the NPT was negotiated.

The EU's main strategy during the negotiations of the NPT evidently focused on protecting the Euratom safeguards system. At the same time, the EU assumed an active role in strengthening the global safeguards regime from the outset, particularly through the export of technical safeguards standards and routines to the IAEA. While the impartial nature of the IAEA as a global safeguards organization generally makes it difficult to exercise direct political influence through the organization's decision-making bodies (Interview with senior diplomat at the EU's Representation to the IAEA in Vienna, March 2012), the technical working groups and bodies underpinning the nuclear safeguards regime provide a less politicized arena for influence.[13] Here, its technical expertise and know-how in the safeguards realm turned the EU into an important partner for cooperation with the IAEA, which generally showed a keen interest in technical cooperation with Euratom to enhance its implementation capacity (Interview with a senior scientist at the Commission's JRC, March 2012).

When the comprehensive IAEA verification system was set up in 1970, the EU had already accumulated several years of experience in administrating its Euratom safeguards system. After the NPT entered into force, Euratom control measures served as a model the IAEA used when entering into safeguards agreements with third countries (see Mallard 2010: 8). The EU's related research and development activities not only helped it to improve the safeguards routines of the Euratom system, but also played an important role in establishing the technical operability of international safeguards (Guta 1979; Cuypers 1994). The European Commission's Joint Resarch Centre (JRC) and the European Safeguards Research and Development Association (ESARDA), created in 1958 and 1969 respectively, functioned as key bodies to harmonize safeguards-related research in the EU and as a platform for the exchange of information, technology and knowledge with the global research community.[14] Specific know-how generated in the Euratom framework – including on measurement standards for material accountancy, destructive and non-destructive measurement methods, or measures of containment and integral experiments – also inspired standards and routines of the global policy regime. A senior scientist involved in the early research activities of the Joint Research Centre summed up the importance of technological expertise for the development of safeguards by stating that 'in the end victory is on the side of the soundest scientific concept, but it can take several years for that concept to diffuse' (Interview with a senior former scientist at the Commission's JRC, May 2012).

Over time, a dense inter-institutional framework for Euratom–IAEA cooperation developed. In 1981 the European Commission Support Programme was launched, formalizing the cooperation between the IAEA and Euratom in the field of safeguards research. Together with the national support programmes of the Federal Republic of Germany, France, the United Kingdom, Italy and Belgium, the Commission's Support Programme made Euratom one of the largest contributors to the research activities of the IAEA at that time, second only to the US (see Runquist 1986).[15] Cooperation between Euratom and the IAEA on nuclear safeguards was further strengthened through the 'new partnership approach' established in 1992, reducing some duplications in the safeguards efforts of the two organizations through the common use of technology and analytical capabilities as well as through enhanced cooperation in research and development (see Thorstensen and Chitumbo 1995).[16] In 2008, the European Commission and the IAEA issued a joint statement that emphasized the importance of joint cooperation covering several important areas, including energy, research and development, and external relations (Lundin 2012). Euratom–IAEA cooperation provided the EU with an arena for technical influence which it used to strengthen the IAEA's capacity for implementing global safeguards. European safeguards techniques – such as the use of certified reference materials and associated training techniques in mass spectroscopy – were first applied in the Euratom framework and then the experience was exported to the IAEA (Goncalves *et al.* 2010). Further examples relate to safeguards techniques designed for large reprocessing facilities, an area where the EU has considerable expertise. Among other things, the IAEA relies on accountancy verification measurements designed by the EU at the large nuclear reprocessing plant Rokkasho in Japan (Joint Research Centre 2010). Moreover, the support programmes of the EU and its Member States directly contributed to IAEA development needs, several of which included tasks outside the scope of Euratom's domestic verification mandate. For instance, the EU's Joint Research Centre has carried out research tasks to improve the verification of the absence of undeclared nuclear activities, contributing to the evolution of IAEA safeguards techniques in areas such as environmental particle sample analysis and design information verification techniques.[17]

It is important to note, however, that policy transfer between the EU and the IAEA did not proceed in only one direction. The EU's participation in the global non-proliferation regime also necessitated adjustments to its domestic legislation in line with its international commitments and the EU also benefited from technical experience and know-how provided by its partners. As a result of the 1973 Euratom–IAEA verification agreement, a new safeguards regulation was adopted in the Euratom framework (Commission Regulation 3227/76), allowing the Commission to obtain technical information from plant operators necessary for reporting to the IAEA. Following the entry into force of the IAEA's additional protocol in the EU in 2004, the EU once more updated its domestic legislation (Commission Regulation (Euratom) 302/2005) to establish new implementation requirements deriving from the additional protocol.

5 The horizontal dimensions: the EU's promotion of global non-proliferation norms

Besides its vertical interaction with the global non-proliferation regime, the EU also promotes its policy preferences through horizontal diffusion. Yet reflecting a strong commitment to multilateralism, the horizontal dimension of the EU's non-proliferation policy is primarily concerned with promoting the strengthening and universalization of international non-proliferation standards, rather than with horizontal EU policy export in a strict sense (i.e. the transfer of European standards to third countries). The EU's 2003 Strategy against the Proliferation of Weapons of Mass Destruction (WMD) specifically called for mainstreaming non-proliferation objectives into the EU's wider external relations, including its economic activities and programmes (Council of the European Union 2003).[18] Since then, the EU has aimed at the inclusion of a so-called 'WMD clause' in mixed agreements[19] with third countries as well as in action plans developed within the framework of the European Neighbourhood Policy. Based on the conditionality mechanism, the clause allows the EU to suspend trade, development assistance, or other elements of cooperation in cases of third countries' non-compliance with non-proliferation commitments (see Grip 2009). The first part of the clause is considered by the EU as 'essential' and states the commitment of the EU and its respective partner countries to fulfil all of their existing international non-proliferation obligations. The second element of the non-proliferation clause anticipates additional commitments from partner countries – namely accession to, or ratification of, relevant international non-proliferation instruments and the implementation of effective national export controls.

The EU has incorporated non-proliferation clauses into relevant agreements with a vast number of countries and the Council reports on progress in negotiations with third countries in biannual progress reports on the WMD strategy.[20] However, observers have identified important shortcomings of the EU's mainstreaming policy. Importantly, the EU lacks a clear strategy concerning what specific form the clause should take with respect to different third countries and how to deal with resistance to the clause from some of the most relevant countries (see van Ham 2011: 4; Grip 2009: 5). WMD clauses have been preliminarily agreed upon but not signed by a number of important countries, including with China, Libya and South Korea. Thus far however, the only mixed agreements with a WMD clause that have entered into force are the stabilization and association agreement with Albania and the revised Cotonou Agreement that concerns several African countries and the Caribbean and Pacific group of states, most of which are not considered critical countries from a non-proliferation perspective. At the same time, the negotiations of a trade agreement with India gave rise to speculations that the EU (or at least some of its Member States) might be ready to abandon the principle of including a non-proliferation clause in all agreements to promote its trade interests (see Grip 2009: 11). While the EU's horizontal promotion of international non-proliferation standards has certainly put these issues on the agenda of its political dialogue and negotiations with several partner countries, there is little evidence to suggest that the WMD clause has actually led to a change of policy in partner countries.

6 Conclusion

This chapter has looked at the EU's potential for policy export to the global non-proliferation regime. Its focus has been on those aspects of the EU's non-proliferation policy where its domestic policy overlaps with rule-making at the global level, notably on the issues of nuclear safeguards standards and export controls. The chapter has shown that the EU's political role in the non-proliferation realm has traditionally been subject to important external constraints as well as internal limitations, with policy export occurring only at the margins.

The core architecture of the global non-proliferation regime has been the product of the Cold War order during which international security issues were dominated by the US and the Soviet Union. Unable to exercise a meaningful influence in the negotiations of the Non-Proliferation Treaty, EU efforts in the realm of nuclear safeguards – where it has been a first mover – initially aimed for the protection of its regional safeguards system administrated by Euratom. At the same time, the case of nuclear safeguards has shown that through its technical expertise and experience in the safeguards realm, the EU from an early point in time developed some capacity for policy export in technical domains (limited functional scope). Through the transfer of technical solutions and safeguard routines the EU contributed to the progressive strengthening of the IAEA's implementation capacity. Over time, a dense institutional network of cooperation has been established that sustains the exchange of information, expertise and technical solutions between the two safeguards organizations. It seems safe to say that the power of expertise and technological resources have defined the EU's capacity for policy export in the realm of nuclear safeguards more than its emerging role as an international actor.

It is only in the post-Cold War setting that the EU has become a more relevant actor in non-proliferation diplomacy, supporting important reforms of the international non-proliferation regime since the 1990s. In the area of export controls for dual-use goods, where a domestic EU regime was established in the mid-1990s which eventually became stricter than global policy, the EU sought to develop its domestic policy with close reference to decisions taken in global institutions that cover most of the relevant supplier countries. Here, policy import at the global level helped to make the Member States' international commitments more binding. At the same time, by developing its own policy with close reference to decisions of key bodies of the global export control regime (in which the EU is strongly represented), the EU sought to maintain a level playing field for its industry.

The EU also facilitated the horizontal diffusion of global non-proliferation norms and treaties through mainstreaming non-proliferation objectives in its relations with third countries. Clearly, proliferation risks are a global problem and promoting international non-proliferation norms, rather than EU policy export in a strict sense, has been a key objective of the EU's external relations with third countries. Thus far, however, the EU's effort to horizontally promote international non-proliferation objectives through its WMD clause – which introduced the conditionality mechanisms to mixed agreements with third countries – has faced important limitations. At the same time, it has allowed the EU to raise non-proliferation issues in its diplomatic dealings with third countries, underscoring its commitment to an effective multilateral response to global proliferation risks.

Notes

1 The introduction of Euratom safeguards was promoted by the US, on which Western Europe heavily depended for nuclear fuel and technology (see Fischer 2000).
2 As an observer has noted, the Euratom system was designed to prevent undeclared nuclear proliferation, while allowing for checked nuclear proliferation. In particular, European negotiators involved in crafting the Euratom system sought to secretly enable US help for a federate Europe to acquire nuclear weapons capability (see Mallard 2010: 8).

3 Since the Lisbon Treaty these instruments are now all called Council Decisions.
4 In the Cold War era the EU members were part of a system of Western states that coordinated their export policies vis-à-vis Warsaw Pact countries through bodies like the Coordinating Committee for Multilateral Strategic Export Controls.
5 Only India, Pakistan and Israel are not signatories to the NPT. While each state party to the NPT has the right to withdraw from the treaty (Art. 12, NPT), on a practical level the high degree of universality of core non-proliferation principles places pressure on states to respect the treaty (see Lindroos 1997: 333).
6 IAEA safeguards are arrangements to account for and control the use of nuclear materials (especially uranium), verifying that that they are used solely for civilian purposes. The traditional IAEA safeguards system includes inspections relying on material accountability (i.e. tracking all inward and outward transfer of nuclear materials and the flow of materials in nuclear facilities); physical security measures (i.e. restricting access to nuclear materials at the site of use); and containment and surveillance measures, including the use of seals and automatic cameras to detect unreported activities at nuclear facilities (World Nuclear Association 2012).
7 However, the board of governors of the IAEA and the UN Security Council are not independent institutional actors and political divisions can impede effective enforcement.
8 By the end of July 2011, 135 out of 189 state parties to the NPT had signed an additional protocol and 109 additional protocols had entered into force (see Drobysz and Sitt 2011).
9 Besides its informal character, the inability of the global export control system to impose restrictions on countries that have not ratified the relevant non-proliferation agreements has been described as additional weaknesses of global export controls (Micara 2012: 3). Moreover, the global export control system no longer includes all the main exporters of dual-use goods – not least as modernization and technological progress resulted in a situation where an increasing number of countries will be able to supply controlled items.
10 High Representative Ashton and the President of the European Council van Rompuy share the role of representing the EU in international non-proliferation organizations and conferences.
11 The EU comprises nuclear weapons states as well as non-nuclear weapons states, NATO members and non-aligned countries, as well as supporters and opponents of nuclear energy.
12 At the time of writing, all 27 EU countries were members of the Nuclear Suppliers Group (NSG), all EU countries except Cyprus were members of the Waasenaar Arrangement, and 22 EU countries were members of the Zangger Committee.
13 In complex technical areas like nuclear safeguards, policy evolution not only results from political interventions but is, to a considerable extent, driven by technological innovation.
14 The EU Member States had begun to coordinate their nuclear research and development activities after signing the Euratom Treaty in 1957.
15 Carrying out safeguard research work for the IAEA is a demanding undertaking that involves a relatively small number of technologically advanced countries. When the Commission started its support programmes only six countries maintained national support programmes besides the EU. By the year 2009, the number of countries with support programmes had increased to 20, including 10 EU Member States (see Runquist 1986).
16 The new approach was designed to apply safeguards in a more efficient manner in the EU, avoiding unnecessary duplication and reducing the IAEA's inspection effort in the EU while preserving its ability to draw independent conclusions.
17 EU research institutions have also been involved in developing the IAEA's 'Conceptual Framework for Integrated Safeguards' (see above) of 2002, which is the product

of three years of intensive development effort involving the IAEA, national support programmes and external experts. Further EU activities included training of IAEA inspectors on novel detection techniques, information analysis and contributions to equipment developments.
18 Making trade and aid contingent on non-third party compliance with non-proliferation objectives was also part of the EU's 2008 'New Lines for Action' document (Council of the European Union 2008).
19 Mixed agreements include a combination of political and economic elements; they require consensus vote in the Council and the support of the European Parliament.
20 The Council's 2007 progress report (Council of the European Union 2007), for instance, noted that successful negotiations on agreements with non-proliferation clauses had been concluded with more than 90 states, while recent reports state that there has been progress in negotiations with, among others, countries like Afghanistan, Australia, Canada and Kazakhstan (Council of the European Union 2013). Still, The EU's reporting focuses on all agreements under negotiation (not only on agreements that are in force) and does not distinguish between differences in the language of the WMD clause.

References

Bunn, G. (2007) 'Nuclear Safeguards – How Far Can Inspectors Go?', *IAEA Bulletin* 48(2): 49–55.

Commission of the European Communities (2011a) *Meeting Report of the 2011 Dual-use Exporter Conference of 20 September 2011*, 19 October. Online. Available: http://trade.ec.europa.eu/doclib/docs/2011/october/tradoc_148299.pdf (accessed 15 April 2013).

—— (2011b) *Green Paper: The Dual-use Export Control System of the European Union: Ensuring Security and Competitiveness in a Changing World*, COM(2011) 393 (1 October 2011).

Council of the European Union (2003) *EU Strategy against Proliferation of Weapons of Mass Destruction*, 15708/03 (10 December 2003).

—— (2006) *Council Joint Action 2006/419/CFSP in Support of the Implementation of the UNSC Resolution 1540 (2004) and in the Framework of the Implementation of the EU Strategy against the Proliferation of WMD*. Online. Available: http://eur-lex.europa.eu/LexUriServ/site/en/oj/2006/l_165/l_16520060617en00300034.pdf (accessed 15 April 2013).

—— (2007) *Six-monthly Progress Report on the Implementation of the EU Strategy against the Proliferation of Weapons of Mass Destruction (2007/1)*. Online. Available: http://register.consilium.europa.eu/pdf/en/07/st11/st11024.en07.pdf (accessed 15 April 2013).

—— (2008) *New Lines for Action by the European Union in Combating the Proliferation of Weapons of Mass Destruction and their Delivery Systems*, 16089/08 (23 November).

—— (2013) *Six-monthly Progress Report on the Implementation of the EU Strategy against the Proliferation of Weapons of Mass Destruction (2012/2)*. Online. Available: http://eur-lex.europa.eu/LexUriServ/LexUriServ.do?uri=OJ:C:2013:037:0003:0026:EN:PDF (accessed 15 April 2013).

Cuypers, M. (1994) *Twenty-five Years of the European Safeguards R&D Association (ESARDA)*, Paper Presented at the Plenary Sesssion of the 16th Annual ESARDA Meeting at Ghent, 17–19 May. Online. Available: http://esarda2.jrc.it/db_proceeding/mfile/B_1994_024_012.pdf (accessed 18 April 2013).

Drobysz, S. and Sitt, B. (2011) *Optimizing the IAEA Safeguards System*. Online.

Available: www.nonproliferation.eu/documents/other/soniadrobyszbernardsitt4ecd0b3738cb3.pdf (accessed 14 April 2013).

European Council (2003) *A Secure Europe in a Better World*. Online. Available: www.consilium.europa.eu/uedocs/cmsUpload/78367.pdf (14 April 2013).

Fischer, D. (2000) 'Nuclear Safeguards: Evolution and Future', in T. Findlay and O. Meier (eds) *Verification Yearbook 2000*, London: Vertic.

Goncalves, J.G.M., Abousahl, S. and Frigola, P. (2010) *The European Commission Support Programme: Activities and Achievements*, IAEA-CN-184/230. Online. Available: www.iaea.org/safeguards/Symposium/2010/Documents/PapersRepository/230.pdf (accessed 18 April 2013).

Grip, L. (2009) *The EU Non-proliferation Clause: A Preliminary Assessment*, SIPRI Background Paper, November, Stockholm International Peace Research Institute. Online. Available: http://books.sipri.org/files/misc/SIPRIBP0911.pdf (accessed 14 April 2013).

—— (2011) *Mapping the European Union's Institutional Actors Related to WMD Non-proliferation*, Non-Proliferation Papers No. 1, EU Non-proliferation Consortium. Online. Available: www.sipri.org/research/disarmament/euconsortium/publications/EUNPC_no1.pdf/view (accessed 14 April 2013).

Guta, D. (1979) *Ten Years of ESARDA. Proceedings of the 1st ESARDA Symposium on Safeguards and Nuclear Material Management*, Online. Available: http://esarda2.jrc.it/db_proceeding/mfile/P_1979_brussels_001.pdf (accessed 18 April 2013).

Holtom, P. (2007) 'An Assessment of the Baltic States' Contribution to EU Efforts to Prevent Proliferation and Combat Illicit Arms Trafficking', in D. Brown and A.J.K. Shepherd (eds) *The Security Dimension of EU Enlargement*, Manchester: Manchester University Press.

IAEA (1998) *The Evolution of IAEA Safeguards*, International Nuclear Verification Series No. 2, IAEA. Online. Available: http://www-pub.iaea.org/MTCD/publications/PDF/NVS2_web.pdf (accessed 18 April 2013).

Joint Research Centre (2010) *JRC Scientists Monitor Safeguards Compliance of 80 Percent of the World's Reprocessed Nuclear Fuel*, news release, 15 June 2010. Online. Available: http://ec.europa.eu/dgs/jrc/downloads/jrc_20100615_newsrelease_safeguards.pdf (accessed 14 April 2013).

Joyner, D.H. (2009) *International Law and the Proliferation of Weapons of Mass Destruction*, Oxford: Oxford University Press.

Leslie, B.J. (1994) 'Dual Use Goods and the European Community: Problems and Prospects in Eliminating Internal Border Controls on Sensitive Products', *Boston Colledge International and Comparative Law Review* 17(1): 193–211.

Lindroos, A. (1997) 'The Role of Euratom in the Non-proliferation Regime', in M. Koskenniemi and K. Takmaa (eds) *Finnish Yearbook of International Law*, The Hague: Kluwer Law International.

Lundin, L. (2012) *The European Union, the IAEA and WMD Non-proliferation: Unity of Approach and Continuity of Action*, Non-Proliferation Papers No. 9, EU Non-proliferation Consortium. Online. Available: www.nonproliferation.eu/documents/non-proliferationpapers/larseriklundin4f797a687776f.pdf (accessed 14 April 2013).

Mallard, G. (2010) *Crafting the Nuclear Regime Complex (1950–1975): Dynamics of Harmonization of Opaque Treaty Rules*, paper presented for the American Sociological Association Annual Meeting, Las Vegas, 20 August 2011. Online. Available: http://citation.allacademic.com/meta/p503699_index.html.

Meyer, P. (2011) *The 2010 NPT Review Conference: An Assessment of Outcome and*

Outlook, Simons Papers in Security and Development No. 11/2011, School for International Studies, Simon Fraser University. Online. Available: www.sfu.ca/content/dam/sfu/internationalstudies/documents/swp/WP11.pdf (accessed 14 April 2013).

Micara, A.G. (2012) 'Current Features of the European Union Regime for Export Control of Dual-Use Goods', *Journal of Common Market Studies* 50(4): 578–593.

Müller, H. (2010) *The NPT after the 2010 Review Conference: Implications for the EU*. Online. Available: www.nonproliferation.eu/documents/kickoff/muller.pdf (accessed 14 April 2013).

Müller, H. and van Dassen, L. (1997) 'From Cacophony to Joint Action: Success and Shortcomings of European Nuclear Non-proliferation Policy', in M. Holland (ed.) *Common Foreign and Security Policy. The Record and Reforms*, London: Pinter.

Portela, C. (2003) *The Role of the EU in the Non-proliferation of Nuclear Weapons: The Way to Thessaloniki and Beyond*, PRIF Report No. 65/2003, Peace Research Institute Frankfurt (PRIF). Online. Available: www.hsfk.de/downloads/prifrep65.pdf (accessed 14 April 2013).

—— (2004) 'The EU and the NPT: Testing the New European Non-proliferation Strategy', *Disarmament Diplomacy* 78(July/August). Online. Available: www.acronym.org.uk/dd/dd78/78cp.htm (accessed 14 April 2013).

Runquist, D. (1986) 'Improving Technical Support to IAEA Safeguards: Programmes Supported by Member States are Providing Valuable Resources', *IAEA Bulletin* 28(4): 29–31.

Schleicher, H.W. (1980) 'Nuclear Safeguards in the European Community – A Regional Approach', *IAEA-Bulletin* 22(3/4): 45–50.

Schmitt, B. (2001) *A Common European Export Policy for Defence and Dual-use Items?*, Occasional Papers 25, Institute for Security Studies Paris. Online. Available: www.iss.europa.eu/uploads/media/occ025.pdf (accessed 14 April 2013).

Stoiber, C. (2003) 'The Evolution of NPT Review Conference Final Documents, 1975–2000', *The Nonproliferation Review* 2003(fall/winter): 126–166.

Thorstensen, S. and Chitumbo, K. (1995) 'Safeguards in the European Union: The New Partnership Approach', *IAEA Bulletin* 37(1): 25–28.

van Ham, P. (2011) *The European Union's WMD Strategy and the CFSP: A Critical Analysis*, Non-proliferation Papers No. 2, EU Non-Proliferation Consortium. Online. Available: www.sipri.org/research/disarmament/euconsortium/publications/publications/EUNPC_no%202.pdf (accessed 14 April 2013).

World Nuclear Association (2012) *Safeguards to Prevent Nuclear Proliferation*. Online. Available: www.world-nuclear.org/info/inf12.html (accessed 14 April 2013).

11 EU financial market regulation
Protecting distinctive policy preferences

Zdenek Kudrna

1 Introduction

The European Union (EU) is the single largest financial market in the world, regulated by increasingly harmonized rules and governed by increasingly supranational supervisors. Along with the US and Japan, the EU hosts one of the three most important global financial centres in the City of London. This puts the Union at the centre stage of the global regulatory regime in finance.

This chapter discusses the EU's capacity to export its policy preferences into global banking and accounting regulations. It finds that the EU rarely exports its policies because the global rules tend to be adopted first and the EU legislation only follows. This is either because the global regimes predate adoption of common rules, or, more recently, it is politically expedient to tame the EU-level policy conflicts by 'harmonizing globally in order to harmonize internally'. The disunity and frequent clashes with the US hamper EU policy exports; hence, it is often relegated to the mere protection of preferences. The EU uses its powerful position in global regimes to ensure that policy imports contrary to preferences of important subsets of EU Member States are prevented. At the same time, the EU and its Member States stick to their multilateralist commitments and avoid pushing the protection of their preferences so far as to undermine the overall credibility of the respective global regulatory regimes.

The chapter starts with a brief overview of the financial market regulation in the European Union and at the global level. The third section reconciles the existing literature and the theoretical framework introduced in Chapter 1 in order to sharpen the analytical focus for case studies. The four cases include three generations of international banking standards introduced since the 1980s and the last decade of the evolution of international accounting standards. The conclusion highlights the EU's limited success in policy export and promotion, coupled with successful protection of its policy preferences.

2 The EU financial market regulation

Financial market regulation is an integral part of the EU internal market policy. Its goals include removal of the non-tariff barriers to trade in financial services through regulatory harmonization, fostering financial stability across the single market and ensuring a high degree of consumer protection. The origins of the common regulations date back to the 1970s, but they became prominent only in the late 1980s during the run-up to the single market project. The policy covers four key subfields: free movement of capital, banking, insurance and securities. In addition, it also covers numerous auxiliary issues related to financial conglomerates, accounting, auditing, corporate governance or payment and settlement infrastructures.

The Single Market project was only partially successful in integrating financial regulations. The EU framework remained largely fragmented along national lines and its evolution lagged behind market developments (see Grossman and Leblond 2011). Hence, at the time of the adoption of the single currency, there was no single financial market. This motivated the launch of the Financial Services Action Plan aimed at removing the remaining obstacles and updating the regulatory framework with market developments. The plan also triggered a major overhaul of the respective governance arrangements by introducing the Lamfalussy committee architecture (see De Meester 2008). Although increasing gradually, the shift of competences to the supranational level remains modest and the responsibility for the internal market in financial services remains shared between the Commission and Member States.

However, as the Financial Services Action Plan legislation was implemented, the 2007 financial crisis interfered. It imposed a major crisis management effort as well as a subsequent rethink of financial regulations. Instead of the planned focus on the consolidation of existing directives, the EU is in the midst of a major renegotiation of international financial rules, which is taking place under the supervision of the G20. The crisis also highlighted the importance of the financial regulation for the monetary union. The excessive lending to banks and states in the Southern EU periphery could have been prevented by better regulation to avoid severe underpricing of risks by (Northern) financiers. Similarly, any EU-level crisis management framework for banks could have prevented Member States (such as Ireland) from guaranteeing bank deposits which increased their national debts beyond a sustainable level and contributed directly to the Euro crisis (see Kudrna 2012). In short, the crisis revealed the mismatch between national regulation and transnational financial markets in its entirety and thus the importance of more comprehensive EU and global regulatory regimes.

In principle, the EU's capacity to shape the global financial regime is very high. The EU is the largest financial jurisdiction and may require compliance with its regulations as a prerequisite for entry to the single market. This strengthens its bargaining position vis-à-vis the rest of the world (see Drezner 2005). However, the common financial market legislation tends to be politically contested within the EU. Historically, individual Member States developed very different structures of financial markets, which has shaped their policy preferences and has complicated agreements on common rules. Although specific cleavages depend on individual directives, many disputes fall into the 'Northern–Southern' divide between governments aligning behind the 'pro-competitive' views of the UK or Netherlands, or more 'protection-minded' views emerging from France or Italy (Quaglia 2010). This divide – described as the 'battle of the systems' – persists today (see Story and Walters 1997; Grossman and Leblond 2011).

Divided preferences often force the EU to seek detailed policy compromises that increase the depth and bindingness of regulations but also add to their complexity (see Kudrna 2012). Excessive complexity, in turn, reduces the chances of policy exports to global regimes (see Mügge 2010). Moreover, the intra-EU disagreements are occasionally so intense that the Commission promotes global negotiations as an instrument for facilitating EU-level compromises (Quillin 2008). This strategy of 'harmonizing globally to harmonize internally' rests on the experience that global rules – despite their voluntary and non-binding nature – limit the number of feasible policy options about which the EU members can argue, thus facilitating agreements (Rottier and Vernon 2011). In short, the divided preferences make it less likely that EU members will unite behind a common policy position, but also increase their incentives to engage in global policy negotiations.

3 Global regulatory regime for financial markets

The global regulatory regime for financial markets has evolved almost exclusively in response to international financial crises that have forced national authorities to establish cross-border organizations and to agree on the rules of cooperation (see Table 11.1). The basic infrastructure, such as the Bank for International Settlements, dates back to the crisis of the 1930s. The Basel Committee on Banking Supervision was created in the 1970s, when the disintegration of the Bretton-Woods system exposed international banks to new risks. The East Asian financial crisis at the end of the 1990s left behind the Financial Stability Forum as the first attempt to introduce a global financial market architecture. These building blocks from the past have now been extended and deepened in response to the 2007 crisis.

The Forum compiled 16 sets of rules that serve as international standards. These rules are produced by various standard-setting organizations that bring together national and international authorities with some responsibility in the given policy domain (see Table 11.2). In response to the 2007 crisis, the G20

Table 11.1 Significance of governance levels over time (Financial Market Regulation)

Phase	National level	EU level	Global level
Post-WWII	High	–	Low
1957–late 1980s	High	Low	Low
1990s	Low	Medium (Single Market)	Medium (Basel Accord)
post-2000	Medium	Medium (Financial Services Action Plan)	Medium (rules spread beyond banking)
2020 (extrapolation)	Low	High (Banking Union)	Medium (post-crisis re-regulations)

Table 11.2 International standards endorsed by the Financial Stability Board

Issue area	Rule (first adopted in)	Standard-setting body
Sectoral standards		
Banking supervision	Core Principles for Effective Banking Supervision (1997)	Basel Committee on Banking Supervision
	Global regulatory framework for capital and liquidity of banks (1988)	Basel Committee on Banking Supervision
Securities regulation	Objectives and Principles of Securities Regulation (2003)	International Organization of Securities Commissions
Insurance supervision	Insurance Core Principles (2003)	International Association of Insurance Supervisors
Cross-sectoral standards		
Crisis resolution and deposit insurance	Core Principles for Effective Deposit Insurance Systems (2009)	International Association of Deposit Insurers
Insolvency	Insolvency and Creditor Rights (2001)	World Bank
Corporate governance	Principles of Corporate Governance (1999)	OECD
Accounting	International Financial Reporting Standards (2001)	International Accounting Standards Board
Auditing	International Standards on Auditing (2009)	International Auditing and Assurance Standards Board
Technical standards		
Payment, clearing and settlement	Core Principles for Systemically Important Payment Systems (2001)	Committee on Payment and Settlement Systems
	Recommendations for Securities Settlement Systems (2001)	Committee on Payment and Settlement Systems
	Recommendations for Central Counterparties (2004)	Committee on Payment and Settlement Systems
Market integrity (anti-money laundering)	40 + 9 Recommendations on Money Laundering and Terrorist Financing (1990)	Financial Action Task Force
Monetary and financial policy transparency	Code of Good Practices on Transparency in Monetary and Financial Policies (1999)	IMF
Fiscal policy transparency	Code of Good Practices on Fiscal Transparency (1998)	IMF
Macroeconomic data dissemination	Data Dissemination Standards (1996)	IMF

Source: FSB website as of June 2012.

renamed the Forum the Financial Stability Board (FSB) and enhanced its mandate to coordinate an overhaul of standards and address their inadequacies revealed by the crisis.

All of the FSB standards are voluntary and non-binding. They differ in their specificity, which affects not only the degree of their bindingness but also the extent of political controversies associated with them. The least politically contested are technical standards specifying details for data exchange and interoperability of various financial infrastructure systems. They are genuinely technical and adopted on an expert level without the need for political compromises. More controversial are substantive regulatory standards. These affect relative competitive advantages across countries and firms, and therefore generate some distributive consequences. However, many of these standards are defined merely as principles rather than as prescriptive rules. These provide national authorities with considerable leeway in interpretation, which may undermine regulatory convergence on the one hand, but also reduce political contestation on the other.

Finally, standards where the general principles are specified in considerable prescriptive detail tend to be the most controversial. Limited flexibility in interpretation and anticipated changes in relative competitiveness generate predictable consequences for profitability of firms and national industries. Hence, all stakeholders have strong incentives to become involved in politicized bargaining during the standard-setting process. The detailed, prescriptive standards thus provide the real test for the policy export capacity of the EU.

Out of the 16 standards in the FSB compendium (Table 11.2), only two are advanced enough on both the global and EU level to enable the analysis of EU policy-exporting capacity. Technical standards lack politically charged aspects. The standards on deposit insurance, insolvency, corporate governance and auditing are defined as general principles without prescriptive details. In securities regulation, there also remains a high disproportion between the prescriptive EU directive and International Organization of Securities Commissions (IOSCO) principles (see Mügge 2011). The global rules on insurance are slightly more advanced, but the EU rules are in flux as the Commission attempts to complete the ambitious Solvency II directive. Only international standards on accounting and banking are currently defined in substantive detail at both the EU and global level and thus suitable for analysis in this chapter. At the same time, they are likely to be indicative of what is to come in the related policy domains as these advance towards more prescriptive and therefore contested rules.

Although international standards in banking and accounting are non-binding and voluntary, their latest versions were negotiated on the explicit assumption that the EU, the US and Japan would transpose them with no or minimal adaptations. With key financial centres on board, other economies have strong incentives to follow. Moreover, their implementation is also supported through monitoring by the IMF and the World Bank.[1] Nearly all countries, including the US and China who resisted before 2007, subject themselves to these evaluations (IMF 2009). The conclusions from these peer reviews find their way to rating and other assessments of each economy by financial markets, which makes it difficult to ignore international standards despite their voluntary nature (Norton 2007). Hence, both bank capital rules and the international accounting standards are implemented to various degrees in over 120 countries.

4 EU policy exports in banking and accounting

Global regimes in financial market regulation share important characteristics that make some forms of policy exports more likely than others. The literature summarized in this section suggests that the EU strives actively to export its policies through vertical bargaining within institutionalized global regimes. Its bargaining power stems from controlling access to the largest financial market in the world, hosting a global financial centre in London as well as from possessing technical expertise in multinational regulation. At the same time, the success of the EU policy exports depends crucially on unity among its members and the acceptance of EU proposals by the US and Japan.

The key challenge to global harmonization of financial regulations stems from history. National regulations evolved differently in different economies and national actors – regulators, firms and governments – have a strong incentive to promote their own rules for international standards. If others accept them, they can preserve their competitive advantages and avoid adaptation costs associated with the implementation of new standards (see Drezner 2005; Story and Walter 1997; Kapstein 1989). Hence, no negotiation of detailed global standards will be free of contested bargaining in which participants promote and protect their policy interests.

At the same time, these negotiations can never be fully divorced from the concerns about financial stability and consumer protection that are shared by all actors. Hence, the formulation of basic principles is typically driven by expert consensus on the best possible rules. Nearly all actors also agree that having some international rules is better than having a myriad of differing national regulations. This does not prevent sharp conflicts over the detailed specification of general principles, but it moves negotiations from the zero-sum format to some form of coordination game. In this set up, all actors benefit from cooperation, but those who manage to get their own rules accepted internationally benefit more, as they preserve their advantages and limit adaptation costs. This also ensures that actors are prepared to compromise in order to avoid a total collapse of the global policy regime.

The US dominated any standard-setting processes for global financial markets up until the 1970s by virtue of its crucial role in the Bretton Woods regime. In subsequent decades, the US lost its hegemonic role and the process became dominated by the triumvirate of the US, Japan and the UK, with other advanced economies participating through the EU and the G10 (see Quillin 2008; Simmons 2001). The case studies cover this period, hence they focus primarily on the interaction of the EU/UK, the US and Japan. However, future negotiations will have to pay attention to emerging economies such as China, Brazil, India or Russia, whose role in global regimes increased following the 2007 crisis, as is evident from the shift to the G20 as the main source of standard-setting initiatives, as well as from their increased voting power in the IMF.

The policy export and promotion requires the EU to secure an agreement of its key partners within an institutionalized structure of standard-setting organizations (see Table 11.2). Hence, the export pathway is likely to be *active* (see Chapter 1).[2] Furthermore, the highly institutionalized nature of global regimes in banking and accounting is likely to enable *vertical bargaining* among key actors. Indeed, the negotiations of international financial standards increasingly resemble trade talks under the World Trade Organization as political concerns about competitive advantages dominate the technocratic concerns about financial stability (Tarullo 2008; Quillin 2008).

The global financial centres in the US, Japan and the UK concentrate an overwhelming majority of financial transactions. Hence, to facilitate the smooth flow of capital, all other countries face strong incentives to adopt the same regulations (Norton 2007). Thus, if the key actors can agree on a single international standard, all the others are likely to follow in order to minimize transaction costs and reap the benefits of the presumed increase in financial stability. This virtually guarantees a very high take-up rate for international standards across countries.

In turn, the guaranteed take-up rate reduces the question of EU success in policy export to a single dimension: the fit between the global rules and EU policy preferences. Furthermore, the central role of the three financial centres allows for even more parsimonious criteria for judging EU success: success occurs whenever the EU manages to secure an agreement from the US and Japan for its policy proposal. When it fails to have its preferences accepted it is not a case of policy export or policy promotion, but rather a case of policy protection or outright policy import. Or it could simply be a case of complete collapse of the global regime due to non-agreement (see Chapter 1 for definitions). The policy fit between global standards and EU preferences thus provides the key benchmark for the analysis of the four empirical cases.

5 Banking standards

The international banking standards are set by the Basel Committee on Banking Supervision (BCBS) established by the G10 in 1974 and hosted at the Bank for International Settlements in Basel. The BCBS sets voluntary, non-binding rules on bank regulation and supervision. Its membership expanded from the founding 12 countries to 27 economies considered central to the global financial markets. Nine EU Member States retain their representatives on the committee which makes decisions by consensus. The European Banking Authority, the European Central Bank and Commission, along with the Financial Stability Institute and the IMF, were given observer status and participate in the negotiation of respective standards.

The most important international standard produced by the BCBS is the Capital Adequacy Framework, which has existed for three generations. The standard defines what may be counted as bank capital, sets the method for

Table 11.3 Global regime for bank capital

Standard-setting body (founded in)	International standard	Milestones	Total membership and EU involvement
Basel Committee on Banking Supervision at BIS (1974)	International Convergence of Capital Measurement and Capital Standards (Basel I, II and III)	1988, 2004, 2010	27 states (9 EU Member States represented); Commission, ECB and EBA are observers

estimating the riskiness of banking assets and defines the minimal acceptable ratio of capital to risk-weighted assets. The first generation of the Basel Capital Accord was agreed upon in 1988 (referred to as Basel I). The second generation was negotiated between 1999 and 2004 (Basel II), and the third generation was in response to the crisis in 2010. The Basel rules were always negotiated with the view that they would be transposed into EU legislation with no or minimal changes, which makes the EU the single largest user of these standards. Collectively the EU members form the largest block in BCBS, but the unanimous decision-making limits their influence. The following sections analyse negotiations of the most contested aspects of each generation of Basel rules in order to gauge whether the EU has successfully promoted its preferred policies.

5.1 Basel I

The BCBS predates the EU legislation on the single banking market. Nonetheless, the Basel I standard negotiated throughout the 1980s offered the EU an opportunity to reap the first-mover advantage. The global negotiations in BCBS began in 1981 but reached stalemate by 1985. By that time the EU had started to formulate its own capital rules for the single market. Had the 12 Member States been able to reach a common position quickly, those represented in the BCBS may have been able to export the EU rules as global standards. However, the most contested aspect of the Basel I negotiations – the definition of bank capital – divided Member States both at the EU and global level so that they were unable to seize this opportunity (Norton 1992; Quillin 2008).

Traditionally, there were major differences in what counted as acceptable bank capital among the G10 economies, and each was reluctant to give up its approach. Countries often blocked proposals that would require their banks to raise more capital, which turned negotiations into a strenuous process that appeared to be on the brink of collapse several times (Kapstein 1994). The BCBS drafted numerous complex methodologies but nothing seemed acceptable. Germany and France even suggested that it might not be possible to derive a single definition of capital, since the capital adequacy depended on the entire scope of a bank's activities and its management quality (Quillin 2008). Such disputes brought negotiations in the EU and the BCBS to deadlock.

Eventually, the deadlock was broken by the US's and the UK's decision to introduce a bilateral agreement in 1986. Both countries had been implementing regulatory reforms and, if they completed them before the multilateral agreement, their banks would be required to carry higher levels of capital than their competitors from other G10 jurisdictions (Kapstein 1994). The US–UK agreement resolved conflicting preferences over capital definition by a structured compromise, which allowed domestic banks to maintain some forms of capital that the other country did not recognize. It distinguished between Tier 1 capital, which included only high-quality and mutually acceptable elements, from Tier 2, which included idiosyncratic capital instruments of lower quality, such as general bad debt provisions in the UK or preferred stocks in the US. To prevent bias in favour of the second tier, its amount was limited to 50 per cent of the total capital.

The US first sought Japanese support for the bilateral proposal before returning to the multilateral negotiations in the BCBS. It bundled the issue with the then ongoing debates about trade deficits with Japan and argued that weaker capital standards would provide Japanese banks with unfair competitive advantages in the US market (Quillin 2008). At the same time, both the US and the UK stated that they would possibly require compliance with bilateral capital standards for foreign banks seeking to enter their markets directly or through acquisition (Tarullo 2008: 51). Japan chose to support the US–UK proposal, after ensuring that unrealized capital gains would be included in the more flexible Tier 2 capital (Tarullo 2008: 50).

The EU countries considered the Basel negotiations as part and parcel of their own efforts to formulate bank capital adequacy rules in the Own Funds and Solvency directives that had to be adopted before the 1992 single market deadline (Kapstein 1991: 266). When the UK informed its EU partners about the trilateral agreement one day before it was made public, they were not impressed. Some governments even argued that the UK may have violated the Treaty of Rome by striking a separate agreement (Quillin 2008). However, as the proposal now covered the three largest financial centres, it was probable it would become a standard even if other European members opposed it. Hence, the EU governments followed the Japanese example and negotiated Tier 2 adaptations. With such amendments, the final definition of bank capital was formally adopted in July 1988 and, over the course of the next decade, was adopted by over 100 other economies worldwide (BCBS 1999).

The Basel I episode illustrates the importance of internal unity as a necessary prerequisite for successful policy promotion. Despite parallel negotiations in Brussels, the UK broke European ranks and opted for the bilateral agreement with the US, which effectively imposed US-UK policy on the EU. However, the EU as a whole was at least able to prevent unwanted policy imports by securing adaptations to the Basel definition of Tier 2 bank capital. Therefore, the Basel I agreement was not a case of policy export, but of successful protection of important policy preferences.

5.2 Basel II

During the subsequent decade the Basel I rules became outdated. They were perceived as insufficiently risk-sensitive and apt to create some perverse incentives for banks to invest in types of assets that had little economic justification other than favourable capital requirement. Hence, the BCBS initiated renegotiation of the Basel standard in 1999. As was the case earlier, the EU was committed to transposing the Basel II agreement directly into the Capital Requirements directive. Since the onset of negotiations coincided with the introduction of the single currency, EU presence at the BCBS was increased by inviting the Commission, the ECB and the BAC[3] to participate as observers, extending the EU representation beyond the Member States.

At the onset, the BCBS decided to retain the Basel I definition of capital and focus solely on the new rules for risk-weighting of assets and calculating capital adequacy. However, there was a dramatic change in the technical approach, which had important repercussions for the degree of political contestation. Whereas Basel I produced a simple, one-size-fits-all definition of risk-weights, Basel II was to be far more flexible, allowing the banks to choose between three different approaches. The standardized approach was the simplest way of assessing risk, suitable for small banks relying on external credit rating agencies. The foundational and advanced internal rating-based approaches allowed larger banks to rely on their own risk parameters based on in-house models approved by supervisors. This multiplicity accommodated a much greater spectrum of national policy preferences than would have been the case with a one-size-fits-all approach. Hence, it substantially reduced political conflicts during the Basel II negotiations.

Nonetheless, there were two contested issues that rose above the technocratic debate into the political realm. The most high-profile intervention was made by Chancellor Schröder, who warned in 2001 that Germany would not accept risk weighting of exposures to small and medium enterprises as they were drafted at the time (Tarullo 2008:115). Other EU countries shared this concern; hence, the BCBS changed course and adopted less stringent specifications in subsequent Basel II drafts. Nonetheless, some minor adaptations were added when Basel II was transposed to the EU directive.

The second politicized issue arose when US regulators unilaterally announced the intention to adopt Basel II only for internationally active banks, but not for 'non-complex' domestic banks (Tarullo 2008: 118). This was a setback for the EU since it had planned to adopt the standard for all its banks and presumed that other countries would follow. The issue was resolved within the US, when small banks feared they might be disadvantaged in competition with large US banks and successfully lobbied for the adoption of the Basel II standardized approach (Tarullo 2008: 182).

The multi-approach structure of Basel II pre-empted many policy conflicts. Countries with financial sectors dominated by less complex banks were more concerned about a standardized approach, whereas those hosting global banks focused on internal rating approaches. The policy preferences were no longer aggregated on the national or EU level, but rather on the level of the most similar banks across countries. Consequently, there was no distinct EU policy that could be exported to or promoted in BCBS, except the shared concern of several EU governments about lending to small and medium-sized enterprises. This concern was accommodated so that the Basel II negotiations would amount to a successful protection of shared policy preferences, rather than an outright export of EU rules.

5.3 Basel III

The financial crisis began in summer 2007, six months before the final implementation deadline of Basel II. Nonetheless, it quickly revealed weaknesses and inadequacies of both generations of banking standards. The Basel I definition of capital, which had not changed substantively since 1988, proved too permissive of supposedly innovative hybrid capital instruments that failed to absorb losses during the crisis (see Kudrna 2011). Similarly, the Basel II calculations of regulatory capital missed certain types of risks that proved important during the crisis (see Commission 2011). Hence, in 2009, the G20 mandated that the Basel committee propose the third generation of Basel standards that would remedy such vulnerabilities.

The crisis created political momentum for reform, which allowed the regulators in BCBS to propose a rather stringent set of new rules and still get the endorsement of the G20 and FSB in 2010 (see BCBS 2010a). New rules improved micro-prudential regulation to increase banks' ability to absorb a greater variety of shocks. It improved risk management and governance by further increasing requirements on transparency. The most innovative aspects of Basel III were in macro-prudential regulation that reduces system-wide risks, pro-cyclicality of capital regulations and the moral hazard of systemically important financial institutions. The new framework also included internationally harmonized leverage ratios to serve as a backstop to the risk-based capital measures.

The Basel III regulations were negotiated during the immediate period after the crisis, which muted the usual bargaining. The BCBS members recognized that new rules were urgently needed and the costs of the financial crisis dwarfed the concern about the relative impact of the reform on costs and competitive advantages. Moreover, the largest banks were busy responding to the consequences of the crisis and were not in a strong position to oppose significant tightening. The Institute of International Finance and other associations of large banks argued that the costs of new regulation would be high (see Eubanks 2010: 9). However, the Basel Committee insisted that long-term benefits in terms of stability outweighed these costs and adopted the stringent version of rules with very few concessions (BCBS 2010b).[4] Hence, the new rules were agreed upon within a year and the dispute shifted from their content to the implementation schedule.

The timing of the transition to Basel III not only determines the spread of implementation costs, but also impacts on the real economy. Banks have three ways to comply with new capital and liquidity requirements. First, they can raise new capital, but that can be expensive as there are fewer buyers in uncertain times and they demand higher premiums. Second, banks may sell their risky assets, but when all the other banks are trying to do the same, it may depress asset prices thus increasing bank losses, which can further increase their capital requirements in a vicious spiral. Third, banks may issue fewer new loans for the real economy already weakened by the recession and thus prolong the slump. None of these options are particularly appealing to banks and regulators, who need to pre-empt any adverse impact on banking stability and post-crisis recovery.

The US regulators were in favour of prompt implementation of Basel III, because the US economy is less dependent on banks; its banking sector was better capitalized before the crisis and aggressive state aid allowed it to absorb losses faster (CEBS 2009). In contrast, EU economies are more dependent on banks which have less capital and their write-offs were postponed and complicated by the Euro crisis. Hence, most EU countries supported the German initiative to prolong the Basel III implementation period. Whereas the initial proposals suggested new measures be phased in between 2013 and 2015, the final compromise promoted by the EU countries extended this period to 2019 (see Eubanks 2010: 9).

The Basel III negotiations took place under the shadow of a financial crisis that dictated the agenda and muted the politicized bargaining. Although parts of Basel III were modelled on experience from the EU – the anti-cyclical provisioning, for example, was derived from Spanish rules – the EU had no ready-made policy package to export or promote beyond concern over the implementation schedule. The BCBS accepted the deadlines supported by the group of EU Member States; thus, Basel III is best characterized as a case of the successful protection of key policy preferences.

6 Accounting standards

The international accounting standards are set by the International Accounting Standards Board (IASB), which is an independent body based in London and operated under private law as a foundation. The roots of IASB date to 1973, when accounting bodies from nine countries created the organization with the aim of developing simple and robust standards that could serve as models for national standards. These had very limited global impact until the EU decided to throw its weight behind them in 2001.

The EU made the IASB rules – renamed the International Financial Reporting Standards (IFRS) – mandatory for about 7000 companies listed on EU stock exchanges, including the listed firms from outside the Union. This move was motivated by lack of progress in the harmonization of the EU accounting rules that hampered the functioning of the single market for capital. As in banking, the EU agreed to use the 'harmonize globally in order to harmonize internally'

198 Z. Kudrna

Table 11.4 Global regime for accounting

Standard-setting body (founded in)	International standard	Milestones	Total membership and EU involvement
International Accounting Standards Board (1973/2001)	International Financial Reporting Standards (initially called International Accounting Standards)	2001 2005	16 private individuals representing geographic regions; the Commission in the Monitoring Board

approach that limits intra-EU regulatory disputes to a narrow range of policy options acceptable within the global policy regime (see also Mügge 2011; Quillin 2008; Rottier and Vernon 2010).

However, in accounting, the EU and its Member States have much less direct influence on IASB decisions, because these are made by 16 private individuals appointed by the IFRS foundation from within the global accounting profession.[5] This provides the IASB with a high degree of operational independence. Moreover, the IASB relies on financial support not only from states and public institutions, but also from private sector entities such as banks and consulting firms. Hence, the IASB needs to cater to a broader base of stakeholders before adopting decisions by a majority of nine votes.[6]

Nonetheless, the EU is well positioned to export and promote its policy preferences through the IASB. The EU is the most important user of these standards and, collectively, the European entities also comprise the largest funder of IASB (IFRS 2012: 65). Moreover, financial globalization creates a strong demand for harmonized and comparable financial data as well as a powerful constituency of transnational firms and national authorities broadly supporting the convergence process. Hence, convergence is largely a coordination game of finding acceptable accounting procedures. At the same time, it is also not entirely free of effects on relative competitiveness and adaptation costs that complicate negotiations, as was the case with banking.

The EU is a latecomer to the global accounting regime that is traditionally dominated by the 'Anglo-Saxon' approach.[7] The more 'continental' approaches that enter the EU-level policy compromises are not automatically compatible with the IASB approach. The misfit of this type generated the most contested aspect of the IASB debates related to the rules of fair value accounting that are defined in IAS 39 called 'Financial Instruments: Recognition and Measurement'.

6.1 Endorsing IAS 39

IAS 39 specifies the rules of fair value accounting of financial instruments. This principle – often referred to as 'mark-to-market' accounting – relies on current market prices to determine the accounting value of financial instruments on the books. Hence, accounting valuations have to be regularly adapted to changing market prices. This is not a trivial task, as some financial instruments – such as complex derivatives – either lack a relevant market price completely or their price isunreliable due to insufficient market liquidity and depth. In such cases, the accounting value is derived from a similar instrument or, if there is no comparable instrument, the valuation is based on a discounted cash flow model defined by the owner of the instrument.

There are several controversial aspects of the fair value approach. First, it makes valuations highly volatile and pro-cyclical, which may distort, for example, the bank capital adequacy calculations discussed in a previous section. Second, it transmits the volatility of financial markets into accounting systems of any financial and non-financial firms which hold any instrument that needs to be marked to market. Furthermore, when the market price for a given instrument is not available, the firm possesses a high degree of control over accounting valuations, which can be misused. Given these concerns, the fair value approach has been used more sparingly in some economies than in others.

The IAS 39 – when it was introduced in 1998 – extended the scope of the application of the fair value approach well beyond its traditional limits in continental European economies and even beyond US and UK practices at the time (Dewing and Russel 2008). In its full scope, IAS 39 was at odds with the prevalent risk management practices. Marking all derivatives to market would make valuations of financial assets and liabilities – and hence profits and regulatory ratios of financial firms – much more volatile (see Brackney and Witmer (2005) for detailed assessment). Hence, the European banks lobbied intensely against the transposition of IAS 39 into EU legislation. In response, the Commission asked IASB to limit the extent of potential application of fair value accounting of financial instruments (see Leblond 2011; Mügge 2011).

The IASB perceived the request as a challenge to its independence as well as its legitimacy of the standard-setter that aims for the 'best of the breed' rules (Tweedie and Seidenstein 2004). However, the EU threatened to carve out two of the most contested parts of IAS 39 when transposing the standard into the EU legislation. Eventually, the IASB accepted one of the EU's demands, but did not budge on the other. Instead, it agreed to a plan to redefine IAS 39 as a new IFRS 9 standard. Hence, the EU finally endorsed IAS 39 with a single carve-out that was seen only as temporary.

Although the threat of carve-outs seems an effective EU strategy for increasing the policy fit of international accounting standards with its own preferences, it is constrained by the need to preserve IASB credibility. The IASB essentially serves as an honest broker between the key stakeholders in the US and the EU, and its independence is instrumental to the acceptance of IAS/IFRS by national authorities across the world (Leblond 2011; Posner 2009; Dewing and Russel 2008). Moreover, its support from multinational corporations is conditioned on its capacity to ensure EU–US convergence. In the final stages of the EU endorsement process, the IASB signed an agreement with the US standard-setting body, the Financial Accounting Standards Board (FASB), on cooperation towards the convergence of accounting standards. This was supposed to abolish the obligation for EU companies active in the US to reconcile their accounting with US standards (see Leblond 2011). However, when the US approved the equivalence in 2007, it applied only 'pure' IAS rules without the EU carve-out.

The difficulties of IAS 39 endorsement shifted attention to IASB governance. The Commission argued that the IASB should be more responsive to jurisdictions that directly apply its standards (Leblond 2011; Buck and Jopson 2005). The EU pressure resulted in the creation of the Monitoring Board populated by regulators representing the International Organization of Securities Commissions, the European Commission, the Financial Services Agency of Japan, and the US Securities and Exchange Commission. The Board appoints and supervises the Trustees of the IFRS foundation and strengthens the influence of public authorities over the global convergence process.

The rules of fair value accounting remain the most contested issue within the global accounting regime. IAS 39 also rose to the top of the regulatory agenda during the peak of the crisis in 2008, when the US relaxed its fair value rules and the IASB followed with similar changes to IAS 39 after some EU pressure (see Leblond 2011). These ad hoc changes aimed at reducing the volatility in the valuation of financial assets during a deep liquidity squeeze, but also highlighted the need for new rules that would merge accounting practices in the US, the EU and the rest of the world.

The G20 continues to push the IASB and FASB to produce converged drafts, while their respective stakeholders from the European and US markets insist on different approaches to their most contested aspects (IASB and FASB 2013). Hence, the two accounting boards have not been able to propose new joint rules during the five years since the onset of crisis. Instead, in 2013, they started public consultations with two separate drafts; thus the convergence negotiations that could resolve the fair value controversy may be restarted only at the end of 2013.

To summarize, the EU was a latecomer in the global accounting regime and had no pre-existing policy to export or promote. Moreover, the legacy rules primarily reflected the Anglo-Saxon accounting traditions that were often at odds with EU-level compromises. Under these circumstances the EU was primarily in the mode of protecting policy preferences by ensuring that the IASB rules did not include policy imports that would not be acceptable for specific subsets of Member States. In the case of IAS 39, this necessitated a carve-out that temporarily undermined the global accounting regime and the EU–US convergence process.

7 Conclusion

The global financial market regulation has evolved over the past three decades into well-institutionalized policy regimes. Although they do not produce binding rules, the voluntary standards have been taken up by nearly all the economies and are systematically monitored by international organizations such as the Financial Stability Board and the IMF. These regimes evolve primarily in response to major crisis episodes, including the current period, when re-regulation responds to the excessive liberalization of previous decades.

Despite the size of its financial markets and central role in global finance, the EU is no hegemonic actor that could easily export its policy preferences to a global level. This is the case regardless of whether we include Member States in the definition of the EU or limit it exclusively to supranational actors, like the Commission, the ECB or the European supervisory authorities. At the same time, the leverage of the EU supranational bodies is gradually increasing. In the accounting domain, the Commission became the most important funder and user of IFRS as well as a full member of its monitoring board; in banking, the Commission, ECB and EBA received observer status and are currently fully involved in technical negotiations. Nonetheless, the intra-EU disunity and frequent policy conflicts with the US continue to limit the EU's policy export and policy promotion capacity.

The EU is a latecomer to financial market regimes and often struggles with legacy rules which do not match policy compromises that would be preferred at the EU level. Hence, the most characteristic outcome of the EU engagement in the global regime is protection of policy preferences, which prevents unacceptable policy imports. At the same time, the EU tends to avoid overly rigid protection that would exclude it from the global regime or even cause collapse of multilateral cooperation. This approach was observable in banking, where the EU policy protection effort resulted in the inclusion of new capital items into the Tier 2 definition of Basel I, the extension of multiple approaches to the calculation of capital requirements in Basel II, and prolongation of implementation deadlines in Basel III. In accounting, it resulted in the use of a carve-out on some aspects of IAS 39, while simultaneously securing commitment to negotiations of its IFRS 9 replacement.

However, EU engagement with the global regime is never entirely defensive. The EU Member States and supranational bodies enter global negotiations proactively as a means of finding the EU-level compromise. This strategy of 'harmonizing globally to harmonize internally' is a form of deliberate policy promotion. It is also an extension of the two-level games characteristic of EU functioning, whereby the global-level negotiations constrain the venerable EU tendency to produce extremely complex policy compromises that make implementation of financial regulations very expensive. The global arena forces the Member State authorities to stick to fundamental priorities that are likely to be respected by the US and other global partners. The 'harmonize globally to harmonize internally' strategy was behind the UK 'defection' during Basel I negotiations, as well as the Commission support for importing the international accounting standards into EU legislation instead of developing new EU-only rules.

The past negotiations of global standards have established a reliable pattern of when the success of the EU policy export or policy promotion was constrained by internal disputes and US bargaining power. The EU effort was limited primarily to the protection of specific policy interests of Member States for whom the initial US proposals were not acceptable. At the same time, the EU was always flexible enough to avoid veto and collapse of the regime due to its withdrawal. However, this 'globally responsible protection of policy preferences' may not last in the future when the largest emerging market economies such as China assert their role, which may reshape global coalition-building and change the dynamic of global bargaining.

Notes

1 Monitoring is conducted by joint IMF–WB programmes called Reports on Observance of Standards and Codes (ROSC) and the Financial Stability Assessment Program (FSAP).
2 The passive pathway may be in play during the diffusion of international standards to other countries, especially in the EU neighbourhood, but not while rules are being formulated in BCBS or IASB.
3 The Banking Advisory Committee was the predecessor to the Committee of European Banking Supervisors, which in turn was transformed into the European Banking Authority.
4 Some of the new regulations, such as the counter-cyclical provisions, originated from European countries. However, they were not part of the EU regulation.
5 The IFRS foundation is itself governed by the 22 member boards, which broadly provides a global geographic balance.
6 In May 2012 IASB membership was expanded from 15 to 16; the new member came from Germany.
7 The IASB inherited most of the technical standards from its pre-2001 predecessor. To prepare for the EU endorsement, the IASB amended 17 standards and created six new ones by the 2005 deadline. The current total is 13 IFRS standards (post-2001) and 28 IAS standards (pre-2001).

References

BCBS (1999) *Capital Requirements and Bank Behaviour: The Impact of the Basle Accord*, Basel: Basel Committee on Banking Supervision.
—— (2010a) *Basel III: A Global Regulatory Framework for More Resilient Banks and Banking Systems*, Basel: Basel Committee on Banking Supervision.
—— (2010b) *An Assessment of the Long-term Economic Impact of Stronger Capital and Liquidity Requirements*, Basel: Basel Committee on Banking Supervision.
Brackney, K.S. and Witmer, P.R. (2005) 'The European Union's Role in International Standards Setting: Will Bumps in the Road to Convergence Affect the SEC's Plans?', *CPA Journal* 75(11): 18.
Buck, T. and Jopson, B. (2005) 'Brussels Seeks Greater Role in IASB Decisions', *Financial Times* (3 February).
CEBS (2009) *Implementation Guidelines for Hybrid Capital Instruments*, Brussels: Committee of European Banking Supervisors.
Commission of the European Union (2011) 'CRD IV – Frequently Asked Questions', MEMO/11/527 (20 July).
De Meester, B. (2008) 'Multilevel Banking Regulation: An Assessment of the Role of the EC in the Light of Coherence and Democratic Legitimacy', in A. Follesdal, R.A. Wessel and J. Wouters (eds) *Multilevel Regulation and the EU: The Interplay between Global, European, and National Normative Processes*, Leiden: Martinus Nijhoff.
Dewing, I. and Russel, P.O. (2008) 'Financial Integration in the EU: The First Phase of EU Endorsement of International Accounting Standards', *Journal of Common Market Studies* 46(2): 243–264.

Drezner, D.W. (2005) 'Globalization, Harmonization, and Competition: The Different Pathways to Policy Convergence', *Journal of European Public Policy* 12(5): 841–859.

—— (2009) 'The Power and Peril of International Regime Complexity', *Perspectives on Politics* 7(1): 65–70.

Eubanks, W.W. (2010) *The Status of the Basel III Capital Adequacy Accord*, Washington, DC: Congressional Research Service.

Grossman, E. and Leblond, P. (2011) 'European Financial Integration: Finally the Great Leap Forward?', *Journal of Common Market Studies* 49(2): 413–435.

IASB and FASB (International Accounting Standards Board and Financial Accounting Standards Board) (2013) *Update by the IASB and FASB for the Meeting of the G20 Finance Ministers and Central Bank Governors 15–16 February 2013*. Online. Available: www.financialstabilityboard.org/publications/r_130216b.pdf (accessed 20 February 2013).

IFRS (2012) *Annual Report for 2011*, London: International Financial Reporting Standards Foundation.

IMF (2009) *The Financial Sector Assessment Program After Ten Years: Experience and Reforms for the Next Decade*, Washington, DC: International Monetary Fund and the World Bank.

Kapstein, E.B. (1989) 'Resolving the Regulator's Dilemma: International Coordination of Banking Regulations', *International Organization* 43(2): 323–347.

—— (1991) 'Supervising International Banks: Origins and Implications of the Basle Accord', *Essays in International Finance* No. 185, International Finance Section, Department of Economics, Princeton University. Online. Available: www.princeton.edu/~ies/IES_Essays/E185.pdf (accessed 16 April 2013).

—— (1994) *Governing the Global Economy: International Finance and the State*, Cambridge, MA: Harvard University Press.

Kudrna, Z. (2011) *Delegating Contested Reform of the European Union's Financial Market Regulation*, Dissertation. Budapest: Central European University.

—— (2012) 'Cross-border Resolution of Failed Banks in the EU after the Crisis: Business as Usual', *Journal of Common Market Studies* 50(2): 283–299.

Leblond, P. (2011) 'EU, US and International Accounting Standards: A Delicate Balancing Act in Governing Global Finance', *Journal of European Public Policy* 18(3): 443–461.

Mügge, D. (2010) *Widen the Market, Narrow the Competition: Banker Interests and the Making of a European Capital Market*, Colchester: European Consortium for Political Research.

—— (2011) 'The European Presence in Global Financial Governance: A Principal-agent Perspective', *Journal of European Public Policy* 18(3): 383–402.

Norton, J.J. (1992) *Recent Developments in the Regulation and Supervision of US Financial Institutions: The Evolution of Capital Adequacy Standards and the Financial Institutions Reform, Recovery and Enforcement Act of 1989*, Bangor: Institute of European Finance.

—— (2007) 'Taking Stock of the "First Generation" of Financial Sector Legal Reform', Law and Development Working Paper Series No. 4/2007, World Bank. Online. Available at http://siteresources.worldbank.org/INTLAWJUSTICE/Resources/LDWP4_FinSecLegRef.pdf (accessed 16 April 2013).

Posner, E. (2009) 'Making Rules for Global Finance: Transatlantic Regulatory Cooperation at the Turn of the Millennium', *International Organization* 63(4): 665–699.

Quaglia, L. (2010) 'Completing the Single Market in Financial Services: The Politics of Competing Advocacy Coalitions', *Journal of European Public Policy* 17(7): 1007–1023.

Quillin, B. (2008) *International Financial Co-operation: Political Economics of Compliance with the 1988 Basel Accord*, London and New York: Routledge.

Rottier, S. and Veron, N. (2010) 'The New Disintegration of Finance', *Financial Times* (9 September).

Simmons, B.A. (2001) 'The International Politics of Harmonization: The Case of Capital Market Regulation', *International Organization* 55(3): 589–620.

Story, J. and Walter, I. (1997) *Political Economy of Financial Integration in Europe: The Battle of the Systems*, Cambridge, MA: MIT Press.

Tarullo, D.K. (2008) *Banking on Basel: The Future of International Financial Regulation*, Washington, DC: Peterson Institute for International Economics.

Tweedie, D. and Seidenstein, T.R. (2004) 'Setting a Global Standard: The Case for Accounting Convergence', *Northwestern Journal of International Law & Business* 25(3): 589–608.

12 Comparative analysis
The EU as a policy exporter?

Gerda Falkner and Patrick Müller

Given the rise in significance during recent decades of governance layers beyond not only the nation-state but also Europe, it is surprising that few efforts have been made to systematically examine the EU's interaction with global policy regimes. This book provides a unique comparative analysis of the EU's capacity for projecting its policies outward in ten policy domains. Our research highlights that policy export is a demanding phenomenon which faces severe limitations and frequently comes with drawbacks. Still, EU policy export has played a key role in shaping the rules of the global trade regime. Moreover, it has influenced global policy outcomes – at least to a minor extent or in technical aspects – in the majority of the covered policy areas. Overall, however, our study reveals that the EU not only aims to export its policies but to interact with its global environment in a number of distinct ways, including also policy import and policy protection; that is, the strategy to shield its standards from global influence.

The previous chapters discussed the role of individual EU policies in global governance. Do the policy-specific activities of the EU have an impact on the global scale? This chapter will compare the findings across policies and draw general conclusions.

We[1] shall cover the following issues. How much does the EU matter in global governance today (below, section 1)? This 'mapping exercise' was one of our two major ambitions. The other was to study the interaction between the EU and the global levels. To what extent are the EU's own internal policies also projected at the global arena of contemporary governance? Policy export, policy import, and further forms of exchange with EU-external policy regimes will hence be discussed (section 2), to be followed by a systematic analysis of the factors and conditions influencing potential policy export (sections 3 and 4). This invites a discussion of the overall insights of our study and the research desiderata waiting to be covered in subsequent analyses (section 5).

1 Global governance today: does the EU matter?

How significant is the role of the EU within the universe of 'globalized governance'? Our goal was to grasp the development of policies over time at the national, EU and global levels.[2] Even a table of only indicative character should be thrilling – not only for the political scientist but for any subject of governance. Our interest in the policies (as opposed to individual international organizations) involves discussing not only 'multi-task' but also 'task-specific jurisdictions' (Hooghe and Marks 2001: 5–9). In fact, this is extremely variegated depending on what matters for the policy at stake at the 'global' level.

Our mapping is based on qualitative expert judgements. That exact and telling data were not readily available required choosing between a 'softer', qualitative approach (with a limited degree of operationalization and indicative 'measurement') and a much narrower quantitative study that could not nearly have answered the pressing research questions at stake. The rich empirical information produced in the policy chapters of this book results in important general insights about the multi-layered character of the global system of governance. Based on these findings, potential follow-up studies could, in the future, go further in terms of quantification and specific hypothesis-testing.

The 'high', 'medium' or 'low' scores regarding the significance of a governance level serve as heuristic devices that we applied with great care to assure quality and internal consistency.[3] In addition to contextualized considerations relating to the decisive and formative character of rules for the overall regime across all levels, these categories are based on three factors for orientation: functional scope of rules; depth as measured by density and specificity of rules; and binding character of the rules for the regime members, as opposed to purely indicative soft law.

No general aggregation rules were applied, since highly case-specific characteristics and the particular context of a policy (or issue area) may play an important role for the relative importance of the various factors. To optimize data quality, the aggregation of the factors was tailor-made and argued for individual cases, all while being submitted to multiple tests of plausibility in terms of the overall project and the comparator policies.

To capture the long-term trends for the individual policy levels at large, the judgement of the policy specialists regarding the development of the significance for all ten policies studied in this book are aggregated and charted in one overall figure. It needs stressing that Figure 12.1 is not about relative changes between levels; the sum of the levels does not add up to '100 per cent'. Indeed, the categories are absolute for each level individually and a gain in significance by one level thus does not necessarily mean a decline of another level. In principle, all three levels of governance may be of high significance, as has happened in domains of environmental policy from the 2000s onwards. We will discuss in more detail below why the figure should be used for indicative purposes only.

Figure 12.1[4] shows the aggregated judgements for the significance of the individual governance layers over time.[5] The changes in the significance as averaged out across all policy domains reveal, first, that *more levels of governance* became significant over time. In fact, the multi-level character of governance – marked by the evolution of a more institutionalized, rule-based international system and progress in European integration – has without doubt increased over the past decades. Based on our informed extrapolations, we hold that it will continue to

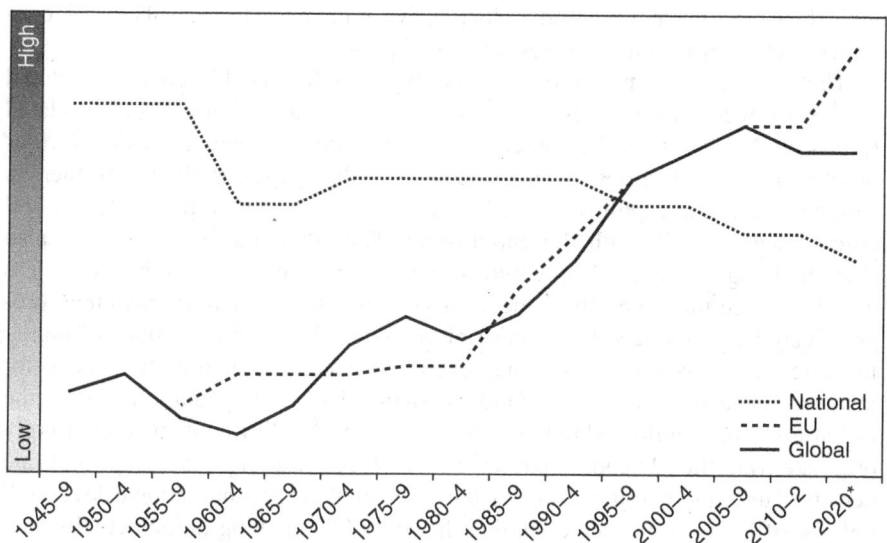

Figure 12.1 The significance of governance levels in 10 policies.

Note
The levels of significance were coded on the basis of the qualitative expert judgements by authors of individual chapters. They were asked to assess changes in the scope, depth and bindingness of respective policy regimes on the scale: low (0), low-medium (0.5), medium (1), medium-high (1.5) and high (2). The coded values across all domains were averaged out for Figure 12.1. However, not all policy regimes have existed since 1945, which affected the pre-1980 averages by producing 'bumps' on the curves every time a new regime was activated with low significance on the European and global level.
* Denotes extrapolation.

increase, meaning that the multi-level character of multi-level politics has further increased and that studying the interactions between governance layers is an important endeavour.[6]

The second crucial observation is that the *national level* is of declining significance, but that this decline is smaller than the rise in global or EU regime importance. The national level has progressively lost significance since the EU was set up. Aggregated across policies covered, the importance today is only medium, no longer high. Overall, the importance of both the EU and the global levels is clearly higher at present. Yet even if the national level is of low significance in a particular area of governance, this does not mean that governments are fully bereft of all powers (on the continued relevance of the nation-state in global multi-level governance, see also Zürn 2012: 735). They represent their states in the EU's Council of Ministers and thereby stay important to some extent, even in fields such as finance, food safety and nuclear non-proliferation policy. The Member States also remain key actors in multilateral institutions at the global stage – primarily because most international organizations accept only states as members. Moreover, while the functional scope and density of rules at the levels beyond the nation-state have been steadily increasing, the national level remains central for rule enforcement as well as the main locus of distributive and redistributive policies, which explains its continued high relevance in areas such as social policy.

That in overall terms, across the ten areas studied in this book, the global level is of even greater significance today than the national level is also related to this book's focus on the source of formative policy content. At times, rules originating from the global level shape the overall regime decisively and then its significance for any policy studied will be high, even if implementation and enforcement are still with the nation-state. The latter may in such cases also show high significance. If, by contrast, the nation-state's function gets ever less decisive concerning substantive decision-making on important rule content, progressively being reduced to managerial tasks and the 'administration' of higher level decisions, its significance may even be graded less than high. This is, for instance, what happens in the field of financial market regulation, where the recent crisis has reinforced the tendency that central policy contents increasingly originate from the EU and global levels, which increase in policy scope and rule density. Here, the extrapolation for the year 2020 is that the national level will only be of low significance assuming that the EU's banking union actually succeeds (see Chapter 11 by Kudrna).

Third, the EU's increasing significance as displayed in Figure 12.1 in fact applies to each and every field studied, as the chapters on the respective policies reveal. The EU level became highly significant in all but four policy areas by 2010 (social, transport, finance and asylum/migration policies). The EU even went from low to high in two out of the ten studied policies: food safety and environmental policy. Trade policy became highly significant immediately after its establishment,[7] while nuclear non-proliferation policy and agricultural policy were of medium significance following the Treaty of Rome and later advanced to highly significant (see Chapters 10 and 3 by Patrick Müller and by Roederer-Rynning and Daugbjerg, respectively). Generally speaking, the timing of the increased significance of the European level coincided with the run-up to the Single Market project since the mid-1980s and there was also a discernible influence of the Maastricht Treaty. The EU has not only been the most important level of governance in the policies covered since approximately 1995; with a view to the authors' expectations regarding future developments, it is worth highlighting that a further rise is actually expected. At the EU level by 2020, a total of nine out of the ten studied areas is expected to be of high significance (only social policy is expected to remain at medium significance).

Fourth, *the global level also increased in significance* in all policies where a change took place, with the notable exception of agriculture. Its significance was only relatively stable in the field of social policy. In a number of policies, the increase in significance by 2010 even meant changes from 'low' to 'high' (nuclear non-proliferation, food safety and environment). In all other policy areas, the global level has at least increased to or remained at medium significance. Interestingly, the timing of policy development at the global level has been driven less by single events than at the EU level, with policy regimes following their particular logics. That the change need not necessarily always go in an upward direction or be sustained in the long run is indicated by the field of agriculture. After being of high significance from 1995 to 2005, Roederer-Rynning and Daugbjerg show that the global regime level's significance fell to medium for the post-2010 period without even being expected to rise again until at least 2020.

A word of caution with respect to the interpretation of our findings is warranted. This analysis focused on (1) the EU and (2) those policies and particularly those issue areas where the EU actually has a corresponding regime level at the global scale. We selected issue areas with an interplay between the levels of governance, and sub-policies without relevance on an international or global scale tended to fall outside the scope of attention. An encompassing picture of each and every existing issue area and policy may therefore reveal a different picture.[8] In any case, *for policies with state-transcending character*, recent decades have very frequently brought about further bottom-up Europeanization and globalization steps.

At large, our findings confirm earlier studies' expectations and arguments regarding a trend towards multi-level governance, but since we focus on the policies which are indeed in place, our findings stand out. We analyse not only the distribution of authority but the realization of policy-making powers, i.e. the de facto governance and not only the governance potentials.[9] In that way, our approach adds to previous studies – some of which also relied on qualitative expert judgements in establishing the significance of different levels of governance across policy regimes. While an increase in the significance of the EU level of governance has also been observed by Schmitter (1996), earlier efforts to represent the EU's significance on the policy level generally excluded the global sphere. This is, we believe, a serious omission, since it invites an overestimation of the EU's role if policies are indeed imported from the global level (see agricultural policy, transport policy, etc.) and possibly underestimating it when EU policies are exported and hence become of global importance.

The trends visible in Figure 12.1 also appear in alternative forms of representation.[10] The robustness of our main findings is supported by Figure 12.2, which is a count of the policy domains that are of high significance at a given level of governance at a given point in time. It shows that by 2010, the team's experts regarded the EU level as having high significance in six policies; the global level in five; and the national level in only four policies. If the same procedure were applied to regimes that have been qualified as being of low significance, the national level would actually show in two cases. This results from the fact that in the areas of nuclear non-proliferation and food safety, key rules meanwhile originate predominantly from the EU and the global levels.

In short, the mapping indicates that the locus of decisive policy decisions has in recent decades tended to shift upward and disperse across multiple levels, with important policies increasing in depth and functional scope at levels beyond the nation-state. A final note: the mapping exercise and Figures 12.1 and 12.2 in particular were designed to convey information in a parsimonious manner without drawing overly bold conclusions from any of their specifics.

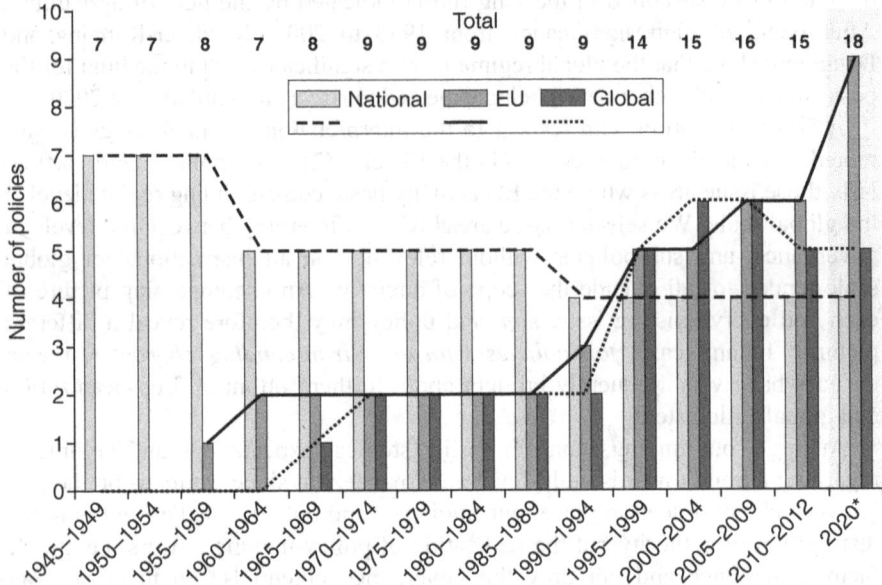

Figure 12.2 Number of policies classified highly significant at each level of governance.

Notes
'Total' refers to the overall number of policies classified as 'highly significant' at any of the three levels (theoretical maximum is 30 for all 10 selected policies).
* Denotes extrapolation.

The project's aim was not quantification but a qualitative study of recent governance trends in Europe that pay due attention to globalization.

2 Is there an ambition to export?

2.1 Global policies from the EU's perspective: vertical export and import

It is a widespread assumption in research on the EU's external relations that the EU seeks to project internal policy solutions to its external environment (Lavenex 2004; Lavenex *et al.* 2009; Schimmelfennig and Sedelmeier 2005; Börzel and Risse 2012). Although the EU's ambition for policy export is generally understood to be less pronounced, less encompassing and less systematic at the global level than in its 'near abroad' (Schimmelfennig 2010), this 'inside-out analogy' of the Union's external behaviour is also frequently applied to its wider international relations (Young and Peterson 2006; Bretherton and Vogler 2006; Manners 2002).[11] A good fit between domestic and global standards is considered to be in the best (economic) interest of the EU, reducing adaptation and information costs while providing the EU with a competitive advantage in global markets. At the same time, the external projection of domestic solutions is also attributed to normative motivations, with the EU seeking to globally export its unique, normative basis.

Our study, however, shows that the EU's interaction with global policy regimes is a complex phenomenon and takes a number of different forms. Evidently, policy export is not always the preferred strategy through which the EU engages with international regimes. EU policies often evolve in close interaction with global-level developments, with both levels inspiring each other and the EU acting as both a leader and a follower. Rather than following a simple logic of projecting domestic solutions to its external environment, the EU has also promoted positions that differed from its domestic *acquis communautaire*, protected domestic policies from external pressures, or imported policy solutions from international regimes. These options are by no means mutually exclusive and frequently occur in parallel or in sequence within individual policy areas.[12] To understand the EU's role in global governance and to put the phenomenon of EU policy export into perspective, it is worthwhile looking into the different EU strategies of interaction with global policy regimes one by one.

2.2 Market-making as the EU's landmark vertical export

Our study reveals that there is indeed one major policy paradigm that the EU managed to export: trade liberalization. Due to its character of cross-cutting economic sectors and its rich spillover potential, it had a revolutionary effect on the long-term development of global governance; indeed, on governance almost anywhere on the globe. From today's perspective there is a danger of neglecting this phenomenon just because free trade has become such a deeply entrenched institution.[13] However, this was different after World War II, when the paradigm of global market liberalization had not yet been institutionalized.

The EU's internal market liberalization was also thought to spread globally from the beginning. The EU's original Treaty of Rome establishing the EEC mentioned the 'progressive abolition of restrictions on international trade and the lowering of customs barriers' (Art. 110). To be sure, the EU's commitment to global market liberalization came with certain protectionist exceptions, notably in areas where important domestic interests were at stake which the EU tried to shield from global pressures (e.g. textiles and agriculture). Still, ever since its origins in the mid-1950s, the core element of regional integration in the 'European Economic Community' (EEC)[14] was the 'common market'. Indeed, free trade turned into a major European export item. Under the post-1947 GATT regime (later the WTO), the US had still been reluctant to open its market borders and had disappointed its European partners. It only changed its position once the EU turned into a strong, unified market and hence into a major player even on the global scale (see Chapter 2 by Dirk De Bièvre and Arlo Poletti on trade policy). The subsequent bilateral EU–US deal on lowering tariffs shaped the outcomes of the Kennedy Round as it was effectively multilateralized to the global trade regime with the 'most favoured nation' principle. During subsequent trade rounds, the EU worked in tandem with the US in writing the rules of the global trade regime concerning issues like anti-dumping policies and the disciplining of subsidy wars, as well as in a range of plurilateral regulatory codes concluded during the Uruguay Round.

In terms of our conceptual terminology, both the take-up rate and the relevance could hardly be greater. Regarding the degree of policy fit, global market liberalization did not exactly mirror the EU's own pattern with regard to a crucial feature. The EU's treaties provided for both market-making and market-shaping re-regulation at the same time in a 'liberalization-cum-harmonization' principle.[15] The latter part was not (or not to a comparable extent) taken up at the global level.[16] As the chapters on competition policy and social standards in our volume indicate, the free trade regime on the global level shows liberalization with much less re-regulation. Very importantly, market-making has not been matched by flanking provisions in areas such as social policy or competition policy to any extent near the EU's, where it has been established on a quasi-constitutional level. This means that on the global scale there is inherent bias towards liberalization as a matter of principle, and that, even more than in the EU, re-regulation of standards hence faces an uphill struggle.[17]

Why did the EU not export its own paradigm exactly as the compromise stood? Various factors may have contributed:

- A more narrow scale of the global-level negotiations (at least, in the original bargains) as opposed to the negotiations on the original setup of the EU which were not limited to certain topics or policies from the start.
- A window of opportunity for those actors who had not preferred the re-regulatory approach of the EU in any case; for example, Germany, which had promoted a free market policy without accompanying EU social policies in the EEC Treaty's drafting (against countries such as France).
- Moreover, trade policy was a core area from the outset, an exclusive competence of the EU, while social policy was a lesser among the shared competences. This meant that the EU only set major activities rather late and it took the EU much longer to establish a unified approach to its external relations in the field. As we also know from other policies, the EU first concentrated on developing internal policy before becoming active in relevant issues on the global level.[18]
- In any case, it appears that global market-making seemed so attractive that sacrificing other goals (particularly since they were not equally promoted by all EU members) was considered acceptable.

Although the EU did not export its own approach of 'liberalization cum harmonization' but merely exported free trade initially, it clearly changed its orientation at a later point in history (when, however, the basic deals could not be reopened). Over the past two decades or so, the EU has become more active in promoting measures flanking global market regulation in a number of policy domains, not least to create a more level playing field for global competition.

Describing the EU's new activism in (re)regulating global markets, Young and Peterson state:

> [T]he EU has been the most aggressive and persistent advocate of a broader international trade agenda and the strongest proponent for developing common multilateral disciplines on the making of domestic rules – what might be termed a 'deep' trade agenda – in areas including competition policy, environmental standards, labour rights and investment rules.
>
> (Young and Peterson 2006: 796)

Embracing an 'inside-out' perspective of the EU's external relations, several scholars have argued that over the past two decades the EU has embarked on a policy approach that promotes a regulatory framework for global liberal markets according to its own domestic model (Woolcock 2005; Baldwin 2006). What is crucial to understand here, however, is that the EU extended its global trade liberalization agenda to flanking measures relatively late in time, at a moment where (1) the basic setup of the global regime was already in place, and (2) it had already lost global influence substantially (see Dirk De Bièvre and Arlo Poletti, Chapter 2).[19] In an increasingly multipolar world, the EU frequently found its pro-harmonization policies lacking support in core multilateral settings like the World Trade Organizations (WTO), particularly from developing and emerging countries. When the EU tried to export not only its 'market liberalization' paradigm but also its twin feature of joint re-regulatory policies to the higher level, it did not succeed with the second element of its endeavour in the crucial GATT/WTO arena. Regarding food safety standards, Chapter 4 by Vessela Hristova shows how the EU tried indeed to have its safety considerations included in the global regime, but only managed to get weak compromise formulae that could barely uphold legal challenges.

It seems that the original deal of market-making with parallel re-regulatory measures (market-plus), as formulated in the EEC Treaty and later extended in subsequent EU treaty reforms, was followed by a global deal of only the first trait, market-making, without significant re-regulation (market-only). Ever since, free trading zones have spread all over the globe – typically without much (if any) re-regulation at the higher level. This brings to mind the latest developments within the EU, i.e. the UK's threat of exit combined with its pressurizing to undo the original EU deal. The Cameron government seemingly wants to continue profiting from the internal market without accepting the previously agreed re-regulatory policies at the same time. It favours a form of 'market-only' integration within the EU. In a nutshell, therefore, the EU could come under severe pressures from both outside and inside, since a liberalized market without re-regulatory action (market-only) is promoted nowadays by both competitive pressures stemming from the globalized markets and some EU members, such as the UK.

That the EU had a decisive impact on the global trade regime during the period of its own inception may come as a surprise to those acquainted with the recent literature highlighting that the EU became a comparatively more unified and active external actor over time. Such a generalized perspective would neglect that trade is special due to the strong external competences and unity of the EU from the outset. Conventional wisdom tends to pay insufficient attention to the long-term perspective we can offer based on our longitudinal approach in the policy chapters. In its early times, in any case, the EU was able to benefit from the initial GATT environment where global deal-making was possible on the basis of intense bilateral cooperation with the US. Nowadays, by contrast, there are many more actors, including the less developed countries, which have recently formed a strong blocking coalition on several issues, and there is also a dense network of rules to be respected. This change in the international environment cannot easily be countered by (some degree of) increased internal unification of the EU.

2.3 *Other cases of vertical policy export and of policy promotion*

With the prominent exception of the free market paradigm, the EU's record of policy export to the global level may be described at best as mixed. In a number of cases we find vertical export of EU policies to international regimes. In selected subfields of environmental policy, including climate change policy (the export of reduction targets to Kyoto) and car emission standards (the export of EU exhaust emission standards to UNECE), the EU succeeded in shaping global policy outcomes along the lines of domestic solutions and preferences.

In a number of areas we learned that success in policy export may have significant drawbacks. On the global level, the result of the EU's efforts to have its policies spread across the globe may well be a non-binding character of the same standards (e.g. in competition policy), a narrow scope of the resulting rules (e.g. nuclear non-proliferation policy), or a low take-up rate (e.g. social policy). In discussing social policy, Guido Schwellnus argues that the EU has been quite successful in uploading its internal standards into ILO conventions in areas with highly developed Community rules, including working conditions or occupational health and safety. Yet success with regard to policy content had to be bought at the expense of an extremely low take-up rate, as 'other countries chose not to ratify ILO conventions with excessively high standards'. At the same time, the EU has shown some ability to export its own policies in technical areas such as nuclear safeguards (i.e. techniques to verify compliance with the international commitment not to use nuclear programmes for weapons purposes) and practices of air safety standards. In the realm of nuclear safeguards, the EU's own experience and expertise in administrating its domestic safeguard system facilitated the export of technical standards and routines to the International Atomic Energy Agency (IAEA), with which the EU established a close network of cooperation. Similarly, the EU was able to capitalize on its top-level technical expertise on issues of air safety and air traffic management, providing technical advice to the International Civil Aviation Organization (ICAO) which turned it into a discrete shaper of international rules.

For the most part, vertical EU policy export has occurred in isolated cases within the observed policy areas and has been limited in functional scope. Several contributions, including those on agriculture, food safety or asylum, report on vertical EU policy export 'at the margins'.

Indeed, EU policy export to global institutions is a demanding undertaking, as illustrated by prominent cases of *failed export*. The EU failed to upload the core of its domestic model based on 'agricultural exceptionalism' to the global agricultural trade regime and it also largely failed to export its stringent policies on food safety. The EU was also unsuccessful in promoting its preferences on competition policy at the WTO, where its initiative on introducing binding minimum standards was soon abandoned. Moreover, it is the US, rather than the EU, that has been most successful in shaping global competition standards in institutions such as UNCTAD, the OECD and the International Competition Network. Even in policy domains where the EU has initially exercised global leadership, such as trade policy or specific subfields of environmental policy, its capacity for policy export has become more limited over time.

Our study also shows that, in various cases, the EU has promoted positions at the international level that have deviated from its domestic *acquis*, opting for a *strategy of policy promotion* rather than policy export. Through policy promotion, the EU seeks to ensure that its common external preferences are reflected in global policy outcomes, even though it lacks the capacity or ambition for a wholesale export of its domestic model. The EU may opt for policy promotion in areas where it did not develop domestic rules that could serve as the basis for policy export; in cases where its domestic rules are too stringent, complex or demanding to serve as a model for global governance solutions; or if it seeks to facilitate the universalization of international rules and agreements.[20] Policy promotion is also central in the external realm of the Common Foreign and Security Policy (CFSP), which, among other things, serves as the central framework through which the EU coordinates its position in core institutions of the global non-proliferation regime.

2.4 Policy import by the EU

Usually, the EU is seen as the 'higher level' in European integration studies and effects are frequently studied in a top-down perspective, with change resulting from the impact of the Union on national policy. However, the EU is only one among many actors in global policy-making and it has developed and reformed its domestic policies along the lines of global regimes. Policy import has often led to 'gold plating': the EU made more of the standards of global governance. At other times, however, the EU has not only imported but also diluted higher level policies. Asylum policy (Florian Trauner, Chapter 9, this volume) serves as a case in point. Considering that the EU prides itself on being a normative power and promoter of democracy and human rights, one might have expected a more impressive balance sheet. However, the EU did indeed fall short of living up to the global asylum standards it originally imported.

From our observations it becomes apparent that EU policy import from the global level has followed different logics. To a considerable extent, policy import by the EU from the global level has been voluntary in nature. In several policy areas such as social policy, transport, certain subfields of environmental policy or asylum (refugee protection), the EU has been a latecomer and developed its domestic policy by importing standards that already existed at the global level. Through the import of international standards into EU regulation, the EU made these policies more binding for its Member States and developed its domestic regime with close reference to international standards and practices.

At the same time, the EU has relied on policy import from the global level as a strategy to facilitate greater intra-EU convergence (transport policy and financial market regulation) or to reform domestic policies. Here, EU policy-making is best understood as a multi-level game with international negotiations providing an opportunity for EU actors like the Commission or individual Member States to alter the domestic status quo through strategic policy import. In the case of air transport policy (see Marcin Dąbrowski, Chapter 8), the Commission was eager to transpose legislation of the International Civil Aviation Organization (ICAO) to ensure greater harmonization across Europe and to consolidate its role as de facto enforcer of ICAO rules. In addition, Zdenek Kudrna argues (Chapter 11, this volume) that internal disputes in the field of EU financial market regulation increased the EU's motivation to engage in global standard-setting, as it served as a means to facilitate domestic consensus.[21]

While the EU overall has shown a strong capacity to prevent unwanted policy import, there were also cases where the EU reformed domestic policies along the lines of international regimes as a result of external pressures. The case of agriculture policy serves as a prominent example where the EU felt pressured to align its Common Agricultural Policy (CAP) with demands of the WTO regime on agricultural trade. While exogenous pressures were strategically employed by certain EU actors to facilitate domestic reforms, the EU's failed efforts to keep agriculture out of WTO negotiations show that it initially sought to avoid pressure for domestic reform. Here, unwanted policy import was facilitated by the particular characteristics of the international setting. As Dirk De Bièvre and Arlo Poletti point out, 'the very bindingness of WTO commitments through the increased judicialization of the world trade regime caused the EU, just like any other WTO member, to be vulnerable to legal challenges'.

2.5 Policy protection

Beyond policy export and import, the authors of this book identified a third pattern: policy protection. The EU can act as a shield against globalization. In several policy domains, particularly in agriculture and food safety, the EU has developed distinct domestic rules and policy preferences which it has tried to shield from global pressures. For instance, food safety is a key concern of EU citizens. Since the EU depends on food imports, it has a keen interest in exporting its standards to the outside world. However, Vessela Hristova indicates that the specific European model of elevated living standards at a high price can hardly be generalized across the globe. Arguing in a similar vein, Carsten Daugbjerg and Christilla Roederer-Rynning remind us that '(s)een from a global perspective, the EU may appear to be a club of rich countries with high regulatory standards that are very difficult to meet'. Accordingly, the EU did not have much choice but to try to at least protect its standards in its own territory.

Our empirical findings suggest that policy protection can take a number of different forms. Policy protection can be a pro-active strategy of preference promotion through which the EU seeks to ensure that global policy outcomes in international negotiations take important European concerns and interests into consideration. As pointed out in the contribution by Carsten Daugbjerg and Christilla Roederer-Rynning, much of the EU's input in global-level negotiations has revolved around protecting core aspects of the EU's unique domestic agricultural regime rather than seeking to export a specific model of agricultural policy. Arguing in a similar vein, Marco Botta describes how the EU has sought to ensure, through its participation in the work of the International Competition Network, the OECD and UNCTAD, that soft law elaborated by these global bodies does not conflict with its domestic competition model. At other times, the EU did not protect a particular policy but the preferences of (some) Member States. Zdenek Kudrna shows how the EU has always been powerful and cohesive enough to mould the outcomes of international negotiations on banking and accounting regulation in a way that prevented 'policy imports that were contrary to preferences of important subsets of EU Member States'.

At the same time, the EU may also delay or block the adoption of agenda items in global negotiations when international standards are not in line with its own policies (see Chapter 4 on food safety). The EU may also protect its interest in a given regime by excluding certain issues from the international agenda altogether, as it successfully did for several decades in the GATT/WTO arena with respect to sectors like textiles and agriculture (see chapters 2 and 3 on trade and CAP). As a last resort, the EU may also deviate from international standards to protect domestic policies, as it did with some of the fair value accounting rules in finance (see Chapter 11 on finance). While our case studies indicate that the EU showed a strong capacity to avoid unwanted policy import, they also demonstrate that, for the most part, the EU tried to be a constructive player aiming to strengthen rather than undermine international regimes.

3 The mechanisms and conditions for vertical EU policy export: what have we learned?

Having looked at EU policy export to IOs in ten selected policy areas, what have we learned? In fact, vertical EU policy export at the global level is a demanding exercise. In several policy domains, EU policy export occurred only at the margins or has not been particularly successful (see above). On a global scale, the EU is not a hegemonic power that can easily export its standards to international regimes and, as we have seen, it does not always intend to do so. Still, there have been prominent cases of EU policy export. In addition, while operating in an increasingly multipolar world, the EU's potential for shaping the rules of global governance is still matched by only a few other countries, first among them the US but also increasingly by emerging powers (i.e. the 'BRICs'). But through which processes and under what conditions has the EU been successful in exporting its policies to global regimes?

3.1 Bargaining

The EU holds significant bargaining power in multilateral settings. Its collective weight in international negotiations is derived from a number of sources, including the EU's large and diversified domestic market as well as its significant share in IOs in terms of membership and financial contributions. This makes it difficult to discount policy initiatives by the EU and its Member States, and prominent cases of EU policy export have benefited from its considerable bargaining power. As Dirk De Bièvre and Arlo Poletti argue in this volume, its bargaining power placed the EU in an influential position to shape the global rule book of the GATT/WTO regime, particularly when it worked in tandem with the US.

At the same time, multilateral settings – which range from traditional IOs to loosely formalized global policy networks – also impose important constraints on the EU. First, rules of membership and representation matter a great deal. With few exceptions – including the WTO and the Codex Alimentarius Commission – IOs only allow states as members, at best giving observer status to the European Commission and at times to other EU actors (e.g. the European Banking Authority and the European Central Bank, in the Basel Committee on Banking Supervision). Besides its participation in some traditional IOs, the Commission is also represented in global networks like the International Competition Network (ICN), where it participates alongside experts from national competition authorities. Still, the particular nature of networks like the ICN – essentially a community of experts – clearly privileges the exchange of expertise, experience and know-how over political bargaining. EU representation in IOs is further complicated by the complex internal division of EU competences. While the case of external representation is relatively clear-cut when the EU exercises its exclusive competence as is the case with trade policy, the Member States have been reluctant to give up authority concerning their external representation in areas of shared competences. Several authors report internal EU struggles over external powers undermining the Union's capacity to speak with one voice and its negotiation potential.[22] Interestingly, initiatives on the part of the Commission to achieve full membership in international organizations received little backing from its own Member States (see Chapters 10 and 8 on non-proliferation and transport policy, respectively). The need for EU coordination at international organizations has further compounded problems of EU disunity, making it difficult for the EU to make effective use of its collective weight.

Second, while the EU enjoys strong voting power if it acts as a block in international settings, formal voting procedures can become a constraint if EU positions become isolated. There have also been situations in which the EU has strengthened its negotiation position in IOs by using its economic weight in a horizontal direction, circumventing global-level constraints. The case of air transport policy illustrates this point. Here, the EU's unilateral decision to extend its domestic Emissions Trading Scheme (ETS) to the aviation sector facilitated efforts to break the deadlock in talks within the International Civil Aviation Organization (ICAO) on emissions trading for international aviation. Similarly, horizontal mechanisms have worked hand in hand with the EU's role in the international organization of the global environmental regime for promoting EU policies (see Katharina Holzinger and Thomas Sommerer, Chapter 7).

Third, procedural commitments may bind the members of international organizations and hence tie their hands for future deals. One example is the 'successive liberalization' agreement in the WTO (see Chapter 2 on trade policy). In particular, legalization and judicialization at the global level may take decisions out of the hands of policy-makers, including the EU or its Member State governments. At times, unclear general commitments are accepted first and this brings about a court or panel decision later which cannot be undone. In a way, certain patterns in the EU which scholars of European integration have studied in depth may also be observed in the WTO arena. As Vessela Hristova points out in the case of food policy, the EU was a defendant in two prominent WTO disputes: the EC–Beef Hormones case and the EC–Biotechnology case, with the WTO ruling against the EU on both accounts. The cases were decided based on the so-called 'SPS Agreement' which was established during the Uruguay Round of trade negotiations, laying down general principles for determining when national food measures may interfere with international trade. The EU is an important trading bloc, and could therefore have reached better deals at times in power-based negotiations than in rule-based institutional settings. This seems to have been the case when the US and the EU still made bilateral bargains, long before GATT/WTO became crucial as a rule-based arena (see Chapter 2 on trade policy).

3.2 Persuasion

The EU is not only a large market power; it has also widely been considered a global role model (i.e. a 'normative' or 'civilian' power) that exercises an ideational influence on its external environment. In this view, the EU seeks to project its 'unique normative basis' – made up of core principles of European governance like democracy, the rule of law, social solidarity, and the respect of fundamental freedoms and rights – through its international relations. While we do not want to downplay the importance of the EU as a 'normative power', our empirical findings point to some notable inconsistencies in the EU's external relations that cast some doubt on the 'inside-out' logic adopted by this perspective. As argued above, in the decisive phase of global trade liberalization following the Treaty of Rome, the EU's external trade agenda departed from its internal policy compromise (which has its basis in the EEC Treaty) that sought to achieve a balance between liberalization and re-regulation through flanking measures. At the same time, Florian Trauner's contribution on asylum policy describes how the EU's restrictive approach to refugee protection undermined the EU's normative authority in this particular policy domain.

Focusing on the specific notion of policy export, this project transcends the focus on more general principles of European governance. From the policy-specific perspective of this book, an aspect of the EU's ideational influence that seems to be of particular relevance is its capacity to persuade others through its technical expertise, experience and know-how. The EU has acquired extensive regulatory competence and technical expertise in a broad range of policy domains. In some cases studied in this book – including such diverse issues as air transport management and safety rules or nuclear safeguard standards – EU expertise has translated into notable influence in international settings. In the realm of nuclear safeguards (see Patrick Müller, Chapter 10), a dense interinstitutional framework between Euratom and the International Atomic Energy Agency (IAEA) has served as an important platform for information exchange and knowledge transfer. Relying on its extensive experience and research activities resulting from administrating its own regional safeguard system, the EU was able to export safeguard routines and know-how to the IAEA. In a similar way, the International Civil Aviation Organization (ICAO) has relied on the expertise and recommendations of the European Aviation Safety Agency, which has developed into a widely recognized authority in matters of aviation safety.

The results of the transfer of EU expertise and knowledge to IOs may range from 'copy-and-paste' solutions to a third country's adaptation of transferred policies to its particular national context. What is more, policy and knowledge transfer through persuasion seems to benefit from expert settings, technical committees and networks at the global level, in which a 'problem-solving' logic prevails. Policy transfer through persuasion thus does not generally apply to the more politicized and contested aspects of a policy and, as our empirical observations suggest, it is frequently limited in functional scope and significance.

4 The horizontal dimension: EU export to other states or groups of states

Overall, our study sustains findings in the literature that the EU's influence is decreasing with geographical distance to the EU (Lavenex 2011; Schimmelfennig 2010; Börzel and Risse 2012). Evidently, the EU's ambitions for horizontal policy export at the global level are less comprehensive and systematic than in its immediate neighbourhood. If we conceive, for the sake of the argument, the entire international sphere as concentric circles with the EU at its centre, it becomes apparent that a number of mechanisms of policy export vary in their intensity with respect to different geographic layers, i.e. the layer of accession and candidate countries, the layer of neighbouring countries, and the global layer.

Empirical evidence in our study also confirms that the conditionality mechanism is probably the most relevant instrument for spreading EU policies in terms of functional scope and significance of the exported rules (entire *acquis*), resulting also in a high policy fit.[23] Still, its influence as a mechanism for EU policy export is geographically bound. It works quite effectively with regard to pre-membership negotiations, where a systematic and wholesale transfer of EU rules takes place.[24] It is already less powerful in the EU's relations with countries in the EU neighbourhood, where the EU relies on policy instruments like the European Neighbourhood Policy (ENP) that offers 'everything but institutions' to partner countries, or other regional frameworks like the European Common Aviation Area. It has only a weak impact in EU Trade Agreements with third countries located in the outer layer.

It appears that the main benefits third countries generally strive for in their relations with the EU are either full membership – an option that is reserved for third countries in the EU's proximity that share its core values and principles – or market access only. It turns out that market access conditionality needs to be directly related to specific EU policies to be an effective and credible instrument for global EU policy export, rather than being incorporated into large package deals, as is the case with EU trade agreements and also EU Action Plans in its Neighbourhood Policy. For instance, Marcin Dąbrowski argues that the EU succeeded in policy export in the framework of the European Common Aviation Area. By making access to the large European aviation market conditional on compliance with the EU aviation policy *acquis*, the EU put a credible instrument in place for rule transfer. Similarly, the EU's decision to extend its domestic Emissions Trading Scheme (ETS) to the aviation sector had a discernible impact on global-level negotiations in the International Civil Aviation Organization (ICAO). In contrast, several contributions to this volume show that conditionality formulated in bilateral trade agreements and through regional trade instruments – like the EU's partnership agreement with the African, Caribbean and Pacific Group of states (aka the Contonou Agreement) or its Generalized System of Preferences (GPS) – has not been very successful. Besides EU trade priorities, these trade instruments may cover such diverse issues as (minimum) social standards, competition policy rules, food safety issues or non-proliferation matters. Yet only in very rare cases has the EU suspended bilateral trade agreements due to third-party violations of non-trade-related contents of the agreements, undermining their credibility and effectiveness as instruments for policy export.[25] The main effect of conditionality clauses in trade agreements thus seems to be in boosting soft supervision mechanisms and dialogue (see also Guido Schwellnus, Chapter 6), rather than the effective use of conditionality.

When looking at the mechanisms of horizontal EU policy export more generally, it becomes apparent that the relevance of EU policy export is more limited in the functional scope of exported rules outside its immediate neighbourhood. Passive EU policy export triggered by external effects of the EU's large internal market is, by its very nature, limited to market-related policies.[26] Katharina Holzinger and Thomas Sommerer, for instance, highlight the importance of external effects in spreading EU environmental standards at the global level, but they also point out that these effects apply to market-related policies only.

Moreover, the EU is not the only player in global politics with a large domestic market. In cases of global regulatory competition with other major market powers like the US, external effects of EU policies may only lead to patchy and sporadic policy export, with distinct forms of regulatory harmonization taking place at different nodes (see Kudrna, Chapter 11; also Drezner 2005).

Concerning EU policy export through persuasion and emulation, we observe that these 'soft mechanisms' are particularly prominent in technical domains and when the functional scope of rule export remains limited (see above). European expertise in aviation matters has provided the EU with considerable persuasive power, with India and sub-Saharan African countries adopting EASA technical norms for the purpose of modernizing domestic regulations and with Singapore copying elements of the SESAR system. Marco Botta points out that in the domain of competition policy, the good accessibility and ready availability of EU legislation in 23 official languages has facilitated the voluntary emulation of EU competition standards as 'best practices' by a number of third countries. EU norms have also been emulated in subfields of environmental policy.[27] As these examples show, there is a significant level of emulation of sector-specific, technical EU standards by third countries that has received little attention thus far in the scholarly literature.[28]

Still, persuasion and emulation generally do not translate into a high take-up rate of the exported rules. In fact, their impact is largely limited to countries that show an interest in voluntary rule adoption, actively turning to the EU to profit from its expertise, experiences and best practices. It is thus not surprising that the voluntary adoption of EU rules by third countries is generally rather haphazard. As far as active policy export through persuasion is concerned, the EU's ability for rule export is most pronounced in its neighbourhood, where the bulk of its external assistance and training programmes take place and where its relations with third countries are more strongly institutionalized.

5 Conclusions

The question of EU policy export has hardly been studied in depth with regard to the global level and with a focus not only on general principles but on specific policies. This book offers a unique assembly of in-depth area studies. We cover ten crucial EU policies in the chapters and, with the sub-policy areas, 18 issue areas in total. In addition, the authors go beyond that level and illustrate 32 cases in some depth. Not only the distribution of competences (as studied in other important large-scale analyses) but the policies indeed adopted are at stake. That our project is not about 'potential governance' but about 'governance realized' makes our results stand out. In addition, our data go beyond quantitative studies which build on statistics about the numerous decisions taken but are qualitative, since our authors analyse policies in depth, evaluate the major decisions and put them in context.

The question of potential policy export was our starting point. However, during our collaborative work we also paid attention to policy import, and the concepts of 'policy promotion' and 'policy protection' were developed. Setting the agenda for future research, the chapters hence also discuss cases where the EU seeks to assure its common external preferences without its own internal policies (or in the absence of a willingness or capacity to export them) as well as issues where the EU shields its policies and members against globalization. It now remains a task for further research to build on these insights and extend the present work in order to draw a fuller picture of the important strategies identified here.

Due to these fresh insights and because the EU did not always have a policy (yet) to offer when the relevant aspects were first discussed globally, the cases of attempted policy export found by our authors are not as numerous as one may have possibly thought.[29] Nonetheless, our cross-comparative look at the material discussed in the chapters has revealed one truly game-changing policy export (trade liberalization in three major GATT rounds), one medium-sized (environmental policy) and six minor cases (see the chapters on air transport, nonproliferation, migration, environmental, food, and social policy) in the vertical dimension. In addition, many chapters mention episodic evidence of policy export at the fringes. It is comparatively easier for the EU to export horizontally to its neighbourhood and particularly to membership candidates, and to export in highly specific issue areas where it has an advantage at the level of technical or other expertise (see e.g. Chapter 8 on transport policy by Marcin Dąbrowski).

As our framework has suggested (see Chapter 1), high unity, high capacity and favourable international settings have all contributed to the landmark case of policy export. With regard to *explaining the success or failure* of attempted EU policy export, our exploratory analysis comparing ten major fields suggests a number of lessons regarding the conditions of relevance for EU policy export:

- There is one *pre-condition for policy export,* as we framed it, in terms of *timing*. There needs to be a EU policy in place in order to project it externally (otherwise it would *per definitionem* be 'policy promotion'). Where the EU is a latecomer, there will typically not be policy export – although it happens that the EU is initially a latecomer at time t1 but then develops issue areas comparatively faster than its environment and, at the later point in time t2, exports part of its policy.[30] We discussed the aspect of a potential first-mover advantage[31] in the category of the international setting because it always relates to the others' timing.
- Another relevant issue in the category of international settings is that several chapters may be read to suggest that, if the EU wants to gain in leverage, it should try to convince the governments to consider increasingly *pooling their powers in IOs*. This may include that Member States give up voting rights in favour of the Commission[32] or that the EU becomes a member of one or the other IO where it is so far only an observer or not admitted.[33] The specific forms and limits of delegation of powers to the European Commission, as relevant in negotiations on the global level, turned out to be an intricate issue and largely a research desideratum (see n. 23).

- We learned from our project that *unity can be crucial*. Zdenek Kudrna (Chapter 11) demonstrates this point for some situations in international finance where, considering all other aspects, the EU could have become the decisive first mover in the late 1980s had it not lacked unity. What matters is not only unity among the EU's Member State positions but also unity among the various Commission Directorates. It is clearly detrimental if there is a visible rift between units, as indicated, for example, in the chapter on environmental policy. At the same time, it seems that unity is not a necessary condition in general terms. Again in the finance chapter, we find a hint that Member States may at times also play 'outside-in' and try, like the UK, to have their way on the global level at the expense of their partners. For sure, this is only easily conceivable in cases where the EU's policy is either not unequivocal or not yet decided. In addition, unity is *by no means a sufficient condition*, as indicated, for example, in the food policy case where high unity is countervailed by adverse international settings.[34]
- The same is true for the *EU's capacity*. A strong Union in terms of intra-EU competence distribution and in terms of bargaining position is clearly helpful. One relevant aspect in particular can hardly be underrated: the preference constellation.[35] Even ideal constellations regarding capacity, unity, timing, and international settings in general cannot bring about success if the EU is an outlier in terms of preferences and cannot persuade others to join its camp (see Chapter 4 on food safety, and agricultural exceptionalism as discussed by Carsten Daugbjerg and Christilla Roederer-Rynning in Chapter 3).
- Finally, looking in general terms at the *international setting*, a major evolution took place over the period covered, as already discussed above. In fact, the EU was one out of only two powerful shapers of the inceptive global level negotiations in the 1950s. By now, it is but one of many 'rather big players' in the contemporary, densely regulated international regime. Although the EU should clearly strive for high unity and capacity in order to maximize its chances to export policies or promote its preferences on a global scale, these framework conditions are setting clear limits. That the international arena has been getting more regulated and in many fields even judicialized,[36] and that new actors have entered the stage whose preferences for structural reasons rarely coincide with the EU's, may explain why policy export may fail nonetheless.

These notable changes in the global-level scenery also invite a final remark. On the level of practical policy recommendations, our findings suggest a 'third way' between two strands of the literature. One recommends a grand new strategy in the vertical direction (Howorth 2010; Jorgensen 2009) since the global situation changed, with the BRIC (Brazil, Russia, India and China) and similar countries gaining more of a say in international institutions. The other would rather recommend to 'go horizontal'. For instance, Erik Jones suggests that Europe's 'deep trade agenda' – based on complementing market liberalization with flanking issues such as environmental measures or social protection – that emerged in the 1980s is a sub-optimal model for its global trade agenda anyway, since vertical policy export (as we call it) has little chance of success. He suggests emphasizing the horizontal pathways (Jones 2006).

Our chapters hint that an altogether different approach is commendable, one that is tailor-making the strategy with the specific circumstances at hand. Each pathway, vertical or horizontal, has its pros and cons, as discussed above. There are trade-offs.[37] The global pathway typically offers a larger take-up rate but more limited policy fit. 'Membership conditionality', by contrast, the most effective horizontal means, works the other way around. It is available only for a few, clearly specified states (low take-up rate) although typically they have to simply accept what the EU has originally designed for its internal use (high policy fit).[38] The good thing is that, in actual fact, the two pathways are strategically not an either-or option and should not be positioned against each other, as much of the academic literature tends to do. The empirics presented in this book suggest that in most cases, the EU can combine different strategies of influence and that its engagement is best tailor-made with each situation judged individually. On that basis, we opt for an alternative in the form of a flexible and comprehensive approach when it comes to optimizing the EU's chances to export its policies.

Notes

1 Thanks to the chapter authors for stimulating discussions and to Zdenek Kudrna and Guido Schwellnus for contributing to parts of this chapter. Helpful comments by Liesbet Hooghe, Sandra Lavenex and Michael Zürn are also gratefully acknowledged. Any remaining shortcomings would be the authors' responsibility.

2 It should be noted that our approach did not include the regional level below the state. Work by Hooghe and colleagues (2010; Schakel et al. forthcoming) on regional authority in 42 democracies reveals that we live in an era of regionalization. Note that ongoing research by Liesbet Hooghe and Gary Marks, to be completed by the end of 2015 (www.falw.vu/~mlg/index.html), starts from the policies, like ours; however, their interest lies with the dispersion of authority away from central states to subnational and supranational levels (ours is about the export of EU policies). Our policy-specific lens stresses the scope and character of policy output on different levels (while theirs is about spheres of action over which a government may exercise authority, hence about attributed policy competences, not the de facto executed policy competences).

3 The team checked the coding for each policy or issue area in depth and the scores attributed by the authors were discussed at various joint workshops and repeatedly between editors and authors.

4 Thanks to Zdenek Kudrna for the compilation.

5 In essence, the presented data seems apt for use in an interval or even ratio scale, and hence for calculating a mean. Crucially, the dimensions have defined outer end points (zero vs. all significant policy aspects on any one governance level) and an intermediate category with roughly proportional distances that is actually meaningful in qualitative terms (with the value 'significant', a threshold is crossed). This is broadly similar to the construction of fuzzy sets (e.g. Ragin 2000: 156). Thanks for Guido Schwellnus' contribution to this part of the chapter.

6 While much attention has been paid to national and EU-level interaction in the literature on European integration, the interplay between the EU and the global levels has thus far received insufficient attention.
7 Note that significant parts of that policy are specified in treaty provisions directly.
8 Although it is mainly a very specific group of internally oriented EU policies that is fully excluded from our focus, notably the promotion of research and development, or intra-regional cohesion.
9 Clearly, major shifts in competences are important. Governance at the EU level starts after the Treaty of Rome (1958) and there is a discernible effect of the 1993 Maastricht Treaty reforms that led to a subsequent increase in the significance of the EU level, at least across the board. As the chapter on transport policy shows, some EU policies may not develop in terms of legislative activity, even though they are explicitly mentioned in the treaties.
10 The overall impression from Figure 12.1's means, as discussed above, is confirmed by the medians which also show that by 2010 more areas studied saw the EU as a highly significant regime level than the global or, even less frequently, the national level.
11 The EU's relations with countries beyond its neighbourhood are less hierarchically institutionalized, less asymmetric in power, and involve a lower degree of dependence by third countries on the EU, constraining the EU's capacity for external projection. An encompassing Europeanization agenda may thus serve EU interests in its near abroad, but it hardly constitutes a realistic ambition with respect to policy export on the global scale.
12 Whether there was an ambition on the part of the EU to engage in policy export or whether the EU opted for alternative strategies seems to depend on a number of factors (the extent to which a EU policy has developed at the domestic level, and the three factors developed in Chapter 1 (i.e. unity, capacity and international settings) also help in an understanding of policy export as well as decisions not to try to export).
13 Note that this is no judgement with regard to the content and effects of the policy.
14 It was only much later that the primarily economic character was somewhat softened and the name changed to 'European Union' under the 1992 Maastricht Treaty.
15 From the outset, the EU found a compromise between some member governments' calls for liberalization and, respectively, for re-regulation, notably in the fields of competition policy and social policy. Both got their own chapters in the EEC Treaty. The competition rules were first among all policies specified, and they were quite specific about preventing distortions of competition and dominant positions via joint legislation (Art. 85–90). The social policy chapter, by contrast, remained rather vague and without specific regulatory tasks enumerated (see Art. 118–124). However, the compromise formulae still formed the basis for the later development of a substantial EU policy with regard to equality between the sexes and – ensuing treaty reforms after the mid-1990s – minimum harmonization of labour law standards (see Chapter 6 on social policy by Guido Schwellnus).
16 It seems that the literature does not answer for all phases (the exception seems to be the Uruguay Round) the question of whether and how intensely the EU (or those who participated and also belonged to the EU) tried to promote the model of 'liberalization cum regulation' during the relevant GATT rounds.
17 This initial deal set the scene for all later negotiations, making it more difficult for the EU to promote, for example, social or environmental standards when it opted to do so later (see Chapter 2 by Dirk De Bièvre and Arlo Poletti).
18 In a way, what the EU exported mirrored its own 'de facto model' by that time.
19 Conversely, it has also been (critically) argued that the EU promotes a neo-liberal agenda, according to its own model of market building and economic liberalization (Wetzel and Orbie 2012).
20 For instance, in the social policy domain, the EU promoted core labour standards of

the International Labour Organization (ILO) through horizontal instruments, which are not regulated at the EU level (see Chapter 6 by Guido Schwellnus).
21 In a similar way, major reforms in the EU's Common Agricultural Policy (CAP) were pushed through in the early 1990s by Farm Commissioner Ray Mac Sharry, using exogenous pressures resulting from the EU's involvement in WTO negotiations.
22 Little seems to be known about the EU's institutional role in different international organizations, with the majority of studies looking at coordination in the UN (Panke 2013; Laatikainen and Smith 2006). Variations range from not being allowed to even be present in negotiations to having the power to vote for all its Member States. Intermediate conditions are being present without voting rights, or voting for those Member States that are present but not for others.
23 The EU's bargaining power is strongest and least constrained in its bilateral relations. Here bargaining takes the form of conditionality and – particularly in its relations to candidate and accession countries – the EU benefits from a highly asymmetric distribution of power and (inter)dependence. Moreover, the Commission enjoys substantial competences in managing the EU's accession process (strong formal capacity) and a high degree of internal unity in terms of the underlying logic and main objectives of the process.
24 Pre-membership policy and neighbourhood policy are ways to 'export' EU policies. This has been studied widely and our authors also stress the importance of this pathway.
25 Conditionality clauses in trade agreements appear to be a last resort measure for extreme cases of rule violation.
26 Damro's (2012) concept of the EU as 'market power Europe' stresses this aspect of European integration as opposed to 'normative power Europe'.
27 Katharina Holzinger and Thomas Sommerer give the Euro norm on car emissions as an example, which was taken up by countries like China, Indonesia and some other Asian countries, Argentina, Brazil, Chile, Israel and Saudi Arabia (supported by positive externality: harmonization of standards in worldwide product market is a positive externality).
28 In this respect, the literature has a strong region-to-region focus (see also our introductory chapter).
29 Please note that the book is not a complete inventory count but that the authors, drawing on their policy expertise, chose illustrative examples in areas considered of relevance (see also the introductory chapter).
30 As indicated, for example, in Chapter 7 on environmental policy by Katharina Holzinger and Thomas Sommerer.
31 See e.g. Chapter 5 on competition policy by Marco Botta.
32 See e.g. Vessela Hristova, Chapter 4, this volume.
33 For example, ICAO non-membership hampers EU capacity in transport policy; see Marcin Dąbrowski, Chapter 8.
34 Most importantly, WTO judicializaton negatively affecting the EU's interests, and by voting procedures providing that only the EU's governments present in the room have a vote in the Codex Alimentarius Commission (see Chapter 4 on food policy).
35 After in-depth discussions we considered it as a part of the EU's informal capacity and all authors cover that aspect in their chapters. Even though it is not a property of the EU, it co-determines its relative bargaining power.
36 Among the noteworthy exception is competition policy (see Chapter 5 by Marco Botta).
37 This argument has been developed in slightly different form by Guido Schwellnus (Chapter 6).
38 More far-reaching horizontal means, in turn, are limited to technical standards or market-related policies.

References

Baldwin, M. (2006) 'EU Trade Politics – Heaven or Hell?', *Journal of European Public Policy* 13(6): 926–942.
Börzel, T.A. and Risse, T. (2012) 'From Europeanisation to Diffusion: Introduction', *West European Politics* 35(1): 1–19.
Bretherton, C. and Vogler, J. (2006) *The European Union as a Global Actor*, 2nd revised edn, London; New York: Routledge.
Damro, C. (2012) 'Market Power Europe', *Journal of European Public Policy* 19(5): 682–699.
Drezner, D.W. (2005) 'Globalization, Harmonization, and Competition: The Different Pathways to Policy Convergence', *Journal of European Public Policy* 12(5): 841–859.
Hooghe, L. and Marks, G. (2001) 'Types of Multi-level Governance', *European Integration Online Papers (EIoP)* 5(11). Online. Available: http://eiop.or.at/eiop/texte/2001-011a.htm.
Hooghe, L., Marks, G. and Schakel, A.H. (2010) *The Rise of Regional Authority. A Comparative Study of 42 Democracies*, London; New York: Routledge.
Howorth, J. (2010) 'The EU as a Global Actor: Grand Strategy for a Global Bargain?', *Journal of Common Market Studies* 48(3): 455–474.
Jones, E. (2006) 'Europe's Market Liberalization is a Bad Model For a Global Trade Agenda', *Journal of European Public Policy* 13(6): 943–957.
Jorgensen, K.E. (2009) 'The European Union and International Organizations. A Framework for Analysis', in K.E. Jorgensen (ed.) *The European Union and International Organizations*, London; New York: Routledge.
Laatikainen, K.V. and Smith, K.E. (2006) *The European Union at the United Nations: Intersecting Multilateralisms*, Basingstoke: Palgrave.
Lavenex, S. (2004) 'EU External Governance in Wider Europe', *Journal of European Public Policy* 11(4): 680–700.
—— (2011) 'Concentric Circles of Flexible "EUropean" Integration: A Typology of EU External Governance Relations', *Comparative European Politics* 9(4/5): 372–393.
Lavenex, S., Lehmkuhl, D. and Wichmann, N. (2009) 'Modes of External Governance: A Cross-national and Cross-sectoral Comparison', *Journal of European Public Policy* 16(6): 813–833.
Manners, I. (2002) 'Normative Power Europe: A Contradiction in Terms?', *Journal of Common Market Studies* 40(2): 235–258.
Panke, D. (forthcoming) 'Regional Power Revisited. How to Explain Differences in Coherency and Success of Regional Organisations in the United Nations General Assembly', *International Negotiation Journal*.
Ragin, C.C. (2000) *Fuzzy-set Social Science*, Chicago, IL: University of Chicago Press.
Schakel, A.H., Hooghe, L. and Marks, G. (forthcoming) 'Multilevel Governance and the State', in S. Leibfried, E. Huber and J. Stephens (eds) *The Oxford Handbook of Transformations of the State*, Oxford: Oxford University Press.
Schimmelfennig, F. (2010) 'Europeanisation Beyond the Member State', *Zeitschrift für Staats- und Europawissenschaften* 8(3): 319–339.
Schimmelfennig, F. and Sedelmeier, U. (eds) (2005) *The Europeanization of Central and Eastern Europe*, Ithaca, NY: Cornell University Press.
Schmitter, P.C. (1996) 'Imagining the Future of the Euro-Polity with the Help of New Concepts', in G. Marks, F.W. Scharpf, P.C. Schmitter and W. Streeck (eds) *Governance in the European Union*, London; Thousand Oaks, CA: Sage.

Wetzel, A. and Orbie, J. (2012) *The EU's Promotion of External Democracy: In Search of the Plot. 13 September 2012*. CEPS Policy Brief No. 281. Online. Available: www.ceps.eu/ceps/dld/7300/pdf (accessed 25 April 2013).

Woolcock, S. (2005) 'European Union Trade Policy: Domestic Institutions and Systemic Factors', in D. Kelly and W. Grant (eds) *The Politics of International Trade in the Twenty-first Century: Actors, Issues and Regional Dynamics,* Basingstoke: Palgrave.

Young, A.R. and Peterson, J. (2006) 'The EU and the New Trade Politics', *Journal of European Public Policy* 13(6): 795–814.

Zürn, M. (2012) 'Global Governance as Multi-level Governance', in D. Levi-Faur (ed.) *Oxford Handbook of Governance,* Oxford: Oxford University Press

Index

Accord Européen sur les Transports Routiers (AETR) 132
Acquis communautaire 33, 42, 94, 99, 102–4, 120, 143, 211
African, Caribbean and Pacific states (ACP) 26, 105, 221
Agreement on the Application of Sanitary and Phytosanitary Measures (SPS Agreement) 46, 61–3, 65–6, 69–70, 73n3, 73n5, 219
Agreement on Technical Barriers to Trade (TBT Agreement) 73n4
agricultural policy 26, 38–57, 208–9, 217
Agriculture Council 42, 53–4
Aid for Restructuring of the Economies (PHARE) 158
Air Service Agreements 133, 137, 139
air transport policy 130–6, 145
Albania 143, 180
Amnesty International 161
Amsterdam Treaty 95, 99, 126, 150, 155–6
Antitrust Committee of the International Bar Association 82
Article 101 TFEU 76–7, 87–8
Article 102 TFEU 76–7, 87–8
Ashton, C *see* High Representative for Foreign Affairs
asylum and migration policy 150, 157
Australia 48, 52, 55n6, 64, 153, 183
Austria 52, 120, 159
aviation policy *see* transport policy
aviation safety list 144, 147n35

Banking Advisory Committee (BAC) 202n3, 195
Barcelona Convention 114
bargaining: collective 94, 96–100, 107; power 9–13, 24–5, 27, 33–4, 143, 153, 218, 227n23, 227n34; rationalist 101

Basel Committee on Banking Supervision (BSBS) 188–9, 192–3, 218
Basel I 193–6, 201
Basel II 193, 195–6, 201
Basel III 193, 196–7, 201
Belgian–Luxembourg Economic Union 22
Belgium 50, 52, 105, 133, 155, 177–8
Belgium, Netherlands and Luxembourg (BENELUX) 22
bindingness 29, 32, 42, 63, 113, 116, 170, 188, 190, 207, 216
Brazil 31–2, 47, 52, 55n6, 120–1, 141, 191, 224, 227n26
Brazil, Russia, India and China (BRIC) 125, 218, 224
Bretton Woods 188, 191

Cairns Group 47–9, 55n6, 64
Canada 28, 30, 33, 55n6, 64, 70, 121, 124, 183
Capital Adequacy Framework 192
car emissions regulation 117–20
Chicago Convention 134–8, 141–2, 146n3
Child Labour Convention *see* Convention Concerning the Prohibition and Immediate Action for the Elimination of the Worst Forms of Child Labour
China 31–2, 120, 141, 144, 170, 180, 190–1, 202, 224, 227n26
civilian power 2, 219
climate policy 115, 117–18, 122–6
Codex Alimentarius Commission (Codex) 58, 60–9, 71–2, 73n3, 73n8, 73n9, 73n11, 73n12, 73n15, 218, 227n33; Codex Committee on General Principles 63; Procedural Manual 65–6, 73n8, 73n9; Working Principles for Risk Analysis 65

Index 231

Common Agricultural Policy (CAP) 24, 38–45, 47–50, 52–5, 216–17, 227n20
Common European Asylum System 151, 155–6
Common Foreign and Security Policy (CFSP) 6, 10, 13, 167–9, 174–5, 215
common market organizations (CMOs) 39–40
Common Security and Defence Policy (CSDP) 2
Community Charter of Fundamental Social Rights for Workers 95
competition policy 13, 31, 76–81, 83, 85–9, 212–15, 221–2, 226n15, 227n30, 337n35
competitive farm regulation 41
Comprehensive Test Ban Treaty (CTBT) 170, 175
Convention Concerning the Prohibition and Immediate Action for the Elimination of the Worst Forms of Child Labour 102
Convention on Long Range Transboundary Air Pollution 113
Convention Plus 160
Convention on the Prevention of Marine Pollution 114
Convention relating to the Status of Refugees 153–4, 157–8, 162
convergence 11, 76–7, 79–81, 83, 86, 88–9, 108n11, 126, 144, 190, 193, 198–200, 216; *see also* policy convergence
Cooperative Development of Operational Safety and Continuing Airworthiness Programs (COSCAPs) 146n7
Cotonou Agreement 105–6, 180
Council of Environmental Ministers 119, 123–4
Council of Europe 95, 135
Council of Financial Ministers 123
Council of Ministers 25, 39–41, 43, 54, 132, 157–8, 207

Declaration on Fundamental Principles and Rights at Work 97
defensive policy import 38, 52
Denmark 52, 112, 160
DG Clima (Directorate-General for Climate Action) 140
DG Competition 77–9, 82, 84–9, 89n2
DG Move 139–40
DG Sanco 67
DG Trade 25, 67, 88
Doha Round 32–3, 49–55, 70

dual-use goods 167–9, 171–3, 175–6, 181, 182n8
Dublin System 150, 155–6

EC-Beef Hormones 69, 219
EC-Biotechnology 69, 219
Economic Commission for Europe (ECE) 73n3, 118–21
Emissions Trading System 134, 139–41
Energy and Environment Council 122
Environmental Impact Assessment 113, 115, 117
environmental policy 111–29, 206, 208, 214–16, 222–4
European Asylum Support Office (EASO) 158, 163
European Atomic Energy Community (Euratom) 167–8, 172, 174–5, 177–9, 181, 220; Euratom Treaty 23, 168, 182n13
European Aviation Safety Agency (EASA) 134, 136, 138, 141–2, 144–5, 220
European Banking Authority (EBA) 192–3, 201, 202n3, 218
European Central Bank (ECB) 23, 192–3, 195, 201, 218
European Civil Aviation Conference (ECAC) 135–6
European Commission 9–10, 24–6, 31, 53–4, 60, 66–7, 77–8, 100, 122, 131, 133, 136–7, 139–42, 144–5, 155–8, 162, 168, 178, 200, 218, 223
European Common Aviation Area 134, 136, 138, 143, 221
European Convention on Human Rights 95
European Co-ordination Centre for Accident and Incident Reporting Systems (ECCAIRS) 142
European Council on Refugees and Exiles 155
European Court of Human Rights 155
European Court of Justice (ECJ) 59, 64, 77, 94, 132–2, 138, 150, 155, 169
European Economic Area (EEA) 104
European Economic Community (EEC) 20, 22–3, 39, 150, 211
European Free Trade Association (EFTA) 104
European General Court 77, 86
European Neighbourhood Policy (ENP) 33, 159, 179, 221
European Parliament (EP) 40–1, 43, 54, 73n7, 105–6, 108n9, 119, 126, 133, 183n18

European Safeguards Research and Development Association (ESARDA) 178
European Social Charter 95
European Social Model 93
European Steel and Coal Community (ECSC) 20, 22
European Union (EU) Charter of Fundamental Rights 96
Everything-But-Arms (EBA) 31, 38, 51
export competition 46
external projection 1, 6, 14, 167, 211, 226n11
extra-territorial approaches to refugee protection 159–60, 163

failed export 215
financial market regulation 186–204, 208, 216
Financial Services Action Plan 187–8
Financial Stability Board (FSB) 189–90, 200; Financial Stability Forum 188
Finland 53, 120, 155
Food and Agriculture Organization (FAO) 9, 61, 73n8
food safety policy 43, 58–75, 207–9, 213, 215–17, 221, 224
France 22, 52, 84, 105, 119, 132, 170, 178, 188, 193, 212
free movement 76, 94, 149–51, 155, 187
Free-trade agreement (FTA) 33
functional scope see scope

G10, 191–4
G20, 33, 187–8, 192, 196, 200
General Agreement on Tariffs and Trade (GATT) 20–30, 32, 34, 34n1, 38–40, 44–5, 47–9, 52, 54–5, 100, 105, 211, 213–14, 217–19, 223, 226n16; Article XI 44
General Food Law 60, 64, 68
Generalized System of Preferences (GSP) 21, 26, 105, 221
geographical indications (GI) 32, 163n3
Germany 22, 53, 78, 84, 90n19, 105, 111, 119, 122, 124, 132, 160, 163n3, 177–8, 193, 195, 202n6, 212
global approach to migration 153
Global Commission on International Migration (GCIM) 152
Global Competition Initiative 80, 82, 84–5
Greece 52, 123, 155, 162
Group of Rapporteurs on Pollution and Energy (GRPE) 118, 120

Guterres, A see UN High Commissioner for Refugees (UNHCR)

Health and Safety in Agriculture Convention 102
High Representative for Foreign Affairs 174, 182n9
horizontal diffusion 11, 99–100, 103, 105–6, 179, 181
Hungary 52, 55n6

India 31–2, 50, 120, 140, 143–5, 180, 182n4, 191, 222, 224
Intellectual Property Rights (IPR) 31–2
Intergovernmental Panel on Climate Change (IPCC) 122
internal market 12, 20, 22–3, 25, 32, 51, 55n5, 59–61, 95, 169, 186–7, 211, 213, 221
internally displaced persons (IDP) 157
International Accounting Standards Board (IASB) 197–200, 202n2, 202n6–7; IAS 39, 198–201; IFRS 9, 199, 201
International Air Transport Association (IATA) 135
International Atomic Energy Agency (IAEA) 168, 170–3, 175, 177–9, 181, 182n5–6, 182n14–16, 214, 220
International Civil Aviation Organization (ICAO) 131, 134–42, 145, 146n7, 146n16, 214
International Competition Network (ICN) 76–7, 82–6, 88, 215, 217–18
International Competition Policy Advisory Committee (ICPAC) 79–80, 82, 85
International Criminal Court 9
International Financial Reporting Standards (IFRS) 189, 197–201, 202n5, 202n7
International Labor Organization (ILO) 93–4, 96–103, 105–7, 108n10
International Monetary Fund (IMF) 189–90, 192, 200, 202n1
International Organization for Migration (IOM) 152
International Organization of Securities Commissions (IOSCO) 190
International Trade Organization (ITO) 44
Ireland 52, 187
Italy 22, 52, 84, 119, 132, 160, 163n3, 177–8, 188

Joint Aviation Authorities (JAA) 134–6
Joint Resarch Centre (JRC) 178–9

Index   233

Justice and Home Affairs (JHA) 150, 159, 163n3

Kennedy Round 20, 24–5, 211
Kyoto Protocol 115, 123–5, 214

League of Nations 96, 153
Least Developing Countries (LDC) 50–2, 55
Lisbon Treaty 40–3, 96, 150, 174, 181n2
Lomé Convention 21, 26–7
Luxembourg 42, 53, 169, 177

Maastricht Treaty 93, 95, 112, 126, 208, 226n9, 226n14
MacSharry Reform 43, 53
MacSharry, R. 49, 53
mechanisms: active mechanisms 8–10; bargaining see bargaining; coercion 3, 8; constructivist 8, 10–11, 13, 101, 104; logic of appropriateness 8; logic of consequence 8; passive mechanisms 8, 145; persuasion 8–14, 53, 67–8, 72, 87–8, 104, 117–18, 126–7, 131, 140–2, 144–5, 157, 219–20, 222; rationalist 8–9, 11, 13, 101, 104
Members of the European Parliament (MEPs) 54
merger control regulation 78, 84, 86
Missile Technology Control Regime 176
modes of EU interaction 7, 14; see also policy export; policy import; policy protection
Montreal Protocol on the Protection of the Ozone Layer 113
most favoured nation principle 25, 211
multilateral trade negotiations 20, 23, 27, 34

National Competition Authority (NCA) 77
National Competition Authorities (NCAs) 76–7, 218
The Netherlands 22, 53, 122, 132–3, 160, 177, 188
New Zealand 55n6, 64, 120
non-governmental organizations (NGOs) 82, 125, 161
normative power 2, 215, 219, 226n12
Norway 117, 121–2, 143
nuclear non-proliferation policy 13, 167–85, 207–9, 214, 220
Nuclear Suppliers Group (NSG) 168, 171–3, 175–6, 182n11

OECD Environment, Health and Safety Programme 114
Open Method of Coordination 95, 151
Open skies policy 133
Organization for Economic Cooperation and Development (OECD) 76–7, 81–6, 88, 114–15, 122–5, 152, 189, 215, 217

Paris Treaty 22
Parliament versus Council 133
pathways of export 2, 6–7, 14–15, 64–5, 70, 72, 99, 107, 138, 192, 225; horizontal policy export 33, 107, 158, 220; vertical policy export 7, 9, 27, 29, 34, 99, 116, 214, 225; see also policy export
Poland 52, 96
policy: convergence 8, 116–17; diffusion 3, 104 (*see also* horizontal diffusion); export 1–14, 21, 24, 27, 29, 32–4, 50, 58, 66–8, 71–2, 73n10, 74n14, 87, 93, 99, 101, 107, 111, 116–17, 120, 125, 149, 153, 156, 158–9, 162–3, 167, 174, 179–81, 186, 188, 190–2, 194, 201, 205, 210–11, 214–18, 220–5, 226n11–12 (*see also* pathways of export); fit 6, 14, 69, 103, 107, 126, 138, 192, 199, 212, 221, 225; import 5, 7, 14–15, 38, 52, 55, 72–3, 93, 98, 180–1, 186, 192, 194, 200–1, 205, 215–17, 222 (*see also* defensive policy import); networks 10, 153, 218; promotion 74n14, 192, 194, 201, 214–15, 223; protection 7, 14–15, 23, 26, 33–4, 68, 70–3, 83, 86, 176–7, 192, 201, 205, 216–17, 223
preferential trade agreement (PTA) 21, 23, 33, 51, 106
Promotional Framework for Occupational Safety and Health Conventions 102
Protocol (Geneva Convention) 154, 156, 158, 162

qualified majority voting 95, 132

refugee protection 149, 153–63, 216, 220
regional protection areas 159–60
Regional Protection Programme (RPP) 161
Rome Treaty 20, 39–43, 59, 76–8, 84, 94, 98, 112, 130, 132–3, 194, 208, 211, 219, 226n9
Russia 125, 141, 153, 170, 191, 224

scope 5–6, 8, 14, 28–9, 31, 33, 39, 42, 46, 59–60, 63, 83, 86, 88, 97, 105–6,

234 *Index*

scope *continued*
  112–14, 116, 126, 130, 134–5, 154, 162, 169, 170–2, 179, 181, 193, 199, 206–9, 214–15, 220–2, 225n2
Singapore Issues 31–3, 79–80
Single European Act (SEA) 95, 112, 119
Single European Sky 134, 136, 142
Single European Sky Air Traffic Management Research (SESAR) 142, 145, 222
Single Market 1, 12, 24, 42, 78, 94–5, 112, 130, 149, 169, 187–8, 193–4, 197, 208
Single Undertaking 28, 30, 49, 52
social policy 93–110, 208, 212, 214, 216, 223, 226n15, 227n20
Soviet Union 154, 172, 176–7, 180
Spain 52, 123, 160
Sweden 53, 113, 120, 160
Switzerland 117, 121
Système de Stabilisation des Recettes d'Exportation (STABEX) 27

take-up rate 6–7, 14, 15n8, 100, 103, 107, 126, 154, 159, 192, 212, 214, 222, 225
third country nationals (TCN) 149–51, 163n2
Tokyo Round 21, 25, 27–8
trade policy 1, 4, 13, 20–37, 51, 208, 211–12, 215, 218–19
transport policy 130–48, 209, 216, 218–19, 223, 226n9, 227n32; aviation policy 130–48, 221
Treaty of Amsterdam *see* Amsterdam Treaty
Treaty establishing the European Community (TEC) *see* Maastricht Treaty
Treaty on the Functioning of the European Union (TFEU) *see* Lisbon Treaty
Treaty of Lisbon *see* Lisbon Treaty
Treaty of Maastricht *see* Maastricht Treaty
Treaty on the Non-Proliferation of Nuclear Weapons (NPT) 168, 170–7, 182n4, 182n7
Treaty of Paris *see* Paris Treaty
Treaty of Rome *see* Rome Treaty

UN High Commissioner for Refugees (UNHCR) 153, 161

United Kingdom (UK) 50, 78, 84, 105, 124, 137, 159–61, 163n3, 171, 188, 191–4, 199, 201, 213, 224
United Nations Conference on Trade and Development (UNCTAD) 20, 26, 76–7, 81–4, 88, 215, 217
United Nations Economic Commission for Europe (UNECE) 118–22, 214
United Nations Environment Program (UNEP) 112, 114–15, 122
United Nations (UN) Framework Convention on Climate Change 9, 115, 122–3
United Nations (UN) Security Council 171, 182n6
United States (US) 7, 20–5, 27–30, 32–4, 34n2, 39, 44–51, 64–7, 69–70, 74n15, 77, 79–89, 105, 111, 113, 116–17, 119–25, 131, 133, 136–7, 142–3, 152, 168, 170–2, 176, 178, 180, 181n1, 186, 190–5, 197, 199–201, 211–12, 214–15, 218–19, 222; Federal Trade Commission 82, 85; Financial Accounting Standards Board (FASB) 199–200; Trade Expansion Act 24
Uruguay Round Agreement on Agriculture (URAA) 21, 28–32, 44–7, 49–50, 52–3, 62, 69, 79, 212, 219; amber box support 46, 49; blue box support 46–7, 49–50; green box support 45–6, 48, 50

Van Miert Report 79–80

Waasenaar Arrangement 173, 175–6
Weapons of Mass Destruction (WMD) 167, 169, 171, 179–81, 183n19
White Paper on Food Safety 60
World Bank 189–90
World Health Organization (WHO) 61, 73n8, 114
World Trade Organization (WTO) 9–10, 21, 23, 28–34, 38, 40, 44–7, 49, 51–2, 54–5, 55n1, 58–63, 65, 67–70, 72–3, 74n17, 76–7, 79–82, 85–6, 88, 93, 96, 100, 105, 107, 192, 211, 213, 215–19, 227n21, 227n33; WTO Agreement on Technical Standards and Trade 28